FOREWORD

BY

FLOYD MAYWEATHER

I must take my hat off to my first fighter I ever had from the UK. He's the first guy that Mayweather Promotions signed from the UK. He was with us from the beginning.
He was my first UK fighter.

I was very pleased with Ashley during his time at Mayweather Promotions.
When he first came to the boxing gym, before I even signed him. I looked at him, he looked tough, we boxed, he had what it took to become world champion. We put Ashley on the right path. He came to the US, with just his luggage and with a dream. They say the US is where the tough competition is. Ashley was over here holding his own. I take my hat off to Ashley. He's a true champion!

During my biggest contract in sports history, Ashley helped me. He pushed me in training, gave me good work. He is a solid competitor. Ashley will not lay down. If he goes down, he'll get back up. He's a fighter. He has heart, boxing skills.
He's a great guy.

Ashley is no push over. Ashley is barbaric, tough and gritty. I said, if I work with you and you do what you are supposed to do. I'll get you the title shot. That's what I did.

I'm very proud of Ashley. True champion. True gentlemen.
He'll always be part of my team. He's a true warrior.

BASED ON A TRUE STORY

RAISED BY THE HOOD

INTRODUCTION

I feel like coming from where I do it is only natural for me to write a novel about my life and hopefully inspire someone, be it an adult or child. As a teenager I saw no future for myself, when you are a kid, you have hopes and dreams. With every passing day, millions of kids lose hope and just settle for what life gives them. Not me!

Many guys I went to school with are in jail, no longer alive, in a dead-end job or have no job at all. Those in prison are doing long stretches for various crimes including murder, manslaughter, armed robbery, kidnapping, drugs to name but a few. This is the kind of environment I come from, where close family members and friends are also in prison for committing those kinds of criminal activity. In my family I looked up to robbers, thieves and drug dealers, along with numerous uncles imprisoned for serious crimes, so what was I expected to be? If I had doctors and lawyers in my family maybe I would've had different ambitions or goals in life. Sometimes I thought that I was cursed to be born into a family with so much negativity. When I was young I was proud to say I'm a Theophane and the older I got I realized that there was nothing to be proud of. I thought as a youngster being from a family of criminals that I automatically had hood stripes, maybe I did but what does that mean in the wider world? Nothing! I must say I am very proud of many of my Theophane and Treasure cousins. I come from a community where a lack of hope is instilled in parents and passed down to their kids. It's starting to change but the blocks in front of us to succeed, are still there.

I used to talk to my cousin Tyrone Theophane about us not turning out like some of the older members of our family, that inspired us to make a better life for ourselves and our next generation. Tyrone was a cousin that I could count on and who had my back. Darren Theophane was also the same, we supported each other. I remember taking a coach as a kid to watch him in his boarding school play. I was the only family member to make the trip and he never forgot that. There were two shows that day, Oliver Twist and a play set in Rome. Darren could act and I wish that he had taken it up seriously, but he finished boarding school and returned to the hood, where that negative surrounding discourages you, especially a talented person. The hood has no respect for talents or aspirations. I do believe it is harder for anyone from an underprivileged background to become a success, but it was not impossible. I believed with hard work anything can be achieved. You will always have things stopping you from achieving something but that does not mean you should not attempt to fulfill your dream or endeavor. The whole point of life is to live and try see what we can do and what we thrive at. You may never know what you are capable of if you don't try. My mother was seventeen when she had me. My father was 24 years old. He wanted her to get an abortion but for whatever reason my mum never.

My mum had very little money at the time, but I had what I needed along with love.
I remember at school I was always ashamed when we came back from Christmas and we would write about what we got for presents. Everyone had big gifts and it sounded amazing whilst I would majority of the time get clothes or the odd toy. I always

remember that I wanted a Nintendo when it first came out. I got it a year after everyone had got it. I was always the one who didn't have anything out of my family and friends. I didn't get my first branded pair of trainers until I was 14 years old and only then because I was a fully-fledged young criminal by then. When my parents split up, we survived on beans on toast for a while. Sometimes the electricity would run out and we would spend the night by candle light. My mum had credit at the local shops sometimes when she didn't have any money. I would be sent out with a note from my mum asking for bread, toothpaste, normal basic stuff. When I think back to my childhood it seems a world away from how my life is now but many kids I guess live like this all around the world. Some kids would be raised in that environment and fall into it for themselves. So they would repeat the lives of their parents. I didn't enjoy those times of my childhood. My mum was and is a great mother. She handled her responsibilities and always tried to better herself. A parents job is never done and it is the hardest job anyone will have to do in their life. I feel that my upbringing instilled the hunger and drive that I currently have.

I have a never say die attitude as I know what it is to have absolutely nothing. Many times I thought that I would not achieve what I was capable of, not because I lacked belief in my talent but because I had a lack of opportunity. I beat Alan Bosworth in a British Title eliminator and did not get to fight the British champion for four years. That is a long wait but in that time, my hunger and determination grew even more. I am a dangerous man to face as I will give my all. I beat former world champion Demarcus Corley just after he had fought world number one Devon Alexander and I beat him. I only had one hand as well because the month before my finger bone had popped out the socket so I could not use that hand in the gym for a month and I was in excruciating pain with every punch that connected on him but I fought through the pain to get the biggest win and buzz of my life. I thought I was going to get a fight with Zab Judah on the undercard of Roy Jones Jr. Vs Joe Calzaghe at Madison Square Garden. Zab turned me down when he heard about me from some mutual associates. I wouldn't fight in America for another eighteen months. In my life it would have been easy to give up and get a job. I probably would have made a decent living as a personal fitness trainer, but I just could not call time on my boxing career. I had no promoter or anyone willing to give me a shot then John Tandy hooked me up with Cestus management. They got me two fights against Danny Garcia and Delvin Rodriguez. I beat Delvin and lost to Danny on a split decision. Even then no one in Britain believed in my talent. I ended up fighting British champion Lenny Dawes only because they wanted my world ranking. I was never going to lose on that night. The media and bookies strangely had Lenny as the favorite going into the fight. Lenny put up a heroic battle, but I would not be defeated. British boxing had shut me out and I was back to show them what they had missed out on. In the months after that fight. The very best British Promoters tried to sign me. Frank Warren was the first, he got in touch the very next day after I beat Lenny. Mick Hennessey, Eddie Hearn, Frank Maloney and Ricky Hatton would all throw their interest in the hat. How times had changed. When I turned professional, I could not get a main stream promoter to give me a break, now they had saw I was the real deal and were suddenly interested. Most fighters are protected by their promoters through their careers, but I had amassed a good record with wins against some good fighters without a promoters backing. Hatton promotions offered me a great deal and the next chapter of my career would take off. Just where I had come to at that point in my career would have been a success in many people's eyes but in my mind I was just warming up.

Rene Carayol, a businessman got in touch with me after my British title win over Lenny Daws and he guided me for many years afterwards. He believed in my talents as a fighter and saw that I had so much to offer society. Before him and before I was in the public eye I was always working on my novel, I had my clothing line and I was British champion. He just wanted to bring me out of the shadows and into the light. He in himself is an inspirational person and changed many thoughts I had before meeting him. He did not have to help me but he saw something in me and took on the challenge. Many thoughts that my background, surroundings and upbringing would not allow me to think possible, Rene made me believe.

If you have no goals or ambition in life, what is the point of living. As Tupac Shakur would say, "I am a rose that grew from the concrete". Many kids from poor backgrounds see criminals flashing cash, popping bottles and driving expensive cars but that is maybe the upside. The downside you always have to watch your back from other criminals wanting to rob or kill you from your illegally gotten gains but police want you for the same reasons. Most criminals end up with nothing. I can say majority of the successful criminals when I was young are now not doing so well. Some stacked their money, bought houses and businesses but they are few and far between. If you got no education and a criminal record, I guess you have nothing to lose.

It is a shame to see life wasted when we all have our own strengths, but they need to be nurtured through positive development and many poor kids do not have the resources around them like that.

In this novel I want everyone to experience my journey from poverty to a troubled childhood through my criminal activities as a teenager which lead me to being imprisoned. During this imprisonment I had an awakening. I was not scared by jail as I made some good friends in there and I was respected. No one troubled me but I knew that this was not the life for me. I have friends and family who have spent most of their lives in prison. Some people have been in prison so many times or for so long they have become institutionalized and can't cope in the real world where you are free to make your own decisions and have responsibilities. In prison you are told what time to go bed and what time to wake up. You have infringements on what you can do, and you are locked up like an animal. You get exercise once a day and if you are well behaved, they will let you learn through education. You are no longer a human being you are owned by the government. I saw so many youngsters who seemed decent to me but made some wrong choices in life. Who knows if they had responsible parents around them or if they had parents at all?

When I was released from prison, I said I was going to try my hardest to achieve something in boxing. Did I believe I could really achieve anything, I had no idea but I wanted to see. I had previously gone something like two years without a win in over ten fights, So I was not an outstanding amateur. Some fights I may have won but I lost many home town decisions. That did not bother me. My aim was to turn professional. I picked up some wins over my last eighteen months as an amateur, beating some decent fighters along the way. When I turned professional with Mr. Akay we had to wait for nearly nine months to make my debut as no promoter believed in my talent. Many fighters have been turned into journey men through lack of opportunity, so they just step in the ring with anyone. I was offered Lenny Daws in December 2002 but I declined the fight as I knew they would not give me the decision. I researched all the top British boxers and I wrote a list of thirty fighters that had been used to build up young fighters. I had to promote myself as no one else in the boxing industry would. I put out flyers in barber shops, take aways and I handed them outside nightclubs. I even hired flyer distribution companies to also do this. I hired a web designer to make me a website as well. I had to market myself. People in America knew about me even before they had seen my fight as I sent out press releases about myself. My whole life has been hard and could easily not have turned out the way it did but I believe that I was destined for something.

Right or wrong there are many kids like me around the world and for whatever reason they never achieve anything. Some people say I'm lucky to be living my childhood dream, but it is not luck. I worked hard to get to where I am and work even harder to stay where I am.

Colour is an excuse for failure. I used to believe that being black held me back or made life harder. There are people of all different religions, races and cultures that have not had an easy start in life and were born in an environment that breeds failure but you don't have to accept your circumstances.

Many youngsters are angry. Angry with the government and angry that they have no one supporting them in their dreams. Everyone needs help but not everyone gets it. I got help and support when I didn't necessarily need it but it came in handy and helped me to step my game up to the next level.

I feel like I represent people who feel they have no hope in life. I was expelled from two secondary schools and I was on the streets getting involved in drug dealing and robbery. I pulled my first arm robbery at fifteen years old. I push myself so hard because I know I will always be the underdog in my life. I know I will always be expected to fail. I thrive as the underdog. It is all I have ever known my whole life. I don't even think my mother expected much of me, but she was always proud when I achieved something. My mother has always been my biggest inspiration. I feel blessed to have such a great mum as there are many men and women who do not take their parental duties seriously.

My novel is about love, pain, heartache, determination, and perseverance. I want the reader to feel my lack of hope whilst reading but still see that I never gave up on a childhood dream every kid has but many kids never follow through. I am no one special. I am not super talented at anything, but I always had a passion for life and I always have tried to better myself. I make mistakes but I learn from them. I am ashamed of some of the things I have done in my life and those feelings drive me to be a better person.

MY LIFE

I was born Ashley Dean Theophane, son of Lucille and Zachary on 30th August 1980 in Paddington, London at the Old St Mary's Hospital on Harrow Rd.

I try to make the most of my life every day. I am alive, I give thanks, because we can go at any moment.

Growing up, my dad was strict, he is the only man I was scared of, sorry Granddad Theophane, Mr Foster Theophane was another one.

One day I was expelled from Cardinal Hinsley, around 9am I went to check my cousin Tyrone, R.I.P as we were both expelled.

I rang the bell and my Grandad came downstairs, I was trying to say Good Morning but I was so nervous the words wouldn't out; well Granddad put his big hand across my face, shouting at me "YOU HAVE NO MANNERS". Tears rolled own my eyes and I said, "Sorry Granddad".

I tell that story to my uncles and everyone laughs, that was
Mr Foster. Growing up he always made me nervous but when he went back to St Lucia to retire with my Granny. I visited in February 1997. When Granny would go out in the evenings, I would talk to him while he sat and relaxed on the porch. We bonded, we spoke about different things and I would introduce him to girls I made friends with in the village.

Growing up I was shit scared of my pops. He just had a back home (Caribbean) accent and for an English born St Lucian it was scary. It didn't stop me getting in trouble though.

I always had trouble accepting punishment from non-family, for some reason being a black youth in the 1980s, white people just seemed like the enemy. The teachers making me write lines at playtime or Mr Medcaf beating me with the ruler stick. I always refused to cry, I would not give him the satisfaction but as soon as he would leave me in the room, the tears would flow.

I got suspended as an 8 year old child from Our Lady of Dolours and the support class I was going to at Essendine School. I was told I was the first child to be suspended from Our Lady of Dolours, if that's true or not I have no idea. That's what they told me at the time.

Back to my Dad, he didn't really do much for me growing up. As I told my cousins when we were teenagers, "your dad is dead, so you can think if he was alive, things may have been different, if my Dad wasn't here there wouldn't be much difference".

I remember coming home from being suspended in Primary School, I was so scared cause I knew this was a beating predicament; I put on extra clothes to help with the pain. But my Dad never hit me. Not yet anyway. I liked the way he did it; he waited for me to think everything was good. Then out of the blue, my Dad switched and started shouting at me, not even shouting, he didn't do that, but his tone changed and knew what time it was.

I ran upstairs to my bedroom, which I always did, which my mum said I was stupid, because I was trapped. My brother would run out of the house. Guess he was smarter.

The beating routine would go like this; I'd tried to push my bed against my dad, that would do nothing. I would be trapped in the corner. Then take my beating with my dad's wooden walking stick or the buckle of his belt, it was either one he could get his hands on.

Going back a little more, 11 Seventeen Street, that is the first apartment I remember living. It was alright there. My little brother burnt the place down. I got in trouble, how does that work.

I was 7 years old and he was 2 years old. He walked into my bedroom with a lighter. I told him to give it to mum, the next thing I know.

My parents bedroom was on fire and my mum was going mad, she tried to put it out, but it was not happening. We had to flee the apartment, my dad wasn't there. When he found out, he swore at me the next day for not taking the lighter off my brother. Well what was a lighter doing lying around because I never smoked as a 7 year old boy.

So we had to move to a Bed & Breakfast for a little while and move to our next residence just before Christmas of 1988.

I was just a troublesome child. My parents tried to take me to a therapist. We would go to a place for kids with behavior problems. We (me, my mum and dad) would sit down with the psychiatrist with their pen and pad. Then it was down to me to let my feelings out and talk. What I can remember, I never did as my Dad would go mad because I wouldn't co-operate. He would be like we are trying to help you. But what did I need help with? I would never talk to a stranger about my feelings, that was not going to happen.

My mother Lucille, what can I say about her, she gave birth to me when she was 17 years old.
How or why she fell for my father I will never know. My mum was attractive and my Dad, well, I wouldn't call him an oil painting. My mum was friends with my Dad's younger sister Molin Theophane, they were in school together.

My Mum was a good mum, life wasn't easy but she done her best for me even though as a young teenager I was very aggressive and wild, some would say that was because my Dad wasn't around but who knows. I was growing up and finding out who I was.

Looking back I sense the struggle my mum had with baby father by her side not being the support she needed.

My mum would stand by and let my Dad lay down his punishment to me and then tell him to stop when she felt he had done enough.

My mum would not beat me, I cannot remember that ever happening, she was into grounding me or banning me from something I liked doing. That never worked. I would say mum if I am good can I go out and my mum would say no, I would go back to being bad.

I would kick the bin in the kitchen, and throw stuff.
To this day I know I was a handful and my mum easily could have put me in a home with social services but she never. Maybe because her mother, gave up her kids so my mum wanted us to stay as a family.

My mum had 2 other siblings from her mum and father Reginald Treasure, Tony and Denise. They all had separate families who brought them up. My Granddad had many other children worldwide, who I am still meeting today and getting to know to this day.

My mum stuck by me when I was a young teenager, week in week out getting arrested by the police.

There were many times as a young teenager my mother could have put me in care. There were times I was uncontrollable, and I would hear my mother crying in her bedroom asking God what she had done to deserve this. Those memories sadden me to this day and my mother would have had every right to give me to the Government to raise me. My mother wasn't raised with her siblings, so I guess she did her utmost to keep us together as a family. She put up with my father's bullshit as much as she could. I never heard them argue when I was younger so when they split it was kind of a shock to me. I always tell my mother, I don't know what she saw in my father but she was seventeen years old when she had me so she was a child when she met him and probably easily impressed as I would have walked past him if I were her.

People don't understand the importance of choosing the mother or father of your kids. That person is part of your life if you like it or not. Having kids with someone is in some ways more important than getting married as you can get a divorce and never have contact with that person but going halves on a baby, makes that bond with that person everlasting.

Early Days

Growing up as a Theophane in Paddington, West London was interesting. As a kid I looked up to my older cousins and my uncles (my dad's brothers).

I would go round to my Grandparent's house, 149 Fernhead Road, that is a house I will forever remember. I loved being there. I could do stuff there my mum wouldn't allow me to do.

We could stay up late, we could stay out late, and I had so much fun with my cousins, Lawrence and Tyrone. We would have play fights with my uncles. That was fun but we would end up getting hurt in the end.

It was a full house as my Uncles lived there as well, they had stuff I never had. SKY and Nintendo as a little kid that was a big deal. I was always the first to sleep and in the morning my cousins would be laughing saying they put their crusty toes on my lips, what a loving family I had.

We could earn 10 to 20 pence going shop for my uncles, that was a big deal to me. That could buy a Wham, Chomp or 10p packet of crisps.

Sometimes or a lot of times, my uncle Simon who worked at Domino's pizza for a while would bring back pizza after work. 149 Fernhead Road was the place. I would love being there. So much could happen.

My uncle Ron was a playboy and sometimes he would be home with one of his girls and another would ring the bell and my Gran would have to make up excuses for him. My cousin told me once he had to hide underneath his bed.

Growing up and being a Theophane I was destined to be a criminal. We had Robber's, Drug Dealers and Burglars. That's who I looked up to. I didn't stand a chance in life. Some people have Lawyers, Doctors and Teachers, not me. I had the opposite.

My family were my role models and I followed in their foot steps, doing all 3.
One memory I have is that, an uncle robbed a corner-shop and he box's and box's of sweets. As a kid under 10 years old, that is a big deal.

My Granny and Grandad would have a tin full of biscuits in their room, at night we would go and stuff our little faces. Sometimes it's the little things that mean a lot to you when you look back at the fond memories you have.

I used to love staying there and I knew my mum never liked it but never said. I would get my Aunty Molin or cousins to ask her and she couldn't really say no, that would look bad.

Being a Theophane, I felt proud as a kid as it was something special to me. Really it wasn't but as a kid it felt like a big deal. My family would tell me and my cousins, you stick together, if one of you fight you all fight. I held onto that for a very long time, I even went jail for my family, that's another story and nearly got killed in Rotterdam, Holland.

I remember in play centre when we had a fight with some Asians, Tyrone came to my rescue and we ended up getting the better of them. We had each other's back from young primary school kids.

Being at 149 Fernhead Rd, I could stay up late, walk the streets late at night and hang in the park. My mum would never let me do that.

MY GODMOTHER MRS EDWARDS

Dorothy Edwards was born 1934 in St Lucia and died in 2001.

I loved this lady so much; she was my second mum and influential in my life up until today. I think about her everyday and the values she instilled in me.

She was a God fearing woman and I loved her. My Godmother has always been there for me, emotional and guiding me in life. Every Sunday I would go round to her family home. That was Soup day, I would look forward to going there every week for that. I have never had Soup as good as hers.

While in St Lucia in 1997 I walked from Castries to Canaries, that was just under 6 hour walk in baking sun, up and down hills.

The reason, it was Bank Holiday and the cabs were trying to charge me a extortionate fee as I was British. So I thought fuck it and walked it.

My Dad's Aunt, Aunty Alex told me it would be too dangerous to walk to Canaries. That just made me want to do it more. I was a man from London, no St. Lucian is robbing me, I did my thing in London, I was a robber. So I packed my rucksack and head off to Canaries, all for a Sunday Bowl of Soup.

I picked up a stick on the way and walked in my bare feet. I walked past waterfalls, lakes and beautiful views, I felt like Moses, I had just watched "The Ten Commandments" so it was fresh in my mind. When I got to Anse La Raye, I bought some Grapefruit and a drink. I arrived back in Canaries early evening, the locals said only an old crazy man had done that and that was years ago. It was nice experience that I would do again.

Sometimes when my Godmother was still in London, I would visit her in the week and chill with her. She would give me advice and I loved her dearly. She would ask why I misbehave but I never had the answer to that. It was just something I would do.

When it was my first Holy Communion, that was her time. She was into all that Religious stuff. We went to shops to buy my suit, I was so happy. It was grey and I had a white shirt. I was so smart and smooth. I was nervous with all the build up and words I had to remember but it went well and I had a good day. I still have the dictionary what my mum's aunty bought me. It was a shame my Granny never came but years later I was told that she wanted me to have it with my 3 other cousins, Lawrence, Tyrone and Darren. My father and sister had a bad experience when my Granny hosted my sister's communion year before so I think there was still bad vibes there. But my Grandad came so his presence was welcomed and appreciated.

With my Godmother, she was the best cook I ever met maybe I am biased but I loved her food. I remember Christmas at my Godmother's home, so much food and friends, kids and family there. Then I went back home, and mummy had the little table with food on, my humble beginnings was real. I had another meal with some mince pies.

My God Brother Steven still lived at home then and he was cool, kind of like a big
brother I never had. He would beat me up but give me money to buy sweets. He would tell me later in life that I was born to be a boxer as he would beat me up but I would never cry. I don't remember that. I remember begging him to stop and him holding me down and punching my biceps until I screamed out in pain. It is all good memories.

My God Sister Uril was cool as well, a big sister to me in ways. I would chill with her. I remember watching Nelson Mandela's release on TV with her, I never knew who he was but I knew he was important as I saw thousands of people in the streets waiting his release from prison.

TROUBLED CHILDHOOD

My early years were different to say the least. My childhood has probably affected my view on having kids as I had it hard and was always the poorest out of my friends and family. I had food, shelter and the clothing, the basics but I guess we always want more. My mum did her best for me I will say that, so I will always try give back to her.
I went to the Marylands Road nursery in 1983 and stayed for two years until 1985 when I went to Our Lady of Dolours until 1991.

I met many kids at nursery who are still my friends to date which is nice to know. One name that pops out is Shane Mitchell. We would go Nursery and Primary school together. He went on to do well academically in Secondary school and University. He ended up working as a teacher and later a lawyer. We even lived next door to one another for twenty odd years. I was proud of his accomplishments and he was proud of mine. Mutual respect for a brother from another mother. He was also Saint Lucian and a world traveler like myself, so we had a few things in common even though we were totally different people. I would even assist him in 2009 with his white collar boxing fight.

I have fond memories of nursery. Socializing with the other kids and learning the basics in life.

Primary school was another learning curve and I have many friends I met there who are still my friends today.

I wasn't one of the popular kids, but I had many friends there. I have been told I was always getting into fights with my primary school rivals. I got made fun of and I made fun of other kids.
I remember not having a very good relationship with many of the teachers. The headmaster Mr. Medcalf seemed to enjoy beating

me with the meter stick. I remember my childhood friend, Jason Jean Charles and I misbehaving. Mr. Medcalf taking us to the library to beat us. I refused to cry while he pounded me with it but Jason was bawling. When he left us in the room with my ass and thighs burning with pain. The tears started to flow down my checks, but I wouldn't give him the satisfaction to let him see me cry.

My Mother noticed I had a speech impediment before I was 5 years old, but I didn't start speech therapy until 1987. I don't know if it helped as I still have a stammer now but It's good to know that the King, father to Queen Elizabeth and Grandfather to Prince Charles had a stammer and would struggle with public announcements and socialising when he was a young man. You can overcome anything if you refuse to let it hold you back. As a kid in Primary school I don't really remember my stammer holding me back. It wasn't until Secondary school when I had to get up in English and Religious Education classes and read out loud paragraphs from Romeo and Juliet, Shakespeare and the Bible that my stammer affected me. My friends would sometimes tease me but it was all in fun, so it didn't matter. I was probably nervous speaking to girls when I was a teenager just in case I panicked and I couldn't get my words out.

In Primary school, I went to St. Charles health centre in Ladbroke grove around early 1987.
They would show me Picture cards to hear my pronunciation of a cow, cat, spider and work on words, letters or syllables I struggled with. I did several sessions for a good period of time. The speech therapist felt my speech had improved and that no more sessions where needed. To this day I don't know if they helped me, but I know there are technics to help with a stammer. Tony Blair and Gordon Brown have a stammer, but they take their time whilst talking and know what they are going to say before saying it. That's an effective way to help with a stammer.

In the school year 1988 to 1989, my primary school Our Lady of Dolours felt like I was being too disruptive in class and sent me to a morning behavioral unit at Essendine school on Essendine Road next to Paddington recreation ground. I was there for a couple years and it was a pleasant experience. My love of baking came from baking sessions we did regularly there. Now I can bake and cook with the best of them. I made some friends yet again who thirty years later I am still in contact with. I was the first pupil to get suspended from the behavioral unit for going to the corner shop and buying some candy. Frosties to be precise. Our lady of Dolours backed the suspension and suspended me from my primary school for a few days. The headmaster said he was disappointed in me and I was a disgrace to the school as no one had been suspended from there in twenty years. I think they over-reacted by suspending me. A warning from both schools would have done the trick.

My parents relationship was coming to an end and I didn't really see it as they didn't have no big arguments in front of my brother and I so I didn't know it was over until it was done.
My parents went to a family therapist in St. johns wood. It was all about us as a family keeping with a routine and my parents sharing responsibility so that it didn't affect us, the kids too much.
I wouldn't speak to the therapists so I only went to a few sessions as I would sit in silence. My dad would get mad and try shout at me, but my lips were staying shut. My brother went more often as he was younger. I don't know if he spoke to them as I just remember him playing with the toys.

My parents tried to remain on good terms which they kind of have to this day now. That may be a reason why I am friends with majority of women I have had a relationship with. I guess you shared something together so if it wasn't a bad break up and you both respect the decision. You can move forward as friends. It takes time but it can work.

Kids to not realise the importance of getting into a good primary or secondary school when they are young, but it can be life changing and effect the course of your life. Going to a bad school can see many talented kids get sucked in with the bad structure and education of the school which is sad.

Kids that go to productive schools with good exam results can set kids and teenagers on a path of glory and the connections you make with other pupils who are destined for top jobs can help with getting your foot in the door or just having that solid environment and backing.

I come from nothing. I was born dirt poor and I am part of Britain who are expected to achieve nothing in life. Working for minimal pay or being in prison, living at the taxpayers' expense.
Too many people have kids just to get an apartment off the government and get more tax payers money and this sets a trend with the kids as majority of the kids from these backgrounds are influenced by their parents and many just fall into the same trap.

My mum went back to school and got some qualifications. It wasn't easy for her and it took longer than it would have without kids. My mum worked as a school support worker moving on to working with vulnerable people then being promoted to manager. There is so much that you can do and achieve in this life but too many people make up excuses why they cannot do this and that.

I was expelled from two secondary schools. I left school with no education. I went to college and got my qualifications. I went prison for armed robbery. I was found not guilty, but I could have gone back hard into being a criminal, but I slowed down and eventually stopped as I didn't want to go back to prison. I turned professional with no backing from a promoter and I took fights sometimes for no money or sometimes I would pay for my opponents' purse which meant I would lose out on a couple thousand pounds. I built my whole life from the dirt underneath the pavements. I come from nothing, so I know anything is possible if you really believe and just work hard and try your best. That's all I have ever asked of myself to give my all, to try my best and if it isn't good enough at least I know I tried. That's all we must do in life is give our best and majority of the time, things will work out.

SCHOOL DAYS

Cardinal Hinsley

Starting Cardinal Hinsley was a new beginning. I was growing up and meeting new people. The first day was nerve racking. Going to a new school, being on your own. For an 11-year-old that's a big deal. Fortunately, a lot of friends from my Primary School were going to be here plus some cousins of mine.

Duane Warrington and Dean Elie were from my old school and we were in the same class.

I only lasted just over 2 school years before getting expelled.

The first year in Secondary went fine but by the 2nd year I was starting to get in trouble with teachers. I became a regular at detention even Saturday detention saw me, and I hated it.

Being at school from Monday to Friday was enough, to get dressed in your school uniform on Saturday. Damn, that's a nightmare.

I was a bright young pupil. I was a competent artist; I got that talent from my mum as she was pretty good.

R.E used to interest me as did History, English, and Science.

I liked Historical stuff and I had a good imagination. I also liked researching subjects and discovering new information. My mum would help and buy book collection to do with all different subjects.

Science was cool cause you got to make different things and learn how things in life are made. I was always good at sports; I was an all-rounder. I wasn't the best at anything but good at many things.

The first year I didn't get into the football team, which disappointed me, but we had a good team. In the second year a B Team was made and I got into that, which I was happy about.

I had a lot of problems with certain teachers who came at me and I went at them. I had a hard time accepting discipline from anyone who wasn't my family. My Dad would say when I go school the teachers are my parents, but the teachers didn't show me no love. I always felt as if they were out to get me. My dad being from St Lucia, he was raised the old school way. He agreed with beatings from teachers and basically anything they said was the truth. When I'd disagree.

They didn't use physical abuse in Cardinal Hinsley secondary school.
Ms. Carmichael, I did not like and Mr Ward, was a bald headed punk in my young eyes, at the time.

By the 3rd year I was on the streets, robbing and fighting. Anyone who spoke to me in an aggressive tone, shit was going down.

My guys from Mozart estate and Kilburn, knew I was representing and wasn't a youth to be messed with.

I had so many fights with big men when they tried to tell me I was a little boy. I would be like show me. Then big men were getting messed up.

In school when my friends or any other students tried talk to me in a way. We were fighting. I came back from the summer holiday of 1993, very different.

My last few months at Cardinal Hinsley. I got more detentions and more people got messed up. People watched their talk with me.

One day in R.E class Dean and I got into trouble. The whole class was talking but we got pinpointed so we were given a detention. I let it be known I would not be attending unless the whole class was going to be there. At lunchtime, Ms Carmichael saw Deputy Head Mr Ward.
He told Dean if he didn't attend, he would get suspended so Dean said he will attend. I've been a hard head from a young age and he tried to call my bluff. He told me if I don't go to my detention I am expelled. I replied, "I guess I am expelled then."

He took me into his office and tried to call my parents. They were at work, so he called my Grandparents. I headed there when I was expelled. I didn't care as my cousin Tyrone Theophane R.I.P was also expelled so I just saw it as we would just hang out.

I don't remember what my mum said but by the time I was stressing her out with my wild behavior, and I was living with my father.

I can't remember if I held a beating, but it was a beat down occasion.

My mum told my father he had to step up and go the meeting with my head of year Ms Carmichael and Headmaster,
Mr Medcalf. That's one thing with my pops when I misbehaved, he would discipline me and if I was in trouble at school he would come to the meetings.

My Dad went to the meetings, he humbled himself and Mr Medcalf had no manners, no respect.

One meeting we came 5 minutes late because of traffic and Mr Medcalf wouldn't see us. He told my father what kind of example are you setting. Somethings are out your control.

We went to a few meetings and in the end, I felt like fuck it.

So one meeting, the last one, Medcalf was talking and he said to me, "Do you want to be here?" By my body language it seems I didn't. I did not say much but Medcalf said he would put on my record that it was a mutual termination so it wouldn't have expelled on my record, but schools still knew I pushed out.

On the way out my dad went mad and wanted to hit me. I think my mum attended that meeting.

My Dad didn't know what to do with me and asked if something was wrong with me.

ST GEORGE'S SECONDARY SCHOOL

Being expelled. My memories are blurry of that point in my life.

My mum was trying to get me into all the local schools. But the only one which would take me was St Georges and that's the school my cousin Tyrone who was also expelled but from Queens Park Community School got into.

He got in before me but for some reason I started first.

St George's at that time had a bad reputation but was improving as Headmaster Martin Lawrence was turning it around.

Everyone helped me settle in, but the school seemed to lack organisation.
I got into the school football team which I was happy about as I struggled to make Cardinal Hinsley team.

In training I was one of the top scorers and playmakers. I would play in a deep midfield role and make runs. My whole game was improving.

We did a Westminster Schools 5-a-side competition. I was put in the defensive role. I did my job as no goals went past us but our strikers had bent feet so we went out in the group stages, as we couldn't score.

Life goes on……

My cousin joined St George's a few weeks or months later. We didn't hang in school much as we were different years and had different people we hanged with. After school I would go by my Grans home to hang out with him and we would hit the streets and go make money.

One time that was funny to me. A group of crackheads were counting their money outside a chemist waiting for their meth. I snatched a wad of notes and sprinted for my life. I still had my school bag and was in uniform.

When I had got away, I counted it and had a few bills. Which isn't bad for a few seconds work.

I gave my cousin some of it as that's how we rolled.

In the Autumn it would get dark quick so by 6pm we would be looking for people who were leaving work or sometimes on a Friday night, you'd get men walking home from the Pub with their wages.

People would say go and get a job but our mindset then was "I'm not working for £5 an hour."

I did little jobs like handing out cab cards for my mum's friend. My mum tried to get me a paper round and a job on a fruit stall, but it never happened. I feel many try to take advantage of kids. Robbing was a job to me.
The Mozart lot were into doing Taxi drivers and jumping in people's car and taking a wallet or a purse. That never happened with my people. We would pounce on muthafuckas.

When I was relying on my mum and dad, I had essentials, trainers, jeans, the basics but when I was robbing. I was buying my Moschino and Versace's in Selfridges. I stopped buying Versace when he made the comment that if he knew black people would buy his stuff, he wouldn't have made it so I stopped buying his shit.

My little brother was making thousands of pounds at the age of 13.

I knew the group he was rolling with did not know what they were doing. I'd take him with me to make money then I went to prison and he followed behind me for a diamond job gone bad. My mum had her two sons locked up. I felt sorry for her and did not like her being alone.

Back to me being in St George's. I'm getting ahead of myself.

My school work was good but as we were allowed out at lunch which I wasn't used to, sometimes I would go home as I was a 15 minute walk away.

I came back late a lot of times and was also late in the mornings a lot. They used this to expel me.

It's funny, I nearly lost my virginity in a block of flats but the girl who was a 5th year was definitely not my type so when she told me she wanted to fuck me, I was shocked and may be a little scared off by her brashness. I wouldn't lose my virginity until a year later to one of my girlfriend's friends.

I had got into the school football team and was popular at St George's secondary school. One new guy from Ladbroke Grove tried to boy me off and that was a definite no back in 95/96. He had older brothers who were supposed to be a big in Ladbroke Grove. He got busted up by me anyway. I wasn't someone to tolerate that as a young guy. He goes in and out of jail now. His life could have been mine but I guess I was destined for something else.

One day after school, my cousin Tyrone who was known as Duck or Ducky was going to fight some guy. Everyone knew I had his back. I told him if he gets in trouble I'm there. In the end I jumped in straight away. That's just how we were raised. If one fights, we all fight.

Majority of the school were there. We had gone to Paddington Recreation Ground near the tennis courts. It got back to the powers that be in St George's that I jumped in. I was suspended until a meeting with Philip Lawrence. He showed no remorse even though it was the first time I was in any trouble. I was expelled.

My mum was upset and did not know what to do with me. She appealed, the school board said as I had a bad late attendance record, I would not be allowed back. My mum cried and begged them to give me another chance. That upset me as I knew that her tears would not do any good.

I got on with the teachers and most of the students at the school and I never got in trouble in the past but Philip Lawrence was running a zero tolerance policy whilst he was there so I was out. I felt sorry for my mother as my father was in Saint Lucia and she was left alone to hold the fort. It is hard for a woman to raise boys without any male assistance especially when they start getting in trouble in the streets and at school.

I was out of school again and Duck was let back in. St. Georges said it was nothing to do with me so that's why I was being expelled.

As a kid, I was raised as a Theophane, if one fight. We all fight. I kept that loyalty, even going prison for my family. Looking back, I probably made more sacrifices than some of my other cousins. My cousins Tyrone and Darren were always there for me when I needed them. We had our arguments as everyone does but overall when we were teenagers, they were there for me and I was there for them.

BEETHOVEN CENTRE in Mozart Estate

Expelled again! Where was my life heading, I was a street robber and even dabbled in a little burglary, kicking open people's doors, and taking their goods.

It was alright there; one American teacher was cool. She was very friendly and wanted to help the students. We had the basics; nowadays expelled centers have everything. Sometimes more than schools but the teachers helped us or tried to help us. Some kids didn't accept the help and were destined for a life of failure but the students who wanted to change their life, the teachers would assist them with that.

On our end of year test I came 1st out of everyone. I was pleased. It was expected. I won 10 days at Super Camp in Harrow on the Hill. It was a good experience for me. There were a bunch of middle classed Americans and Europeans. My family could not afford to send me somewhere like this, but it was a great experience and showed me something different to what I knew.

£1000 for 10 days of Super Advanced learning was out of my family's price range.

I quickly bonded with some Londoners and I had a queue of US teenage girls who wanted me. I had choice. I had a girlfriend back home but what she did not know would not hurt her.

It was at a Posh private school in Harrow on the Hill and everything was top class.

I even enjoyed playing tennis with some American Italian girl. She could not believe I had never played before. I loved watching Andre Agassi and John McEnroe but that as close as I got to playing tennis on a tennis court.

We had classes of super learning, focusing, achieving things you thought not possible and many more. Some of the stuff I learnt there still help me today. I have a speech impediment so I would hate public speaking. They got me to stand in front of 100 students and talk about my emotions and feelings, that was a big break through.

I had trouble with the teachers, as Ashley Theophane does. Sometimes it got to confrontations and I could easily have been sent home, but they showed me love, patience and tried to offer me some guidance. I was not a bad kid but where I'm from its kill or be killed. Even as I write this, I have a death warrant out for me. People want me dead. I still live my life, but I must wear a bullet proof vest every day.

On one of the last days, my mum, dad, brother, and cousin Tyrone came up to watch the presentation I was going to do. I was nervous but I stood up and spoke about being a leader. The teachers saw something in me and said I am strong minded and if I use my talents for positive, I have qualities to be a leader in life. Who would think that they would be right? I did not believe them, but they saw something in me.

I believe them now because I am into lectures of Malcolm X, Farrakhan, among other great speakers.

I may not be the best speaker in the world but everyone who talks to me sees my drive and how focused I am.

I want to make something of myself. It's not all about money but self-worth, feeling you have achieved something. I have always believed that I have someone watching over me. I have done disgusting crimes and ruined people's lives with the things I have done. I could be in prison just like many other of my peers from around the way but you could say I have been lucky or you could say I have a purpose on earth. I think I have a purpose and I am fulfilling my potential.

While at Super Camp, I liked a Caucasian girl when I could have chosen a black girl. Valerie and I are still cool today. We write and email each other now and again as she is from Atlanta but now living in NY.

She said she thought it was no contest between her and the white girls, but she said I guess you got the Jungle Fever. Jungle Fever is when a black and white person are romantically or sexually interested in one another. Halle Berry and Wesley Snipes starred in a film of the same name.

I felt like I let her down, but my friends mean a lot to me and girls come and go in my life real quick.

After leaving Super Camp and going back to the hood. It was different. I felt I had changed and could see life more brightly and was more optimistic. That did not last long. A few weeks later I took my cousins to the Super Camp school, Duck (R.I.P) and another who I rather not incriminate, and we ended up breaking in and taking some of the electronic goods. The Caretaker caught us and we did not get everything but it was a laugh as he ran us out of there.

They still have Super Camps happening to this day. One day I would love to be a helper or make a guest appearance there. It was a good experience for me, and I would like to have the same effect on a generation coming up and in need of some light.

MAIDA VALE COLLEGE

I could not get into no school after being expelled from Cardinal Hinsley and St. Georges so I was accepted into City of Westminster College, Maida Vale Centre to do my GCSEs.

It was different as it was an adult environment. Everyone there was doing their GCSE's again.

The year was 1995, in my young prime as a Street Robber. I had gold chains and sovereign rings for a 15 year old that was a big deal back then.

I had a support worked by the name of Simon. He was a short plump man and even though I've had no contact with him in 25 years, he's had a role in how my life has gone as he helped me when I was not sure which direction to take. People like this do not get appreciated enough in life but I owe this man my full gratitude.

He was a nice man and was always there to help me with my college work or advising me. People who are nice to me I am always skeptical. I think he was a genuine guy. He even got me work experience when he had finished his work with me. He knew I liked sports but I did not know which direction I wanted to go in. He got me work experience with Kensington Leisure Centre, I stayed there for 2 years and he even advised me to do a Leisure & Tourism course so he had a role in direction of my life. A good honest man.

I did not do too good at the Maida Vale Centre. Again, it was my attitude that was a hindrance to me. I think I was too young as it was an adult environment, you were left to do it on your own and I was still a child.

Primary school to Secondary school and now College. My bad attitude was affecting my relationship with my teachers and then that affects your work as the teachers are there to help you. Students do not understand the importance of their education. When you're nine years old you don't understand that the secondary school you go can have a big impact on how successful you become. You still have college or six form then University to get into. As a young teenager it is better to be around young aspiring teenagers who want to become successful men and women. When you are from the inner city, many kids aspirations are very low if they have them to begin with. Your home life and support from your family is very important. There is only so much that schools and teachers can do.

I never got on with my Math's or Human Biology teachers and I got a U in both classes. I did pretty good in English getting a B and a D in Business, but European Studies I was also poor in. Which was a shame a I always loved History and European studies interested me.

I met some nice people at Maida Hill college, but I was not very sociable even now I am not. I have always enjoyed my own company. I had a crush on a pretty Jamaican girl with a cute accent. We would hang out and take pictures, but she said I was too young for her. I liked her, she was cool. Sadly she died in Tottenham when a car crashed into her. She was a lovely girl.

I would go college in the day and hang on the streets at night.

I would go to Stowe Club for Boxing on Tuesday and Thursday, other than that I might be at Granville Centre or Carlton Centre.

In the Mid 1990's Peel Precinct in Kilburn was the place to be. Girls hanging out and getting laughs with my boys.

I would normally go home earlier because it got late, there was nothing to do. Sometimes we would go out there (which meant to go and rob) and rob a cabbie or a live which was a drunk man coming from the pub. I had money in my pocket most of the times which was a great feeling for a teenager.

MY 1ST CONVICTION AND FOILING DAYS

Back in 1993, I was a young kid who enjoyed going Granville Community Centre and Carlton Centre. That is where the youth from Kilburn and North West London would hang out. We had table tennis and a pool table that was about as much entertainment we were provided with.

Nowadays kids have PS3's, Ipod's, Music equipment and computers, back then it was the basic but it was better that being out in the streets.

My cousins used to play football in Albert Road around Queens Park area. The pitch and youth centre have now been knocked down and made into a million pound apartment complex. I'd tag along and watch, sometimes I'd would join in. I made many friends there who to this day we still stay in touch.

I have no idea how it came about, but some of the youths, were doing something called Foiling. You would get the old 10 pence and some sticky foil and wrap it around the 10 pence and shape it like a 50 pence piece. We would do like £5's worth or a tenner. We would make between £25 and £50.

We would use it in the chocolate machines on the tube stations. Normally we would split up as it would look strange with a bunch of black boys hanging around chocolate machines. So we went in two's and would go all over London from Zone 1 to Zone 5.

Sometimes the machines would reject your coins if not done properly. That would waste time. As you wanted to get in and out, if your coins were rejected, you have to fix them up and that is not what you want as undercover police officers and CCTV are at the tube stations.

Ducky's coins were really good. It was funny cause by the end of the day we would have pockets full of coins heading back to Kilburn.

We would go every station from Alperton to Hyde Park Corner to Lancaster Gate to Brixton. Nowhere was out of bounds.

One day with my cousin, Tyrone Theophane, we were working the machines around West End, Central London. We stopped off at Charring Cross to make our money. It was packed, which was not ideal because you don't know who a commuter is and who is an undercover police officer.

We did what we had to do, it was time to move to another station, but we got too greedy and overstayed our welcome. Some undercover police officers arrested me and my cousin. It was the first time I had been arrested, so I was scared. I won't lie and go on as if I did not care that I was arrested. I knew my Dad would kill me. I was 12 years old, I begged the officers to let me go. Tears running down my face. This was a nightmare.

We were put in separate cells then my Dad arrived a couple of hours later.

We were interviewed and cautioned. That wasn't so bad but my Dad went mad at my cousin as he said he was a drug user, so they had to test him. Of course, they found out he was lying and just wanted to waste their time.

We had to go back a month later to get cautioned officially and that was it.

Tyrone Theophane as you will read through this book, you was there in many bad situations in my life. Maybe we had a bad influence on each other, who knows. But from a kid, we were running around the streets robbing and selling drugs. We shared many convictions and even went prison together. He had my back. Growing up from babies to the day he died, I love that guy. Once I was drunk, I was going to some party with his twin, Lawrence and I told my cousin in my drunken state we are like triplets. I was 14 when I made that statement but their mother, my Aunty knows what I mean. My mum and her mum were school friends and my father was her big brother. From when Tyrone and Lawrence were born, which was only 18 days after me. We grew up together and as a kid I loved being around them. Maybe I felt that bond as a baby. Who knows!

With my first conviction and my mum and dad separating, My mum was under a lot of stress. I was rebelling. My mum could not control me. My Dad was not there as he was looking for somewhere to live. I would see him on weekends. It did not really bother me but may be with my dad not in the same household as me, let me run wild.

When my father got his place near Marylebone Road and he was settled there. My mum basically told him, she could not handle me no more and I would not listen or accept punishment when she tried to discipline me.

If my mum would ground me, I would normally wait for her to forget to unlock the door and run outside. A lot of that time in my life, I cannot remember. Maybe it was so painful, I have blocked it out and made myself regret. I'm sure my mother remembers those times better than me as she was the one under stress.

I lived with my Dad for a long time. It's a time in my life where it is like a big blur. I definitely didn't like it at my Dads but my mum wouldn't take me back as maybe she wanted to protect my little brother from me. Seeing his big brother aggressive all time could make him think it is okay to kick the bin over or throw stuff on the floor.

Living with my Dad was slow and boring. He was very strict and easily would give me a beat down for the smallest thing like letting the bath overflow.

I always remember him telling me to cook the chicken that was in the fridge whilst he went out. No instructions or nothing. I did not know how to cook chicken. Boil an egg sure, but cooking a chicken I had not been taught that yet.
I attempted to cook the chicken. I did not know you had to season it and put it in the oven. I'd never watched my mother or family members do it. I stuffed the chicken in a big pot and boiled it.
It looked wrong when I had finished but again, I had never been taught but I was supposed to know what to do.
He came back and was obviously not happy. I'd say it was his fault but I'm sure I was punished.

I was released from my sentence of living with my Dad when he went to St Lucia for 6 months. I was so happy to go back to my mum's and away from my Dad's military rule.

By the time my Dad came back I was going court for a street robbery I was accused of committing with you guessed it, my cousin, Tyrone and 2 others.

While my Dad was away I had continued to get in trouble at school and was regularly robbing on the streets. I was in by 8 or 9pm in the week. Straight after school I was hanging on the corners with my boys and getting into problems with other boys.

YOUNG THUG

As a young teenager, I was a young thug.

Foiling was the start but that was nothing.

The youngsters I knew started robbing people on the street. It was petty shit but for a 13 to 15 year old it was good money.

I would go by my Gran's and my cousin's would say, "Dem Man" are going "Out there." I was not into that. It did not appeal to me. I would say cool and just chill and watch television but as the weeks and months went by. My cousin and my boys were making money.

We would be hanging in Peel Precinct in Kilburn with the girls but when it got a bit dark. My boys were gone looking for victims. At first I would hang with the females but having empty pockets is no good. When everyone is shopping, I am window shopping. It's not about that.

So eventually I started going "out there" with the "man dem." When we were young, we would roll deep with like to 5 to 10 men. You aren't making money like that. It was fun to us, may be not the victims but we had a laugh.

We would go all over West and North West London. Back in them days we knew of guys from Brixton and Tottenham but that was a world away to me. I only knew my hood, Kilburn Precinct and Mozart Estate.

As time went by, I would roll with 1 or 2 men max. It also had to be a man you trust as back in them days. Whoever got the money would normally say it was less than what it really was.

That's why I normally would roll with one of my cousins or a trusted friend not just an associate.

I made money back then, for a youngster. I had no fear. Police would stop and search us but it was nothing. I didn't smoke and I didn't carry weapons, so I was good.

My convictions as a kid were not for robbing but for assaulting Police Officers. I picked up a few of them along the way.

I wasn't afraid of them. They had their weapons but other than that they were another gang. They are the biggest gang.
Once I got evicted from a bus and the police were called. I remember this like it was yesterday. It happened just off Kilburn High Road. The Police tried to man handle me and after being beat by my Dad. I was never scared to fight no one. I went at them. No doubt 99.9% you will always lose a fight with the police, but I wasn't put on this earth to be abused by police officers.

Police would normally assault someone and change their stories so that it seemed they were defending themselves. If the police were not corrupt, I wouldn't mind them. They are supposed to protect the community. I don't see them as doing that.

One of my boys had an aura of craziness about him. He was like 2 years older than me, but he was a mad brother.

It was best to have him as a friend than an enemy. He was always cool with me as a younger. He didn't like me robbing he would tell me to go Boxing and when I would ask to go on criminal moves, he was hesitant. My brother did 5 years for one of his moves gone wrong.

One day we were in South Kilburn Estate. He was in a flat with some guys. My cousin Darren and I were waiting in the corridor for him. There were raised voices and my boy came outside the flat. He is staring down the 3 guys and me and my cousin are there. I don't know what my cousin was thinking but I was thinking if this kicks off. It's going to get crazy.

Somehow nothing happened but it was a close call.

My boy had an ongoing beef with some next dude.

We burgled his home a few times. One time we booted off his door. There was nothing there as we had taken everything. My boy told me and my cousin to wait outside for 10 minutes and keep watch.

He calls us in and all we can smell is shit. We covered our noses as we continued in.

On the guys front room wall. My boy had written in his own excrement "KILBURN BRATS" and he left poo on the guys pillows on his bed. People get murdered for less. The guy's older brother who was a big man got involved. He tried to talk the situation down but one night in South Kilburn Estate. He got into a fight with my boy.

In the end, the guy was tied up and made to drink my boy's urine. That was the end of the Beef. Game over!

In my mid-teens, robbing was my job. We would go school and when it finished, we would meet up around 5/6pm and go on the hunt. Them days I was training at Stowe Boys Club in Harrow Road on Tuesday and Thursday at 7pm otherwise I was on the road or at Granville Youth Club or Carlton Centre.

From when I was street robbing, I can never remember being broke. For a kid I was comfortable.

We would go up St John's Wood, Queen's Park, Maida Vale. Areas where business people were working and rob them while they were going home. From when I pounced on them if they fought back, I would feel as if the robbing me. I was never violent towards them, but they were I looked at them they backed down.

Sometimes I was a clamper, that's when you put the victim in a sleeper hold while your accomplice dipped the victim's pockets.

I was arrested a few times for street robberies but never convicted of them. Sometimes I would be at the Police Station and they would arrest me on various robbery charges. Some of them I had done and some I hadn't.

I did a few ID parades but was never picked so the charges were dropped, and I was free to go. A couple of the local police knew my name, but I tried to keep low and off their radar.

The one conviction for street robbery was one I never did but was convicted as an accomplice.

I was going round my Gran's house to meet my cousin. I met him by Saltham Crescent. We bumped into 2 guys from the zones we were cool with. They were up for it, but police knew them on a first names basis. We walked down Saltram Crescent, next thing one of them moved to a victim. Police were coming out of all places. It was a set up, an operation. We all run off, but my cousin ran with our 2 friends across the road, I started walking when I got behind some cars. As they were chased down the road I nearly got away, but an undercover police officer popped out of an entrance to a flat. He said he was arresting me. I claimed I was going home. He wasn't sure so he brought me over to another officer. This officer was 6 foot plus, a big muthafucka. He grabbed me and started swearing at me. I thought he was going to hit me but he threw me in a van with a mattress on the floor. I was 14 years old and arrested on robbery. 1 by 1 all 4 of us were arrested and brought to Harrow Road Police Station. My mum came to the station. I was really worried when I never got bail. I was used to getting bail and thought I was going jail for the first time. The fun had gone out of the robbery game.

My cousin Tyrone and I was put in a youth home up near Central London. We got there around midnight. I felt safe with my cousin and more relaxed. The staff gave us a chocolate bar, packet of crisps and a glass of milk. It was Friday night, so we had court on Saturday morning. I didn't know what to expect. Our 2 friends were kept in the Police Station overnight.

We were woken up real early the next morning. When we got to the Youth Court in the Morning, my mum and my brother had come to the court. Our Uncle Simon came for Tyrone and our Co-D's mothers had come.

Everyone except Bull Dog got bail. He was 15 years old and had previous convictions for Robbery. We were happy to get bail, but we could all end up in prison.

As the following months came, I slowed down on robbing.

When it came to trial, my cousin and I said we never knew our Co-D's and that we were just on the same road as them.

The police officers had all different statements. There were holes all in their reports. It was 3 judges who were deciding about our case. Obviously, they went for the police but it was an undercover operation and we were caught up in it. We were always going to get found guilty.

A lot was going on in my life at that time. My Dad was in St Lucia for 6 months while the robbery had happened. When he came back, he tried to leave off where he had left our relationship and beat me. That recording was playing no more and I fought back.

We had a few fights over a couple of weeks. I was ready for my pops, but he messed up my face digging his nails in my skin. We weren't really talking for a while, but my Dad still came to the trial.

I was in the Unit for expelled pupils at the time, so my life was real low at that moment.

We all got 24 hours Community Service which was nothing as we basically had to go a Youth Centre for Criminals every Saturday for 2 hours, that was our punishment. It was a joke.
Tyrone went to St Lucia with our Grandparents for a few months, so I wasn't going alone. I never went. When he came back, we started going. It was cool.

I even beat up some guy who had stolen my walkman. It was a cheap one, but it was the principle of the situation. I had to wait a whole week to get this punk. I saw him in the centre, walked straight up to him and moved him up. No problem, he got fucked up. They called the Police but he didn't want to press charges, so it was nothing.

When I was young, people knew I had a short fuse and would move up someone if they stepped out of line. I wasn't a bully. I just stood up for myself. I even made a few hundred pounds one going to the Youth Centre for Young Criminals. There was a bag at a bus stop. The person had jump on the bus by the time they had noticed I was off. A quick change before I did my 2 hour punishment at the Youth Centre.

In the end of year exams for the Beethoven St Centre for expelled kids I came first out of my year. The prize was 10 days in Super camp in Harrow on the Hill.

It was strange for me leaving the Hood to do this thing. Middle class kids from Europe and America. It was a Cultural change for me.

I clashed with the tutors in the camp. Looking back, I was a hard kid to get to. I was nearly thrown out. Bit by bit we found an understanding and we got on.

It was nice to meet kids from all over the World. The American girls got along with me just fine. They noticed I talked different to all the other English kids. In class we would learn speed reading. Ways to study our fears and problems with oneself.

My problem was my attitude. I had to break a plank of wood with the word ATTITUDE written on it. I kept the 2 pieces of wood for 13 years. I had 3 girls who liked me. 2 white and 1 black girl. I kissed the white girl afterwards the black girl told me she thought it was no competition as we both black so she thought I would have gone for her. While I was there, I tried not to see race but Camilla said I got a case of Jungle Fever, referring to Wesley Snipes film about White and Black couples relationship. It was a good 10 day event, it showed me there was more to life than what I had experienced so far.

At the end of the 10 day event, everyone had to do a speech. I was nervous as I am not the strongest public speaker. I was told while I was at the event that I was a natural leader. This is what I spoke about. I still keep in touch with Camilla. A few weeks later 2 of my cousins burgled the venue where the event was held. That shit was funny to me.

BEEFING WITH THE TWINS

Back in 96, we were good. Hanging out in Peel Precinct, making money. We felt good.

Carlton Centre was open those times. They had dance for the girls. A music room for the guys and the chill out area with the Pool and TV.

That was our shit. One day, it was over the School Holidays because I remember it was midday. Two guys came in, looked around and left. As they were leaving one of them bounced me. Man died for less in those days. We had a stand off and he left.

He came back with more men an hour later. They tried to trap me on the stairs. We were outnumbered so we bounced.

I forget who I was with. But I remember I went to my Aunt's home. Her sons had my back. I went for my cousins Darren. His big brother Dollar gave me a big meat chopper.

I rounded up my cousins, Grim and Duck, told them what went down.

Back in the day, we did our thing. No one knew who these guys were, so we walked around Kilburn for a few hours looking for them.

We never knew the guy had a Twin. Its around early evening and we see this guy. Looks exactly like the guy who tried it on me earlier on.

We move to him. He doesn't know what the fuck we are on about.

We rough him up and let him go. We walk back to Carlton Centre. It was me and Grim trailing behind. We see 3 muthafuckas running at us, shouting. I turn to them and start telling them let's do this. I had my Chopper, so I was good. Grim had nothing on him so wasn't so keen. I look around Grim is heading for Carlton Centre and I got 3 guys brandishing knives running towards me. I legged it to Carlton Centre as I knew I had man in there.

I ran upstairs, shouting at them behind me. Somehow, we end up in the music room.

I got my Chopper out and the 3 guys surrounding me with their knives out. There was a group of kids behind them who were in the music room and my cousins Darren and Grim. I felt let down as they stayed on the side, but they didn't have no weapon. My cousin Ducky, love that man for life. Took off his fucking belt around his waist and stood by me. Ready for action.

They told him they only want me. Step back and they won't touch him. Ducky wasn't having it. He said he's man's blood. Duck has his belt out and I have my Meat Chopper. We are facing these 3 scumbags who have 3 big kitchen knives and it looks like it's going to be a blood bath.

I had many near death experiences when I was young.
This was one of them.

One of the youth workers tried to calm the situation down. I said my chopper isn't coming down unless these guys back up. It was tense. I was sweating. Not sure if I'm going to die. But they backed off and left the building.

Went back for my cousin Dollar told him what went down. He came over to Peel Precinct. Crazy came as well with some of the elders.

We found out where they lived, and my cousin Dollar tried to boot off their door. 3 of them were barricading the door, shouting and laughing at us that we wouldn't get in.

They were in our hood so we would see them again. A week went by and Ducky told me Crazy had squashed the beef with them. We saw them near the Petrol Station me and Ducky. We were going to have it out but it was just a stared down. Me thinking the Beef is over. I see them a month later in South Kilburn estate. I was walking over to Precinct.

I walked pass a Jeep that was parked on the side of one of the buildings. I didn't even notice them. One of them called at me. "Are you Ash?" I was like "No" Next thing I know he swings a punch at me, and his boys try to grab me to throw me in the Jeep.

My fucking heart is jumping out of my chest. I get loose and run round the back of the shops. They split up to trap me. I ran so hard. I knew if I was caught it was over so I ran to Crazy's apartment but he wasn't in. This is before everyone had mobiles. That was a luxury back in the mid 90's.

I went to a next man and asked if he had heat. He was an older and didn't want to give it to me. I can see why the kids are going prison for murdering each other now cause if I had got the gun. I would have killed them and maybe be in prison. I've known kids as young as 13 and 14 who have shot someone. You can live in the same city and different neighborhoods be like different worlds.

I told my mum. We had to leave the area but she didn't take my situation seriously. Next thing I hear those two greasy scumbags were in prison for rape. They even got released cause a few years later I read in the national newspaper that they had struck again. Rot in Jail!

ON THE RUN

I was getting reckless and I started to slip. I was ripping loads of 18k Rolex's and Cartier's. I was nicknamed the 18k kid. It all started when Crazy wanted my bike and I was saying I'm going out there myself, he laughed at me and said, "OK"
I was destined not to fail. Well, at least I thought I wasn't. I went around Kilburn, Maida Vale, Little Venice, St.John's Wood, Primrose Hill, Bayswater. I could not see nothing. I did not want to go back to Kilburn Precinct with my tail between my legs. Then I saw a man walking with his shopping bags. My eyes fixed onto his watch. My radar did a quick assessment and it came up positive. It was all systems go. I parked my bicycle near my getaway route and jogged back to the road where my soon to be victim was. There was some building work going on opposite where he was walking. I was just fixed on the watch. I grabbed his wrist before he knew what was going on. He was on the floor shouting that he had been robbed. The builders didn't even have time to chase me. I was off. I was competing in Athletics at the time and was reigning Westminster Champion. I was in shape. No beer drinking builder would be a match for me. I ran round the building to where I had parked up my bicycle. Image if my bike would have been stolen, I would have had a long run back to the manor. Lucky for me, my getaway transport was waiting for me. I was a 10 minute bike ride from Kilburn Precinct. I rode as fast as I could. My heart was beating out of my chest. I was happy that I had got away. I looked at the watch, scoped the gliding of the Rolex ticker to assure me it was real. I put my head down and peddled hard. When I got back to the Precinct. The whole crew were there. I told my cousins what I had done and where I had been. They told me to keep it under wraps as Virgil was around.

He was an older man who robbed younger guys. I didn't really know him then. I asked Crazy if he had got anything today as he had been "out there" as well. He said,"Nah" and I showed him what I had got. He smiled. I said, "I know you didn't think I had it in me." It was the first time I had got one on my own. I had got with Bighead in the past and with next man but this was where I grew man balls and got my own shit on my own. I didn't care who you were. If you were wearing a Rolex or Cartier, you were a target. Black or white.

While I was with Jessica, I kind of stopped robbing. I never told her what I did before I met her. We had a close relationship. She told me stuff I would never repeat out of my mouth, but we were cool. I was with her a little bit after Nicky, who was my first childhood girlfriend.

Rahel came after Jessica and would last on and off for many years.

I had like a year out of robbing. While I was with Jessica, it was just athletics, boxing and her. I was a broke in that relationship. All my cousins and friends would tell me what they were doing how much money they were making but I was just
 doing a morning cleaning job. I started in 1996 and stopped in 1999 when I was with Rahel. Rahel would stay round overnight, it was the first girl I had really doing that on a regular basis. I didn't want to leave her in the morning, so I gave up the job and one of my family members did it. That cleaning job had done me good. It was in a designer store and I would break into the different stores and steal their expensive suits and shirts. I stole clothes worth a few grand from there. I got a suit which was over £600, some real smooth 3 piece suit. I wore that to my Grandad's funeral in 1999.

When I met Rahel, I was in full flow of my robbing. It was like my job. My cousin Tyrone and I would sometimes leave in the morning to look for victims. Sometimes you wouldn't get nothing until the end of the day. Shopping centers and high streets in rich areas where good to go as we would follow the potential victim for up to 2hrs. We could have been private investigators because we were pretty good.

By now I had a 250 Kawaski Motor bike which I had bought off a business associate I went high school with. I had bought a Ford Fiesta XR2i and a few other things. We nearly fell out over a fake Rolex he got off his friend which I bought from him. I let it go, over looked the situation because I didn't want the guns to come out over his friend tricking him as well, so at a time I had a GT Turbo Renault, a Ford Fiesta XR2i and my Kawaski 250. I was balling for a 18 year old kid. I started selling drugs again as Baby man had advised me to flip my robber money so I sold Ash, weed and crack. I tried to work with everything. I was about money then. I always tried to have my finger in loads of different ventures. Some flopped but you never know if you don't try.

I was doing some loose Rolex robberies, too close to home. I had started getting tattoos by now and summer time was the prime time to strike on victims. I could be walking shop or checking a friend down the road, if I saw diamonds or Rolex's. They were gone. I was a predator. I would rip your arm off if I had to but I was like a surgeon. I would step to you and before you knew it, the 18k Rolex or Cartier was in my hand while I ran off. I used to tell women I was interested in, that I dealt in antiques, buying and selling them. People knew I was gain, which meant up for it. I used to hang around Kilburn Precinct, we felt like we ran shit. South Kilburn guys couldn't tell us nothing and neither could the Mozart Mexicans as they called themselves. Some of them I went to school with so they would try holla at me to go out there with them cause they knew I was making money. Some of them made money with me, some of them didn't. Whoever was with me would get a cut, sometimes I was too generous. They would get 30% of what I got paid for my jobs just for being there. A lot of times I would pounce on the prey on my own but I would want someone there just to look out and in case of any heroes. Some guys have been to prison just because of heroes. I never had a big problem with heroes, but I know a few guys who have done prison time because someone would grab them and shout out for others to help them. I had my backup just in case a problem arose.

One afternoon in May 1999, I was outside of my mums' home with my 13 year old brother. I was showing him how to ride my Kawaski 250 motorbike. Police were surprisingly driving by and saw us on my mum's road. As soon as I saw what police officer stepped out of the car, I knew we were in trouble.
PC Allen Mills was notorious in West London. He put a lot of guys from the area in prison. He knew everyone's name and details. I had only had a couple of run ins with him, but he knew who I was. My brother and I were filming each other riding on the road with my new Sony camcorder. PC Alan Mills came towards us and asked what we were doing. We replied. I knew he would be going to arrest us. My brother was like 6ft tall at the time, so he looked older than his years.

I was told to come near my front door. PC Mills asked to see my new Sony camcorder that was the last time I saw it. It had incriminating footage of me boasting about being the biggest 18k rob- ber in the area and it had my other cousins boasting of what they do. Even one of my older cousins who is doing big stuff now building houses all over the world, he had said a few bits about being a boss. Lucky for us they never checked the footage because they never came back at us for that and they would have.

A police van was called while they were questioning us, so I knew we were in trouble. The backup cops came to chat to me while Alan Mills went over to my brother. He punched my brother while questioning him and pounced on him with other officers. I

was pissed. My bike collapsed to the floor, damaging the paintwork. We were man handled and thrown in the police cell. We were there for a few hours; my brother was released way before me. I had my solicitor come. It was a legal aid one appointed by the police station. They were a firm from Southwest London. I was charged with a robbery of a gold and silver Rolex that had been robbed. I knew about the robbery. I thought that I was not getting bail and that I was going to prison. I was getting nervous. It was summer and it was not the time to be in lockdown. I told the police that I was studying in Paddington college and that I am innocent of the crime. I gave them a fake name. Back then they sometimes did not fingerprint you so when they gave me bail, they were never seeing me again. I was off. When it came to go court, I never went so I had jumped bail. Police where contacting my mum and my solicitor was advising me to hand myself in. They even went to my college. That hurt me as I could not finish my GNVQ Advanced Leisure and Tourism. I even helped my boy Joseph passed his course work as he copied some of my work. He went onto University and to work for a Sports Unit in London and my old primary school. He got married which I was so proud of him for. While he was in University, he would sell cannabis and hashish for me there. We made money; he controlled the distribution until too much competition came and tried to undercut us. It was nice while it lasted.
He was running the University, controlling majority of the supply and I was the man feeding him. I liked it, we were making money and doing what we do.

I was running out of places to lay my head. My girlfriend at the time Rahel, lived with her family so that was not going to happen as they were Eritrean and very old school. My cousin Darren had me for a few days but that was still in the area and I needed to get out of west London. PC Alan Mills would find me, and I would be incarcerated. I hadn't spoken to my ex Jessica in a while. I got in touch with her, to tell her my situation. Lucky for me her family were away on holiday. I was so happy for that. I was there until I found somewhere else to stay. I was seeing Rahel now for nearly a year. Jessica left to go work at JD Sports for the day. She said she would be back around 6pm. Rahel was coming around that day to see me.

Rahel came early afternoon. She was my ride or die chick back then. She wanted to help me. She was scared for me. She didn't want her man in prison. We chilled for a bit then we slept together in my ex-girlfriends' front room. Imagine if my ex-girlfriends' parents walked in and saw us naked having sex on their family sofa. We did it a few times, got showered and chilled until Jessica came back from work. They didn't really say anything but mumble at each other. I told Rahel not to be disrespectful because she was helping me out. She replied, "I bet she is." Rahel stayed for a little while longer and left me to be alone with my ex-girlfriend.

Jessica had a male friend stay over that night.
On Sunday morning I thanked Jessica for her hospitality and headed back down to west London. I called my mum, she told me that the police came by a couple of times so I stayed at my cousins again.

When I was 17 years old, I had started driving and bought myself a car. I partied a lot in South London. Sometimes I would bring my brother, sometimes I would go with my boys or sometimes I would roll solo. I was driving so I went where I wanted to go.
My first car was a Fiat Uno, platinum color.

I met Chinade at the Fridge bar in Britain. It was an under 18s event where Boy Band, Another Level were performing. We'd become friends, I took her to the Ginuwine
concert in Shepherd's Bush and I hanged out with her at her mother's place in Fulham. Her mum was a nice lady and very

pretty. She had a kind heart and liked to joke around. I have fond memories of her. I kept low in Fulham for a bit.

I had just got my first tattoo on my right bicep; I was with my friend Tafari. He had got his tattoo up Burnt Oak at Rock-it Tattoos studio a few months earlier, so he recommended Tony the tattoo artist to me.

Tony was a nice guy, he used to do martial arts, so he was into fighting and fitness. He had put on a little bit of weight since his fighting days, but he was still interested in what I did. I was getting a tattoo of a boxer and I was happy with the job. I would end up getting addicted to tattoos. 3 years down the line in 2001, Tony would sponsor me. When I was out of jail he asked how my boxing was going and how much it cost. He said he would pay for my training costs. He backed me for many years to come, from to 2001 to 2011 he helped out. He is a nice guy and very supportive of me. I had goals in boxing, to win the World and European titles but for him If I fought for the British title I would dedicate that belt to him. When I won the title, he was over the moon and very proud of me. It was nice that someone that did not really know me other than speak to me when he gave me tattoos, believed that I could win a British title and he believed that I should be on the World stage. Tony is another special person who walked into my life and I am very grateful to.

I had just been swindled out of a kilo of skunk, that was around 3600 pounds. I was selling drugs to a guy I knew from Harlesden, his cousin. We made contact in prison and when we both got out we did business together. He would later introduce me to his cousin. His cousin was buying drugs off me for over a month. He was only getting little bits but one night, he asked for a kilo. I had it there so I dealt with it. He did me dirty. He was in a car full of man. I met him near Malvern Road Post Office. We normally met there so it was not unusual. He got out the car and told me to give it to one of the guys in the car the kilo. Looking back, it was dodgy but I didn't think he would pull that on me. As I got out he gave me a black bag tied up with what I thought was money. I got home and untied the black bag. I could not believe what I was seeing. I thought he had made a mistake; it was newspaper cut in the size of money and wrapped in elastic bands. I kept calling his phone. He let his phone rang and I left messages. I called his cousin up who had made the connect. He got back to me saying he will show me where his sister lives. My cousin Tyrone was one of the people who made calls and said its on me what I want to do. I knew I had to move to him, he didn't know where I lived. I wanted to see him to put him through some pain. I didn't want to go to his sister's place, and he was not there. Back in my teenage years I would have done it easily. I was trying to focus on my boxing and stay out of trouble. I didn't need a war right now. I just wanted to make money on the low.

Decisions were made, the guy who made the connect would be murdered in Harlesden a couple of years later, the cousin who swindled me, was never seen or heard of again. This situation would never happen again.

I met Rahel at Hackney Downs in May 1998 while I was talking to Chinade. I didn't have a mobile phone then, so I gave her my dad's house number. Rahel would call like once every 2 weeks but would never leave her number with my dad. By September Rahel left her number with my dad. I was so happy when my dad said she left her number as I thought she was so beautiful. When I saw her in Hackney Downs, I thought this girl is out of my league, but I thought fuck it I'm going to make a move. She was friendly and took my number. I never expected to get a call from her so when I did, I was beyond happy. We spent many years together, had good and bad experiences. She has been my business partner in the past and we still stay in contact to this day.

I would stay a night at Chinade's mums place while I was on the run. She advised me to get a good Lawyer and hand myself into the police. I told her I would do that but that wasn't going to

happen. I had jumped bail. I knew if they caught me, I would be put in prison. I spoke to my aunty up Euston. I told her the situation. She told me I could stay. That was good for me. The police would never think to come up to Euston for me. Rahel would come up there and we would spend time together, taking my nephew Jerome to the park or my little cousin Simone football training. I chilled out there for a week or so. My boys from college told me that the police had come to our college. I was studying Advanced GNVQ and the police had told the teachers to call them if I show up, I had to rush in some course work and ended up failing the course when I was looking at a B (merit). That hurt me not passing as I had worked hard for 2 years on that course. I had met a nice teacher by the name of Yve Ming. She was cool and gave us advice. My friends Joseph and Ryan would pass the course.

My aunt said I could sleep on the leather sofa which was cool but after the first night. I
decided to sleep on my cousin's bedroom floor with a bed sheet. I heard something running across the front room floor. I struggled to sleep that night. When I told my cousins in the morning, they laughed at me and said, "We thought you knew." Tyrone would leave me and his brother sleeping in the bedroom, he would tell us to come with him to the youth housing services in Sommers Town in Euston. They help youth people get accommodation. Within 2 years Tyrone had his own place.
Staying at my aunts was cool. She would sometimes cook for me which was nice. I didn't really care about that. I just wanted a roof over my head but food was a bonus.
I stayed away from my mums until it was time to go Ibiza with the lads. It was me, Ryan, Joseph and one of their friends. I had

grown an afro whilst being on the run and added some more tattoos to my body. I was on the run from the police but still making my drug money and robbing the rich folks up in the suburbs. I was back around Paddington and Kilburn now but keeping a low profile. I was wearing sweatshirts and jumpers in the summer heat, sweating my balls off. I even had started to jerry curl my hair. I looked totally different.

Around that time, I had to back my cousin Darren as his apartment had been burgled. He called me when he had noticed it had happened. I got over to his place quick. I didn't know what I would do if that happened to me. He handled it pretty well. I told him to think of anyone it could be and I would back him. He had no idea as he had no enemies. I told him that we would go around Mozart estate in the afternoon and see what everyone says and move them up if need be.

Around 6pm we went over to Avenues Youth club, everyone was there. I spoke to some of the older guys first. They were cool. They went on like they didn't know anything about it. We would have got the same response if they had done it. One guy, Ricks shouted out "I did it." I went over to him and warned him not to joke because I would drop him. He smiled in my face and said, "What!" The elders came over and broke us up. He said he never had anything to do with it and was kidding. He was one of the younger guys who was doing his thing. He robbed and sold drugs just like me. Most people either did one or the other. He had the area on lock back in those days. We would later become friends, but he would be in and out of prison from robbery to selling drugs to failed kip-nap attempts. I was a lucky guy as I did the same shit as him but only ever touched prison for armed robbery and got acquitted in the end.

People just don't understand, I grew up in this shit. All my people, my uncles, my cousins, it's just what we did. We lived this shit. It traps you. It seems like there is no way out. Crime surrounds you. It takes a strong person to walk away from that life especially when they are making money. Being a criminal, financed my professional boxing career. I didn't need no manager or promoter to finance me. I put a whole heap of money into my career over the first 6 years as a pro. When you think of it, I wasn't bringing back no income from boxing for the first six years, so it was all an investment. I believed in my ability and it would pay off.

IBIZA

Being in Ibiza was great at first. 4 young guys on a 18-30 holiday expecting fun with loads of women. It would not work out like that.

We were homeless within the first 5 days and we had to buy some knifes from the army shop as there was some racist energy in the town. Nowadays it is more welcoming to blacks but in 1999. Ryan and Joseph's friend were called a nigger on our first 2 days there. The trip started off promising. We went to a foam party on the first night. There were women everywhere. I haven't tried to chat up so many ladies up in my life without some success. I was getting no play. I remember we went out to some trance party. We were dancing with the girls and making the most of the night. Joseph had his tongue down a few of the drunk ladies without it going further. We laughed at him afterwards. Kissing strange girls for the fun of it, what was he thinking. We would go for KFC most nights after a night out. I was drunk every day, drinking everything. Thinking back it was nice to get away with 2 of my best friends but for a man of my sexiness, it was a shock to my system to be in a place where there was 3 to 1 more women than men and I wasn't getting no action.

Ryan tried to chat anything that moved. The guys were hungry in town, so the women had choice and we were not their flavor.

We had paid for a day out to a winery, go karting and a drinking session. It was baking hot and we met up with everyone who was going on the trip in the morning. We first went to the winery. I found this boring. Why would I care about this stuff? I couldn't wait to get out of the place. We jumped back onto the coach and went to some big open space of sand with the sun beating down on us. One by one we got on our knees, tilted our head back and was drowned by pure Vodka. It was not a good sight being drunk and the day was just starting. It was only noon and the next stop was the Go-karting track. I was wearing my blue and white Iceberg waistcoat and shorts with a dirty blue helmet. I was confident of winning, but I would come 2nd place as my drink driving skills were not as good as Ryan's.

By the bar, we saw a group chanting, so we went up closer and to our amazement we saw a girl on her knees giving some guy oral sex. There must have been 40 people around them filming it and trying to take photos. We had a slow start to being in Ibiza but seeing this truly gave us a false sense of hope which would lead us to being disappointed time and again with knock backs.

After seeing the oral sex skills of a stranger, our coach headed off to a restaurant bar where we would have unlimited amounts of sangria. I took it easy as my head was still not good after the night before and the Vodka being thrown into my mouth earlier in the day. I enjoyed my fish and chips and the day trip was over. We got back to our hotel early evening and would chill out then get ready for the nighttime festivities.

It was like spot the black man there and we would always be happy when we would see some black folks during the daytime or even out clubbing. There were few R'n'B nights but Twice as Nice, which is a big party in the UK, was doing a rave there once a week so that was good because we would hear the music, we were comfortable with. That dance and trance music was driving me crazy but by the end of the first week. We were in our new residence on the strip of San Antonio in Ibiza as playing with our knifes got us thrown out the hotel we were staying. I had come at my friend with my knife, he picked up his mattress, I grabbed it off him and threw it outside the hotel. It landed on the hotel owners car. Just missing him as he spoke outside to one of his

staff. He called police quickly, we had seen a drunk English man get slapped by a short fat police officer the night before for dancing in the police man's walking space so we knew that we had to be on our best behavior with them. We tried to apologize but the owner of the hotel was not having none of it. He over charged us for his side view mirror on his car and threw us out with nowhere to stay. We were on the side of the road, homeless in Ibiza with nowhere to go. We spoke to our 18-30 representative Becky but she could not help until the next day. We were on the streets for the night. What a nightmare! The heat did beat down on us while we sat on the wall like idiots wondering what our next move was. Down the bottom on the hill was a plush
hotel. Our luck would have it there was no reception in the front, so we slipped into the waiting room. That would be our bed for the night, but the Twice as Nice party was on. Ryan and Joseph's friend Michael was the one I chose to stay and watch our bags. He protested but I told him if he chose to leave the hotel and my bags where taken. He would have to pay for everything in my suitcase. Joseph and Ryan thought I was wrong for that but he was not my friend and I wanted to go out partying.

We had a good night. We were homeless but still raving it up. When we got back around 4am, Michael was fast asleep. The next day, our 18-30 representative Becky found us outside our new hotel chilling. She got us a new apartment on the strip which had it perks, we just did not have a swimming pool like in our old hotel. We were happy to have a new place, so the stress was over. It was like something was always going wrong and getting worse. That night Michael and Ryan went out to one of those dance parties, we had already paid for it on our first day as our 18-30 rep did a good job selling the whole Ibiza events to us but come a week of hearing dance and trance music, it was not for me so Joseph and I passed on it. Instead we went down to the amusement centre and queued for the bungy jump. It was opposite. Instead of jumping off a bridge. You went into a metal bubble which was throw into the air at a very fast speed. We were strapped up in it and the guy operating it, shouts out "There is a loose cord" and pushes the button and we fly in the air. I am screaming that we are going to die and Joseph is just screaming out swear words. After 20 seconds we were safe again. My heart felt like it was going to jump out of my mouth. That was a scary moment. I was glad we did that instead of going to another rubbish dance party.

After the excitement of being thrown into the air, Joseph and I went out for a meal at a nice restaurant. If I was with my lady it would have been real nice but unfortunately I had a short chubby half Philippine half Moroccan man dining with me. We had a good time and the food was nice.

We went on a club crawl later that night, going to most of the bars in San Antonio, we passed by our regular club, Kremlin. They had a garage night and it was better than some of the others. We were downing alcoholic shots, drinking brandy and coke adding vodka and red bull. We were smashed that night. I had met a mixed race girl called Natalie from Shepard's Bush in London. She was cool and we would meet up at Kremlin on some nights. She was feeling me but I could tell she had been hurt in the past. I was on holiday, so I wasn't looking at anything serious.

We went out with the whole of the 18-30 party crew. It was a night out with sex games, sex show and all sorts. It was another night to get drunk. I have never drunk so much in such a short space of time. You had girls getting their breasts out doing sex games on the stage. Another game was girls showing off their dick sucking skills on dildos. I tried to get hypnotized, but it didn't happen. The other 4 guys did but I didn't so I am not sure if that stuff works. Later in the night some red faced girl, who was drunk out of her head was on Joseph and me. We could have had a threesome going on, but she was not for me. I let Joseph take over and he left us and went with her. He would later say that he thought he was going to get jumped by a group of white guys as they seemed a bit too rowdy for his liking. I told him, we see them on the holiday we will deal with the case. He said she was from South London and used Heroin. She sounded like a loose one, happy I let that one go. I'm sure he had a nice night though.

The next day we would go out and get drunk again. Joseph went onto the balcony to look over the beach strip. I locked the door and Joseph went wild. Banging on the door for me to let him in. Ryan and Michael where across the hall in their room. Next thing I know Joseph picks up a chair and tells me he will throw it at the glass sliding door. It was one of those steel chairs so certain to go throw the thin glass door. I smiled at him and stepped back. That sent his blood boiling and he threw the steel chair at the door. He smashed it near the latch to open it and stuck his hand through and turned it and slid the door open.

I didn't care because that was on him to pay for it not me. Now we were facing getting thrown out another hotel and we had a few days left. This holiday just kept getting worse. To see that Joseph is now married with children, working in a school, he's come a long way.

BACK ON THE STREETS

I would go back to robbing as the cash flow was running low and my boys were making money without me.

I was selling drugs more and more these days. It was a sideline to the robbing. Robbing wasn't a steady income as you had to wait for opportunities but when I got something it would be a few grand at a time. I was getting hashish from my people down Goldbourne Road or my friend in Kilburn. I would get weed and skunk as well. I messed with everything. If you needed it, I could get it. I built up a steady flow of customers. I was going in and out of my mum's place too often. I felt like the police where watching me.

One evening I was off to meet a client, I had a good portion of an illegal substance on me. I had a feeling that I was being followed by the police, so I jumped on a bus to try lose them. A couple of minutes later, on Shirland Road at the junction of Elgin Avenue in Paddington, there was police sirens going off. We were at the traffic lights so I was sweating and I thought this was it, I was fucked. The police car blocked off the bus. I was waiting for the officers to come upstairs but I heard them speaking to the driver and the next thing I knew was that the bus started to move again. I couldn't believe how lucky I was.

After that incident I would store my kilos at one of my family members apartment for safe keeping. Even that was risky as he lived in a crime ridden area where police where always stopping youngsters but I would take cab when transporting big portions. I would use his apartment until he got married and I had to give him back the key.

THE MOMENT THAT CHANGED MY LIFE FOREVER

GETTING ARRESTED & GOING PRISON

The day was June 18th, my brother's birthday. I had gone athletics in the morning with Michael Flavien. He used to coach me in Athletics when I was younger, and I was helping him out with the kids coming up now.
I did the session there and came home. My cousin Tyrone came round to see how I was. He was supposed to help me reload so I had to go get the money as I didn't have enough around me. He followed me down to Halifax bank in Whiteley's shopping centre down Bayswater.

It was a nice day, so the beautiful girls were out. That was always something my cousin and I had in common. I got the money I needed to add to get my box (kilo) and we headed back. We jumped on the 36 Bus to my mum's place.

As the Bus came to our stop on Chippenham Road, we jumped off outside Domino's pizza and started to walk back home. Now I didn't know this dude called Casper but my cousin knew him as he had stabbed his twin in the leg the previous year in a tussle they had up Euston.

Casper was driving a Black BMW, Tyrone saw him pass us on Chippenham Road. There were a few cars parked up as the traffic lights was red so Tyrone was like, "That is the guy who stabbed my brother." He told me to move to Casper from the driver side as Casper knew him so he was running on the pavement to come to the passenger side. My good friend Trevor was outside his window on his balcony watching us. I shouted out to him and kept it moving as we were on a mission. We got to the car. My cousin opened the passenger door, there was a female there and she just yelled out in fear as he had surprised her. I opened the driver's side. My cousin was telling me to pull him out the car, at that stage in my life I was a robber and I saw his Rolex and Cartier diamond bangle, so I was going to rob him. I pounced on him, he didn't know what was going on. Back in the day, if I moved to you to take your stuff, it was over. I'm taking it. I ripped the watch off his wrist, and I got the Cartier bangle off.

It was crazy, my cousin was over the female in the car, attacking Casper and the girl in the passenger seat was a girl he used to date a few years before. Sabina from Latimer Road, I remember her because I liked her younger cousin. Casper thinks we have just moved him up and he doesn't know why because he didn't click on that it was over Tyrone's twin.

We run off, but where the fuck to go. I didn't want to move to Casper because it was across the road from my mum's and the road was packed with cars as it was a Saturday afternoon in June. We where right in front of Chippenham Road Park. It was just crazy but I had to go with my cousins lead, that was my partner. When we ran away from the scene, where would we run to? I wanted to run down Grittleton Road to Elgin Avenue, but my cousin went straight to my mums house so I had to open up. Even though it's one of the dumbest moves a criminal could do and I was pissed. It worked in our favor in the end as Casper said I took out a big gun and was waving it around. No gun or Jewelry was found so in reality they had no case but being a black youth the British justice system is against us, innocent or not.

We are at my mum's place, with the jewelry, hiding out. We call my brother and my cousin's Twin. They come rushing round and we tell them the story of what happened. 10 minutes later, we see Police cars driving around the roads. Now we are thinking he doesn't know us so he won't know this is where I live and we were thinking Sabina's from the inner city so she won't open her mouth.

To our surprise she opened her mouth, giving my name and my cousins name. The police had put two and two together that we ran down a certain Road and disappeared. My name was on the Police system from the age of 13 so they knew where we went. As time went by, more and more police came. They blocked off both sides of the road. The Armed Police came so the big guns were out. People started to gather around. It was like a scene out of a movie. We had the jewelry, what the fuck was we going to do. We were going to jail, I couldn't believe it. We were thinking what we could do, where can we hide it. Nowhere seemed good enough to put the stolen jewelry.

Out of all 4 of us it was the youngest, a 13 year old boy who said, hide it in mums' curtains. It had some design where you could put stuff in at the top of the railings. I thought it would never work but I reluctantly agreed. It looked like if the Police shook the curtains it would fall out and we would be doing 5 years easy and as they were saying Armed Robbery, it may have been 8 years.

So now we are inside, the Jewelry has been hidden but my drugs are still here. I had a half box there (500grams/18 Oz's) so where the fuck was that going to go? There was a balcony at the back of the apartment where we used to store all my old BMX bikes from when I was younger. I used to put bikes together, it was one of my pastimes as a child.

So I thought why not. Police had come to this crib a few times and never gone outside there. I jump out the back window. Now opposite is the back of other houses so no one can really see me except people in their homes. They wouldn't think anything of me being out there so I thought it was a good idea.

I put the drugs behind some bikes and my cousins shout out "don't move, there is Armed Police pointing their guns at you". I looked and I saw them behind a wall. I was 4 floors up but I could see them. I moved so slowly, I didn't want a bullet in my back and I didn't want them to see me do any sudden moves. When the police kill a Black person, nothing ever happens to them.

I climbed from the back window into the house. We are stuck! The big guns are all around us. We are looking outside the living room windows and kitchen blinds and seeing how dangerous it is looking outside. The police emptied all the neighbors out from the three other flats in the building and they were ready to come for us.

My cousins and my brother knew they were coming so we just waited. We were calm and knew what we had to do. We heard the police coming up the stairs. They are shouting out to us; they start to break open my mum's front door. I am now swearing at them. "You fucking pigs, you broke my mum's door". I let a load of obscenities come out my mouth, I was revved up and pissed off. I have always had hate for the police due to being targeted by them as a teenager. That's how it is for many black boys in the inner cities. Good or bad, we are targeted.
My cousins are telling me to be calm as I was making a bad situation worse.
The police told us to put our hands over the balusters one by one. I was the last one to leave. We went downstairs and we were handcuffed.

There was a massive crowd outside watching us put into the police van, some people who I know generally cared about my wellbeing and some were nosy neighbors.
I remember the time because the European Championship was on as we arrived at the station, I asked one of the police officers the results on the game I wanted to know about.

They treated me ok on the way to Paddington Police Station, sometimes you get an asshole.

We were booked in at the police desk at the back of Paddington police station. My brother, two cousins and I charged with Armed Robbery.
Then we were put in separate cells and they were away from each other so we could not communicate. It was messed up. I sat in my cell thinking about all the mad things I had done in my life, I am going jail for this crime. This was bullshit. It wasn't my call, I had to back my cousin. It's how we were raised. If one fights, we all fight. I remember my Aunty Molin telling me that at our Granny and Granddad's house, when I was like 8 years old. She was sending Tyrone and I to the local shop on Kilburn Lane, she said we must always have each other's back. Many times, Tyrone had my back and I had his as well.

I am looking at the 4 walls in the Police cell and thinking, so many times I have been here but my luck has run out. I knew I was bang to rites. The Rolex and Cartier Diamond Bangle was at my mother's place. They would find it as there was so many of them and they think a gun is in the house, so they are going to rip the place apart. We were fucked.

A few hours went by and we were going to get checked by a Doctor, I was escorted out of my cell and led down the corridor to a door on the left as we walked out the corridor. I saw my brother with our father. My brother was 13 years old, so he had to have an adult present. My Dad was aggressive as usual. My brother was wilding out, he wasn't having it from the police as they were trying to man handle him. I told him to calm down, everything will be okay.

I went into the Doctors room, he's checking me out, making sure

I am ok but really, he didn't give a fuck. I said my wrists were sore. I could hear my brother getting agitated and our father was swearing now, telling my brother to calm down and be quiet. Next thing I could hear was a commotion, I thought they were on our father, so I jumped up, opened the door and I see a bunch of officers assaulting my 13 year old brother. Our father was telling my brother not to fight them. I wasn't standing by and watching them on my little brother, they must crazy. I jump on them, trying to pull the officers off my brother but more came and restrained me. They got me in an arm lock and threw me to the ground. Now I look to the side and I see them pushing our father to the wall and they have his face against it and his hands behind his back. That made me even more mad as my father was sick. PC Allen Mills punches me in the face a few times and tells me to shut up. It was crazy. Zachary and his 2 sons all in the police station getting man handled by the pigs.

Our father was pushed against the wall with his hands behind his back and face pressed on the dirty wall while my brother and I was led back to our cells. They told my father to calm down. What the fuck do they expect a father to sit down calmly while his sons are assaulted. It would have been nice. My brother, my father and I fighting the police but my father has been sick since the late 80s, early 90s. I have heard so many stories from the elders in the community about back in the day, my father fighting racist children in school, skinheads, and racist police officers. Through my father's life, racism was normal, hence as a young child he told me to never accept it.

A promoter/manager who I worked with early in my career, Johnathan Feld. Told me that a UK promoter who has now had a sex change had started a rumor that I was racist. Things like this can hold back your career.

With African and Caribbean's coming here since helping Great

Britain in the World Wars 1914 to 1918 and 1939 to 1945, African Americans that fought in the wars would often stay here as Britain wasn't as bad as the USA. Racism still existed, white women that had relationships with blacks were often ostracized. Life was hard raising mixed race children.

Whilst in prison on remand, I told my lawyer to bring a case against the police for assault. Funny, on that day the cameras was not working. As always, the cops were dodgy as fuck.

I woke up in the police station realizing that of all the things I have done, I had done some crazy shit and never been caught. My good luck streak had finished. The police were going to find the Rolex and the Cartier Bangle in the curtains where they had been hidden.
I had to back my cousin, but I was still mad at myself. Tyrone, had always backed me so it is something that sometimes you may not like but you go along with it. I was mad that my cousin ran straight to my mums apartment but he did it and in the end it worked out for the best as the police knew we had run straight there so the Rolex and Cartier bangle should be there as we didn't have time to hide it anywhere else.
Thankfully for the police not doing their job properly, they never found it and their case was always going to be an upward struggle. As I was known to the police from years ago as a robber. They were always going to come at me hard. When I was younger and would get stopped by police, saying my surname would always be a bad thing, as my family were known. From my uncles to my cousins, a family of criminals was what I was proud of.

My brother and Tyrone's twin were given bail on the Saturday night as the alleged victims did not name them as their attackers.

My cousin Tyrone Theophane and I had our clothes taken from

us as part of the police evidence. I had changed my clothes anyway and my cousin had changed into some of my tops. We were experienced in police practices and knew what they do. We were given the white all in one jump suits to wear in the meantime.

Sunday morning, the day after getting arrested. My lawyer had told me because of the seriousness of the alleged offensive we would be kept in custody until Monday morning so we could go to court and be sent to a Young Offenders Prison.
I can't lie I wanted to cry. I was really sad and I knew I was facing a long time in prison. I had heard a lot of jail stories. It seemed like hell on earth. I was about to find out.

I was interviewed later in the day. I did what I always do. I said No Comment to majority of the questions, but I made a statement saying I had coached kids in the morning at Paddington Recreation Ground. I used to help out with my old Athletics coach Michael Flavien. I told them, my cousin Tyrone Theophane came to visit me as I was going down to the bank in Whitley's Shopping Centre to take some money out. We said we walked back so it couldn't have possibly been us as we wouldn't have made it back in time. We had cameras all over the shopping centre see us but funny they couldn't find us on there. Legal aid solicitors (Public Defender Lawyers) are garbage, might as well represent yourself.
I told the police in my Interview that guns and I do not go together. My solicitor told me they had not found no gun or the alleged stolen jewelry. I knew in reality they should have given me bail but it was at a time when a lot of celebrities were getting robbed and Tony Blair had said he was going to go hard on robbers and he had instructed the judges to enforce that zero tolerance through sentencing. That lost Tony Blair my vote in the 2002 General Election. I was locked up with no evidence against me.

I used my one phone call to call home. I spoke to my brother. He let me know nothing had been found. That was joy to my ears. It had been passed onto my cousin so it could get sold.

It was our word against theirs. No way should we have been kept in jail because someone says they were robbed. It was broad daylight and no witnesses had come forward. The British law system is a joke.

Tyrone's mum, my auntie sent Sunday food for me and him. We also got some sweets, Sunday Newspaper and some juice. I hadn't eaten at all. I could never eat police station food as I would never trust that they wouldn't spit in it.

I had been reading the police code of conduct manual of what they are supposed to do for you whilst you are under their care. I was making myself a nuisance whilst there. I advise anyone arrested to do the same. Make sure these police do what they are supposed to do.

When Monday morning came we were woken early. We had a shower and put on our white paper tracksuit, provided by the police force. I thought we would have been taken to Marylebone Road Magistrates court but instead we were driven to Horseferry Road court. We shouted from our cells, trying to communicate with each other. We were down in the court cells all day. When we got to the court room, we were there for a few minutes. Some of our family came with my girlfriend of 2 years and Tyrone's girlfriend of 2 years. We waved to them and had quick words between each other. The judge said no bail and we were led back down to the cells. My cousin had been prison for contempt of court before with his twin for a few days so he had a feeling of how it was going to be. I just had the stories of jail fights, men getting raped and robbed. I was nervous and mad at myself but nobody forced me to make the decision I made, so off to prison we went.

The Prison van reached Feltham young offenders Institute early evening. All the new prisoners where lined up in a single line and one by one we were enrolled in her Majesty's prison system. We were given a prison number and we were told to forget our name as we are now a number. I still remember my number today FB7185. Being in jail made me who I am today. Focused and determined to make the most of my life.
My cousin Tyrone Theophane was FB7186. My soldier till the end. It pains me that we didn't grow old together.

We were put in a holding cell with the new arrivals and the prisoners who had gone Court in the morning. It felt weird being with hardened criminals, well they felt hardened to me as it was my first time in prison. I was with my cousin, so I knew we had each other's back.
FB7185 was called and I walked into a room where one officer took all my items and my belongings then put them in a bag with my number on it. They gave me a strip search; I was made to squat naked which was dehumanizing. I had seen it in the movies but doing it myself was an animalistic feeling, something I would have to get used to.
I was given some blue denim jeans and a white shirt with blue strips. I even had the checkered red and white boxers. I kept my trainers but wow, thanks for that. I would have rather kept my own boxers.
I was led into another waiting room where we were given some bed sheets for our cells and led off to the Induction prison wing.

As we walked down the hallways to the wing. It was kind of strange the way it looked. It was like hallways that you could see outside into the prison grounds, but the halls had bars so no way of escaping.

We were given a cell on the ground floor of the wing in the corner. It was pretty big but plain. Two single beds on the floor, a toilet in the corner and a sink opposite our windows. We had one window above each of our beds. I chose the bed furthest away from the cell door. I sat down on the bed, thinking I am trapped and lost in the system. Nowhere to go. Locked up like an animal. I wanted to cry but the tears wouldn't come out. I had been in trouble with my cousin Tyrone many times before. We had fought together, robbed together and cried together but now it had gotten serious. In jail for an Armed Robbery, It was no joke.

The night went so slow. We talked about what our story would be and how we will go about it. We had two different lawyers, from two different companies. We would have to have a story and stick to it. They had no evidence, but we had to prove we were innocent.

We were woken up around 7am for breakfast and told from now on we would have to make our bed and be up for when the cell door opened at 7.30am.
Breakfast consisted of cereal, some bread, jam and an egg with a carton of juice, which was called juice box by the prisoners. Nothing special but it was better than nothing.
It was our new home and we had to make the most of it and get used to it, fast.

The time moved so slow, it was crazy. I was thinking what I am supposed to do for all these hours just sitting in our cell watching the four walls. Around 11am, we were let out our cell. We did a 2 hour Induction which was cool. It got us out of the cell, and we got to meet the other prisoners.
One guy, who was from Hackney. Told us his story that he was stopped with his girl and he had rocks (crack) in his car. He was banged to rights. Looking at a 5 year sentence. He was only recently seeing the girl. Like a few weeks. I would have ran off

and left her there. He also said she looked like J-LO (Jennifer Lopez) but we saw her on a visit a few weeks later, she was far from J-LO, more like Courtney Cox. We always laughed at that when we saw them together during our visits. Even my girl at the time would laugh. Each to their own, he was in love so that's all that mattered.
His father was also in jail and serving a double sentence, so it was a cycle, hopefully his kid doesn't touch jail.

Later in the day, mid afternoon my cousin and I where switched to Nightingale Wing. It was normally the first stop after you did your Induction.
We were put again in a corner cell but this time on the second landing. It was okay for a cell, very spacious. I had the bed near the window and my cousin took the one near the cell door.
We would spend just over a month in that cell.
We met some nice guys there. Many of them where from South London, which had a respected reputation on the streets. Somewhere from Brixton, some from Elephant & Castle and a few white boys from Bermondsey who were looking at double digits for attempted murder. It was crazy, people would sometimes go for sentencing and get hit big, anything over 5 was seen as a lengthy stretch.

It was summertime being June, so it was always hot in our cell. This drove my cousin mad. He would sometimes look outside the cell windows and talk about what we could be doing instead of caged like two animals. I would just lie in bed and say outside doesn't concern me. I tried to block out the outside world as I didn't know when I would be seeing it next.

We tried to get a job, doing anything but it seemed on Nightingale wing that it was the white boys who were given the jobs. Sometimes new blood would arrive and within a few days they would get a job. The screws would laugh at us sometimes and say, "Theophane, you know you don't want to fucking work. You just want to get out your cell". I would think that is why everyone wanted a job. We got paid 50 pence a day for being locked up but if you worked you could get a tenner extra. I laugh at that now but when you are in prison. You need everything you can get. We were both sent money, so we were cool. My mum sent me some and I had people selling drugs for me outside. My cousin would sometimes get some weed or hashish from our people. We had an argument once as he was selling it for canteen and would be nice but it was my hashish, so I felt like I was entitled to some of the extra canteen.

We had each other's back in there. He was my cousin and CO-D so if you fucked with me, you fucked with him and vice versa.

One time we offered out a prison officer in our cell. He nicked us for threatening behavior and we were sent down to the block. We had agreed to say he was racist to us. Two prisoners' word against one screw. In the end the Governor just let it go as the officer had no proof and we were backing each other.

On the way to the block, I was told to stand up by a wall. I was leaning back on it and a screw who was walking past told me to stop leaning on the wall, I was smiled at him and ignored his instructions. He stood in front of me and jumped on me. He called for assistance from the woman screw who had led me to the block. They had me in a hold and frog marched me to a cell in the block. He was basically throwing his weight around. The block is where you'd find all the troublemakers. The prisoners who could not behave was held here. It was called D Block by the inmates.

There was one guy there called Sparks, he was known on the streets. I had heard of him from when I was a kid robbing. He was from South London, but his name was known across London. He was also an amateur boxer. If he was good or not, at that point I did not know as he seemed to always be in prison. He had bussed various serious cases. Crazy had gotten his Rolex watch years ago in Feltham, back in the mid to late 1990s. I was there with H when Crazy gave over the 18k Rolex during a prison visit. I don't know how he cheeks that, but he did.

Back to the story at hand. I had just been manhandled and Sparks was my next door. He didn't know me and tried to laugh at the situation with one of his boys. I let him know my situation wasn't a laughing matter. Obviously, he didn't take kindly to my words. He had interrupted me talking to some guy from Kilburn who would get bail and end up getting convicted with my 13 year old brother for a diamond robbery. He was always in and out of prison.

Sparks started threatening me, telling me what he was going to do, I was goading him, "I would like to see that." The guy from Kilburn was trying to calm the situation down. Telling Sparks, "Be easy" and Sparks was like "warn your boy." I knew who Sparks was but I couldn't show no fear. The screws let the prisoners out for association and led them to the yard. I was kept in my cell. 10 minutes later I was brought to see the Governor.

Going to see the Gov was mad. They had a screw next to me and two next to the Gov. You were read your rights as if you were in Court or at a police station. You were asked do you plead guilty or not guilty. Then he would say what he found you and the punishment you would get.
You had to wait in block whilst you waited to see the Gov. It was basically a mattress on the floor and maybe a table and chair, nothing else. You just had to go into your own world. I guess they try to break you so you have to be mentally tough. Some people spend weeks or even months down there. I spent a week there once after a riot in Qual wing, but I'll get to that.

After that there was no way that the Nightingale screws where going to give us a job.

The guys from Brixton used to rap battle each other at night time through the windows on Sundays. It was normally boring, or more than usual I should say.

I remember when one the prisoners had a child born, he was so happy but sad at the same time as he couldn't be there and was locked up.

We wanted to do mechanics, but that course was full, we were willing to do anything to get out of our cell for 3 hours in the morning. We did a Math's class for a while. I got 95% on my exam on that. My cousin had his GCSEs so that didn't mean much to him as he had a higher qualification in that subject. We passed Math's class and started our cleaning course.

It's funny, I did garbage in my GCSE math's but sometimes my cousin would call me to work out certain sums for his drugs business. He never got how I worked it out, but I could do certain sums in my head quick without a calculator or break down big numbers. I would always tell Tyrone; I was proud of him as we came from nothing and had no help in this thing but we weren't bums. He didn't want to do crime forever, but it was a way to make enough capital to get out and start a business.

When DJ WestWood had his radio show on Fridays and Saturdays on Radio 1, practically the whole wing would be listening in their cells and kick their doors when a popular tune was played.

I was in Nightingale wing with a guy who used to train at All Stars Boxing Club with me. He was like my big rival there when we were kids. He was good but were I chose to do the boxing thing when I was released, he went the other way and kept doing crime and going in and out of Jail. He was a nice guy though.

Quickly after the issue my cousin and I had with the screw, within a few days we were transferred to Qual wing. I think they did that to scare us as Qual wing was for murderers and violent criminals. It was the most serious wing in the prison with all the top guys being housed there so they obviously wanted to fuck us over.

My cousin was only in Qual wing for a few days. We were lying in our bunk beds, just chilling and chatting shit. He got told by a screw that he had got bail. I didn't know what to say. I was happy for him, but I was sad as it was nice to be there with him, having each other's back. He told me to change my lawyer to his as they were trying get us to go against each other and blame one another, which would have meant we did it or where there. A conviction for both of us would have been likely if we did that. We would stick to our story that the police had a vendetta against us. Tyrone left me his canteen and was off to fuck, be free and make money.
I just told him make sure we get found not guilty. Do what you must do. That was my message to people on the outside. Friends and family from Ladbroke Grove, where one of the accusers where from, had spoken to them.

The other inmates would ask how Ducky is, like the old boys from Nightingale wing. I would say I haven't seen or spoken to him since he got bail which was like a month. They thought it was bad as I was in jail for something which wasn't my decision. I had backed him in a beef. I was raised like that so I do it without thinking. My family all fought for each other. The other prisoners would say it's bad he hasn't seen me, but I would say I don't care as long as he handles business and I am found not guilty. It really didn't bother me. If anything, I wanted money for canteen as my money was low. I was disappointed with one of my cousins not Ducky, when I asked for 15 pounds, he replied I thought you had money. I said I haven't been making money and my mum was the only one sending me some. I feel that it shouldn't have been an issue. I was in jail for his beef not mine. My dad's excuse for not sending me money was that he was not making Prime Minister Tony Blair money. He didn't understand I needed money for toiletries. I was disappointed my cousin made that comment but he did send me money when I would write him and say I need it. My girlfriend had turned down jobs so she could visit me every day. I told her that I owe her for life cause whenever my back was against the wall. No matter what state our relationship was in even if we weren't together. She would have my back.

My girlfriend came to see me nearly every day so I was good. She was my rock at that time in my life. She kept me strong and gave me focus that I was coming out to something. That kind of saved our relationship as we were going through a bad patch and I was promising to be different. I failed when I was released but the love was there. I just couldn't act right. We are still friends to this day though. We grew up together, good and bad. She was there for me in many struggles I had in my life. She helped me when I was down and believed in me. She's a good person.

Over the next week I had a change of cellmates. I had some white boy from country. He was like 17 years old and an idiot. He was only with me for a night and was moved in the afternoon. He was acting crazy, from when he came to my cell. He kept asking when they are going to let us out again. I was like we will have dinner around 7pm then we are locked up for the night. He could not stand that. He kept pacing up and down all night and talking to me. I didn't feel safe with him in my cell even though he was a little idiot. It was Friday night, so it was a Westwood thing on Radio 1 but he kept on talking. The next day I had decided to get him out of my cell. All through the night, the night screw would come and look in our cell through the flap. He had already told them he would kill himself so I would play on that.
After we had lunch, my cellmate asked when next would we be

out again, I told him, later on in the day. He couldn't take it so I told him to ring the bell and tell the screws you are going to kill yourself. He did it, it was so funny. I was on my bed reading a book and the screw came in the cell and said, "You shouldn't be ringing the bell, it's for emergencies". My cellmate was like "I'm going to kill myself". He started poking his skin with a fork. The screw rushed over to him and grabbed the fork and started poking it hard into the prisoner's forearm. I was lying in bed, laughing to myself. He had only been here for a couple of nights and he was cracking already. I will admit, I was feeling hurt when I first arrived in Feltham but I was like a vet now. It was nothing. I was doing my time. People say young offenders' institutes are a playground, I beg to differ. Majority of the time I was locked up for over 20 hours a day and a few times we did 23 hours in a day so believe me, that isn't no playground.

The screw told him "you are bothering Theophane, get the fuck out of here" whilst slapping him in the back of the head and pushing him out the cell. The screw apologized to me, "Sorry for the inconvenience and walked out of my cell." I found the whole situation funny.

I would get another cellmate Kristian Fraser. Our friendship would last beyond the prison cell bars. The first day he came, we had a talk and he told me he was beefing with some guys from West London. A few of them were my cousins from my Grandma's side. A few days before Kris came there was a guy called Jermaine Abbott on our wing. He had a reputation as a stickup kid. He was feared on the roads as he had robbed guys from Acton to Croydon. I personally saw a few guys kiss his ass in jail. I'm the type of guy if I don't know you or have anything in common, I have nothing to say.

I spoke to guys who were from West London, South London, a few Tottenham and Hackney boys. The guys who thought they were hard I didn't say shit to them if they didn't say shit to me. One of my top boys had robbed a few of them as well so when I said I was from Harrow Rd; Kilburn area I knew I was a target. The first day that Kris and I was on association some guy from Ghetto which is what guys from New Cross called their area back then in 2000. Some tall dude, he was like 6'7". I forget his name. He was tall and skinny and down with all the guys who thought they were hard. I was still new to the wing and had only been there for over a week, so guys tend to see who they can push and what they can get away with. I made my stand, I wasn't no punk. He was a blatant bully because when I stood up to him, he tried to stand strong but when he saw I wasn't playing, he backed down.

There was a queue for the people playing pool, for whatever reason he missed his turn. He tried to come and say I'm next. I was like fuck that. I'm next. He said, "We shall see." Now I know, if I let him go and play before me, man will try and take me for a fool going forward. So my time was now. I had heard of these jail stories of snooker balls flying all over the place when a fight broke out and it was now my turn. I had met a few prisoners with big coconut bumps on their foreheads from getting a snooker ball in their forehead. I knew the stories were true!

He grabbed the snooker cue when the loser had finished and tried to set up the balls. I said firmly, "You are not playing." I grabbed a few balls and told him, "If I don't play, no one plays." Voices started to get raised and the whole wing sensed a fight was about to break out. Even the prison officers didn't bother to try stop the argument, everyone was quiet and watched, listened and waited for the fight to happen. It didn't happen, the freakish tall punk backed down and said, "I'm next then". I was happy it didn't kick off because going to the Block was not an enjoyable experience. After association Kris said he thought it was going to get messy as there was a lot of South London guys on that wing and a few where from Ghetto which was the nickname for New Cross in London. He said he would have backed me; I don't know about that. He knew me for less than 24 hours but now I had respect on the wing. The other prisoners knew now who I was but now they knew I was not a punk and would not be pushed around.

That night when my cellmate and I were locked up. A screw opened the cell door and said, "Enhanced association". My cellmate got up out of his bed to go as he had just moved to this wing from another wing and he was enhanced on that wing.

Enhanced was for the screw boys, the guys who kissed the prison officer's ass. The prison officer told him not you and said, "Theophane, I will lock the door if you don't want to come". I started to laugh and laughed at my cellmate as I got up to leave our cell. I don't know how I got the bump up to enhanced status but I wasn't going to turn it down.
Prisoners on enhanced status could play computer games, watch tv and get little other perks like an extra shower. My cousin Tyrone and I had caused havoc on Nightingale wing so I don't know how I earned enhanced but maybe they were trying to keep me happy, who knows. Fuck it, I had it and that's all that mattered.

Over the next few days guys would approach me and we would get talking. One guy from South London called Tooth, he was a cool guy. There was the Anderson family also from South, who were good people. There was a Yardie based in Tottenham, who was a joker. I wasn't friendly with a lot of the other London gangsters on my wing. We would swap pleasantries but nothing more. If I didn't have to talk to them I wouldn't. They did not try and talk to me so fuck them. It wasn't in my make up to kiss ass. My mum would always say don't cut your nose off to spite your face, whatever that meant but I always stood on my own as a kid and as a man continued that. I depended on me. I was not good at asking for help or accepting it.

One of the prisoners who was a cleaner, Mario, would always piss me off. He would clean out in the yard and a lot of prisoners who did not like him would shit on their prison jumper and throw it outside the window. He would have to clean it up. Sometimes he had up to 5 jumpers outside waiting for him. I was tempted to do it but I wasn't an animal like that. I would just warn him that he would get moved to if he continued his cheek. He laughed at me many times until one day in the computer room. It was me, him and Tooth. Tooth was bullying him, and he tried to stand up to me. He was 6ft plus and I am 5'8" so I was looking up and he was looking down. I jumped on him and I started laying in punches on him. I picked up a PlayStation and slammed it on his head. He staggered back to the wall, I moved to him and put left and right hooks against his chin. He was in a daze. A prison officer came in and I stepped back. He didn't see any of my violence on Mario but he could tell he had just got a beating. He told me afterwards that everyone wanted to beat up Mario so good on me.

Mario would piss all the prisoners off and hide behind his status as a red band which meant he could go anywhere in the prison and was allowed out from morning to night. He was a number one ass licker.

When everyone found out I moved up Mario, they were like, "You are crazy. You are on enhanced level, fuck risk losing that privilege." I did not care. I had taken too much from him so I had to show him what time it was. He wouldn't step out of line again. The cellblock prison officers started doing competitions every day. They would look for the cleanest cell. Kris and I won a few times but our cell were rundown so we could only make it look so good but others had newly painted prison cells started to win all the time. When we did win, my cellmate Kris Frazer and I would often argue about what we were watching. It got so bad that sometimes that I would say if we don't watch certain programs, nobody doesn't watch television so we would often not watch anything and just listen to the radio. Looking back, it was childish and stupid but being locked up like an animal can make you act like one.

We were in a cell not much bigger than a public toilet; we had our bunk bed and a little table opposite it. Our toilet was on the left as you walk in. It was not perfect, but it had been my home for 6 weeks.

Having dreams of a positive future whilst on remand for Arm Robbery can be seen as being delusional but my mind thought that as long as I am found not guilty, I will follow my passion. I'll finish college and pursue my boxing career.

Who would think, ten years later I would have beaten a former world champion who had fought Floyd Mayweather Junior, DeMarcus Corley. World number three Delvin Rodriguez who had fought for the World Title a year earlier and I would become British champion. All from a teenage life of robbing, selling drugs, kidnap attempt on me, guns held at me, hit put on me, going training wearing a bullet proof vest for a year. Against the odds I have achieved what people never thought was possible.

I look back at my time in prison positively. I used to see it as a wasted six months of my life but without that happening in my life I wouldn't have been so determined to succeed. I
witnessed so many young men wasting their lives. I even offered to go and speak to the inmates after my British title win but Feltham Youth Offenders Institute turned down my offer. I find that disgraceful as I could give the young prisoners hope that after leaving, they can still achieve their goals and a life of crime doesn't have to continue.

RIOT

I'll remember this day for the rest of my life. I was on the phone with my girlfriend during association. An argument broke out between a prison officer and a prisoner. The next thing I notice, his co-defendant jumped into the argument and jumped the screw. The alarm goes off and the screws start to run out of the wing. They shut and lock the main gate to the wing which I was out of. I'm laughing on the phone with my girlfriend, giving her play by play of the action. Minutes go by, the alarm is pounding out and I can see there are guards suited up in riot gear. They are outside of our wing, waiting to rush in. I'm still on the phone, they come to me and start barking orders at me. I tell them I've done nothing wrong. It is nothing to do with me. They didn't care, I'm a prisoner. I'm the enemy. They rush me and pick me off the floor. Four of them have my arms and legs. I'm brought out to the hallway. Orders are shouted at me and I'm told to crouch. A prison officer punches me numerous times in my face. I shout at him, that I'm not scared of them.

I can only imagine that I got off easy. There was a gang of them, ready to rush the wing. All down the corridor, I'm in an uncomfortable position all the way to the block. They dehumanize you. You're an animal and act like that. You must adapt. I was the first of the prisoners in the block. One by one, I heard them being assaulted and thrown in a cell.

I spent a week in the block. I was used to my surroundings now. I spoke to the governor again, but I had done nothing so they could not punish me. In the block, you can easily go crazy. You can shout from cell to cell and speak to the other prisoners you are cool with. I just asked what happened when I was taken out of the wing. All hell broke loose on the wing. What did they expect, everyone was there for murder or gun offenses, It was a wing that could blow at any time and it did. A wing of hot heads is a recipe for disaster.

HMP LEWES

Half of Qual wing was transferred to Reading prison and the other half was transferred to HMP Lewes. I went off to HMP Lewes. It was in Brighton so it wasn't too far from London. I got visits from my father, Rahel, Tyrone and his girlfriend Tameka. I had adjusted to life in prison now.

In HMP Lewes, you would either get gym or education in the morning. I tried to get education but it was full, so I got an hour of gym instead. It was weird the way it was worked out as one day you would be banged up for 24 hours. We would just come out for our meals and the other day you would get two hours association which was good. It would alternate like that. I spent nearly three months at HMP Lewes. It was a mixed with adults, which was different to Feltham as that was a 100% juvenile prison so the oldest there was twenty-one years old.

One of the inmates told a group of us on association that he was masturbating to a sex magazine when a male prison officer opened his cell door. He had just ejaculated when the door opened so he was frozen with his dick in his hand and semen shooting out in front of the officer. The stuff that happens behind those walls are sometimes too
disturbing.

Everyone always says how easy prison is and that it is a holiday camp. I had no tv and no stereo. So I had to occupy my mind with writing and planning my life for when I leave. I was determined to make something of my life or at least try. I was going to go back to college and finish my second year of BTEC Media then turn professional. That was my plan.

RELEASED FROM PRISON

When I was finally released from HMP Lewes, I could not believe it. The charges were dropped and I was a free man. I did not expect to be released as I had been denied bail at Horseferry Road court by all the judges and Guildford crown court opposite the Houses of Parliament.
My girlfriend at the time Rahel, my cousin Tyrone and his twin Lawrence were as shocked as me. I phoned them as soon as I walked out of the courthouse. I told them I would meet them back in West London, but they told me to wait as they were on their way.

Police constable Allen Mills had taken another day off working in Wales to try and tell the judge once again how dangerous I was and that I should not be released from prison. The victims who were also the only witnesses had gone missing over the last two weeks. The police had arrested them, and the judge had threatened them with prison if they did not attend the trial. They had tried to drop the charges against us, but the police were not allowing them to do that as they had signed a statement which stated an armed robbery had happened.
When they did not attend the first day of trial, the judge said he had enough and was dropping the charges and was finding us not guilty.

I would see the girl who accused my cousin and I a few years later in Wembley Market. Tyrone had been gone a few years now and anyone from the inner city would expect me to slap the shit out of her, she even expected that as she looked scared, but I just gave her a hug. She didn't know what to expect from me, but I had let go that anger in my heart. Without me going prison, I may not had been so focused on my boxing career. I locked many people off on my release from Prison, so it is an experience I would not take away. Too many people dwell on negatives in their life instead of taking the positive out of it.

THUGLIFE

I had been out of prison for 6 months now and the money was rolling in. I first picked up a half kilo of marijuana from Roy. Some dude I knew from Mozart Estate since I was a kid. He gave it to me for a nice price and from then I started to get back my clients. It was a slow process, but I went through my numbers and let them know the kid was out. The muthafuckas couldn't keep me in prison. I had buss case. I laid low for a month or so then I hit the block hard. I wasn't starting back college until September, so I just touched base with Claire Grey at Westminster Kingsways College. She seemed happy I was out, but my Media Tutor seemed pissed I was out. I didn't care anyway as I would roll in for the morning classes and leave in the afternoon. I still got a Merit which was basically classed a B grade, so I was happy with that. I told the teachers as long as I pass the course, I am happy. They wanted me to go University as they saw how easily I came through the course, but University wasn't for me. I would have loved to have made my mum proud of me, but I would make her proud another way. My kids will go and make us proud. I could have been the first Theophane out of my grandparents Foster and Catherine's kids but my Boxing dream was a bigger desire for me, at the time.

I had been hardened by being in jail. I don't know if the Government think jail is rehabilitation, but I was just locked up especially in HMP Lewes, I only came out to go gym and get my food. Somedays we were locked up for 24 hours a day. That shit is crazy. I am a very strong person mentality so they just made me more focused and determined to make me be successful in life. I was going to make money, be known and lay my legacy down.
I threw myself into my Boxing when I came out. I got some good results and improved. I would stay amateur for one more year

until June of 2002, then I would make the move to go professional.

Bighead had been out of jail since May 2000 and it felt good to have my side kick back. When he came out, I went in but that was crime for you. He was back on his feet and making money now by the time I came out. We had some quality time when he first came out. I was supposed to take him shopping but I got locked up by the time we had planned to go out up Oxford Street so that never happened.

Bighead and H were two of my closet friends growing up on the streets. The summer of 2001 Bighead and I was rolling tight together. He would be selling his crack and heroin, I would have the skunk, marijuana and hashish. I was shifting a few kilos a week and I was making money. Robbing had now slowed down. Most of the robbers where now selling skunk or crack. I hated being around crack heads so I stuck to the softer drugs. I would sell cocaine and crack to other dealers but I didn't like dealing with the crack fiends.
I would go round with Bighead to his crack sells, I wouldn't want to touch anything in their apartment as it was dirty and disgusting but he also had crack sells in Maida Vale and Fulham so he had both sides of the pond. He sold to some Doctors and Lawyers so everyone fucked with that drug.

For a year I stopped driving while I got myself back on my feet. Bighead would let me drive his Ford Puma if I needed to. I was stacking those grands every month and I was in a healthy state. Rahel and I was not going perfect since I got out of jail as when she wanted me to come up to East London, I would say I had to stay down in west and make money. She was always traveling to see me. She truly loved me, and I was her world. I didn't appreciate that until we would split.

Bighead was making a lot of money and people were starting to take notice. He was making a lot of enemies among other crack dealers as he was stealing their sells. On 24th December of 2001, he was kidnapped. Christmas Eve was maybe the worst time to get got. His girlfriend at the time called me to say that Lippy had called her and said that Bighead had been arrested and that the police would come and search the place so he should come and get his crack stash and money. He came round to her place. She played dumb and only gave him a few hundred pounds and a few crack rocks. He wanted bighead's gun, but she said she knew nothing of it. She said it seemed fishy and Lippy wasn't the smartest guy on the block. So she called the police stations and asked for him and his alias's. Nothing came up. I even took her down to Paddington police station in Edgware Road. There was no trace of him. I told her to get some sleep. The next day came and Bighead's mum got a call saying he had been taken.

Some of Bighead's closet friends from Kilburn got together and we went by Lippy's apartment in Kilburn but there were secure gates around it so we could not get into his door. V made some calls to some of the local criminals in the area but some of them were not answering their phone and some said they did not know what was going on. We would later find out that some of them were part of the kidnapping.

In the end, the guy who kidnapped him wanted to sell Bighead's car back to his friends.
Everyone was nervous to meet Crazy as they thought he may take them too. Even one of my cousins who got along with Bighead turned round and said they weren't that close.

I received a call from Crazy and I said that I would meet him. My cousin who would not meet Crazy told me to be careful. I told my brother the situation and asked him to come with me. He said

Crazy wouldn't do anything to me. I believed that but my cousin sounded nervous and put those thoughts in my head. I met Crazy on Chippenham Road near the park. He said he didn't want to take no money off me, but the other dudes involved wanted money. He told me that the car was on Warlock Road. I ended up giving him £500, which was much less than he wanted. The car was worth around £10,000. Crazy called one of his accomplices to say he did not want to take money off me but the guy on the phone wanted the money. I have a feeling it was Ricky, who years before had gone on as if he had something to do with the burglary at my cousin's apartment. We had a standoff in the local youth club about it.

Crazy gave me the car keys and we parted company. Bighead was left in Northwest London earlier in the day and I would drop off his car the next day. He was shaken up which was to be expected.

My cousin Tyrone would get shot a few weeks later as Crazy had kidnapped a drug dealer from South Kilburn estate. Crazy had learned from Bighead's situation. He would now ransom the guys he would kidnap to their friends. They were all drug dealers so they wouldn't go to the police. The drug dealer from South Kilburn had business partners from Harlesden and Stonebridge. Tyrone went to school with a few of them so when he saw one of them up Harlesden one weekend, he enquired about the kidnap situation. He was shot in his leg as a result in front of his eldest child. Tyrone was shot as he was friends with Crazy. With my cousin getting shot, it would lead to a long running feud with a business partner of the South Kilburn drug dealer getting killed near Scrubs Lane and an innocent man being shot in the neck at KFC in retaliation. He would later die.

Kidnaps were now common, and many drug dealers were getting kidnapped by Crazy and his crew. No one was safe.

My brother goes to prison again. This time for an armed robbery, Crazy had set up. They robbed a jewelry store and got away. Whoever's job it was to set the getaway cars on fire and burn the evidence. Didn't set the cars on fire. He had dropped the lighter. Evidence and fingerprints were left and they all got arrested. It was a wild time in North West London. Shootings, kidnappings, and murders were happening too often.

My brother was in a police station up Watford. I'd drive up there to give him some food. He would be the only one to go guilty. He wasn't interested in fighting a case he knew he did and that he'd mostly likely be found guilty of. The rest of them went to trial to fight the case. I attended the trial most days. I spoke with Mr. Isola Akay, my first boxing coach and founder of All Stars Boxing Gym about helping my brother out. Mr. Akay was awarded an MBE in 2000, he was a respected and recognized member of the community. He wrote my brother a letter for sentencing. That was a winner as the judge said my brother couldn't be such a bad person for this man to do this for him. He got sentenced to less than half of what the others got but he also pleaded guilty from the start and was under 18.

My brother did his sentence and was released from prison. By that time, there was an all-out war going on.

My brother was in prison when our cousin Tyrone had gotten shot in the leg, whilst holding his daughter.

He didn't waste time in confronting members of the gang that were friends with the guy that did the shooting. The situation didn't end well which led to my car getting set on fire outside All Stars Boxing Gym hours later.

I can remember the day so clearly. I came out of my mother's home and saw two guys walking opposite. I knew their faces;

they were in war with childhood friends of mine and were part of the gang that had shot my cousin. Why were they there? I was alert as I got into my car and drove off on the main roads in case, they tried something. Going down the side roads as I usually did, wasn't the wisest thing to do. I'm watching them in the rare view mirror as I drive down Harrow Road. I park up on First Avenue, right next to Allstars Boxing Gym. I walk into the gym, Serge had his boxing class on Wednesday mornings, during this time. So I greet everyone in the gym and I go into the changing room to put on my workout clothes. I didn't even get a chance to take my clothes off. Members of the class came to me panicking.
"Ashley, your car is on fire." I was calm as I knew who did it. I walk outside, I see the streets are packed with people, looking at my car on fire. Flames everywhere. What could I do?
Nothing, I walk off down Harrow Road and call my cousin. I tell him what just happened. He told me my brother was at his place and they did it for retaliation for the altercation earlier. I head to my cousin's place to speak to my brother and my cousin. He could have at least given me the heads up. I was clueless to what had happened. I was now in danger and a target.

MURDER

Whilst away in Florida with the number one contender for the World WBA Junior Welterweight title Dmitriy Salita during March 2007. I got a call one morning from my cousin who asked me where I was. I told him I was in the USA. He said that was good as some crazy stuff had went down with the South Kilburn guys. One of the brothers had been killed in his car and a backlash was thought to happen. I was safe as I was in the USA but when I got back to London a few weeks later. I found out what had gone down. It was a long running saga. They had set my car on fire, nine months earlier.

My friend H would call me a few months later to warn me that my life was in danger as the South Kilburn guys had trouble getting who was responsible for the murder of one of their own and the police had not caught no one. I was doing well in my boxing career so I would have gathered a whole heap of paper inches if they were able to murder me. H told me that the person who told him I was a target thought I was a good guy and he didn't want to see me go out like that. H didn't tell me who it was, but it was obviously someone who had known me for years. The insider was at a gang gathering when my name was mentioned as a possible target. I already thought I was a natural target as it was common knowledge of my relationship with everyone involved. H gave me a police force issued bullet proof vest, that would follow me on my morning runs and when I would drive to Canning Town to go Boxing at the TKO gym. After six months I stopped wearing it, but I would be vigilant for years to come.

In the early hours of Saturday 22nd May 2010 a family member of mine would go to the KFC takeaway on Harrow Road in London. The next morning I would find out that a guy from the area was shot in the neck 15 minutes after my relative left. He struck a scary resemblance in height, skin color and hairstyle. He was even wearing the same style T shirt. Being midnight, the assassin's obviously saw my relative in the KFC takeaway with his friend, they went to get their gun and by the time they came back, he was gone but this young guy who looked similar had turned up by then and his life was taken. He was a hardworking young man who was not a criminal, but his life would be tragically ended.

I would drive by the crime scene the next day as I was driving around West London looking for my girlfriend's presents for her birthday which was the next day.
Police had closed down the KFC restaurant and the local store next to it to do their forensic tests.
It spread like wildfire through the area that my relative was in the takeaway 15 minutes beforehand and friends where coming up to me asking if it was true.

11 days it took for the police to come round to my apartment. They had obviously looked through footage of who was in the restaurant beforehand and they knew it was my family member. It would not take a genius to realize that he was probably the target.
Detective Pete Delvin would ring my bell. I looked out the window and did not see anyone and I was not expecting a package from one of my sponsors. I had a feeling it was the police, so I was not surprised when it was them and they wanted to talk to me. I told them I had nothing to say and was busy. The police got in through the front door from one of the two other apartments and started to knock the door. I opened the door and said, "Can I help you?". I said I am Ashley Theophane so you have no need to speak to me. The detective Pete Delvin said he was looking for my family member as he believed his life was in danger. I said I would pass on the message. The Detective said he is glad he did not have to get a warrant. I replied,

"Because I did not want to speak to you. You would break down my door to give me a piece of paper with your number on it." He said that I pay his taxes and even if I would not appreciate a broken door, a lot of taxpayers probably would. I told him to stay outside the door and do all his talking there as I did not like his kind. He went on to say he doesn't like me and probably wouldn't like my family member he was looking for. He thanked me for my time and left. I passed on the information and gave the detective's card with his name and number on it and left it at that.

Exactly a month after the attempted murder of my family member I saw an associate of the guys who did it in the gym. I had known him since we were teenagers, so we were good. He was working out with one of his friends for an hour while I was there. When his friend left, he came up to me and asked what I thought of the Kilburn and Mozart situation. I said it was stupid. He said he just wanted to tell me he is not involved in it and is staying out of it as he knows people from both sides. He asked me if my family member had told me he had an argument with him the other day. I said he didn't tell me anything. He went on to say that he had words with DB9 and let him know that the Kilburn guys are his friends, but he is not part of the beef with Mozart. It was weird as he was born and raised in Mozart but working with the enemy of his area.
He went on to say that he had spoken to them about me and said to leave me out of the gun battle as I had a career and was nothing to do with it. He said when he asked them not to do stuff, they went against what he said. They told him that they had tried to run me over one time in Kilburn, that must have been a lookalike as it certainly was not me. He said the area was proud of me and that to keep doing my stuff.

On the evening of Wednesday 30th December 2010, I had finished running up Holland park hills as I trained for my fight with Lenny Daws. I headed to the family home to get some soup as my mum was making dinner. My ex-girlfriend was there as she was dropping off my mums Christmas present and picking up her one from my mum.

We were all talking about all kinds of stuff when my cousin who had been staying over, shouted out for me to come. He had just come through the door. I didn't hear him so Rahel said my cousin wanted me. I went to see what he wanted and I saw blood all over him face. The first thing that came to mind was that the guys that shot that guy in KFC had jumped him. My cousin asked me to get a towel, so I took one out of my sports bag. We went straight into the bathroom. The flesh coming out of the deep cuts around his left eye. His left eye was closed and swollen. He had deep gashes around his eye socket and blood leaking out of it. I told him we need an ambulance. He said I couldn't call one as the incident had gone down very local. I was going to call a cab but then I said Rahel is here, she can drive us. He agreed and she took him to her car. I was in my boxers as my clothes were soaking with sweat and I hadn't bathed yet. I had to throw jeans and a hoody on and run outside. I was worried as he was disorientated, and he had lost a lot of blood. Rahel drove us to Paddington Hospital, we went to the "Accident and Emergency" department. I walked straight to the desk and showed the receptionist my cousins face. She went straight to the back and found a doctor. They got me to register him then we went to where the beds where. They got him to lie on a bed and took his heart rate and pulse from the machine and connected him to a drip.

I couldn't look at him as it was a scary sight, seeing my cousin with blood all over his face and not knowing if he had lost his eyesight. I was trembling a little bit as I was scared for him. God knows how he felt. Rahel stayed with us for 2 hours but left as she had work early in the morning. That woman has always been there for me even if I didn't deserve it. We got transported to the eye hospital on Marylebone Road just before Kings cross. The nurse gasped as she removed the bandage from my cousin's face. I took some photos for him so he could see it. The doctor came and did some eye tests at Praed Street hospital in Paddington, my cousin could only see light and shadow from his left eye but the doctor at the eye hospital gave him some instrument that made him able to see a little bit. That gave me a sigh of relief. The doctor said my cousin had damaged muscles in his eye but pupil was not damaged which was positive news. The doctor said he is a lucky man and should thank the man above. I hope he takes this advice. We were at the hospitals for over 7 hours, from 9pm to 430am. That messed up my training for the next day but I just had to swap around some training sessions.

I'm someone who learns from mistakes. I hope my cousin does too.

AMSTERDAM

Amsterdam for New Years with my younger twin cousins and two other guys from the area. It was a fun trip. We were 22 years old, seeing in the 2003 abroad. What could go wrong? You had the red light district, sex shops, cannabis cafes and late-night partying with a bunch of Brits that flew in to celebrate.

We were staying in Rotterdam but the adventures happened in Amsterdam. The trip was a blur as we had some wild nights partying, surrounded by beautiful women.

On New Year's Eve, we were dressed in our best outfits, smelling good, looking good, having fun, dancing, flirting with women.

There was a crowd from Peckham, they slapped one of my cousins in the back of the head. So we confronted them. Within seconds, one of them bottled me. I staggered back and felt my head, I saw blood on my hand, and I saw red. I look around and grabbed a champagne bottle. There's now twenty of them shouting at the five of us. I throw the bottle at them; it smashes in one of their faces. Blood splatters from his face. I hear one of my guys say run. We were outnumbered. We run down the escalators as a shower of champagne bottles come raining down after us. We get outside and jump into a waiting cab. We get back to our hotel. We later hear that there were gun shots fired as we left so people thought it was us. That would be the last holiday I go with the guys. Trouble just seemed to follow us.

FROM THE CRADLE TO THE GRAVE

I was away training in the USA. I spoke to Rahel, she would tell me Tyrone my cousin was sick again. I called Tamika, the mother of his children but she was at the Notting Hill Carnival in London and she was with their kids so she said she couldn't really talk. I would later find out that my cousin Tyrone who was basically like a brother to me, was in a coma. My heart sunk, I was so scared, so confused. I had no one to really open up to in training camp. I would suck it up and put my frustrations into my boxing training.

This was the start of what would see my cousin fight as hard as he could. He had a rare heart disease that couldn't be healed. He'd have a heart transplant that would give some hope to give him a longer life. He had three beautiful children who he loved and adored.

Tyrone would be a cousin that felt like a brother to me. He was always by my side as a kid and teenager. When we became young adults, he'd live his life but support me and my career.

Visiting him at the hospital was always saddening but his spirits were high. He was a strong determined person, so I know he fought till the very end.

I'd find out from the mother of his children that my cousin had died. She came to pick me up from my mother's home and we drove to be by his side. His soul had left his body. He was no longer here but I hugged his body and cried. Monday 11th September 2006 in the early hours of the morning, Tyrone had died. He would forever have a place in my heart, and I was determined to make him proud.

THE AMERICAN DREAM

Coming to America was a dream come true for me. Since I was a kid, I had dreamed of coming out here and boxing. It was a huge step for me. This is where champions were made. The big fights in Las Vegas and the historic fights at Madison Square Garden were stuff of legends to me. I was taking this major step and seeing how good I was. Most British boxers like to stay in their comfort zone but that's how you never excel. I didn't know how good I was or how far I could go but I wanted to see. I wanted to find out what my limit was. No one expected anything off me in Britain, so this was all for me. I had just lost my first fight, a couple months before so my pride was dented a bit, but I had won my comeback fight a few weeks later so at least I was in better spirits. Who would have known that I would meet some of my closet friends, on my adventure in the United States of America and that it would open doors in my career.

The night before flying I stayed up, making sure I had packed everything I needed. I was not sure that I would be let through immigration at JFK airport, so I was extremely nervous as the queue got smaller and smaller. The immigration officer was firm, abrupt and watching me closely. I felt nervous. I felt like I had done something wrong and he was trying to get it out of me. He took a photo of me and fingerprinted me. They do this to everyone so when and if you visit again. They have you on record with your prints and photo so no one else can try come as you.

I made it past the immigration officer and I let out a sigh of relief. I had to get my luggage. I waited for about ten minutes until I got both bags. As I walked towards the exit, I saw that I had to get checked by another officer before walking out. I was nervous again. To make matters worse, he wanted to check my luggage.

He asked me what I was doing in New York. I told him; I had come out here to train at Gleason's gym. He looked in one of my suitcase's and saw my boxing gloves and some shorts. I guess that was enough evidence for him and he let me go through.

Celine Sentino, who was related to me through marriage. My aunty Doreen was married to her uncle. Desmond Treasure, my mum's half-brother on her father's side had got in contact with Doreen and asked if she knew somewhere where I could stay. My aunty Doreen would ask Celine and Celine said yes. Celine and I's relationship would start off sticky as I wondered why someone would be so nice to a stranger and open up their home to that person. I had never witnessed kindness like that before in the United Kingdom so it made me uneasy. I told Celine that none of my family in the UK would open their doors to a stranger the way she had to me. Our friendship would blossom, and she would become one of my best friends.

I walked out into the exit area of the airport. There were people with names on cards for people who had just flown into New York. I didn't know how Celine looked and she didn't know how I looked but I walked past these waiting people like I had flown into New York many times. This threw Celine off as she was expecting some tourist looking English man.
Somehow, she stopped me and asked if I was Ashley. She always says that my accent was cute for the first five minutes after that it was whatever.

Celine likes to bring up how when my aunty Doreen said I was a boxer and that I was good looking. She expected me to be some big six foot man, but I was barely taller than her.

On the drive from the airport, I was like a little boy in a candy store. Looking around the scenery of New York City, well in fact

Brooklyn. It was exactly like I had expected. It had its own essence. I didn't stay at Celine's that night as I had already made a reservation at the YMCA in Greenpoint, Brooklyn.

For about 7 years, New York City was my home. I felt more at home in Brooklyn than I did in London. The people, the atmosphere and the environment were positive, helping me grow in my career and as a person. I had some great experiences which were a dream to me. A kid from Harrow Road against the odds pursuing his goal, trying to better my life and achieving that feat.

Training at Starrett City Boxing Gym and Gleason's Gym in Brooklyn, I'd make friends with Francisco Figeruoa and spar him up Morris Park in The Bronx. The L and A train got me around town.

Yuri Foreman, Luis Collazo, Paul Malignaggi, Joan Guzman, Dmitriy Salita, Argenis Mendez, Raul Frank, Chris Smith were some of the fighters I sparred in New York City. I was so hungry and determined. No one wanted it more than me. I was willing to die in that ring.

Jihad Abdul Aziz, Harry Keitt, Lennox Blackmoore and Francisco Guzman were four coaches that without them, I wouldn't be the fighter that I became. Hours, weeks, months, years working with me for little money. I'm happy I could repay Harry and Jihad with Trips to Las Vegas and London. They helped me become British champion, world number four and be good enough to join Mayweather Promotions.

Fast forward to 2011 when I told Celine about Rene Carayol and how he was helping me. She said how it is strange how my life is, as I do not trust people who genuinely want to help me as was the case when I first came to stay with her. I was shocked and bemused why she would show me so much love and try to help me out. I would ask her what she wanted from me or was trying to get from me. She said she was just helping me as I'm not from America. We would have heated disagreements when I would tell her that I do not need her help. We would find our common ground in the end. As the years went by, Celine would leave me to do my thing knowing if I truly needed something I would ask, and she would help in any way she could if possible.

I had known Celine for over five years by the time Rene was in my life, so Celine knew me well enough to know that I do not allow people to walk into my life offering help. She thought as I had worked so hard that I deserved support from someone in Rene's position. Celine knew that money was not my goal. I fought in America for very little money and which just about covered my training costs.

I fought future world champion Danny Garcia, former world champion Demarcus Corley and world title challenger Delvin Rodriguez for under $30,000 combined. My British title reign was about $100,000 over four fights. Mayweather Promotions gave me $100,000 alone for my first fight with them plus Floyd had paid me $20,000 just for sparring him. $120,000 off Floyd for my first fight with him, was life changing for me. Plus a $10,000 check from Al Haymon's office.

The moral of the story is when you don't do something for money, the money will eventually come, and it did as part of "The Money Team". I earned it, for years I didn't care about the money. It was my goals, my passion to make something of myself. I was already successful before Floyd but signing with Floyd was the icing on the cake.

BOXING & THE HOOD

Spring 1988 was when my love with Boxing took off. My father took me down to the local gym to see if I really wanted to do it. I spoke to a man with a Baseball cap on and great swagger. He was joking around with me and told me to come down and see if I had what he takes. Mr Isola Akay would later become a man I looked up to and who was always there for me when I needed help with anything. From my boxing career to my personal life. He always had advise for me, he was proud of me and how successful I had become, when all odds were stacked against me. He saw me going through trouble in school to selling drugs to being a robber, but he never turned his back on me. As much as my mother was a strong influence on me. He will always be up there as an important person in my life.

A few days later my dad took me again and one of the boxers Cassius took me through a boxing routine of skipping, hitting the bags, pad work and some groundwork. I still remember to this day doing pads in the old ring in All stars with Cassius on my first day and I jumped up to hit the pad with a left hook but I hit Cassius in the face. He smiled and said, "You are going to be a champion one day." He wasn't wrong.

I continued going to All Stars for the next 2 years. I was pretty good for a kid under 10 years old. I would strike up friendships with Mikel and his brother TT. Mikel was a little older than me and would go on to be the young star of All Stars. He would later stop and move in Martial Arts. It was Mikel fighting that pushed me to leave All stars and join Stowe Boys Club. I was always asking Mr Akay if I could fight in competitions. He would say I was too young and to wait but I saw Mikel fight, so I wanted to. I would leave for Stowe Club and end up waiting for another 5 years to make my amateur debut, even though I was always there.

Trevor Joseph was a family friend who used to box and took me down to Stowe Boys Club to see if I liked it and I ended up staying there.
It was 80% full of Irish kids, mostly travelers. I would build friendships with them. I would later end up in Secondary school with one of them, Patrick. He was the same weight as me and very good. He would always get the better of me and even a lot of the other Irish boys used to beat me up. I felt like a punch bag when I first went there as they were very good. I would go home with my head hurting me and my stutter being even worse from the beating I took from them in sparring.

The years went by and I would get better and start holding my own with the boys in the gym. Billy Corcoran was a member of the gym as his family went there. His little brother Eddie would later go on to be a successful amateur and he joined me at the TKO Gym in East London when he turned professional.
He was better than Billy. I sparred Billy once and outboxed him as a 15 year old kid. We wouldn't spar again. He was the star of the Stowe Club and I think the coaches didn't like that I had outboxed him with ease.

I was at Stowe Boys Club from 1990 to 1996. I had a good time there but with just three fights in that time I had to move on. I was pushed before I could jump as Tom the head coach told me I could no longer box for the club as bullies are not welcomed here.
I had an argument with my friend Trevor and it got out of hand. We ended up having a little tussle. My brother was man handled by one of the staff and I told Trevor I was coming down to sort him out. He said he couldn't let me do that. I said if you get involved then you become part of the problem. I always told Trevor one day he would get involved in some other people's business

and he would end up getting hurt. So I went down to see the staff member. I put it on him, telling him not to touch my brother again or he will have to put his hands on me. Trevor tried to hold me and I got mad as I had made no movements towards his boss so I went at Trevor and we ended up rolling on the floor. I would not speak to Trevor for a couple years after that. We would walk past each other in the street until one day I saw him and just stopped him and started speaking to him. He was my boy and sometimes you must be the bigger man or just see you were wrong. Good friends are hard to come by and in my environment, you pick your friends carefully or you could end up in the back of someone's trunk getting ransomed.

Tom threw me out of Stowe Club for having an argument with a man who is 15 years my senior and who attacked me first. So be it, Allstars was my home anyway.

I wanted to go back to All Stars but I was nervous. I would pop in the gym sometimes. Mr Akay would recognize me which was nice as I had left years before. All Stars used to be an intimidating place. Some of the hardest guys around wouldn't want to go in there.
After making a few trips there I summoned up the courage and asked if I could come back.
Mr Akay didn't think twice. He told me to come back on Monday. He let me spar with the current club captain Bruce who was a Welterweight. I was nervous as he was aggressive and coming at me. But I bust him up. I was too quick, skillful, and strong. Mr Akay welcomed me back and that was the start of a decent amateur career for the club.

I lost my first fight with All Stars Boxing Gym to Manus Barber from Fitzroy Lodge amateur boxing club. I thought I won but we would go onto have a trilogy. My only trilogy in my amateur or professional career. I only won one of the three but it was all a learning experience for me for when I wanted to go professional.

My time at All Stars Boxing Gym as an amateur was mixed. I clashed with many of the coaches except for Tony, he was a cool guy and easy to work with, Mark who was from my father's country St. Lucia and Mr. Akay, who was the boss. I had the utmost respect for him. The other coaches I nearly came to blows with them and we are talking like 8 trainers through the years. A few of them complained to Mr. Akay and after a while I was asked to leave the gym. I looked for a couple gyms. I even started to train with top British boxer Ian Nappa at Crown Manor in Hackney as we had a mutual friend in Samuel Buckman but I would go back to All Stars with my tail between my legs. I asked for forgiveness, promised to change and I was back in.

I have seen many boxers come and go but I have been a faithful servant to the club. No one has done what I have done fighting abroad beating former World, African, British, Commonwealth and English champions along the way.

I was never a favorite at the club. I was told I was too rebellious but all of the club favorites I would see flop one by one. I liked being the underdog and I am used to being under appreciated but I work hard for me not approval of other people. I met some great guys at the gym. Our club captain when Bruce left was Tony John. He was Saint Lucian and a great guy. He was one of my favorites over the years. He died in St. Lucia while on holiday. We had great history with loads of fighters winning regional and national titles. Taju Akay aka Tee Jay and "Big Bad" James Oyeboya were two of the club's top amateurs and professionals. They outdid me when it came to amateur success. Taju won National titles in amateur and professional. He even went to the Olympics, representing Ghana. He lost to Evander Holyfield in the quarterfinals but he had good success. He was a playboy and lived a lavish lifestyle. Both him and James were offered deals in

America but they turned it down for their own reasons. James and Taju both died young. Taju of a heart attack and James was shot at a wine bar for asking some guys to put out their cigarette as a smoking ban had just been introduced by the Government. They leave legacies that their children can both be proud of. Watching Taju and Mr. Akay in his corner on ITV inspired me as an eight year old kid. I wanted that to be me. I wanted Mr. Akay to be in my corner. He was for many years until I went to work with Johnny Eames as he had his own team but I would take Mr Akay to my fight in my father's homeland of St, Lucia.

I went 2 years without winning a fight as an amateur boxer. It was disheartening but I kept running, going gym and boxing. I was putting in all my effort but the judges didn't like me, my style or thought I actually lost the fight. The officials would always comment on my Thug Life and Out Law tattoos. I knew they didn't like my persona. I had an attitude and thought everyone was against me. I wanted to turn professional from the age of 18 years old but Mr. Akay told me I was not mentally ready for the seriousness of the professional game. I was wild and quick tempered. I had bitten a few opponents in boxing matches. Their coaches had told Mr. Akay and he had warned me that if they go to the Amateur Boxing Association board I would be banned and my dream of being a professional fighter would be over.

I got to the North West London Division ABA Finals 3 times and lost three times. My first time I had dropped the weight the worst way possible. I didn't eat for 2 days. I just had a 250ml cup of water on each day and that left me too weak to compete. I was on target to make weight on the weekend but I went out with my girlfriend at the time Rahel for Valentine's Day. It was on a Sunday and we went to Trocadero in Piccadilly Square in Central London. The Candy tempted me and I thought my weight is cool so I had sweets and that put a couple pounds on me.
People thought I hadn't trained for the tournament. My body

could not do what my mind wanted it to do. I lost to a Welsh Champion who lost in the London final.

I would also lose to one of the Irish, Barrett brothers and ABA Champion Lee Beavis. The fight with Lee was probably one of my most memorable fights as I had to beat gym mate and friend Jamal Morrison to advance to the North West division finals. I had grown up with Jamal and his brothers so I knew him before he started boxing. The pressure was on me to win as I had been boxing the longest. I won and it was a decent fight. I just had too much overall experience for Jamal. I would fight Lee Beavis in the final. He was from Ladbroke Grove so it was another local rivalry. He was strutting around like he was in the London finals already, as he was in the England Squad, he felt like he was the man. He beat me, but he had to earn it. He had to fight every minute of every round. It was a good fight but it was another loss. 2002 was my last year in the amateurs. I felt I had achieved everything I could possibly do. Every year I went for tournaments and I lost so it was time for another challenge.

I had told Mr Akay and he was supportive this time. Since 1998 when I brought it up. He had seen me go prison and come out more focused than ever. I was still on the roads but I had knocked robbing on the head as it was too high risk and I had focused more on the narcotics business. Most of the robbers of my generation had change direction and gone into that as well. Only a couple dudes would stay robbing and they would focus more on legal businesses or rob drug dealers as drug dealers are not going to report getting jacked to the police.
Majority don't even retaliate as they are all about money not violence. There are some guys who have done very well from robbing and selling drugs. They have opened restaurants, shops, set up legal businesses and either got workers handling their day to day business. If you are born in a crime ridden environment, you do what seems normal to you. Sometimes there seems no way

out but when you make enough money to come out and do some legal business, why not. Most criminals end up in prison. Just being a criminal to be a criminal is a waste. If you study, go college then university you will make more money than 99% of the criminals in your hood. It just takes longer but your education is for life and will help you get a job until you are ready to retire but with crime it is like sports, it is a short career and you have to get the most out in such a short time but you get caught you will end up broke or in jail or even worse, dead. Life is for living and too many kids in inner cities just see the glamour side of crime, by the time they realize there is more to life than prison and pocket change they are making on roads, they have a criminal record and most high level jobs will not hire them. When you go jail you are supposed to have done your time but your record stays with you for life even though you may have changed as a person. That time in your life will always be what certain people judge you on.

I turned professional at the age of 22 years old in October 2002. Mr Akay was my manager and John Tiftek was my trainer. John had come in one day and asked to work with me. That was the end of it. We had great chemistry and I loved what he was teaching me. He was letting me fight the way I want to fight but making my style more professional.

Mr. Akay was struggling to get me fights. It was harder than I thought and totally different to amateurs. The promoters didn't want nothing to do with me. Frank Warren, Mick Hennessey and Barry Hearn all passed on me. Mick Hennessey offered me a fight with Lenny Daws but he was the National Amateur Champion and I wasn't going to take that fight as my first fight when we could meet for a championship with more money on the line in the future. I didn't get to make my professional debut until June 2003 when Eugene Maloney, brother of Frank offered me a space on his show. I was so happy and I had been in the gym for a year straight with no fight. I had gone out once for my friend Yousef's birthday party in Luton back in December. I had stayed focused. I thought Lee Biddel who had given Chas Symonds a hard fight, a couple of months before and he had only lost once with a couple wins on his ledger. It was a hard first fight but nothing is ever easy for me.

Mr. Akay and I had gone for a couple meetings with Eugene Maloney and it was fairly promising. He was giving me the break no one else was willing to do so I have to respect him for that. A whole load of people from West London came to support me. It was a crazy feeling. The crowd roared and my body tingled all over. I was backstage in my black boots and black shorts. Our changing room was a toilet in York Hall in the East end of London. I would go on to have 30% of my fights there so it was like my hometown venue. I looked at myself in the mirror and told myself it's your time Ashley. It is all about now. My whole life had been directed to this moment. I could lose and my career would be over but win and anything was possible. I hyped myself up and we walked out to Elephant man's bad man a bad man. I walked to the ring feeling like I had 100 men walking with me. I entered the ring and the crowd went crazy. There was no way I was going to let Lee Biddell beat me. From the word go Lee came at me swinging. He wasn't looking to win on points, he was looking to knock me out. I tried to box him but I had to fight fire with fire. We went at it and I took a lot of punishment. Lee took more. I stopped him in the fourth round dropping him three times along the way. I was so relieved to win, I just hugged Mr. Akay when he came into the ring. The crowd started to chant "Ashley, Ashley, Ashley". While coming out of the ring, one of the officials asked Mr. Akay why I didn't wait until after the 2004 Olympics. I just laughed. They had me for years in the amateur system and I only received a call up to the British squad training once. It was their loss. I had bigger fish to fry. Eugene Maloney asked me if I would fight in July. It was only a month away but why not. I was on a roll now. I beat a Junior Middleweight in my next fight. Mr. Akay wasn't happy about it but I said I would outbox the guy. He wanted a no risk performance and that's what I gave him. It was opposite to the gunslinger approach I took in my first fight and it showed I can box and fight. I would go away to Cuba in August for 2 weeks. I had a great time. I needed a holiday as I had been in the gym for a year straight. It was good to take time off. Cuba was fun. I was supposed to go Cancun, Mexico with my cousins and some friends but they were all unorganized so we ended up going nowhere and I ended up going Cuba on my own. I had the best time ever and met some great people.

I was scheduled to fight in October up Tooting Bec in South London but that was cancelled so Eugene told me I could fight on his December show. When I got to the venue, they told me that my opponent from Birmingham was stuck in traffic and wouldn't make the show. They offered me Henry Castle. He was only a Super Featherweight at the time but he had won the National ABA tournament. I said yes but his team declined saying I was too big. I was offered a Junior Middleweight but this guy was still a live fighter. My fans were disappointed but I could not take such a risk on my third fight. Eugene Maloney told me I would win as the fighter was under orders to lose but when you are in the ring, he could think fuck it and try come after me. Eugene said he would never fight for him if he didn't follow instructions. He even got his brother Frank Maloney to assure me saying that we have to be careful how we say this but you will win. Maybe I should have trusted them but where I come from trust is not so easily given. It was hard for me as Eugene was the only promoter to give me a chance.

I would take the rest of the month off going to Cuba with my mum for 2 weeks but Stacy Warren from my team sent out DVDs to promoters in Europe, America and Australia. I had interest from some promoters but the most concrete was from Dave Coldwell from Koncrete promotions. I went up to meet him in Sheffield with my girlfriend at the time. I sparred with one of his fighters and we got down to talking. Rahel was in the meeting as I wanted a witness to what was going down. She was acting as my representative. We spoke about what my aims were and he agreed. He said he didn't want to promote me though. He wanted to manage me. I would have to speak to Mr. Akay as he was my manager. He gave me the British Boxing Board of Control contract and I had to get Mr. Akay to sign. I spoke to Mr. Akay and he was willing to let me go. I told him I didn't want him to go and I wanted him to be part of my team. He agreed and I let him know that Dave Coldwell would be getting me fights from now on. So everything was good. Dave had a list of 30 boxers I was willing to fight until I was 15-0 and then I would fight anybody. My first fight with him was with David Kirk who had beaten Matthew Hatton, Ricky Hatton's brother. It took place in Nottingham. It was a small show but my first in 9 months. I was a bit rusty but I got the win. I would be on Matthew Hatton's next fight card which was in Barnsley. I won there as well. Next up was a Welsh fighter by the name of Chris Brophy. I was back in London for this one. The main event was Bobby Vanzie vs Graham Earl on a Frank Warren promotions. I stopped Chris in the third round.

My brother was in jail at the start of my professional career so I would send him DVDs in the post of my fights. On the way to visiting him I would receive a phone call from Harry Holland, matchmaker for Audley Harrison's A-Force promotions. He said he had seen me fight the night before against Chris Brophy and he was wondering if I was free to fight two weeks later at Alexandra Palace on Audley Harrison's WBF Championship fight. Of course I was available. Audley was doing big things back then. I fought Arv Mittoo also known as Pineapple head in the boxing circles due to his hairstyle of dread locks. His boxing style was very awkward. He was the one journey man I didn't want to fight but that's who they chose as my next opponent. He had 100 fights

winning only ten. It was a win but I wasn't happy with my performance.
Harry Holland was happy with my performance and was said he wanted to sign me to A-Force promotions. That never came to anything as straight afterwards Audley would lose his television deal with the BBC. They had felt their millions had been wasted on Audley's poor choice of opponents.

Dave Coldwell would struggle to get me fights for the next six months. He was trying to make me an opponent and I promised myself I would never do that. It is different if you are fighting for a championship but not when you 6-0. He wanted me to go Scotland and fight their prospects. He may have been in the same gym as World Champions Johnny Nelson and Naseem Hamed but their talent didn't rub off on him.

Dave Coldwell amassed a record of six wins and thirteen loses. His best win was against Tommy Craig who was 1-0. He lost to decent boxers Mickey Cantwell and Hussein but other than that nobodies. He was trying to turn me into what he was as a professional and that wasn't going to happen so he would say there is nothing around but then try get me fights where I would basically lose. The last straw was when he offered me a fight against Michael Jennings. I was only 7-0 and had only completed one six rounder but Dave Coldwell wanted me to fight Michael Jennings. Dave was like, it's for five grand Ashley. So he was just thinking about the 625 pounds he would have out of my purse. I turned it down and I know that
frustrated him. There is a time and place. I asked for 15 fights, that was only another 8 fights away so that could be in 18 months for more money if you think of the bigger picture. I would get a fight on former Commonwealth Champion Derek Williams debut promotion at Crystal Palace centre after Dave Coldwell struggled to do anything. I was stepping up to fight Keith Jones. He was a tough cookie and had been in with everyone. It was my first six

rounder and I was stunning the first four rounds but Keith's body shots took their toll and I had to fight it out for the last two rounds. I won in the end and to come through the six rounder was a great feeling. Derek Williams wanted me on his next show and he had high expectations of me.

Three months later at the Hackney Empire, I would fight Judex Meemea. I beat him in my opinion but the referee went against me and it was my first loss. I was heartbroken. It felt like my woman had left me. I was Judex's first win in five fights. Derek tried to appeal the decision but the British Boxing Board of Control just said to have a rematch.
It was a terrible decision. The fight was messy but I had clearly beaten him. That kind of hurt my fan base for a while. People thought I wasn't as good as they first thought so people or haters as is said nowadays were happy, I lost. It always saddened me when people I knew would ask how the fighting is going and all I say is I am winning. It is like it made them unhappy to see me doing good. I learnt to say it's going okay because people who follow me know how my career is going. If you need to ask, then you don't need to know.

That same night I lost, Saturday 26th March 2005 my cousin Tyrone told me he had not been feeling well and had been in the hospital for pains in his chest. He went to the hospital and his GP many times but they said there was nothing wrong. When they did finally admit him. His health drastically dropped. He died 6 days before his birthday. He left a twin and 3 beautiful kids behind. He supported me even when he was sick so he will always be with me and he is a reason I live my life to the max. I try to have very little regrets.

After I lost to Judex Meemea I asked Dave Coldwell over the phone if he would release me from my managers contract. He sounded shocked and bemused. He obviously thought he had done a good job when he hadn't got me a fight since I beat Chris Brophy on Saturday 5th June 2004, that was ten months ago. I had fought three fights but that was down to me not him. That was Stacy Warren from my Hood Stripes team making movements for me. Dave told me to go to the board to sort it out. Everyone told me that he was a wanker for doing that and if a fighter wanted to go, they would just rip up their contract and let them be free.

I went to the board with Mr. Akay as he owned 12.5% of my boxing winnings. My girlfriend at the time Rahel came as she was a witness to the initial meeting I had with Dave Coldwell and witnessed his promises. The Board told her she would not be needed and asked her to stay outside.

Mr. Akay spoke to them and they spoke to him with disrespect. I was not happy. I was asked to speak and they tried to shoot me down at every turn, telling me that the list of fighters I had given Dave Coldwell didn't mean nothing as the fighters were not waiting for me to fight them and they could be busy so Dave could get me other fighters he deemed fit. If that was the case, how come when I took over from Dave Coldwell, I got fighters from my list with no problem. So the British Boxing Board of Control told us that I could manage myself but had to give Dave 12.5%.

I would go on to have a bad 2005 dropping 2 losses in 6 fights to boxers beneath me in the rankings and beneath me talent wise. They were both bad decisions but that is boxing.

I would start to work with promoter/manager Jonathan Feld that would be a relationship that transcends boxing, I had three fights with his promotions beating David Kehoe twice and Jus Wallie. My last fight with my boxing team of John Tiftek and Mr. Akay would end with my points win over Duncan Cottier on a Derek Williams promotion at Elephant & Castle Leisure Centre, Saturday 19th November 2005.

When I had beaten Jus Wallie on 12th June 2005 and amassed a 10 fight record with one loss I thought now is the time to go to the USA or I will never go. I was told from a young age that I was good enough to be a World Champion. A trainer from Gleason's Gym in New York was at All Stars Boxing Gym for a couple of months and he spotted me out from the crowd and praised my talent. Mr. Akay and him promised me a trip to NYC but it never happened so I was going to finance it myself. My uncle Desmond was proud of me and would always come to my fights when he was around. He had a sister in New York and he asked her if I could stay with them. She said yes but she was Upstate New York and I needed to be in the city as that was a 3 hour drive every day to get to Brooklyn. So my aunty Doreen asked her husband's niece Celine if I could stay with her in her three bedroom apartment. She said yes and that was my home for years to come. At first, I had my back up with her but as time went by we built a friendship which has lasted till now, she is a genuine nice person. I wasn't used to people being like that so it threw me off as where I am from, people don't help people just for the sake of it.

For the first couple of nights I stayed at a YMCA hostel in Brooklyn. It had a strong polish community around there. I wasn't comfortable at the YMCA hostel as there was a lot of homeless people staying there and I felt homeless. The whole place was grimy. I was paying for the luxurious suite but I wouldn't stay there again unless it was that or the streets. They had a nice gym and a decent pool but the building and my room were less than suitable for me. Celine called me my first night to see how I was. I settled in quickly. I had been on holiday in Cuba on my own so being in New York City was no problem. It was just like I had seen on television. The Cosby Show and New Jack City sprang to mind. America had been a destination I always dreamt of going as a kid. Being a fan of US shows like from Saved by the bell, In Living Color and Fresh Prince of Bel-Air, America seemed the place to be. American boxers like Marvin Hagler, Meldrick Taylor and Pernell Whitaker had influenced my boxing style as a teenager so it was only right that I hit the big apple in the chase of the American dream when I was a professional boxer.

I went down to Gleason's gym when I was settled in and asked if I could train there for a month. They told me the prices, I paid and was made a member. It was a big gym. They had like four boxing rings and ten heavy bags. The gym had a grimy feel to it. Champions had come and gone from there. Fighters like Mike Tyson and Muhammad Ali had trained there. They had World champions Wayne Braithwaite, Zab Judah and Vivian Harris training there at that time, world ranked fighters, future World champions Paul Malignaggi, Yuri Foreman and Elio Royas also plying their trade there. It was everything I had dreamt of. I was nervous but I needed a trainer whilst I was there so I took an hour and looked round the gym, watched the trainers and their fighters and enquired about who was doing what in the gym. Lennox Blackmore seemed to be respected and he was training Vivian Harris who I had a whole load of respect for and Cruiserweight champion Wayne "Big Truck" Braithwaite with hugely talented Elio Royas. There was also trainer Harry Keitt there who was training the Irish stallions John Duddy and World Amateur Bronze medalist James Moore with future World Championship challenger Dmitriy Salita also in his camp.

Respected trainer Hector Roca who got Hilary Swank in boxing shape for her Oscar performance in Million Dollar Baby had trained many World champions Arturo Gatti being one of them. I took all into account and I went to Lennox Blackmore. He was from Guyana just like Vivian Harris and Wayne Braithwaite with Elio Royas being from Dominican Republic. So I felt at home with my Island people as my family are from Saint Lucia and Jamaica.

I always thought I was a good boxer with abundance of skills but when I started to work with Lennox, he taught me so much. Relaxing, feinting and setting up my shots. It was hard at first but I got it bit by bit. I sparred with some Russian boxer and he just tried to bully me throwing me on the ring canvas and throwing punches after the bell. I out boxed him and made him look stupid. He was not amused nor was my trainer Lennox Blackmore, he said if someone disrespects you in the ring you disrespect them back. If he hits you below the belt you return the favor. I would take those words with me for the rest of my career. If a man hit me below the belt even by a mistake, I would repay him with one back.

I would walk in the next day and there was some kid in the far ring with a headband on. I didn't know who he was then but after our sparring session I would find out that he was 21-0 and he had a loudmouth. I asked Lennox who he was and Lennox said, "Does it matter?" I replied I am here to learn so I will spar anyone. I had forgot my sparring equipment so Lennox said, "Those are your work tools and this is your workplace. Don't forget them again". Lennox kitted me up and told me to pressure this kid as he hates pressure. I would later find out that Vivian Harris knocked him out cold and Zab Judah beat him up so bad that he started crying. That wouldn't shock me as I saw him weeping when Ricky Hatton beat him up and he comes across a bit melodramatic. Paul Malignaggi had 21 wins with no loses and I had ten fights with one loss so you would expect him to get the better of me but that was not the case. Lennox told me to show him no respect, feint him and come with combinations and hit him to the body. I did that for three rounds and at the start of the four Paul spat at me then started shouting and cursing at me about my dirty tactics. He wanted to try rough me up but didn't like the same treatment back. He would go on to be successful winning the IBF World Title and his biggest win was against former Lightweight Champion Juan Diaz. He would lose his two biggest fights to Miguel Cotto and Ricky Hatton but there is no shame in that when you are making bucket loads of money in the process.

Paul ran at me like a girl and I restrained him. His trainer started talking mess about he will go to the penitentiary and he isn't scared to do time. A bunch of trainers and fighters in the gym separated us and kept him in the gym and took me out of the ring. He ran to the ring ropes and spat at me, I jumped back. He started wining and I just said you're a bitch. That was all I could say. He kept going on and on. I felt like my lady was shouting at me.
The guys at the gym said he was just upset because I beat him up and he thought I would have been an easy workout. He knew who I was now.

I called my cousin Tyrone back home and he just told me to be careful. No matter where I went trouble followed me. When I got to the gym I saw Paul with two of his Italian sidekicks and some dodgy looking black dude wearing black outside the gym so I waited for them to go inside as I didn't want them to try jump me outside as I already knew he couldn't take me on his own.

When I got into the gym, I couldn't see them but they were in the changing room with Paul. When I got in there, I knew I had to change right next to them to show no fear. Through the session I had my eyes on them at all times but some of the dudes in the gym said if it kicked off, they had my back as he was a nasty muthafucker for spitting at me. I finished my workout and completed my abdominal work next to them in the gym as they chatted and joked amongst each other.

I would later do various interviews and I would mention Mr Paul Malignaggi and how he acted like a broad whilst we were sparring. I was later told he was not happy with me mentioning his name and he would confront me at Mike Arnouatis fight in Manhattan a couple months before his fight with Ricky Hatton.

He told me to tell it how it happened and not my version. He said he got upset with me because he had been out with an injury for 18 months and it was a week away from his comeback fight and he didn't want to get injured. If that's the case don't try to rough me up and you'll be good.

I asked Lennox if I could spar with Vivian Harris but he said I was not ready yet and that Vivian only spars one way and won't hold back on me. I still didn't mind as I wanted to test my skills against him but at least Lennox was trying to look out for me. He let me spar with Elio Royas though and boy, was he a talent. He was a Super Featherweight but strong like a Junior Welterweight. He had skills, speed and great ring generalship. What Lennox was trying to teach me, Elio was doing effortlessly. He was a pleasure to watch train and spar. He would beat up everyone his size so he had to spar with bigger guys and I was more than willing. We sparred a few times and I held my own which was good. His manager Antonio Tineo wanted to sign me but my co-manager at the time Dave Coldwell wanted $10,000 so that was a stumbling block and put an end to Antonio managing me.

My first trip to America would begin my love affair with the USA. I met family I had never seen before. My mum's sister and her family treated me great. It was nice to meet some more of my Treasure family. I had made some new friends with Celine being the one that would last the test of time.

I came back to London full of confidence and promoter Jonathan Feld got me on dodgy small time promoter Roy Hilder's show facing his fighter Oscar Milkitas. I would lose on points in a fight I easily won. Oscar's face was busted up and mine was still smooth like a baby's bottom. I was hurt and felt that some underhanded stuff had gone on but it was pointless going to the BBBofC as I knew they didn't have my best interests at hand by now. Three weeks later Jonathan Feld put me on his promotion which was at Hammersmith Palais night club. I beat David Kehoe again nearly stopping him in the third round.

I went back to New York City as I had applied for the Contender boxing reality show and I had gotten through to the Interview stage. I had sent them video footage of my girlfriend at the time Rahel and my mother. I knew if they were doing my weight category, I would have a chance. I went to the Interview at a hotel in Manhattan. I would see Paulie Malignaggi there. He acknowledged my presence and kept it moving. There were loads of boxers trying to get on the show. I went there with my Gucci hat, Gucci shoes with Armani pants and my Prada jacket. I knew the way I was dressed was London style and I knew they would love it. They told me that they loved the footage of my family. They interviewed me and I was a hit. I was certain to be in it if it was my weight. Michelle McNulty who worked in the casting process told me that Paul had told them about our altercation in Gleason's gym. I laughed when she told me that as he was the name out of us two so if anything it should have been me trying to use his name to get in but that wasn't my style and I didn't want to achieve anything off the back of this name but he didn't have the same principles.

He wasn't allowed to do it as Lou Dibella, his promoter wouldn't release him which turned out to be a smart move. I got through to the next round and was given the contract to look over. The contract was thick like a textbook. After one of the contestant's partners tried to sue the company in charge of production on behalf of their unborn child, I guess they had tightened up the contract. It was like signing away your life and career. Most of the contestant's careers have nosedived or they have been very inactive after the series. I couldn't get a visa in time for shooting and I guess it turned out to be a godsend as in 2006 I had seven fights with three being in Germany. I joined Johnny Eames and Peter Swinney at the TKO Gym and my career would take the next step up towards a title shot.

John Tiftik my trainer had built up his stable of fighters and even though he started with me and learnt a lot with me he was trying to do his managerial thing as well as train fighters. He joined up with some guy who knew nothing about the business but had a bit of money and was willing to back John and his fighters.
They wanted to manage and train fighters so John's investor told him that I was taking away valuable time from their other fighters. John told me he couldn't train me no more. The funny thing was, when he called to tell me I kind of knew as I was talking about it the night before that I may have to look for a new trainer soon. I wasn't shocked. John and I discussed trainers I could work with. Johnny Eames, Brian Lawrence and Tony Sims were mentioned. John said Brian Lawrence who was training Ian Nappa and Ted Bami at the time. I knew Johnny Eames had a lot of guys my weight so he was my top choice. John thought Johnny wouldn't be for me and I said, "Because he's white". John thought I would be more comfortable with Brian Lawrence as he was black and trained a lot of black fighters. That wasn't on my mind. Johnny Eames had Lee Beavis, who I had lost to in the amateurs. Ross Minter, son of World Champion Alan Minter. British, Commonwealth and WBU Champion Graham Earl and a host of talented other fighters. I got Johnny's number and gave him a call. He was cool and said to come try us out for a week and see if I like it.

PRIZEFIGHTER

Monday 5th October 2009, I received an email from the head of boxing at Matchroom Sport. They asked me if I was interested in taking part in their Prizefighter boxing series. It was popular in Britain but outside of this country. No one really cared. All the winners hadn't gone on to do anything major. It was a launch pad if you were interested in fighting for the British and Commonwealth titles but nothing else would really come from it. You got paid 32 thousand pounds which would come in handy but fighting 3 rounds of 3 minutes was not for me. I hated amateurs and I hated 4 round fights. I am a Championship fighter. That kind of offer was 5 years too early. If I was 35 plus, I would take the challenge on but I still had fire in my belly and I had plenty of miles left on my clock. I was hopefully 33% through my career. I would be happy to retire by 40 years old. Shane Mosley, Bernard Hopkins and Roy Jones Jr still had success to their late 30s and I hope for the same kind of longevity in my career.

I had turned down two British Title shots in early 2009. One was at ten days' notice and the other was a few weeks but at Welterweight. I never got no love from the big British promoters so I would never do them no favors when they called. Mr. Akay tried to get some of the big boys to sign me when I turned pro, but none was interested. British National Amateur champions Lenny Daws and Nigel Wright both turned professional at the same time as me, but I ended up being more successful and more respected worldwide than them. They had big promoters behind them with big budgets. I had me, myself and I financing my career. Street money funded my career and it did me well, but I had kind of stopped so the funds was not flowing the way it used to.

MR ISOLA AKAY MBE

This man has been there for me like a father, throughout my life. I have known him since I was 7 years old when my dad took me to All Stars Boxing Club in spring of 1988.
He has seen me grow from a boy to man. He has seen me as a wild teenager doing criminal activities, to a focused man working hard to achieve his goals.
Mr. Akay had written me letters to judges to help me stay out of prison when I was convicted for assaulting four police officers. His letters also helped my brother when my brother pleaded guilty to armed robbery.
Foreign boxers would sometimes come over and Mr. Akay would help them with visas and all sorts. Many boxers have had trouble with the law and Mr. Akay would be there for them.

Mr. Akay knows the hard work I have put into my Boxing.

His son Tee-jay was a British Champion as a professional fighter and a National Amateur Champion. He died of a heart attack in his 40s. He was also a good guy who was always supportive towards the boxers.
James Oyebola was a Heavyweight National Amateur Champion and WBC International Champion as a professional. He was shot when the smoking ban in the United Kingdom was enforced. He asked some young guys at a wine bar if they could put their cigarettes out. They took it as if he was being disrespectful towards them. They walked off to get their gun and came back shooting him and killing him in the process. That was two loses to All Stars. They were fighters I grew up as a kid seeing them in the gym and wanting to follow in their path. James and Tee-jay could have gone to America but turned down the opportunity. Mr. Akay told me Tee-jay was seeing a woman at the time and didn't want to leave her. He was a playboy and ended up splitting with her anyway. Tee-jay was talented and probably never reached

his potential. He would be partying at night then and come back, change and get ready to go for a run. He was a character, a really good person.

Many Champions had walked through the doors of All Stars Boxing Club, Lennox Lewis, Azumah Nelson, Roy Jones Junior, Badou Jack, Tim Witherspoon, Ricky Hatton, Joe Calzaghe, Michael Nunn, Mike Tyson. The list goes on. Even 50 Cent came for an interview once.

When Mike Tyson came to All Stars for some training sessions before knocking out Lou Saveresse, I was in prison. I would have loved to have seen him then. My brother saw him and visited me in prison teasing me about this. Shit happens. Prison was a life changing experience for me and I don't think I would change that part of my life as I learnt many things about myself and the company I was keeping.

Mr. Akay has done a lot for many people, young and old in his lifetime and when he goes. His legacy will live on.

On Sunday 8th November the day after David Haye won the WBA Heavyweight Title, I felt inspired and went for my morning run down Holland Park to do some hill sprints. A couple of hours later I went to All Stars Boxing Club to do an hour skipping with some shadow boxing and speedball work. Mr. Akay was taking the amateurs through some drills. I was watching them as I had to choose some of them to take some products I had received from HIGH5, Wellman and For Goodness Shakes to help them in their build up to the Mayor Cup that Mr Akay had started a year earlier.

Mr. Akay looked his usual self while instructing the amateurs on what he wanted them to do. There was no concern in his health from what I knew of. After I had finished my hour skipping and the amateurs left the ring to hit the bag. I was getting ready to go in the ring and do some shadow boxing.

The amateurs had done a round on the bag before I heard someone scream out to me that Mr. Akay had collapsed. I was kind of in shock and just stood there stuck to the ground, frozen. As some of the boxers ran past me to call an ambulance, I collected myself and ran to Mr. Akay. I told Badran to put him to his side as he did that Mr. Akay came awake. He said he was okay and tried to get up. We held him and I told one of the boxers to get him a chair. Mr. Akay sat on the chair and gathered his thoughts. A boxer gave him a banana and some Lucozade. I gave Mr. Akay a HIGH5 energy bar which Mr. Akay smiled at knowing I am always plugging my products I use. Mr. Akay started to joke and said he was fine but he had rushed out of his house this morning without eating as he was running late to open the club for the amateurs. Obi called 999 to speak to the ambulance. They would not come as we didn't know his health history, which I thought was stupid. If a 76 year old collapses for no reason at all. I would think it should be a priority to come and see he is okay.

Mr. Akay told the amateurs to go back to training, they didn't want to but he insisted so I stayed with him and spoke about the great job David did last night against the World Champion Valuev. David had come to the first annual Mayor Cup and had said to Mr. Akay he would come again to the second one with his WBA World Title.

When the amateurs finished their workout and came back over to Mr. Akay, I got a mat and did some abdominal work. Then I went to shower. Badran had asked Mr. Akay if he wanted a lift home but Mr. Akay said he can drive home. I knew I had to accompany him home as it would haunt me forever if he blacked out and got in an accident. I asked him for a lift to his house. He said I would drop you home, I replied that I want to visit my cousin who lives on his road. He drove home and when he was parking up. I said,

"You know I just wanted to make sure you got home safely." He laughed and said, "I know!" We said our goodbyes and I made sure he went through his front door. A few hours later I received a call about him neglecting his health as he is so busy. For a man in his 70's he works everyday with kids and adults. He is a good hearted person and many people see him as family. Many people love him. He is an inspiration to me.

The All Stars volunteers nominated Mr Akay for the BBC Unsung Hero Award in early 2010. The BBC confirmed in November that he won the (regional) title; BBC were at the gym on December 1st doing interviews and presenting him with the Award, it was shown on Sunday 12th December. He also attended the BBC Sports Personality of the Year Show in Birmingham on 19th December as this Award is a part of that nomination, he did not win the National Unsung Hero Title but Mr. Akay was the man to me.

I know that I shocked him with the success I had. I was not an outstanding amateur but I believed in myself and worked hard. Mr Akay's son was the most successful amateur to come out of All Stars with him winning the National Amateur boxing competition and going to the Olympics and getting to the quarter finals, only to lose to the eventual winner and future great Evander Holyfield.

I was by far the most successful professional to come out of All Stars. I had fought in Germany, St. Lucia and America, I had won various championship titles and the British championship. I had beaten former World champion
Demarcus 'Chop Chop' Corley, World number three Delvin Rodriguez and British champion Lenny Daws and former European Champion Jason Cook, who Sky Sports had said was one of the best British fighters over the last ten years.

There were not many people I look up to and respect but Mr.

Akay is someone I would say is an Inspiration to me, just like my mother is.

Mr. Akay was a torch carrier for the London Olympics in 2012. He joked that he wasn't even British and that Ghana wouldn't be happy. This man was migrant who started a boxing club in his hallway for the local black kids who could not use the local boxing clubs forty years ago. Mr. Akay is the perfect example that if you want to make something happen, you can. He is in his seventies and is still receiving awards and achieving goals. Most people his age are in a rocking chair, this man is living his life to the full.

2019, Mr Isola Akay sadly passed away, a few days after his birthday. He was in his 80s. The man has left a legacy. All Stars Boxing Gym is now managed by Mufu Akay, his son. I hope they can continue being a positive environment for the community and continue the great work that Mr. A started.

I hope to start Treasure Boxing Club and follow Mr. A's lead and hopefully have the same success as him.

CESTUS MANAGEMENT

I signed with Cestus management on 31st August 2009. I was happy signing and optimistic about the future but that would soon turn to displeasure as I would be unhappy with their management of me. I know they did pretty good with Mike Arnouatis but when it came to me it didn't go that well.

I was first going to sign with Cestus management in November 2008 but I decided against it as I felt like they were trying to jump on my deal to fight former Undisputed Welterweight champion Zab Judah and I didn't want them to get the limelight for my hard work and pass it off as theirs. The fight would fall through anyway.

I was then supposed to sign with Stuart Duncan who had worked with and produced a lot of champions. He is Australian and was going to get me fights in Australia and the States then get me a World title shot. That fell through. Then I was left in Britain and I had two keep busy fights with Left jab promotions.

I contacted the CEO from Cestus about me signing with them. They were happy for me to come on board but it took them over 2 months to get a contract to me which was blamed on their attorney being busy then I signed at the end of August and month after month was told to keep training. It is impossible to stay on top of your game. No one can train intensively for months on end; you need to have a date to build towards.

I was offered fights in Ukraine, Canada, America, Germany and Britain whilst waiting on Cestus management. It was frustrating waiting on them and by the end of November I was ready to leave them. I had said to myself that by February I would ask them to release me out of the contract. They would say that they have loads of influence in the World of boxing but were unable to get me a fight. They told me that a lot people do not want to fight me and have a lot respect for me. That comment showed lack of knowledge of who I am. When the European Champion and number one contender for the world title will fly you to their country to have you spar with them to help them, get them ready for their important fights. I am a fighter who is respected by his peers. I have beaten a world, African and English champions. I have sparred with loads of World Champions and World rated fighters. I have earned my respect, it was not given to me and by them saying they were struggling to get guys in the ring, showed me that they did not have the influence they thought they had. I was managing myself for years and doing very well but I needed a management with more contacts than me and I thought they could do it.

I had waited four months after signing the contract and Mike would always come with stories of how he is working on this and that but nothing ever came to fruition. I decided to take a trip to New York, December of 2009 for a couple of months to make my presence felt in New York in hope of something happening. I had no faith in Cestus management by now. They talked a lot but did very little.

In January Mike Michael from Cestus Management and I had a big argument which would forever damage our working relationship. For months, my frustration grew as Cestus failed to deliver any fights to me. When they did it was a fight that I did not want but I had been out of the ring for so long that I would take anything.

One Saturday afternoon Mike called me to get a hold of the media contacts that my team Hood stripes Entertainment had. I refused to give him them, I said that he could use his own contacts as when I joined Cestus they boasted about their connections in the boxing world, If you have so many contacts you do not need mine. As we spook our discussion became more heated and I told him how I felt and he started to put me down saying after 30 fights that I am not ranked in the World and that I have not made any purses of value. I put my own money that I had made from the streets and financed myself. Paying for opponents and sometimes making no money from fights. I invested in me. I believed that I would get back what I put into my career. I had paid for trips to the USA, spending thousands of pounds on training, equipment, food and general living costs. All this is very expensive and majority of it came from my finances.

I joined Cestus Management to get big fights in the USA, it would be down on me to use my judgement because all they cared about was the 25%, they were entitled to. I was just a fighter and after me they would have more fighters so I had to look after me.

After I lost to Danny Garcia I went back to the United Kingdom and I would not take a big fight until I had won a fight and got back some confidence. I traveled to Germany and picked up the IBO International Title. Cestus Management would call me after my fight and ask me when I would be ready to fight again. I said within 6 weeks. They offered me Delvin Rodriguez and I knew I had to take it. I was never given a chance but I knew I was the better fighter. He was an ABC fighter and I had talent which was up there with some of the world's best.

After beating world number three and two time world title challenger Delvin Rodriguez in Oklahoma, USA, I had finally gatecrashed into the World rankings. My relationship with Cestus was not any better. I had spoken to Mike the week of my fight but I kept it short and sweet as I was not happy with the way he had spoken to me in January when we had an argument. He said how he felt and I said how I felt. It would now be a business relationship and Gina would do all the talking and have the only contact with me. I will not tolerate anyone talking down to me. If he had said the things he said to my face and not over the phone, we would have swapped punches.

When I signed the contract to fight Delvin Rodriguez. I had reservations about signing the contract with options in it as I had a bad relationship with Star Boxing when I lost to Ali Oubaali. They kept contacting me and saying how they had options over me even when they did not. Cestus management said Star Boxing would let me have my fights in Europe if it did not clash with fights that they had for me in the United States.
I had planned to fight on Miranda Carter's Left Jab promotions show from June and when Cestus Management heard about me fighting on her show they asked if I would get it taken off the internet as the IBF wanted to nominate me for a world title eliminator against former world champion and the current IBF world number 2 Randall Bailey. I got Left Jab to take it off the website, I knew I was still fighting on October 10th and that the world title eliminator would have to be at a convenient date for me. They wanted early November and that was not good for me. I wanted an early 2011 date. I was offered $20,000 and that was not good enough for me either as I had to give out 35% to my management and trainer plus training costs so I asked for $25,000. They said that the money was not there so I said I would pass.

Cestus Management were upset that I had turned down various fights but they had lost my faith. I wanted to fight Kendal Holt in February and Cestus Management wanted me to fight Danny Garcia instead which proved to be a bad fight for me as I did not think much of him as a fighter and I had no motivation.

I turned down fights against Said Quail and a fighter in Canada called Greco. I wanted to fight big name guys and guys who were 140lbs not 147lbs. I had taken the Delvin Rodriguez fight because I was unhappy with the way Stan Hoffman and Lou

Fosco had treated me 2 years previous. Lou did not fully prepare me for my debut in the USA and I got paid just over $3,000 for the fight against Ali Oubbali and after 35% deductions and other expenses I was left with $1,750. That was the hardest fight to date and I was paid garbage money for it. So even though I did not want to take the fight against Delvin Rodriguez I took it for personal grudge. I knew I was fitter and better conditioned than Delvin as the training Lou Fosco does in camp was very basic and too easy. If Delvin changed trainer, he would probably be a world champion by now.

Cestus management had proved that they could not take me to where I wanted to go.
I wanted to fight Kendall Holt but Mike Michael talked me out of it. He said fighting on a Golden Boy Promotions show would be huge and when I win, they would have a two fight option on me so I could get a fight on HBO. I saw the logic in it but fighting an unknown fighter like Danny Garcia did nothing for my appetite.

I would fall out with Mike in the buildup. We wouldn't talk until my fight with World number three Delvin Rodriguez. I wasn't a welterweight but getting back at Stan Hoffman and Lou Fosco for their treatment of me two years previous spurred me on. Delvin was trained by Lou and management by Stan. Stan was good to me, giving me my first break at America but I lost to Ali Oubaali and he never gave me a second chance. Stan wanted me to train with Lou as that was his in house trainer but I had no connection with Lou and didn't rate him highly as a trainer. I wanted to train with Harry Keitt and Francisco Guzman who were training James Moore and Dmitriy Salita up in the Poconos Mountains which wasn't too far away. I had trained with them before and they knew me, were as Lou Fosco was told by Stan Hoffman I have qualities to be a world champion and he'd just do three rounds of pad work with me and leave me to do whatever else I wanted to do.

After beating World number three Delvin Rodriguez. My relationship with Cestus eased a bit but I would not speak to Mike Michael on the phone until April 2011. I saw him the week of the Rodriguez fight but other than that, nothing.

I beat Delvin Rodriguez on the Friday on ESPN's Friday Night Fights. The Monday after I was back in the gym. Two weeks later ESPN would call Cestus and ask if I would top their bill as their main event for the end of season show had fallen through. It was in Montreal, Canada so I was looking forward to going.
ESPN would turn down ten opponents for me and in the end, they had a garbage main event.

The IBF put me as world number four in their August rankings. I was over the moon. I would go Las Vegas for my 30th birthday. I had a great time.

Whilst in New York City, I received an email from John Ingle, match maker to Mick Hennessey from Hennessey Sport. He obviously knew about my big win and World ranking so he asked if I would be interested in a fight with John O Donnell. I said I wasn't interested. He took offense and said just because I beat the world number three, I would not be getting a fight with Mayweather or Paciquao. I told him I'm interested in a fight with Lenny Daws. He said he would get back to me.

On my arrival to Britain in September I was offered a world title eliminator with Randall Bailey in Belgium on 5th November. I wasn't happy with being offered $20,000 for such a hard fight so I told the IBF I wasn't available. They were supposed to go to the available fighter and so on. I was dropped 10 places as the IBF were unhappy, I took a warmup fight instead of fighting in the world title eliminator.

British champion Lenny Daws was ringside at my keep busy fight and I obviously impressed him as he asked Mick Hennessey to make the fight with me.
He thought he would over run me with his work rate.

The fight was due for mid-December before Mick Hennessey changed the date to February 5th, when the new year came, he pushed it back by another 2 weeks I was starting to wonder if this fight would go ahead.

In that time Cestus had sent me a letter of fight offers and my rejections. Cestus had basically made Mike Arnaoutis a
fully fledged stepping stone and that wasn't going to be me. They would offer me fights in Canada for $12,000 against the home boy and wonder why I say no.
After beating the World number three I would think they would get me to sign with a promoter but they were happy to pimp me out like a whore to a promoter willing to pay. I tried to like them but I felt I was paying 25% for a Personal assistant.

After I beat Lenny Daws. I had a meeting with Frank Warren. Cestus kept ringing my phone wondering what was going on. I didn't answer as I had an argument with Gina the Wednesday before the fight as I didn't want to go to the press conference on Thursday as I had a bad cold. Gina went onto Hennessey side saying how unprofessional it was. I told her not to contact me and I didn't go.

So now I've beaten the World number three, British champ and lost a split decision to World number nine Danny Garcia. Cestus are still contacting me with late notice fights for a few thousand dollars. It's like these guys do not see the bigger picture.

I should be signed to a promoter who can maneuver me into a world title shot.

I got late notice fights to fight Lamont Peterson in a world title eliminator and Joel Julio on an ESPN Friday night fights main event.
With Peterson I got ten days notice and Julio was seventeen. As much as I would love those fights. I had to turn it down. I could beat both of those guys with a months notice so I'm not going to short change myself. If I lose, I get judged on my performance. No one cares that I took it short notice. ESPN were still in my bad books so I wasn't going to do any favors for them as they treated me bad over the Montreal fight and their fight analyst Teddy Atlas is always going against me.
Cestus of course are always unhappy with me turning down fights as all they want is their 25%.

On Tuesday 7th June 2011, Golden Boy Promoters contacted Cestus management about me featuring on the undercard of Floyd Mayweather vs Victor Ortiz against their rising star Jessie Vargas.
It would be part of the Pay Per View show.
I turned it down instantly as I saw it as disrespectful. I am not a steppingstone for some rising star. I took the Danny Garcia fight as I hadn't fought in nearly eight months but I was not up for the fight so even though a lot of people thought I won I knew I could have done better. Jessie Vargas may be a rising star but I have never heard of him. I want to fight other world ranked fighters, not unknowns. It's a shame as it's a great opportunity to fight on the

same show as Floyd Mayweather.
Cestus obviously rang my phone down. I let it ring and just text Gina to say my decision was final. All they care about is their 25%, so fuck them.

Gina had asked me the day before if I would like to meet up as she will be in New York City with Mike. I told her that I didn't want to see Mike, as my feelings have not changed since we had an argument back in January of 2010. He called me back in May, I only answered the phone as I thought it was Gina. He spoke to me for an hour about how some millionaire was interested in signing me but I had to be an opponent for Lanardo Tyner first in an Intercontinental title fight for the IBO. The man was a joke. He had made Mike Arnaoutis into a world class opponent and he wanted to do the same to me.

I agreed to the Lanardo Tyner fight as I could not see him beating me in a million years but the promoter in Chicago moved the fight by three weeks so when they sent the contract I stalled for two weeks as I was waiting on Hennessey to finalize the deal with Tyson Fury v Derek Chisora. Mike and Gina tried to harass me by calls and texts but I never replied. I was only getting paid $9,000 to fight Tyner but they wanted me to sign. Luckily, I didn't as Mick Hennessey would confirm the deal with Chisora and Fury and I was the co main event on the card. Cestus probably wasn't the worst management around but they thought so small that they would forever be a nickel and dime bag management.

I hadn't spoken to Gina since July 1st, 2011 she had sent me emails to see how I was. I didn't reply to none of them. After my fight with Jason Cook, she sent me four emails congratulating me. I didn't reply. She sent me an email saying that her and Mike were not against me but working for me. Two fights in two years was a poor job. I had gotten the Lenny Daws fight myself as Hennessy Sport matchmaker had emailed me about fighting John O

Donnell and I had told him Lenny Daws is the only fighter I want to fight so he said maybe December but he would get back to me. He did and Cestus finalized the deal and got 25% for doing basically nothing. With the Jason Cook fight they were not going to get 25%. I was ready to make the move to get them out the picture. Lawyer Liz Ellen and Rene Carayol would be heading the task. I went away to Cuba for two weeks, hoping the situation would be nearly finished by the time I got back.

With top US promoters wanting to sign me, I knew Cestus would be seeing dollar signs. Therefore I signed with them but in two years they had failed to do that. I wanted them out of my life. I liked Gina as a person but I disliked Mike Michael. They were a team so they had to go.

Gina had called me and left a voice message and she sounded nervous, like she knew the axe was coming down. She wanted to know if I was going on vacation and when I would be ready to fight as the new US promoter wanted to make the deal. I didn't reply. She texted and emailed me. I forwarded the relevant information to Rene and left it in his hands. In five months of working with Rene, he had done more for me than Cestus had done in two years. I was willing to make him my agent. I no longer needed a manager. Cestus were surplus to requirements.

Cestus were making all the right moves now and saying all the right things. This is what I wanted from them two years ago. Our relationship was too damaged to move forward. Golden Boy Promotions wanted me on the Floyd Mayweather. Jr v Victor Ortiz, Star Power card again. I guess my win against former European champion, Jason Cook made people sit up and take notice that I was good enough to be a world champion.

I hadn't spoken to Gina since our argument about the rematch clause in the Jason Cook bout, she had been harassing me with calls, texts and emails before and after the win. Liz Ellen from law firm Mishcon de Reya made her move a month after my win. I was in Cuba recovering after my fight when Gina emailed me saying how she had received a letter from my attorney. She said she was shocked as Cestus had done everything possible to aid my career. She seemed to think I wanted to part company with Cestus because of the Jason Cook contract situation. Gina thought I was still under contract with Cestus but I had never signed a contract and it was never rubber stamped so I knew I wasn't under contract. Gina said in her email that Cestus still wanted to work with me, of course they did. They got 25% for making phone calls. I always wanted a promotional contract with an American promoter but I hated Cestus so much that I needed them out of my life.

Gina copied Liz Ellen into the email she sent me and Liz copied me into her reply which said no contact will be made through Ashley Theophane unless it's through her.

DMITRIY SALITA v AMIR KHAN

Friday 25th November 2009

Dmitriy had asked me to help him out with sparring a week before his fight with Britain sensation Amir Khan. It was something I was happy to do. We were supposed to spar in Finchley at My Gym boxing gym but for some reason Dmitriy had to go up to Newcastle ahead of schedule. I was not looking forward to going up to Newcastle but I wanted to help him out and it just felt nice to be part of the team for the lead up to his World Title fight. The biggest of his career.

This was a fight that Dmitriy had waited for a long time as he had amassed an undefeated record of 30 wins and 1 draw. It was a Jewish fighter versus a Muslim fighter and even though this had not been mentioned really in the buildup, I am sure it was on both fighters mind. The Sun newspaper mentioned it in passing.

I hope that Dmitriy wins as I've known him and have worked with him closely in four fights. He's flown me out to the States twice. I have not been a part of his training camp for this fight so I don't know how his training went and what form he is in. I will make that decision when we spar together over the weekend.

Saturday 26th November 2009

I arrived in Newcastle at 6pm. Two members of Dmitriy's coaching team came to pick me up from the train station. We were staying at the Copthorne Hotel which was only 1.9 miles away.
Bob Goodman from Square Ring promotions welcomed me in the hotel lobby. I told him I knew his name from somewhere and he gave me a quick background on who he is. The man is rocking a

hall of fame ring so you don't get that for nothing.
We went up to Dmitiry's room and it was nice to see him. I haven't seen him in over a year as I had been in the United Kingdom since being in training camp with him for his fight on the Roy Jones Junior v Joe Calzaghe show. I feel happy to be here to assist him and it would be a great feeling for him to be World Champion.
We got ready straight away to go to the gym so I put my boxing stuff in a bag and headed out to the car.

We did a few rounds skipping to warm up then gloved up. Francisco Guzman who is Dmitriy's trainer said that we would be doing 4 minute rounds with 30 second rest. I had already done a 2 hour boxing workout at All Stars Boxing club that morning, taking part in the KO Circuit which is a good workout.
We completed 5 rounds at a decent pace nothing hectic. I moved around like Khan and shot out sharp jabs and left hooks which landed majority of the time to my disappointment. I hurt Dmitriy in the 5th round so I stepped back as he had to take a 30 second rest and there were people from the gym watching so I was weary of that as I didn't want the word to get out that Dmitriy was not looking too good. When I stood in front of him, he would throw rapid combinations, he caught me with some good body shots. After the session I filmed clips of Dmitriy training and just enjoyed being part of the team.

The best sparring partner Dmitriy had was Jorge Teron, a lightweight from New York who I don't think was the best preparation for Khan. I wish Dmitriy had used me as I feel his preparations could have been better and with just a week ahead, I hope he puts everything together. He moved his feet too slow and was not cutting me off. Sparring is just part of your preparation so if mistakes will be made it is best to be made in the gym.

Francisco, Orlando, Stuart and I went for dinner in the hotel restaurant afterwards. Had a lovely steak meal with apple pie and ice cream. We chatted away for an hour then Francisco and Orlando went to their rooms. I accompanied Stuart out to the Town centre. We went to 3 clubs. The first one was like partying with my grandmother and her friends then we went to another one that played 70's and 80's pop songs then the last one was more up my alley way. We stayed for 30 minutes and headed back to the hotel.

I found out that Dmitriy didn't have the best camp with him and Francisco falling out as they usually do but this time Francisco said he quit but they worked out their problems in the end.

We got back to the hotel room after 2am. Israel was still up so we chatted about the fight. I ended up going bed at 3am and I had to be up for 7am as I was going for a run with Orlando and Dmitriy along the riverbank.

Sunday 27th November 2009

Today Dmitriy, Orlando and I went for a run along the riverbank outside the hotel. We ran for 48 minutes as a nice slow jog as Dmitriy is just working on dropping weight now.
I asked Dmitriy why he did not fly me over to New York for his training camp. He said he wanted to but his trainer was happy with the talent in New York they were going to use. Going by our first session, his sessions with the New York boxers did not prepare him enough. Dmitriy is a good guy so I just want him to do well.

He told me how Square Ring who promote him wanted him to hire Emmanuel Stewart for his fight as Amir Khan has Freddy Roach. Emmanuel would not make no difference. Francisco is a good trainer and probably under rated.

I had breakfast afterwards and a two hour nap before we left for the gym at 3pm.
Francisco said we would do seven 4 minute rounds. In the end we only did three and a half rounds. Francisco stopped the sparring, when Dmitriy hit me with a right and shook his hand as if it hurt, the sparring was stopped. Today was good. Dmitriy boxed well. He fires off great combinations but he seems to sometimes lose focus and not work enough in the round.
The Dmitriy I am seeing in the ring; I am not happy with and it upsets me as I would love Dmitriy to be World Champion and I hope it happens. I have been talking about him since we first sparred together in August 2006.

There was a reporter from the Israel Times that came along to the boxing gym with Bob Goodman from Square Ring promotions. He worked with Don King promotions for 30 odd years and spent 13 years working with Muhammad Ali through Don King promotions.
Bob has been all over the World and now works with Square Ring promotions. He is 71 and has so many stories and experience in life, you just can't help but listen when he talks. Reminds me of my time with Stan Hoffman. Bob asked me who I am signed with, I told him no one. He gave me a business card as he liked what he saw in the sparring session with World number one contender Dmitriy Salita.

Bob talked about current fighters on the scene and I think he sees the determination in me to succeed.

Monday 30th November 2009

Whilst eating in the hotel, Bob Goodman came to have breakfast so he sat down with me. We spoke for over 30 minutes and it was great to have his time. We spoke about many things in boxing, how things had changed, what his roll is for Square Ring and what he did whilst working with Don King. This man has lived life and is an inspiration just like manager to the Champions Stan Hoffman and my Boxing mentor Mr. Isola Akay M.B.E.

He mentioned that he keeps up to date with the boxers around and has been following my progress for a while. He told me not to make the boxing business dishearten me and to stay focus. He said that I am a highly skilled fighter who just hasn't had the breaks. That was nice to hear it from a man who has been in training camp with boxing legends Joe Louis, Sugar Ray Robinson and Muhammad Ali. He has seen them train in the flesh so that meant a lot to me.

He told me that I can't do it on my own and I will need help to reach the top. I know this and I told him for 2010 I want to sign up with a promotional group to leverage me into getting big fights.

I wanted to get ready to run with Dmitriy so I excused myself from the table but it was an honor to speak with this man. This alone was worth the trip.

Saturday 6th December 2009

Dmitriy was stopped in 76 seconds in the first round against Amir Khan. Who knows what happened. It was his first loss and he can come back. He just needs to make some changes.

NEW YORK TRAINING CAMP

Sunday 20th December 2009

I arrived in New York City on Tuesday 15th December. It felt good to be back. Hopefully, I can fight whilst I am here as that is the whole point of this trip.
Spoke to Gina and Mike from Cestus management. They seem optimistic but I have been with them for 4 months, so I am not as hopeful as them.
They talk about a lot of dates. I don't care about dates. I care about fights so hopefully early January I hear something.
I will be training at Starrett City for a month then I plan to go Kid Kelly's Boxing Gym to train with Francisco Guzman.

Wednesday 20th January 2010

I had a great day at Gleason's Gym today completing 8 rounds with Jorge Teron at a frantic pace. I have 5 weeks to go so I am happy with my progress. I spent 5 weeks training at Starrett City in Brooklyn working on the technical aspect of my game. So now we are stepping it up and increasing the intensity of my boxing sessions. Today I did skipping, shadow boxing, sparring, bag work, speedball work and strength and abdominal exercises at the end.

John Duddy and I have the same trainer, so I see him a lot in the gym. He was telling me that Julio Cesar Chavez Junior and him could fight later this year. That would be a good fight for him and I am sure he could come home with a win.

I met up with my management in the evening to sign the bout agreement for my fight with Danny Garcia.
I think Golden Boy overmatch many of their fighters as in 2009 Victor Ortiz, Juan Diaz and Alfredo Angulo lost when they were

put in the wrong guys. It is my aim to show that Danny Garcia is not ready for this level.
I am chasing fights with Golden Boy's other 140lb fighters. Nate Campbell, Victor Ortiz, Juan Diaz and Vivian Harris are all on my hit list. I believe you never fail as long as you try and you fail if you never try so I am just making the most of my opportunities. There are not many British boxers who have won in four different countries as a professional.

I haven't fought since last June but I haven't been out of the gym for more than a day.
I have sparred world number three Ajose Olusegun, European Champion Paul McCloskey and world title challenger Dmitriy Salita so I have been getting in world class sparring, keeping my tools razor sharp.

Friday 22nd January 2010

Two time World Champion Joey Gamache was in the gym today and he told me that he liked the "Treasure Hunter" piece the Boxing News did on me a year ago. He mentioned that London boxer Mark Alexander did very well in sparring while he was at the Kronk Gym last year.

Sunday 24th January 2010

I got lost on my run this morning in Brooklyn. Ended up doing a ten mile run instead of an eight miler.
Lucky for me I had a massage midday to ease out my sore muscles. I met up with Dmitriy afterwards as I was in his part of town. We had a quick chat and I left him to go do his strength conditioning workout with his trainer. I haven't seen him since helping him out in Newcastle before his World title challenge to Amir Khan. Personally, I feel he will redeem himself. People will criticize him but Amir Khan was knocked out cold just over a year

ago and came back to win a world title. It happens.

Wednesday 27th January 2010

Conditioning was the topic of the day today, got through a six mile run, spin class, yoga session and thirty lengths swimming in the morning. In the evening I ran up a twenty floor tower block seven times. That was murder but great strength work for my thighs.

When I was asked to fight Danny Garcia. I was like who? He is still learning his game and this is the best time to fight him. I wouldn't have choose this fight if it was down to me as fighting him is like whatever to me but it gives me a shot at redemption on ESPN as last time I dropped a close decision to Ali Oubbali. This time I can't throw away the first four rounds. I will have to be aggressive from the get-go. Harry Keitt works on offensive so that works out good for me. No stone has been left unturned in my preparation.
I will be ready to fight one of America's top prospects come 26th February.

Thursday 28th January 2010

US Olympian Sadam Ali is fighting in a week so I got Harry to organize sparring for Saturday. Jorge's trainer, Mark Breland wants one last session with me so we will mix it up.
Our sparring session was filmed today and watching myself I have World class skills. It is all about translating it to fight night. Luis Abregu is an Argentinean welterweight in the gym that is rocking a 28-0 record. He looks like a brick with muscles coming out of his fingers. He has been banging out the rounds also and I want to get some rounds in with him. He is strong but slow. Today's workout was good. I love putting in the work in the gym. I am feeling in great shape.

Saturday 30th January 2010

US Olympian Sadam Ali couldn't make the sparring session today so it was just Jorge Teron and I.
Jorge's manager came to watch his last session so obviously he would expect a show from his fighter.
I boxed decent. My trainer Harry Keit was happy with my performance saying I was on form today but I felt like I was better on Thursday. My stamina has been very good. I am sharp at the minute and my timing is coming together. I am blocking a lot of shots and my distance, reflexes and confidence in the ring is all on point.
I have done 48 rounds with Jorge Teron and I have four weeks left of training and three weeks of sparring to go. Jorge has been good work and it has been very competitive. Hopefully he wins his fight with Brandon Rios.

Sunday 31st January 2010

Went through the DVDs of Danny Garcia today. He is talented but makes mistakes as all fighters do.
I am not too bothered about concentrating on him as long as I bring my A game I will win.

Wednesday 3rd February 2010

Nigel Benn victim former World champion Iran Barkley was in the gym today doing some cardiovascular work. John Duddy came back today after his win at Madison Square Garden and Junior Middleweight champion Yuri Foreman was in the gym doing some fitness drills.

In the evening I went down to one of the local housing estates to do some drills. It took forty-two minutes to run up the eighteen floors ten times. This is great work on my thighs and a good cardio workout.

Thursday 4th February 2010

Watched Melissa Hernandez and Belinda spar today. I am not a fan of female as the level is low. But I have been watching these girls for years and I have not seen any females with the talent they both have in the UK. Watching them you forget they are women because they are so good and enjoyable to watch.

It is two years since my last outing on ESPN in America. Since then I have beaten a former African, Commonwealth and World Champion. Danny will be looking to put on a show and so will I.

Friday 5th February 2010

Danny Garcia has been protected in his first 15 fights. I am not here to be part of somebody's learning curve. He has a fight on his hands and his pity pat shots won't have me tumbling to the ground like a sack of potatoes like his previous KO victims.

I saw popular NYC Junior Welterweight Edgar Santana in the gym. He holds an identical record to mine. He is making a comeback after some unforeseen circumstances made him take a break from the ring.

Saturday 6th February 2010

Jorge Teron who I completed 48 rounds of sparring with for my fight with Danny Garcia got stopped in three rounds in his fight today against Brandon Rios.
Every fighter loses; it is how you come back that matters. Nate Campbell, Carlos Baldomir and Glen Johnson all suffered losses coming up the ranks so it happens. You learn from the losses,

make adjustments and work harder in the gym to improve your game.

Sunday 7th February 2010

Went for an hour run this morning. Felt like I was ice skating as the snow from yesterday had frozen.
Got my weekly fix of Danny Garcia footage. I usually win my fights with my speed and skill. He has both so I will have to win with my ring smarts and tactics. It will be all about killing his speed and quickness as they are his best assets. They are great assets to have as all my favorite fighters have them. He makes mistakes and I will look to capitalize on them.

Monday 8th February 2010

People talk of Danny Garcia like he is some future boxing star. He is a talented fighter but what does that mean. He has fought guys who looked scared before they entered the ring and guys who get hit with one punch and hit the ground like a sack of potatoes. That surely is not me. He is very beatable from what I see and far from a future Shane Mosley or Floyd Mayweather Junior. I have seen many talented fighters not make the grade through bad matchmaking or just not good enough. Golden Boy Promotions are not the best at bringing along talent. I have to find out the odds on me winning this fight. Might be worth a little wager.

I was called a veteran today. That is funny. I am 29 years old with 29 fights. What would you call Bernard Hopkins, Shane Mosley or Glen Johnson then? Old age pensioners!

Glen Johnson is a fighter who perseverance was the key. I am sure many people did not believe in him early in his career, but he did and his hard work, determination, and belief in his self-brought him success.

Fighters like him inspire me. Nobody thought I would get this far in the British boxing scene. Goes to show how much boxing journalists and boxing experts know.

Tuesday 9th February 2010

Had my first sparring session of the week with Gabriel "Tito" Bracero. We completed 6 rounds which I was happy with after a full morning of training. At this minute in time I am working on my tactics for the fight in sparring.

Friday 12th February 2010

Ran up 18 floors of a Tower block ten times tonight. I feel a sense of accomplishment when I am finished as it is a murderous workout. In total I ran up 2520 steps and 180 floors. I finished in 41.51:90 last week and 39.36:84 tonight. I took off 2 minutes and 15 seconds from last week's session. I'm very happy with that. I feel improvement with my fitness. Next week will just be maintaining and tweaking little things.

Tuesday 16th February 2010

Snow rained over New York City once again. I woke up to inches of snow covering everything.
Went for a 50 minute run while snow beat down on me. When I arrived at Paerdegat gym, I started off with 30 lengths in the swimming pool before taking part in a Pilates session and finished off with a strength conditioning workout.

Received my boxing outfit from Boxfit UK this morning. It is Royal Blue and Gold with the flags of Saint Lucia and Britain. It looks good!

The fight will be shown live on ESPN2 which is televised across the world.

Wednesday 17th February 2010

Completed ten rounds sparring with highly respected Gleason's gym resident coach Hector Roca's young prospects Dean & Scott Burrell. Hector was not there so World Champion Yuri Foreman's trainer took over their corner advising them on tactics. Dean & Scott Burrell both have quick hands and fast feet, so they give me a good workout for ten rounds.
I worked on my ring craft and boxing tactics which I plan to take to the fight.

In the evening I ran up a Tower Block's eighteen floors ten times. It was the third week in a row that I was doing sets of ten after starting on five in January. I forgot my music which was a nightmare as it takes my mind off the pain going up the stairs. Maybe that made me work harder as I could not wait to finish the session. Three weeks ago I did this session in 41.51, last week was 39.36 and this week I shaved another 3 minutes off to 36.36. That's five minutes in the last three weeks I have shaved off so my fitness is not an issue with just over a week till I fight the 2008 US Olympic alternate.

I have completed 85 rounds of sparring so far with one more session on Friday.

Ten weeks in training camp is coming to an end and all the hard work is nearly done.

The mental preparation is now the final part of the puzzle to which can earn me a notable win on my record.

WINNING THE IBO INTERNATIONAL WELTERWEIGHT TITLE

Following the weeks that I had lost to Danny Garcia in a split decision on a Golden Boy promoted show in El Paso Texas. I wanted to get out quick and put that loss behind me.
Cestus management had thrown up names like Zab Judah, Julio Diaz and Jesus Chavez but they were unable to get anything concrete on the table. That meant I had to do their job for them and I secured a bout in Munich, Germany for the IBO International Welterweight Title.
I trained solidly for ten weeks for the fight. Sparring with former British, current Commonwealth and World number two at the time Ajose Olusegun, International Masters Champion Yassine El Maachi and young prospects from All Stars Boxing gym. I did over one hundred rounds and I felt ready and good to go.
My opponent has only nine fights with seven wins and one lose and one draw. I did not overlook him as he was the home boy even if he was from Afghanistan, he had been based in Germany for years.

I had been working with All Stars coach Dave Brown and he helped me get in shape with some good pad work.
We left for Munich, Germany the morning of the weigh in. I stayed round my girlfriend at the times apartment that night and she dropped me off to my brother's apartment to pick up my suitcase. My brother was sleeping but I woke him up to leave him some birthday money. He told me how our Aunt had not picked up our mother from JFK in New York the day before as she was supposed to. My mum was going to visit her family for the first time as it was her nephew Keno's wedding. My mum had to stay in a hotel and I was not happy at all. On the way to the airport I was texting her and emailing my friend Celine who's uncle was married to my aunty Doreen to try find out where my mum was and help sort out this mess. I did what I had to do before getting

on my flight and heading to Germany. I had no reception on my cell phone so I could not contact anyone until I got back on Sunday midday.

My fight with Harasch Hotaki for the IBO International title over twelve rounds was being held at Messehalle in Burghausen, Munich with one thousand people in attendance.
We stayed in a small hotel called Hotel Glockrlhofer. It was a village kind of town but the people were friendly. It had a feeling of a vacation place for senior citizen's as it had the biggest castle in the world there and very old historic buildings.
The supervisor from the IBO Mr. Benedetto Montella from Italy was a fine guy. He spoke to me many times and he said that I could fight for the IBO's World title in the future as I had a good record.
Mr. Montella had worked for the IBF boxing organization for over twenty years until the IBO offered him a job. He told me he had brought Italian referee's and judges as the last show which had German referee's, was an appalling standard. He said one fight was stopped when the home fighter threw body shots that had hit his opponent's arms. He was very down to earth even telling me how he lived in London when he was eighteen years old and was a waiter in Shaftesbury Avenue, working for one pound a day with free food and lodge.
He thought I would have no problem with Hotaki as he had never beaten a fighter with a winning record or never gone past four rounds. The referee even complimented me at the weigh in as having a good record. They could see I fought all over the world and had handled some of the World's best.

The day of the fight I stayed in my room until it was time for our driver from the Audi car lot to take us to the venue. I went down for breakfast around 8am which consisted of scrambled eggs with a roll, some granola cereal, and some fruit. I would spend the day watching other top fighters. Herman Ngdoujo v Julio

Diaz, Cotto v Yuri Foreman, Marvin Hagler v John Mugabe and Miguel Cotto v Shane Mosley. Just to get my mind in that fighting mode.

I gave my shorts to the cleaner at the hotel to iron on my IBO badge for the fight. When I went to get my shorts off her. She said she had given it to some blonde guy who spoke German and said he was with me. I did not have a clue who she was on about. I wanted to keep my mind on the fight and not get stressed with the situation. I spoke to her again and asked if she had seen the guy she gave it to. She had not but she checked the rooms for me on our floor. I told her if she saw him to call me straight away. Dave would speak to the manager and he said they were trying to find the guy. In the end I took Dave's shorts to wear as I did not have a backup. When we arrived at the venue, the Czech boxing team coach gave me my shorts. I gave him a big hug as I thought they were gone.

They had me in the away corner but the IBO team had been so good to me I felt like I just had to do what I do and I would get the win. This did not turn out to be the case. I won the fight by four rounds, two rounds and one scorecard were a draw. If I did not finish the fight as strong as I did, I would have lost. I nearly stopped him in the last two rounds. It was a shame I kept it so late. In between corners I asked Dave what round it was and I thought he said round six and I got off my stool and heard round ten so I had to put my foot on the gas and start showing the judges what I can do. All through the fight I busted him up with my jab and left hook. His whole face was swollen, his nose was busted up and bleeding and he was very tired. I had a safety first approach as the promoter had told me that he has a strong right hand. He struggled with my movement and by round six when he did catch me flush, he had nothing left in him. I knew he was desperate and just looking for the haymaker and I was not going to let that happen.

After the fight he would tell me because he had fought rubbish opponents, he believed he was better than he was. When he saw that he had hit me with his best shots and I was still there he knew he was in trouble. I told him that I had lost four times and that you just have to learn from your loses and become a better fighter. He said I was very skillful and he hoped that one day I would become a World Champion.

His trainer said I was very smart as I was moving around and biding my time. I had my game plan. It worked but I wanted the stoppage. Dave told me to throw my right hand but I neglected it. I basically won with my left hand.
I was worried about my urine sample test after the fight as I was loaded up with caffeine and I had taken 400mg of pain killers to numb the pain in my right hand that I sometimes got. Everything turned out fine but it didn't stop me from worrying.

Dave and I stayed until the very end as I wanted to know who was driving me to the airport in the morning as it was over an hour away and I knew Mario didn't care how I got back as he left my former trainer Peter Swinney and I stranded in Berlin when I won a Welterweight championship there.

He spoke to Florian Wildenhof after he won the GBC Junior Middleweight title and he agreed to drive me to the station. I was not sure if he would as he was the star of the show and I thought he would be partying through the night.

I took loads of photos with people after the fight and many of the fight fans enjoyed my fight. Maybe it took too long to warm up but it got there in the end.

Florian Wildenhof and his girlfriend Sylvia came to pick us up 8am sharp. I told him I was not sure if he would come as I thought he would have partied after the fight. He went on to say that he had to clean the venue as Mario had left him to do it and had not hired cleaners. He told me how he did not get paid and that he gave the sponsorship money to Mario. I let him know that he did not need Mario as a promoter as the people of his town came to see him not any of the other fighters so he could work with another promoter and do a deal to get 25% of the gate receipts. He was a nice guy who aspired of fighting in America. Boxing fucks fighters all over the World. Florian called Mario the Berlin Don King for screwing fighters out of money.

He went on to tell me that he does security work for night clubs sometimes and that some of the clubbers start fights with him because he is a prizefighter. His woman was beautiful and he was a good person. It was a shame boxing didn't care how good a person you were. It fucked everyone if it could.

Florian was told by Mario that he was going to fight me for the IBO International title in March, a few months before. He watched me on You tube and said I reminded him of Floyd Mayweather Jr and I got a sense he did not fancy a fight with me. I had more than over 20 fights than him so he wasn't wrong.

We got to the airport just after 9am with a scheduled 11.30am flight. Florian and his girlfriend could have dropped us off but they made sure we got to the right check in. We took a couple of photos and made plans to train together when he came over to London to workout and his girlfriend to shop.
They are nice people.

Our flight was postponed by two hours which didn't sit nicely as I hadn't slept and was very tired. It was Father's Day as well so I would have to see my father.

DELVIN RODRIGUEZ TRAINING CAMP

Friday 9th July 2010

I sparred WBO Junior Welterweight champion Timothy Bradley's opponent Luis Carlos Abregu on Thursday at Gleason's gym which was good.
Abregu is ranked 5th in the world so I wanted to see what he was made of. Everyone said he was strong but lacked boxing skills. They were right. He must be the worst 29-0 fighter I have ever seen.
We completed five rounds and I was pretty much happy with what I had done. I am fighting IBF number three Delvin Rodriguez in exactly three weeks so it is full steam ahead. After my IBO International title win, I am glad I only took the one day off as now a great opportunity has come about and my fitness is on point.
It is a Welterweight fight which I am not too happy about. I tried to get it made at 144lbs but my manager Mike Michael called Delvin's manager Stan Hoffman to see if they could do anything on the weight and Stan said he couldn't. It is whatever as I'm good enough to hang with Delvin.

I've been in New York City a week and they are experiencing a heat wave. The weather has been over 100 degrees. It is good for my training as it makes it that bit harder but in general, I hate it.

The winner of Delvin and I will be fighting IBO World Welterweight Champion Lovemore Ndou, that is a fight I would love and one I know I can win.

I am very unhappy with the contract Star boxing gave me. They

are only flying out one of my trainers, wanting a three fight option on me, not meeting me at a catch weight and not giving me what I am worth. They are telling me that John Tandy, who I am cool with can be my cut man for the fight but he had no faith in me when I fought Danny Garcia so why do I want people around me who don't believe in my talent.
Gina from Cestus management wanted me to send the contract to them ASAP but I told her I was not rushing or going out of my way for Star boxing and that I would send it on Sunday.

Hector Roca came up to me in the changing room and told me he likes me as a fighter because I'm a real man. I'll fight! He said Luis Carlos Abregu was too soft.

Monday 19th July 2010

The nearer I get to the fight the more excited I get. I beat Delvin Rodriguez and I am a step away from a World Title shot. I believe in myself I know I can do it.

Thursday 22nd July 2010

When I turned professional, I dreamt of being in big fights in America. You never really believe it will happen or that you will be good enough.
With little support from people in the boxing world I have achieved something I thought was unattainable. With perseverance I am doing my whole life's ambition. It is truly a great feeling to realize the low points where I thought it would never happen or where I lose belief in myself for a minute. I don't need to be a star as that was never a goal of mine. I am happy where I am. Knowing one big win will put me on top of the tree.

I did really well in boxing today. The last 2 days I have done 9 rounds sparring. Today I sparred with Raul Frank who fought for the world title twice against the late Vernon Forrest. He is 20lbs heavier. He started out just boxing and the more frustrated he got the harder he would hit me and he hit me low a few times and, on my thigh, as well. My trainer Harry Keitt got upset but I wasn't bothered as I knew I was doing something right. Finished with 4 rounds of pads, 3 rounds of skipping, 3 rounds on the speed bag, some dips and chin ups then 1000 crunches. I'm feeling ready baby.

Friday 23rd July 2010

I did 8 rounds sparring with the identical twins Dean and Scott Burrell. I can never tell who is who. I like their speed and skill. I did 4 rounds pads afterwards and even my trainers commented if I am on that Manny Paciquao juice as I am in great shape. I did the speed bag and 1000 sit ups afterwards plus I warmed up with 9 rounds of skipping and shadow boxing.
I am feeling great. Body, mind and soul.

Sunday July 26th 2010

Talking to Jamal this afternoon I realized I was in prison 10 years ago for armed robbery. Young Offenders Institute Feltham and HMP Lewes. I would never have thought 10years later I would be one fight away from a world title fight. That's emotional! So many kids go prison and it is the start of a life of crime. I went to prison, passed my BTEC Media first year and I even wrote a book whilst I was there and took courses when I could go to the education classes they had there. I was determined to change my life if I was found Not Guilty. When I was, I didn't look back. I locked off a whole load of friends I used to hang out with and it was the start of a lonely existence for me staying focused on my dream to be a Boxing champion and to fight the best in the world. There was times I did not believe in myself and times when I wasn't making no money but I wanted no regrets. I had qualifications to fall back on whatever happened with boxing. If I achieved my goals or not I would still end up okay. I had plans for after boxing and I was looking forward to it. I gave my life to boxing, I may have missed out on partying with my friends and having a normal life but I gave myself to 35 years old then I would begin the next chapter in my life. Getting married, having kids, owning my own home. When I want something, I get it. I dedicate myself to that goal.

I have to appreciate my life. I was on a road to nowhere and experiencing that time locked up. Even though I was found not guilty it was a big wakeup call not to waste my life.
I need to go to prisons and talk to these kids. People can change. I am the perfect example. I will contact some young offender jails as I can maybe help a couple of kids.
I have gotten so much support from people for my fight on Friday. So many people believe in me. I never think anything of me. I'm just Ashley who is always on his own. I am like many kids who have a dream. Most never reach it but I'm living part of mine. I am grateful for life. The struggles and hard times only make you stronger.

Tuesday 27th July 2010

A lot of people at Gleason's gym feel I can beat Delvin and so do I.
I got my haircut early afternoon and I headed off to the Royal Day Spa for my 3 hours plus of pampering before my fight. I had an hour massage to start with then I had a 30 minute pedicure then I had a 90 minute facial and a manicure to finish off with. I felt like Floyd Mayweather Jr. I'm a fighter, I should look after myself and treat it good as it goes through so much punishment to get into

shape.

I came back home for an interview with Big Dog Radio. It was good, the host said that my fight with Danny Garcia was one of his favorites of 2010. He thought I did enough to win.
They said Delvin was looking past me and calling out the big names in the division. He is a fool to do that as he lost twice last year against ordinary but strong aggressive fighters.
I learnt that former World champion Demarcus Corley who I beat 2 years ago is fighting Marcos Maidana for the WBA Interim World Title. That just shows that I am in the mix.

Went for breakfast 7am. I saw Delvin's trainer Lou Fosco as I came out of my room. He trained me for my US debut with Ali Oubaali so we knew each other.
I told him good morning and asked how Manager Stan Hoffman was. Stan had a heart attack a few days earlier so needed a quadruple bypass. Lou said he came through it and was recovering. Stan had got me my first US fight so I would always be appreciative to him for that. He had worked with or made 30 World champions so he had a good eye for talent. He said I had good eyes like Whitaker and Mayweather Jr. Many people have said that about me so I knew it was true.

Delvin would want to win for Stan and I know he wants to make a statement as he wants the big fights. He feels I will feel his Welterweight power and start running. I am looking to take his power and back him up.
Andre Berto is looking for an opponent so I beat Delvin and I will call him out.

I had an apple, orange, a yogurt and some fruit and cereal. As I left, Lou said I look in shape. I said thanks and went back to my room to relax until 2pm when we had the press conference, weigh in and ESPN interviews.

The press conference was good. Local TV where there to plug the show.
I spoke about Chop Corley fighting for a title and Delvin was my way to that.
Delvin spoke about his tough 2009 being the victim in bad decisions. I am used to it and make no big deal about it. 3 of my 4 losses I feel I didn't lose but that happens in sport. Bad decisions are what makes real fighters. It's how you come back that matters.

My TV interview with ESPN went well. I spoke about my goals to become a world champion and they asked how am I going to get the decisions in tough fights in the US as they seem to go against me all the time. I said, I'm just keeping focused and working hard.
I ate a chicken pasta for dinner and some Pedialyte to get those electrolytes into my body.

Friday 30th July 2010

Pre-Fight Diary

I had dreams about my fight through the night. Believing in myself is the key.
Went for breakfast around 7am. Ate some fruit bran with raisins, toast with honey and 2 small pots of yogurt.
I watched some films on HBO whilst watching some fights on my laptop. Miguel Cotto v Yuri Foreman, Marvin Hagler v John Mugabe and Ashley Theophane v DeMarcus Corley.
I received so much support from people in the UK and US, it was very touching. Over 100 messages which I read all of them.

Delvin has stopped no one in 3 years and that was against Keenen Collins who I've never heard off. He says he is hungry but I've always been hungry. I feel this fight will be one of my best.

Marvin Hagler who is one of my favorite fighters and he never won a World title until his 50th fight so I know I will get my World title shot in the end.

I'm on my journey, on my own, so when I do achieve my goals to fight the best and win a World title it will be so sweet for me.

Teddy Atlas, Mike Tyson's former trainer and commentator wished me luck when I saw him on my way to get my Shrimp pasta. I know he loves Delvin so his commentary will be one sided as always.
All the boxers had their weigh in just before 6pm, it was a hassle but has to be done.
I feel ready, just relaxed and topped up with my High5 bars through the day.

Saturday 31st July 2010

Beating the IBF World number 3 was a great feeling. I knew I could do it but many didn't.
It was a somewhat tough fight but as I am always prepared. I was losing the fight and the last 3 rounds I finished strong grabbing a Majority decision 95-95 96-94 96-94.
I am know in the big boy leagues. To think I was locked up 10 years ago just shows how far I have come.

Sunday 1st August 2010

This morning I went to the Ear and Eye Infirmary in Manhattan on 14th. I had been there 2 years previous when I beat Demarcus Corley when he burst my left eye drum in battle.
Nancy King MD was the doctor given the job of cutting open my eye, draining the excess blood and stitching it up. She was 30 years old and previously worked in the financial market before becoming a Doctor. She said she made more money when she was 23 years old than as a 30 year old woman. I asked her how it was to save a life, she said after a few times it becomes normal. She was doing the weekend shift and would be working for 48 hours straight. I asked her how she did it. She said why complain when it is something you want to do. She seemed like a focused woman. I love meeting hard working ambitious people. They always inspire me.

Wednesday 4th August 2010

I have received a fight with Chad Bennett in Australia for September 24th and John O Donnell on September 10th. Neither fight appeals to me. My management have mentioned Joan Guzman and Zab Judah for the IBO title. That would be great but Zab is not high on my list of opponents as he pulled out of fighting me twice.

Dmitriy Salita called me to see if I was free to go Catskills, NYC on Sunday to help him with his preparations for his comeback fight on September 1st. It will be his first fight as a promoter which is great. I'm glad he is finally fighting. It's well overdue.

Monday 9th August 2010

On Friday, my management spoke to Zab Judah's promoters Main Events and they agreed me as his opponent for October 2nd in New Jersey unfortunately he turned round and said maybe after this next fight. He is trying to get a world champ in the ring and sees me as a threat to upset that.

Wednesday 11th August 2010

Stuart, Dmitriy's friend who I went out on the town in Newcastle when Dmitriy was in the UK drove me up to Catskills to spar Dmitriy for his upcoming fight.

Monday 16th August 2010

Today my manager called me to say that ESPN contacted them to see if I was available to be main event next week in Canada. I jumped at the chance but I need to wait until tomorrow to find out. I'm excited, I hope it happens.

Saturday 28th August 2010

Ashley Theophane v Emmanuel Augustus was not seen as TV worthy but they put some Lightweight by the name of Lundy in our place against somebody. It was a shit fight and ESPN should feel shame with putting on a poor quality show like that.
I'm off to Las Vegas for my 30th Birthday on Monday so it is celebrating time now.

Wednesday 3rd November 2010

Hennessey Promotions for whatever reason are not finalizing the fight between Lenny Daws and I so I have given my management 10 days to get the deal done or I will have to look for a fight elsewhere. I am in good shape and have dropped 7lbs in just over a week but I can't train intensely if nothing is 100% and I will not go into the fight giving any advantage to Hennessey promotions and their fighter.
I will vacate the title straight away as I see the British Title as a step down from the level I have campaigned at.

Dmitriy Salita & British Title Training camp

Friday 19th November 2010

Midday Dmitriy Salita picked me up to go Universal Boxing gym for sparring. He was with Javan "Sugar" Hill, who is Emmanuel Steward's nephew. Dmitriy had been training at the World famous Kronk gym in Detroit to get ready for his fight with Mike Anchondo for the IBA Welterweight Title on December 16th. He spent a month there working with Emmanuel Steward and Sugar Hill.

I hadn't sparred since my win over Willie Thompson 6 weeks earlier but I had been doing 25 hour training weeks for the last month. I paced myself working on my defense, movement, ring generalship. I tried to pick my shots. I got through 6 rounds of 3 minutes with a 30 second rest. My fitness was good, I could have done a couple more rounds. We have three more weeks to go so it is a good start for my preparations for British Champion Lenny Daws.

Monday 22nd November 2010

I sparred with Dmitry Salita at Universal gym in Queens that evening.
Afterwards Dmitriy commented that I'm hitting harder than ever. He said 4 years ago no one except for myself believed what I was capable of but now people in the boxing world know who I am. Dmitriy saw my talent from when we met in August 2006. After our first spar he took me to training camp in the Poconos Mountains, the following year he flew me out to Florida and later that year I went to Catskills with him where I met Stan Hoffman and impressed him enough to fly me out to NYC to get me my first fight in the USA.

I asked Dmitriy how many fights he wanted next year. He said two fights and a big money fight then he will concentrate on Salita promotions. I'm sure that Dmitriy will make a living out of his promotions and stuff he does outside of boxing in his community.

I remember in Florida, Dmitriy said that we would come together in the future as promoters and work together. It's nice to see him moving forward on something he had in his mind a few years ago. Being a promoter was never a goal of mine. When I'm finished from boxing, I may have no job in the sport as being a trainer is very hard to make money as you need a few world class fighters. If I do anything in boxing I would move into management. My mind is focused on building my personal fitness company when I retire from boxing.

Nermo, trainer to former World Welterweight Champion Luis Collazo and Dmitriy's current trainer thinks that WBC Welterweight Champion Andre Berto would be a good fight for me. My management spoke to Andre Berto's promoter before his fight with Freddy Hernandez but Hernandez got the call before me.

Wednesday 24th November 2010

Multi Weight champion Joan Guzman is training at Gleason's again. His trainer asked me if I would do some sparring with him as he is fighting on December 11th. I'm a big fan of Guzman. I accepted a fight with him for the summer for the IBO Welterweight Title but that was another fight that didn't happen.

I saw my friend WBC World Junior Welterweight number one Ajose Olusegun at Gleason's today. He has a World Title Eliminator soon and is struggling for sparring here. I told him I'll help him out next week.

He wants to move to America to pursue his boxing goals. He spoke to John Duddy's manager but he hasn't come up with anything as yet.
Friday 26th November 28 2010

In three weeks' time when I leave for London I will be 80% ready for my fight. I would have had sparring sessions with Dmitriy Salita, Ajose Olusegun, Joan Guzman and Sadam Ali.

Jihad asked me how Britain would receive me if I won a World Title. I said they would probably love me as I haven't done it like most British fighters who stay in Britain and do the safety first approach. I'm abroad mixing with the World's best so when I do win a World Title, I would have deserved it as no one is going to do me any favors.

Even the IBF have dropped me from World number 4 to 11 in three months just because I passed on the World Title eliminator as I wouldn't have been fit enough to compete in it and I wasn't happy with the purse.

My trainer Jihad called me to get my opinion on a situation. He said Ajose asked him if he could hook him up with a promoter. Jihad told me he had Lou Dibella as a backup but he had a link with Golden Boy promotions. GBP are the best place to be for a Welterweight as they have a good crop of them. I would love Ajose to get a deal with a big promoter here, he deserves it. Jihad wanted my opinion on if he had done anything wrong as Ajose had asked Harry first to hook him up. I told him Ajose asked you as well and it would be good to have as many contacts as possible so Ajose could choose someone, he felt suited him. Harry probably would want a manager or promoter who he had a good relationship with so they wouldn't try make Ajose leave him but I hooked Harry and Jihad up with Ajose and Ajose can choose who he wants to train with. Harry took it hard when John Duddy left him for Don Turner so when I beat Demarcus "Chop Chop" Corley, Harry was probably as happy as me as he got one up on Don Turner. After in the cab to the airport, Demarcus Corley was in our cab and Harry kept talking and dissing Don Turner to Corley. It was funny but you could tell it hurt him even though John had moved to another trainer since and has now gone back to Harry.

Saturday 27th November 2010

Jihad told me today that Ajose cancelled the sparring session they had planned as he is in Las Vegas. I think Jihad thought he had another trainer interested in him but I said Ajose had been Wildcard in Los Angeles but came back to New York so I doubt it is that. He is looking for a manager or promoter so told him that is probably the reason he is in Vegas,
I said Ajose is a loyal person.

Sunday 28th November 2010

Dmitriy and I sparred for nine rounds this morning at Universal boxing gym in Queens, NY. I spoke to Dmitriy about Ajose Olusegun wanting to get an agent, manager or promoter over here in America, He said he would speak to Square Ring promotions about him. Ajose told me in the day how he had flown out to Las Vegas to meet Samuel Peter's manager. He wanted a five year contract so Ajose said that's where he lost him.

British Title challenge

Wednesday 1st December 2010

I completed a good workout in the gym today. Joan Guzman was sparring as I was finishing up. He was sparring some overweight, slow and technically rubbish amateur. He might as well have been hitting the bag. I told his trainer why he would cancel sparring with me and use that garbage boxer. He said the dude he is boxing is trash, on that dude's level so that's why. He said we will work when he steps up. It's funny how highly thought of I am in the gyms across the USA. I blow hot and cold but on my day I can beat the very best fighters out there.

Friday 3rd December 2010

I received the contract for the fight with Lenny Daws. Everything is good in it, I just want the options clause to state that I can have interim fights anywhere in the World as it only says I can in the USA. I ran up the Spring Creek Towers twelve times today. I usually do ten which is murderous already but I need to be better than my best against Lenny Daws when we fight. I feel like a foreigner boxing him. This is my homecoming to prove the doubters wrong. I need to show how good I really am.

Tuesday 7th December 2010

The IBO president's assistant contacted my representative from Hood stripes Entertainment today as he wants to talk to me personally about fighting for the World IBO title. I'm 12th at the minute in their rankings and their International Champion.

His assistant said he was in transit on his way to Germany for Klitschko's defense of his World titles which include the IBO's version but he would call me when he arrived.

Thursday 9th December 2010

Nirmal, former world champion Luis Collazo's trainer thinks I could beat World champion Andre Berto. Its nice to come to a different country and have trainers see the talent in me. In Britain I think they try to make you think small. My mind has always been on the world stage and my UK trainers never liked that. I turned down a British title challenge 3 times. It's never been a big ambition of mine to win it.

Friday 10th December 2010

Harry Keitt, one of my two man training team I train with in New York said I have improved a lot since I came here in 2005 and I am definitely good enough to win a title. I said what British or World. He said World of course. I need to get past British champion Lenny Daws first then get back on the World Title picture.

Victor and Tunde flew in today to film the American footage of the documentary they are making on me. They filmed me in Canarsie doing my run up Spring Creek Towers. I beat my time by twenty one seconds. I feel this documentary could be really good. They are obviously serious. Terri Kelly filmed me for a year and nothing came of it. Wesley Mcleod filmed me as well and production suddenly stopped. I hoping third time lucky with this one.

Saturday 11th December 2010

Filming at the Universal gym in Queens went well tonight. They got some shots of my training. The owner of the gym, Moses spoke to them and Dmitriy also did. They asked him if he would ever fight me if he won a World title. He stopped and looked at me. I laughed and said I want to see if we are on the same page D. He said he would never fight me. Victor who was filming told him that I said the same thing. Some friendships wouldn't be the same. I fought Jamal Morrison in the ABA Northwest division semi finals. I beat him but we were still cool after it.

Sunday 12th December 2010

Trainer to over ten World champions Hector Roca saw me in the gym on a Sunday morning after a hard weeks work and said, "You are going to be Champion man, you work so hard." He went on saying I just need to box more as I am strong and in condition. He thanked me for helping the Burrell Twins as when they need sparring no one helps out but they help when it's the other way round.

This is what I have chosen to do so I'm going all out to be the best I can be. Wherever that takes me I don't know, but trainers of champions say I have Championship attributes so they believe I can achieve that goal. Only time will tell.

Friday 17th December 2010

Today is my last boxing session at Gleason's gym until the New

Year.
Thinking of flying in Harry to do my corner work on the fight. I have decisions to make.

Saturday 18th December 2010

My flight to London was cancelled and as you can imagine not happy at all.

Sunday 19th December 2010

It took me 24 hours to get through to the Virgin Atlantic help line. I have to spend an extra 5 days here but on a good note they have upgraded me to Upper class.

Monday 20th December 2010

Boxing Monthly magazine contacted me to do a big piece on me for their January 2011 issue. In their 2010 issue they named me as the 140lb British fighter who could make waves this year and they got it correct.
Dmitriy is off to Israel with his wife and kid for a break. He asked if I would be interested in fighting there in the Spring against Steve Forbes. If my World Title eliminator doesn't come off against Randall Bailey. This is be a good back up plan.

Wednesday 22nd December 2010

My flight was cancelled for the second time in 5 days. The lady from Virgin Atlantic tried to say I could fly on Sunday 26th. I said that would be eight days that I've been stuck in New York City.

Tuesday 1ST February 2011

My trip to Liverpool to spar former English champion Steve Williams went very well.

I arrived in Liverpool just after 2pm.
I went to the gym an hour early as I wanted to warm up and do all of my exercises.
Steve's trainer was pleasant to me and asked me how I find the States and what first made me want to go there. The other boxers were friendly which is always good. I did 10 minutes on the cross trainer then I stretched. I went on to do 30 minutes of skipping, shadow boxing and work on the speed bag. 10 minutes of each. Steve and I completed seven 3 minute rounds with 30 seconds rest. It was hard work, well it started off hard but by the 3rd, I got to grips with his style and the tempo of the spar. Steve is a very aggressive fighter who throws some good body shots. I took them and gave him some of mine. I practice moving around the ring, boxing, fighting, defensive work and trying to back him up. It was a very productive session.
Afterwards I completed 22 minutes on the heavy bags which was pretty much 6 rounds straight including the 30 second rest which I worked through. Afterwards I did some strength exercises and one thousand crunches.

I met up with my friend Lisa from Liverpool afterwards and we went for a meal at a nice Thai restaurant called Yeerah. She showed me a few tourist spots then I walked her to the train station and went back to my hotel in the city centre.

Tuesday 15th February 2011

Adrian Dodson told me today after my training session not to worry about the win per say but my performance, doing what I need to do each round.

I have trained as hard as I could have possibly done. It's all about handling the nerves now and dropping the last few pounds.
I can beat Daws but his fitness is very good. It will be a hard fight and it is all about getting the tactics right on the night. I would like to walk him down and try break him but at the same time I am tempted to try to outbox him. Even though I don't class myself as the challenger as I'm the one who is world ranked in this fight I am seen to be challenging for his British title even though he can keep it. People's belief in me is a little overwhelming but I have sacrificed a lot in the last three months so I need to go out there and bust this guy up.

Dean Powell, match maker for Frank Warren gave me a call in the evening. I wondered why he was calling me as we were never really close but I thought I would see what he wanted. What he said to me meant a lot. He told me that I have proved him wrong over the last eighteen months to two years with what I had done over in America. He said a few years ago he didn't think I had what it took but I had done really well knuckling down to get some good results. He told me that Friday when I weigh in I will be the challenger and to remember that as no one does anyone any favors.
Dean said that for 47 minutes I just have to concentrate and do what Don Charles tells me and I will be fine.
He said he hoped I win as it would be great for Mr. Akay, Dave Brown and the whole of the All Stars gym. He said my co-trainer Don Charles had great belief in me and he hopes I wake up on Sunday the new British champion.

Sunday 20th February 2011

I woke up this morning as the British 140lb Champion. It feels great as many boxing writers and fans doubted me and said that I was hype.
Even the commentator Steve Bunce was saying how I shouldn't be shouting out loud that I spar with Dmitriy Salita as he lasted 7 seconds with Amir Khan and that a lot is being made of my sparring champions in the gyms of New York City plus a couple wins over former World champion Demarcus Corley and World title challenger Delvin Rodriguez. By the last three rounds Steve Bunce's attitude towards me had done a 180 degree turn. He said the hard sparring in New York had paid off and that this was a good performance from me. Bunce and his co commentator called me arrogant before the fight and that I was disrespectful to Daws for not showing at the press conference.
I was sick so I didn't want to give Lenny Daws a mental boost seeing me ill and my tactic of not showing up worked even if he said it didn't. I made it seem like I didn't care about him and I kept calling him a keep busy fight so he would think I'm over looking him. After I beat Lenny I went into his changing room and told him that I didn't mean anything that I said in the media and that I rated him as a fighter and had a loads of respect for him. I do. I wish Lenny didn't fight me as he could have picked an easy voluntary and got to keep the Lonsdale belt. He came up to me and told me to look after it. The Lord Lonsdale Belt!

I felt confident stepping in the ring before the bell went off, but for the first two rounds Lenny Daws had come out like a champion. He wasn't giving up his title without a fight. I was missing shots and he was countering me. I had planned to bully him and back him up but Lenny was stronger than I thought he would be and his Lightning nickname was justified. Lenny was hitting me with rapid combinations as I made mistakes. After losing the first two rounds I thought I might as well box him for a round as my Plan A, did not work. I had success this round with my jab and counter punching Lenny on the back foot. I walk back to my corner tired. I thought that I couldn't do that shit for nine more rounds but Lenny was struggling to deal with my boxing on the back foot. By round six I was probably two rounds down but commentator for Premier Sports Steve Bunce had me six rounds down after six rounds. He must have been watching a different fight.

Round nine is where everything changed. I caught Lenny with a lead left uppercut which staggered him. I followed up with two crunching body shots and a chopping right to the side of the head which sent him crashing to the canvas. He got up for the count of eight and I rushed to finish off the job. He held on not before hitting the canvas for the second time in the round.

I was blowing myself after trying to finish Lenny off, so for the next three rounds I just out boxed him and picked him off. I knew I had won the fight but you never know with the judges.

As Lenny and I stood beside the referee as he held our hands to raise the winners. I kept saying to myself "And the New" over and over again.

When the ring announcer said, "And the New British Champion." I leapt two foot off the canvas with delight and ran to the corner jumping on the ropes and waving to my friends, family and supporters.

If I hadn't got the double knock down I may have got a draw or even loss. They had it that close. Nevertheless it was a great win and a stunning performance.

I was interviewed afterwards and I said that Teejay Akay had been an inspiration for this as he was British Champion 23 years ago. I also gave my cousin Tyrone Theophane a shout out. The interviewer asked if it was true I would be vacating or would I defend my title in Britain as it would be nice to see me on home soil. I said I don't know what I'm doing yet but I'm very proud to be British champion.

Monday 21st February 2011

I got a call last night from one of my trainers Don Charles, trainer to Derek Chisora about Frank Warren wanting a meeting with me. I instantly thought they want me for Frankie Gavin or Kell Brook.
Don Charles said just go there and listen to Frank and see what he wants. So I met Charles up My Gym in Finchley.
We drove down to Frank Warren's office. His match maker Dean Powell congratulated me on my win over Lenny Daws as we sat in the waiting area. Whilst I was sitting in the waiting area Cestus management emailed me to say that the Randall Bailey fight had been offered to me again. Hennessey Sport had obviously heard that I was in a meeting with Frank Warren as I had posted it on my Facebook status and tweeted it so they requested to follow me. Hennessey Sport were going through a bad time as European champions Darren Barker and John Murray had left them. Three of their top fighters had lost over the weekend, John O Donnell, Lenny Daws and Junior Witter. After ten minutes we were walked through to Frank Warren's office. Frank congratulated me on my win as I walk through the door. I had been on Frank's shows when I was coming up but he never gave me no notice. Beating Lenny Daws had obviously made me seem official to the people in British Boxing.
I asked where should I sit and Frank replied anywhere your arse will go. I sat quietly and listen to Frank. Don Charles mentioned how he thought I would turn down the meeting as I'm my own man. I told him I couldn't turn down a meeting with Mr Frank Warren. My progress just shows how far I have come to have Frank Warren ask to have a meeting with me the day after my

British title win. I told them I would be on holiday from Tuesday so they fit me in on Monday.
I knew Frank wanted the British title for Frankie Gavin but I wanted to hear what comes out of his mouth.

Frank told me that I could defend the British against Frankie Gavin or vacate the British so Frankie could have it and he would let me fight for the WBO 140lb Intercontinental title on his Wembley show against someone of my choosing in the WBO top 15. That was tempting but I wanted to defend my British title at least once. To walk in the ring as the British champion would be amazing but I told Frank Warren how Mick Hennessey had options on me as British champion but if I vacate I'm free.

I left the office feeling great. Meeting Britain's number one promoter and one of the best in the World.
On my way out I saw Dean Byrne who I knew from my time at TKO gym. He had gone to Los Angeles and Freddy Roach was managing and training him for the past three years. I even sparred him when I went to the Wild card gym in November 2008.
Dean said he was here to ink a deal with Frank Warren. Dean had been calling out Frankie Gavin so maybe that fight was in the reckoning.

Dean Powell took us to lunch but had to cut it short as he had to get back for the meeting with Dean Byrne who he thought would be trouble even before signing him.

Cestus management were obviously nervous of what I was doing and I hadn't taken a call from them since Friday after we had a disagreement about the press conference.

They had offers of $15,000 to fight David Estrada and a World title eliminator with Randall Bailey. I had been offered $20,000 to fight Bailey last year so unless they increased that fee. It wouldn't be happening.

Amy, an ex girlfriend had told me even if there was positives, that fighting under Frank Warren probably wouldn't work as I'm not a good team player and I'm used to doing things a certain way.

My friend Danielle Elie emailed that night to say that I should stay on my original path of fighting in America and not get sidetracked by getting in bed with Satan for extra money or whatever false promises he makes. I agreed with both Amy and Danielle but I would sleep on it and see how I felt after a couple days in the sun.

Tuesday 22nd February 2011

My two weeks in Dominican Republic with my mum starts today. I need a rest after killing myself in the gym for this fight.

I'm thinking to vacate the British title but get Frank Warren to give me money to do so and to get him to promise me two WBO Intercontinental fights for the same amount of money what Hennessey had promised me for two defenses of the British title. I don't want to be promoted by Frank Warren long term but I'm willing to do a two fight deal so I can still fight in America.

Training Camp for Jason Cook

Thursday 2nd June 2011

As I walked through the doors of Gleason's gym I saw Keisha McCleod and owner Bruce Silverglade. Bruce welcomed me back and Keisha told me that I had put on weight.
Nothing like a welcome in Brooklyn.

My trainer Harry Keitt walked in just after me. I know he was glad to see me back. I changed in the locker room and we got to work. Everyone seemed pleased to have me back in the gym and the coaches congratulated me on my British title win.

My friend Dmitriy Salita called me today to see about my availability on his monthly boxing shows he is currently doing. I asked him to hook up some sparring with former World champion Luis Collazo as they train at the same gym.

I also spoke to my friend Francisco 'El Gato' Figueroa to arrange some sparring. I'll go down his gym, Morris Park in the Bronx in two weeks time.
Frankie fought in a World title eliminator against Randell Bailey a couple years back. I'm glad he is back in the gym and giving it another shot.
Tuesday 7th June 2011

Golden Boy Promoters contacted Cestus management today about me featuring on the undercard of Floyd Mayweather vs Victor Ortiz against rising star Jessie Vargas.
It would be part of the Pay Per View show.
I turned it down instantly as I saw it as disrespectful. I am not a

stepping stone for some rising star. I took the Danny Garcia fight as I hadn't fought in nearly eight months but I was not up for the fight so even though a lot of people thought I won I knew I could have done better. Jessie Vargas may be a rising star but I have never heard of him. I want to fight other world ranked fighters, not unknowns. It's a shame as it's a great opportunity to fight on the same show as Floyd.
Cestus obviously rang my phone down. I let it ring and just text Gina to say my decision was final. All they care about is their 25% so fuck them.

Friday 10th June 2011

Today I sent Rene an email saying that I had come to America for solitude and that the Carayol's team email's and text's even though wishing me well, seeing how I am and just contacting me on issues about Brand Treasure were too much for me.
Jackie's text about my afterparty for VIP's only was the last straw for me, as my family and friends were my VIP's and I probably wouldn't be where I am today without their support.

When my career is finish, they will still be there whilst Carayol's VIP's would have moved on to the next hot thing.

I had drafted an emailed to Rene stating reason's for team Carayol and I to split. I never got to send it to Rene as he emailed me back with some calming advice about my feelings of being overwhelmed by the constant emails from his team. I felt better about the situation.

Tuesday 14th June 2011

Today I received great news from my lawyers, Mishcon de Reya. The European Boxing Union were overturning their ban on me. I contacted them straight after beating Lenny Daws who was number one in Europe at the time and they told me that i would not be ranked by the European Boxing Union or fight for their title. Rene came on board and got Mishcon to write to them stating what they were in breach of and a month later they back track, saying any boxer who fights for the GBA or GBO in Germany will be banned for a year meaning that I will be in their European rankings for July. Great News!!

Thursday 16th June 2011

Whilst I was there, Gina from Cestus management emailed me and messaged me on my blackberry to say that Mike and Mick had been working on me fighting for the European title on July 23rd. I found this offense as I knew what had been going on. Rene and Luke had been working with Mishcon de Reya on getting my ban lifted from the European boxing union. Cestus come in when the ban is lifted and go on as if they had done this their selves. I told Gina that my lawyers had got the ban lifted and she acted like she didn't know.

Cestus are something else. Why didn't they go in their pocket and get lawyers to lift my ban. I can't stand them.

I watched Denis Shafikov, who I would be fighting and he is decent but I would beat him.

Wednesday 22nd June 2011

Former European and IBO champion Jason Cook has been announced as my opponent for my first British title defense. I wouldn't have picked him as an opponent as now I don't know who will be fighting Nigel Wright in the eliminator to fight me. Jason is aggressive and goes for the knockout but with fourteen knockouts out of 28 wins, he is not really a knock out artist. He will start quick and fade. I will stop him or dominate him after round six.

Wednesday 29th June 2011

Hennessy Sport still hadn't come up with a contract that I agreed with.
As usual Cestus were happy to do business as all they wanted was there 25%.

I never saw what manager got 25% for basically making calls. They're glorified personal assistants in my opinion.

I was unhappy with the clauses in the private agreement. As the five months would have past. I would be free from Hennessy Sport's two fight option clauses.

I had missed out on fights because I never knew when Hennessy would arrange the fight between Tyson Fury and Derek Chisora. I was supposed to be the chief support to the fight.

I wanted to get the other fight option changed for three months as if I waited on Hennessy and He didn't do another show in five months. I would be out for the rest of the year.

The rematch clause also stated that it was up to Hennessy Sport who Jason Cook would fight in his first voluntary if he had won, even though I knew he would not win. I wanted to back myself up. Jason Cook had mentioned in an interview that if he won he thought Hennessy would try get him to fight Lenny Daws in a rematch instead of me and I thought the same thing.
I refused to sign the contract unless they changed it to what I wanted.

Vicky from Hennessy's office said that they had been accommodating to all my demands and that the contract stated a rematch. It did but it also said it was up to Hennessy if I got a rematch. Hennessy was trying to treat me as an opponent and I wasn't having that. He needed me. I didn't need him.
Gina didn't like that I wouldn't accept calls from her and Mike but they had pushed me away with treating me like an opponent.

Thursday 30th June 2011

Cestus do not have my back as usual. All they want is their 25%. They are saying I'm missing out on a great opportunity to become a star as the fight is being televised in America as well as Britain.

I never came into boxing to be a star. I came to achieve various goals. Fighting the best in the World and seeing what my full potential was. Money was never an issue. As long as I can live. I'm happy!

My relationship with Cestus was on edge as it was. It was time to cut them loose.

I was used to being on the outside looking in but now I had the British title, I was a target for upcoming British fighters and the old boys looking for one last shot.

Monday 4th July 2011

Gina emailed me around 11am to say that Vicki from Hennessy Sports had been in contact with Mick and he had said he wouldn't be changing any of the terms of the agreement and that if I don't sign I would be turning down the fight.

I forwarded the message to Rene and he got Liz from Mishcon, onto the case.

Liz had a conversation with Vicki and smoothed over everything. Liz had said that I had issues with Cestus and that was a big issue in the negotiations as I didn't trust them. Vicki said she sensed that through her discussions with Cestus.
At the end of it, Liz said that all communication would be going through her from now on.

Cestus had forced me to fight for the British title and in doing that, lost me as a fighter.
I didn't have a valid contract with them and I was now self managed in the UK.

I finalized the deal with Hennessy Sports by the evening and I have to email the British Board Of Control to say that I would accept Nigel Wright as my Mandatory challenger as I was fighting Jason Cook who was supposed to fight Wright in an eliminator so I was fighting the number one and two as my first two defenses to win the Lonsdale belt outright. That was unheard of but I always have to do stuff the hard way. That's just my life!

Wednesday 13th July 2011

Top British trainer Joe Gallagher read my blog on my website and sent me a message. Sometimes as a fighter the nearer a fight gets, you start to doubt yourself and your abilities. Having people around you, who believe in you and have a positive mindset is key. Joe has had many British champions and went 49

wins straight before losing to World champion Felix Sturm in Germany with Matthew Macklin. It's nice that I am highly thought of amongst my peers.
"Thanks for your support and tip for this weekends fight, much appreciated.
Big fan of yours and your work ethic. Good luck in your Career. Joe Gallagher"

Wednesday 20th July 2011

Today was the Media workout at the Crown Manor Hotel. Tyson Fury and myself were the only fighters due to attend. I was not looking forward to it but it ended up being very enjoyable.

Former fighter Jane Couch, who was the first female British professional boxer. She went onto being awarded an M.B.E. She interviewed me for her website and she was hilarious. She's a lovely woman and I admire her for what she achieved in boxing.

I did interviews with iFilm London, Seconds Out TV and a host of newspapers and boxing websites. I even jumped in the ring to do some shadow boxing with English champion Tyson Fury, who fights British champ Derek Chisora on the same Wembley show as me.

Friday 22nd July 2011

Jason Cook weighed 139.75lbs and looked terrible. Very fleshy! Southern Area 154lbs Champion Ryan Toms said he asked Cook how training went and straight away he replied making weight was hard. Who knows if that is the truth. I don't care! He has a decent punch and will be dangerous in the early rounds.

I got interviewed by Al Bernstein after the weigh in as he is commentating on the televised fights. It was a pleasure to meet him and speak to him.

Took some photos with fans and did the normal pleasantries with the boxing fraternity.

Harry Keitt arrived from America last night and was in attendance.

I'm glad he is here. He's been in majority of my big fights, so he knows me well.

Darren Wilson, trainer to Jason Cook keeps saying that Jason has been hitting harder than ever. That will not win them the fight. My defense is excellent and I have a solid chin even if he did get through. If they are relying on that they are in for a surprise as I hit harder than my record suggests.

Jason Cook was with his girlfriend at the weigh in. Me personally, I would leave my woman at home as to me that's a distraction but everyone is different.

I've been so focused I haven't had sex in seven weeks.

Sunday 24th July 2011

In the last year I have beaten three champions. USBA (United States Boxing Association) champion and World number three Delvin Rodriguez, British champion and European number one Lenny Daws and now Welsh Champion and European number six Jason Cook. Next on my list is a World champion.

Jason Cook was one of my best performance up to this date. I started out slowly as I normally do. He came out firing as I expected. I just tried to box him and keep a high guard. I blocked majority of his shots, the first four rounds were fairly even. I kept tapping him with body shots. I could tell they were getting to him as he kept complaining. By round six I was deducted a point by the referee. I thought my body shots were on target and that he was play acting but looking back, a few did stray low. Come round seven I was more vicious. I knew what I had to do. My trainer Harry Keitt, told me to stop going to the body for the next couple of rounds so I started to head hunt Jason Cook and I was pin point. I was relaxed and started to ooze the star quality that I have.

By round nine, Harry told me to go back to the body. I was breaking Jason Cook down. He was looking for a way out and in round ten I gave it to him. I ran out towards him in the tenth round and started letting off hard shots.

I hit him to the body with a left upper cut that my UK trainer Dave Brown and I had been working on and I threw a looping right hand that sent Cook crashing to the canvas. He tried to get up but the referee waved the fight off and I regained my title.

One of the British Board of Control officials came up to me afterwards and said that two of the officials had the fight a draw after eight rounds and one had me winning all eight other than the point deduction.

He said that he was glad I won and was getting nervous when he was seeing the scorecards. He asked if that was my plan to give away the first rounds and come back. I said I knew it would be close after six rounds but I had hoped to be taking over by then. He said not to scare him again and I replied, "Yes sir."

Ian John Lewis was a judge for my fight. Whilst I was in the ring he said that he is proud of me and that I have come a long way. That meant a lot as he refereed my second
professional fight. Even then he said, "You're that Theophane kid, you're supposed to be alright." I would always feel confident that I would win my fight if Ian was there, as I knew he would score it fairly and I would be more than likely the winner.

The fight was televised in the USA and there were US promoters interested in signing me to a promotional deal after this fight.

STEVE WILLIAMS TRAINING CAMP

Sunday 12th February 2012

I have had a hard first week of training in New York City.
I have a set routine that I do whilst I am here. I've been doing the same preparations for the last two years and I am always in tip top shape.
I came here weighing 160lbs and I intend to leave here weighing around 148lbs.

Monday 13th February 2012

I've decided to go to Floyd Mayweather's gym in Las Vegas for two weeks. I need a change of scenery as I want to get that nervous feeling of having to prove my talents all over again. I'm known and respected in New York now. I want to get my weight near to 150lbs so I go there feeling great. I'm excited about watching Floyd Mayweather train as he is fighting Miguel Cotto soon, so he will be in the gym.

Tuesday 14th February 2012

I woke up this morning to hear the news that my promoter Ricky Hatton was coming to London today to book the venue for my fight in April. That got me excited as I have not been to happy with the loneness of getting a fight date.

Wednesday 15th February 2012

Ajose Olusegun is back in New York. It was good to see him at Gleason's gym. He told me he wouldn't be fighting as he was going to sit on his mandatory status as world number one so he could fight the winner of Erik Morales and Danny Garcia.

Dmitry called me when I got in from the gym to give me the low down on his career and see if I wanted to spar next week.

Paul Malignaggi had turned down the opportunity to fight the WBA champion and Dmitriy had done a deal with the promoter to step in but Paul was offered more money and accepted the deal to fight the champion in Ukraine.

Rene emailed today to say that the BBBofC are being difficult, saying I need to fight Steve Williams to win the Lonsdale belt outright as you need to fight a mandatory challenger.

It is not my fault Nigel Wright failed his brain scan. Jason Cook would have been mandatory anyway as they were due to fight each other until Mick Hennessey and Channel 5 chose Cook as my opponent.

I'm willing to fight Lenny Daws in April and Steve Williams in June. I'm not bothered, I'll beat them both.
I'm not happy with the slowness that Hatton promotions dealt with the Nigel Wright situation at the start of the year and how they are dealing with my first fight with them. I don't feel like a priority.

Thursday 16th February 2012

This morning at Gleason's gym, Harry came up to me whilst I was wrapping my hands and ask if he could wrap my hands. I told him I'm nearly finished so it is pointless. He got a near by chair and said he's been meaning to talk to me. I smirked knowing what he was going to say. Harry asked me to listen as I tried to interrupt him. He went on to say why do I always disrespect him and talk down to him. I laughed and denied the accusation. He said I see how you speak to other people and you don't speak to me in the same way. He asked if he had done anything wrong to me. He said all he wants is the same respect he gives me. I've thought for a while now about letting him go. Harry is a cool guy and he has been involved in all of my big fights but I don't have the same situation with Jihad. Sometimes people's personalities clash and I think ours does.

Harry told me if he thinks I should tone down the way I train or maybe think of moving up to 147lbs. I told Harry that I had got so far training the way that I do so why change. I explained to him that all the best fighters in the world have one thing in common and that is their work ethic. That separates them from the crowd. Floyd Mayweather Jr. , Bernard Hopkins, Sergio Martinez and Manny Paciquao are all known for their conditioning. Marvin Hagler and Pernell Whitaker, two of my favorite fighters were also gym rats.

Friday 17th February 2012

Last night Mrs. Sentino made some Banana fritters. I love anything with banana in it and just could not help myself. She laid them on the table and told me to take some if I want. Before she could walk back into the kitchen which was only three steps

away, I was already over the plate of banana fritters. They were freshly made and smelt so nice. I grabbed four then I remembered I'm supposed to be losing weight. I put back one of them and threw the other three in my mouth.
I gave my approval to Mrs. Sentino. She was already at the sink washing the pans, bowl and plates she had used. She said, "Oh you've taken one?" I replied "I took three." She laughed and carried on with her washing up.

After scoffing down the three tasty but fried banana fritters, I knew I had to go for a run. I did a six miler around Canarsie, Brooklyn listening to Jagged Edge on my iPod. I rather enjoyed the run and burnt off the tasty but fritters.

I woke up this morning weighing 156.5lbs which means I have dropped 4lbs since arriving in New York City twelve days ago. Two pounds a week is my target and I'm on course. I have just over two weeks unless I go Floyd Mayweather's gym in Las Vegas and I would love to drop more 6lbs by then just incase sparring came up I would feel light, quick and in shape.

Sunday 19th February 2012

I woke up this morning feeling in good spirits.
Celine woke up around midday and said she had something she wanted to talk to me about. I thought she was going through more dramas with her boyfriend as nearly every other day she had a story to tell me. It was something regarding her boyfriend but regarding me. I was shocked and bemused as I should have nothing to do with their relationship. He was a Haitian 24 year old who lived with his cousin. He was in a low paid job but studying in college for a well paid career at the airport as one of those workers who signal the planes whilst on the runway.

Enough about him as he is not an important person to consume many pages of my novel. Basically he felt that I stayed too often and too long at Celine's apartment and he was not comfortable with the situation. He was supposed to stay at Celine's for a month when Celine's mother left for Belize. He said he would not be staying whilst I am there. I was with my girlfriend Amy at the time, she flat shared with her male friend in Queens Park. He was not my friend but it did not bother me as I trusted my girlfriend and if she said they were friends that was it. I felt let down by Celine as she had basically been seeing this guy for less than three months and he was dictating to her already. I felt that our friendship couldn't be that strong if I was being pushed out by some newbie. I had seen boyfriends come and go during our friendship. Some of them I liked. Some didn't take the time to know as it was nothing serious. Celine felt like a few of her ex boyfriends made the same comment but this was the first guy to make a big issue about it and make a stance. I told her that I never wanted to meet him or have no contact with him. She was on some if we get married will you not come. I replied of course not. Celine was like if we split up you are always welcome back. I let it be known that I would not be back as I was disappointed in her weakness towards this new guy. I got too comfortable and that was my fault. Celine was a true friend to me. At first I stayed because I did not have enough money to rent out an apartment but now I was in a position where I could rent out an apartment but I stayed at Celine's as I liked her and it felt like my home away from home. She was family to me but I can not lie, I felt hurt. The last time we had a big disagreement like this was four years earlier before I went to Los Angeles for my trip to Wild-card.

Wednesday 29th February 2012

I want to be known as a Great, British champion and the only way to do that is to win the Lonsdale belt outright. I've fought the best what Britain has to offer in the form of Lenny Daws, Jason Cook and I was supposed to fight Nigel Wright before he failed his brain scan. Ben Murphy did a great job putting in maximum effort. Next up is Steve Williams.

I believe I am destined for something special and I'm working hard to make it come true.

Sunday 4th March 2012

I completed just under thirty hours this week training. I pushed my body to the limit and it felt the strain but I soldiered on.
I'll be heavier than I wanted to be for the Vegas training stint but I'm sure Hatton's matchmaker Richard Poxon won't stick to his words when he said I would fight on April 21st.

I'm hoping I don't let myself down in Las Vegas but I'm in shape, I'm mentally shape and I usually rise to any obstacles I encounter. I would love to spar Floyd Mayweather but even watching him train will make the trip worthwhile.

Tuesday 6th March 2012

I landed in Las Vegas last night and checked into the Monte Carlo Casino on the strip. I went straight to bed. I woke up around 530am and had a shower before heading down to the Hotel's gym. The gym had everything I needed to complete a two hour strength and cardiovascular conditioning workout. I went to the hotel Buffet, I shouldn't have but I had a big lunch. It will be the last time I go there as I need to watch my weight.

I went back to my room and took a nap.
When I woke up I went on the net to find Mayweather's Gym address. I found it but there were many posts of people being turned away as it is a private gym. I hoped that I would not be turned away but I had Johnny Tocco's gym as my back up where Floyd Mayweather Senior trains his fighters.

The cab got there within ten minutes and I tipped him twenty percent. I walked in and saw some guys lounging on some sofas. I asked where do I pay to train and the guy said I have to see Roger Mayweather first. He took me to Roger who was on the gym floor and Roger looked me over, asked me some questions and told me to get changed so he would check me out.

I went to get changed and came back ready to workout. Jeff Mayweather was training some fighters there. Two fighters came up to me and asked if I was Ashley Theophane. A boxing reporter also introduced himself and took some photos of me working out and did a short interview with me. Former world champion and now Boxing trainer Cornelius Boza Edwards called me over and said that he knew who I was and that I was linked with a fight with one of their fighters Jessie Vargas. Cornelius started his professional career in Britain in 1976. He won the WBC world title in 1981 in America. He fought boxing greats Alexis Arguello, Bobby Chacon, Hector Camacho and Jose Luis Ramirez.

Kofi Jantuah who is a two time world title challenger and a former WBC International champion trains at the Mayweather Gym as well. He has been in with some good fighters. He is also from Mr. Akay's homeland of Ghana.

I completed my boxing workout which included shadow boxing, skipping, heavy bag and the speed bag.

Floyd's bodyguards asked the boxers working out to finish up their workouts as Floyd will be coming in soon.
I was doing my abdominal crunches so it didn't affect my workout. After I finished my workout I sat down to wait for Floyd to enter.

Floyd Mayweather walks in the gym and I'm sitting down, watching him in awe. He is around my size. He just oozes confidence. Straight away his team are warming him up and loosening up his muscles. There is a fighter in the ring to get some sparring rounds off Floyd.

I had the best seat in the house. I was sat with Floyd's friends and family whilst he was sparring then when he went to hit the heavy bag and finished off on the pads with Roger. Normally I watch Floyd training on the television but I was ringside in his gym for this.

Floyd spoke a lot whilst he trained like to hype himself up. I get a sense that he enjoys being the number one in the boxing world. His training session and Floyd himself was entertainment in it self.

Floyd talked aloud "How you going to be pound for pound king and you've never been a multi weight world champion.
I'm all natural, baby. I don't cheat. Just hard work and dedication. I'm nearly forty and I still look good".

50 Cent walked out of the boxing area after Floyd finished sparring. I never even noticed him before but it was nice to see him anyway.

Whilst I was sitting down Roger Mayweather asked me to come over to him. He gave me various instructions, blocks and other defensive moves. At first I didn't understand some of his instructions but when I got it I was blocking, slipping and bobbing and weaving his shots. He said we would do pads tomorrow. He said he had been watching me workout. I'm looking forward to pads tomorrow but I'm not sure how good I'll do with his style of pad work.

I go back to sit down to wait on Floyd. Some of his female friends and family were rather good looking. I noticed that, but what red blooded male wouldn't.

Floyd had finished his workout and was chilling with 50 Cent in the lounge area. I was walking past as I was leaving to go back to my the Monte Carlo Hotel and Resort. Leonard Ellerbe was standing next to 50 Cent.
Floyd saw me walking as I had to walk pass him to get by. He looked at me and said hey. We shook hands and he asked who I was and what weight I fight at. He went on to ask me my record. He heard my accent so he said where you from. Leonard Ellerbe said London. I laughed as I'm always getting that. My London accent stands out here. Floyd went on to say that he isn't fit yet but he will do some sparring with me and test out my skills. I told him I'll be training at his gym for the next two weeks so we can do that.
I walked out the gym and headed back to my hotel.
I've had the best first day that I could have asked for. Roger and Floyd Mayweather both showing me love and offering to give me work. This is why I came here. I would have been happy to train at his gym and watch his workout but I have got the best result.

pad work with Roger and possible sparring with Floyd, my training camps just keep getting better.

Many people say I'm lucky to do my dream job. I disagree! Many people want to do something but just talk about it. I try to make my dreams reality. Everything I have ever achieved has come through hard work.
I never want to lose and think I wish I had done this or that.
I bust my ass in the gym so I have no excuse other than I'm not good enough and so far that has never happened.

Wednesday 7th March 2012

I completed my normal two hour gym session at 6am at the Monte Carlo Hotel gym. Strength and Cardiovascular conditioning followed by one thousand abdominal crunches.

I had some breakfast at the hotel buffet then I went to have a nap for a couple hours.

I woke up, got my training stuff together and jumped in a cab for the Mayweather Gym.

Yuriorkis Gamboa was at the gym today. He is supposed to be fighting Brandon Rios next month but he has skipped the last two press conferences and there is a rumor he is joining Mayweather promotions. Mayweather has said that him or Adrian Broner will succeed him as pound for pound king. I shadow boxed in the ring whilst Gamboa was doing his pad work. He is a Cuban fighter, they breed the best.

I completed a two hour boxing session which was identical to yesterdays workout. I went for a shower and sat down to wait for Floyd Mayweather to come in and do a workout.

I went over to where Roger was doing pads with a fighter and he asked me if I wanted to do some work. He didn't know I had already been working out for two hours. I was tired but I'm not going to turn down the chance to work with one of the best trainers in the world.

He gave me some moves he wanted to do and I struggle badly at first then I started to get into my groove then I was doing what he asked. He said I was too slow and that his seven year old students can do these moves. I replied "I know. I watched them yesterday." My conditioning wasn't a problem even though I was tired. I was in the zone. After working with me for 15 minutes he told me to hit the heavy bag and double end bag whilst he watched.
Afterwards I thanked him and told him I would be see him tomorrow. He replied "I'll be here." I'm not sure if he thinks I'm a good fighter or not as I didn't really shine but he could tell I was in great shape as he was trying to get me tired and that was not happening.
Roger said, "My nephew Floyd isn't the biggest puncher in the world but he is the smartest puncher."

Thursday 8th March 2012

I woke up just after 5am this morning. The last two mornings I had completed a two workout in the Hotel gym so I wanted to gym it up so I went for a run on the Vegas strip.
I started from my hotel which is the Monte Carlo and I ran to the Stratosphere Hotel. It was a round trip of seven miles which I did

in 58 minutes. It was nice to take in the sights of the strip.

At 10am I jumped in a cab for the Mayweather Gym. I was the first one there and no one would come for an hour or so as the opening time is 11am but the gym manager said he would be there from 10am if I wanted to come early.

I warmed up, wrapped my hands and started to skip. I completed four rounds then I jumped in the big ring to do six rounds of shadow boxing. I love that Floyd Mayweather, the pound for pound king uses this ring as well. Even though I was in the gym alone. The atmosphere just oozed of achievement. Floyd's fight posters surround the gym walls.

Yesterday was so cool shadow boxing in the same ring of world champion Yuriorkis Gamboa. There are not many fighters that I feel are special but Mayweather and Gamboa fall into that category just as Joan Guzman does. Training amongst great fighters inspires you. You get to watch them at close quarters. Two things what they all have is amazing talent and great work ethic in the gym. I have talent not amazing but enough to trouble the world's best fighters and my work ethic is amongst the very best in the business.

I'm respected coast to coast across America. Whatever gym I walk into, fighters and coaches know and respect me. How many British champions are known across America. Very few! World champions Carl Froch, Joe Calzaghe, Amir Khan, David Haye and Ricky Hatton are all known and respected. I intent to add a world title around my waist. Be it a WBC, WBA, WBO or IBF. British fighters normally only travel to challenge a world champion and nowadays they lose. They give a good battle but lose all the same.

I've traveled America to fight anyone. Three of my biggest fights have been in America and I won two of them and lost one on a split decision that most people thought I won and that fighter is now fighting for a world title. Since then I have won IBO International Welterweight and British Junior welterweight titles plus beaten the World number three welterweight and a former European lightweight champion. I'm on great form right now.

I went onto the Heavy bag and double end bag. I worked those for twelve rounds then I finished up on the speed bag. I did my usual one thousand abdominal and back crunches then I did a ten minute strength workout.

I worked hard for two and a half hours. I'm not at the Mayweather gym to play around. I came here in great shape and if I can get sparring rounds with Gamboa or Mayweather I will. I will be there everyday so I live in hope.

I feel like I'm destined for greatness. Publishing a novel based on my life, opening a Treasure boxing gym, having a successful boxing career and launching my own clothing line. I feel that nothing is impossible. You just need to believe and work towards making your dreams a reality.
Against all odds I have achieved so much but now the hard work begins. I have one life to live so I am doing all that is possible to make my dreams come true.

Friday 9th March 2013

I completed a two hour plus Strength and Cardiovascular conditioning workout followed by twelve hundred abdominal and back crunches in the Monte Carlo Resort and Casino hotel at 6am to

830am.

I got to the gym for 1pm as one of the trainers at the Mayweather Boxing Gym said he would have sparring for me today.

I warmed up with twelve rounds of skipping, shadow boxing and stretching my muscles.
He came back to me and said no one wants to spar me. One guy Mike Rue wanted to but he had just had an operation on his jaw under a month ago so I wasn't going to risk messing up his jaw so soon.

I asked the trainer who sorts out the sparring for Floyd. He said that I would have to speak to Cornelius Boza Edwards. Boza hadn't been in the gym for the last two days and nor had Floyd. I know Floyd was sparring at a gym in Los Angeles against some up and coming middleweight. The trainer said I may get hired for as a sparring partner if I impressed Floyd. I didn't care about that I just wanted one session with Floyd. Roy Jones Junior and Floyd Mayweather Junior were my favorite fighters in recent memory so to spar Floyd would be amazing. I will speak to Boza. Everyone in the gym knew I wanted to spar Floyd and Floyd had told me he would do some rounds so we will see what happens. I love training in Floyd's gym anyway. I've come a long way. I'm known worldwide and many people Stateside believe I'm capable of becoming a world champion.

I finished up with twelve rounds on the heavy bag and three rounds on the speed bag. Five hundred abdominal and back crunches with a ten minute stretch was how I finished my workout.

The Mayweather gym works for three minutes with a 30 second rest. My fitness feels like it is improving. Minimal rest is the best work to build up your fitness.

Saturday 10th March 2012

Today I woke up at 5am and was in the hotel gym by 6am. I completed an hour on the cardiovascular machines then I completed twelve hundred abdominal and back crunches then I finished off with an hour strength conditioning workout.

I was at the Mayweather Boxing gym by 1230pm. I weighed 153.5lbs before training and afterwards I was 151.5lbs. I'm happy with my current weight. If I can stay this weight for the next week I can drop it to 150lbs by the time I head home to London. I'm not trying to drop weight whilst here, just maintain.

Today I pushed hard again. I warmed up with four rounds skipping followed by a stretch then I completed 15 rounds shadow boxing in the big ring. I love the feeling of using the same ring that Floyd Mayweather uses. I worked on my movement, defense, power punches, speed, fighting from the southpaw stance and counter punching.
I finished up with three rounds on the speed bag and some abdominal work.

Sunday 11th March 2012

The Mayweather Boxing Gym is closed today so I just completed my regular two and a half strength and cardiovascular conditioning workout with one thousand abdominal crunches.

I went for a 90 minute massage to refresh my muscles as I intend to go hard for my remaining week at the Mayweather gym and I need to be at my best. My weight is good and my fitness is on point.

Monday 12th March 2012

It is like an event when Floyd is in the building. There was fifty people there to watch him train. Many were friends and family but there were also former world champions Eddie Mustafa Muhammad, Zab Judah and Hasim Rahman in the building. World champion Yuriorkis Gamboa was there earlier in the day. I enquired if he would be sparring this week as I would have loved to of traded punches with him. His coach said he would be leaving tomorrow so it would not be possible.

50 Cent was also in the building. Supporting his friend, Floyd and Fiddy seem inseparable these days.

I myself had completed a two hour workout. After I had finished Roger told me to hit the Heavy bag for five rounds then go onto the double end bag finishing up with three rounds on the speed bag. Overall I completed twenty rounds on the heavy bags, six rounds on the speed bag, three rounds skipping, four rounds shadow boxing and one thousand sit ups. This was all with 30 seconds rest. I dropped over three pounds through my workout.

I watched at close quarters as Floyd sparred with middleweight Omar Henry. Floyd was incredible. He was fast, strong and his defense was on point. They worked for around twenty minutes only stopping every five minute for a sip of water. They were supposed to have a 30 second rest after the five minute session but Floyd would take a sip of some fluid and say, "That's enough. Work time." He broke Omar's heart. Omar tried but Floyd had to much for him. Floyd's mean streak comes out whilst he is sparring and he tries to hurt his sparring partners. He is very aggressive.

Floyd told Omar "Get out the ring, bum. Put another bum in the ring for me to beat up." Some short, muscular, dark skinned middleweight jumps in the ring and straight away Floyd starts to goad him. Floyd is more cautious with this sparring partner as he boxes more but when there is an opportunity Floyd unloads his powerful hooks and uppercuts. Watching Floyd on this performance with eight weeks to go. He is yet to hit form. Floyd Mayweather should stop Miguel Cotto and I have always been a Cotto fan but Floyd is the greatest of this era and one of the Greatest pound for pound fighters of all time.

Floyd finished sparring then he went to hit the heavy bag I was hitting earlier on. Whilst Floyd banged away on the bag his team shouted out "Hard work Dedication." Floyd seemed to react to these chants by working the bag even harder. After 20 minutes of hitting the bag, Floyd went back into the ring. I was on the ring apron.

Floyd was dripping of sweat, eyes focused, his mind obviously thinking of Miguel Cotto floating around the ring. First he worked with Roger Mayweather then he work with the assistant trainer Nate. He banged the body of Nate and Nate could feel the power of Floyd. For twenty minutes Roger and Nate alternated whilst Floyd worked his magic.

Floyd went back onto the heavy bag for another ten minutes then went back into the ring to work with Nate and Roger again.

He then completed some strength exercises alternating with skipping. 80's soul blasted from the speakers. There was a joyous vibe in the Mayweather Gym. Floyd is a winner and I can see why.

I've had the pleasure to watch Manny Pacquiao at Wildcard gym in Los Angeles in private sessions and I've had the pleasure now to watch Floyd Mayweather train in private sessions at the Mayweather Gym. Both times I have been inspired by the experiences but Floyd is exceptional.

I inquired about sparring Floyd Mayweather as he said he would spar me and test my skills last Tuesday. I asked Roger and Boza who hires majority of the sparring partners for Floyd. Boza even spoke to Roger about it in front of me. Boza said that Floyd was only sparring middleweights in this camp and that he was in the zone now. I told Boza I didn't expect Floyd to take it easy on me. He said it had nothing to do with that but all sparring partners had been hired. He said that if I was here two weeks earlier it would have definitely of happened. He said in the future it could happen.

I was happy to watch Floyd workout as that was something special in it self. Not many people get to watch Floyd up close so I do feel privileged.

I have definitely taken in loads from his two workouts I have seen over the past seven days.

Tuesday 13th March 2012

Las Vegas was very warm today. I was sweating in the cab ride to the boxing gym.

The trainer who tried to get me sparring last week asked if I wanted to work. Which is a term for sparring, I said, "Of course that's why I'm here."

After skipping I stretched, loosened up and wrapped my hands. Otis Pimpleton Jr, a former fighter and trainer at the gym, saw that I had the face protector head gear.
"One pussy coming up." He shouted this out around five times. I laughed as it was gym humor. He said to me "tell them you're the champ." I replied to him "They already know who I am. Records don't lie. They know I'm official."

I knew that people would be watching me as they know I have been in the ring with some elite American fighters. I got in the ring to trade punches with this young hungry fighter and I noticed he was a southpaw. Lucky I've had the best southpaw sparring around for the past eleven years. WBC world number one and mandatory challenger to the WBC world title Ajose Olusegun. I worked on different things. Countering him, feinting him, defense work, foot work and pressuring him. It was decent work. I was just warming up and I saw he jumped out the ring. We had completed three rounds. Next time I will request two to three fighters as I'm a twelve round fighter. I don't even start breathing until the fifth round.

I completed a two hour workout. The heat in the gym was energy sapping but I am glad I pushed myself through it.

I'm in the locker room. I've just showered and I'm basically in my underwear. The door opens and in walks the pound for pound king Floyd Mayweather. I was so surprised. I spoke what entered my mind. "Oh shit" leapt out of my mouth. Floyd was cool. He said, "What's up" and spudded me with a clinched fist. I hurried to put on my jeans and a bunch of quarters and dimes fell out of my pockets onto the floor. Floyd looked at me and I just picked up the loose change that now lay on the floor.

Two members of Floyd's money team came in and started talking to the world's best fighter. Floyd just changed conversation and started talking about how he fights at whatever weight he is walking around at. He went on, "What other fighter you know who does that. Fuck that! I'm not starving myself. I'm going to eat eight times a day if I want." Floyd is a funny character just like his father Floyd senior and Roger. He randomly starts talking about how great he is and what he does that other fighters don't.

I went out back into the gym and sat where I usually sat to watch Floyd spar. I'm normally surrounded by the female members of his family so most of them acknowledge me and say hi.

Music blaring and beautiful women in attendance to watch Floyd train. The atmosphere is more of an adults get together then a gym workout.

A Ghanaian fighter sparred Floyd today and he made Floyd work. He refused to back down and because of that Floyd let him continue doing rounds. I got the feeling that Floyd wanted to knocked him out for having the audacity to stand and trade blows with him. Floyd was backed to the ropes numerous times during their six rounds of five minutes with 30 seconds rest. Floyd hit him with some knockout punches. It was weird seeing Floyd stand and trade toe to toe as you rarely see him do that in his fights. This was a gym war and one that Floyd Mayweather shined in.

Everyone in attendance spoke about the gallant effort he put in against Floyd. He certainly earned his two thousand dollars a week. Floyd has six middleweight sparring partners. They don't know if they will be sparring the champion or not until he turns up at the gym. A Mexican who has been here since I arrived has yet to spar with Floyd.

Floyd goes to the Heavy bag and pounds away for around twenty minutes straight. Only stopping to drink some fluid and jive with his team. "Some guys do it in the gym. I do it when it counts. Under the bright lights". One of the money team shouts out "in front of thousands of people. You got to do it under those bright lights."

Which is very true. Many fighters get excited because maybe they got the better of someone in sparring. So what! I don't get paid for shining or beating someone up in sparring. There are gym fighters and show time fighters. I'm a show time fighter. Sparring is when I practice stuff I've been working on with my team. Sometimes I've already trained for three to four hours in the morning, if I'm sparring in the afternoon. All I want to do is get the rounds under my belt. If I can spar whilst tired. Imagine what I can do on fight night when I've had thirty to forty-eight hours rest.

Floyd goes into the ring to do pads with Roger and Nate. Today Floyd was on fire during his pad session with Roger. Scintillating speed. It was great to see in person what I've seen on HBO's 24/7 fight build up reality series. Floyd was banging in those body shots to Nate. Nate was feeling them and he had a protector on.

"This is easy work" Floyd says. If this is easy work. I'd hate to see what he calls hard work.

Floyd shouts out "I've slept for one hour. Two hours max. Me and

Fiddy was partying last night and look what I can do. I'm not even in shape yet." That is the frightening thing. Floyd for a normal professional fighter is in great shape. It was a hot day in Vegas and the gym was even hotter so for Floyd to do what he did was amazing and educational. Floyd drinks Powerade a lot whilst he is training but at the end of his workout he likes some soda. If it is for show or not is to be seen. He is a phenomenal athlete either way.

I feel like I'm learning from the master. Just watching Floyd you see what it takes to be a great fighter. Floyd is obviously talented but his work ethic is what makes him the great fighter he is.

Wednesday 14th March 2012

This morning I woke up to rumors that promoter Frank Maloney had won purse bids for my fight with Steve Williams. It will be in Liverpool on Saturday 19th May on the same show as David Price.

I wasn't happy but I'm not surprised Hatton did not win the purse bids. I feel like they don't share my same ambition.

Rene was working in Chicago so I let him know about the rumors. He wasn't happy as would be expected. He feels Hatton promotions have let me down. He said he would have a meeting with them on his return. The gloss has fallen off signing with Hatton promotions and the reality is since signing with them in September, all they have done is give me free Hatton clothes which I don't need as I have my own Treasure sports wear. Steve Williams is the last thing on my mind right now. I'm enjoying training at the Mayweather gym in Las Vegas. I have

dreams of big fights Stateside.
Signing with US promoter would be a dream come true, my main focus is to keep winning and get paid well in the process.

After updating Rene with the rumors floating around the internet about me fighting in Liverpool, I went for a run on Las Vegas Boulevard. I ran from my hotel, Monte Carlo resort and casino to the Sahara hotel and casino. I completed it in my quickest time yet. A fellow runner sped past me so I wasn't having that. He kept a nice pace for maybe just under two miles. I stayed maybe ten to twenty meters behind him. I saw him start to slow down and I overtook him. Sometimes we all need a little kick up the bum to raise our game. I took off five minutes off my last two runs along the Vegas Strip. I'm in great shape.

Michael Jackson's father was in the gym today. So was comedian Alex Reid and former Heavyweight champion Hasim Rahman. You never know who is going to turn up to watch Floyd train.

I worked with Floyd's assistant trainer Nate Jones today. He is the coach always wearing the body bag. Floyd normally does speed work with Roger then hits the body bag with Nate.

I worked of a few technical things with Nate and he tried to tighten up a few things I could perfect. I know he was impressed though. Certain moves I needed to do slow motion a few times but when I got it, we went full steam ahead. Nate is a good trainer. Being patient is a key to any good trainer and he has that.

Earlier in the locker room I was speaking about Bastie Samir performance yesterday. Nate said that Floyd is just warming up and Bastie will be shipped out soon. He also said that Omar Henry will be gone soon as he is just taking a pay check. Omar boasted to me later in the evening when I gave him a lift in my cab to the Gold coast resort. That he used to be signed to Top Rank but because of his friendship with Floyd their relationship soured and he is now with Don King. I told him that was a risky move but he said as he has a pretty good name out there that he can get on other people's shows.

Floyd beat down Bastie today and just like Nate said earlier, he will surely be gone soon. Floyd out boxed him and picked him off at will. It was easy work for Floyd.

Floyd's security told me he saw me running at 7am along the strip.

Thursday 15th March 2012

I sparred with three fighters today. One was the southpaw I sparred with yesterday and two other skillful fighters. I completed six good rounds. They had different styles and different strengths. There is a lot of fighters at this gym around my weight which is great and they all want to learn and improve. I'm a senior, more experienced fighter to them but they are hunger which sometimes can override that. It doesn't in my case as I'm as starving as when I first turned professional. Back in 2002 when no promoter would give me a chance to now where many people dislike what I've achieved which is weird as I give hope to fighters who didn't turn professional with a silver spoon in their mouth. I've gone off my own back to America and beaten respected America fighters with zero support. What could I do if a promoter believed in my talent and backed me.

I did some pad work with Floyd's assistant coach Nate Jones again today.
He knows Floyd from the amateurs as they were in the US team together. He went to prison and two years after getting out, he was in the US Olympic team. He said he told his fellow inmates he was going to go to the Olympics but they didn't believe him. He said he ran round the yard and did loads of exercise in prison to keep himself in decent shape. I understood him as I had that same experience when I was 19 years old. Life is too short to be chilling behind bars.

I weighed 152.5lbs before training and was 150lbs afterwards.

Floyd made two of his sparring partners spar today. They went to war. One was a Mayweather promotions fighter. It was an entertaining five round sparring session which had the on lookers shouting in excitement.

Floyd took a day off sparring which was wise as he had sparred three days in a row.

Floyd started to talk aloud in the ring as he does often, "I'm yet to hit my A game. I've been beating fighters on my B game."
"There are too many cheats at my weight 147lbs. Catch weights and fighters sticking needles in their arm. We need a clean sport".

The highlight of today's pad session with Roger was when both of them closed their eyes and moved in perfect motion. "Mayweather's on another level" was shouted from the crowd of on lookers.

After hitting the Heavy bag and working on the speed bag. Floyd went back into the ring to shadow box. I love how he floats around the ring, feinting, slipping, sliding, bobbing and weaving.

Everyone has their eyes glued on Floyd and there were many fighters watching the master at work. Floyd took time out to tell us some of his views on various subjects.
"I took two years off, came back and beat that bum Marquez and Paciquao struggles against him after me."

Ali is not the greatest of all time. You have to leave boxing with your faculties in working order. Lying on ropes, taking shots, that is not wise. Defense wins fights. Don't get hit wins fight. He didn't go through no weight divisions like me."

Floyd is still shadow boxing whilst talking to his admirers.

"I make money when I sleep. I don't have to fight to make money. I got real estate in New York City. It is over crowded there so people will always need accommodation. It is a great investment."

I listened with interest as Floyd has done everything and is the money man in the boxing world.

"These young fighters can keep the belts. I want that money. You have to get that first world title though. You need you one of those titles to establish yourself and get some leverage with the television companies. Promoters give you money, but don't worry they are going to take it back and more. One way or the other,

I've been burnt but I'm smarter now."

Floyd saw me watching and listening to him with interest from outside the ring.
I was wearing a white t shirt with Treasure going across the front with London underneath it.

"Treasure. I like that t shirt, man. I went over to London and they show me so much love. 5000 people came to watch me train at a gym. We partied. Boy did we party. I went onto one of those bendy buses. We had a hell of a time in London."

He starts chanting "There's only one Floyd Mayweather. I smile and he smiles back at me."

Whilst I was watching Floyd. Leonard Ellerbe, Floyd's adviser comes over to me. He says what's your name again. I tell him Ashley Theophane. He said, "That's it". He asked if I had sparred Jessie Vargas whilst I had been here. I said I hadn't done rounds with him yet. He asked how long I would be around in Vegas. I told him I'm here until the weekend then I'm off to New York for two weeks then back to London. I gave him my business card and I said I'll be back.

He seemed like a cool guy and he showed interest for whatever reasons. I took it as a positive as they know who I am now and I had shined in all of my sparring sessions.

As I was waiting for my taxi to come. Floyd Mayweather had arrived at the gym, he was talking and joking around with his family and friends. I said, "Floyd, I need a photo with you to take back to London." He told me to give my phone to his photographer and we took a photo. We shook hands and I left the gym saying that's made my day. Leonard Ellerbe smiled as I strut past him.

They made me feel comfortable and at home in the gym.

Friday 16th March 2012

I ran on Industrial way this morning which is basically the street parallel to the Vegas strip. The only landscape that the eye can see is highways. This part of a boxer's life that is the lonely. Running six in the morning with just your inner thoughts to keep you company. I covered eight miles in under seventy minutes.

I went down to Floyd Mayweather's barber afterwards as I met her at the gym the day before and she invited me down to get my hair done.
She worked her magic on my hair and I was looking sharper than the day before with a fresh haircut by Las Vegas's master barber.

I sparred one of Roger Mayweather's fighter this afternoon. He looks real good on the pads with Roger. He is a decent fighter. He has speed, skills and power. I was breaking him down with my body shots and in the fourth round he wanted to stop sparring midway through the round. He worked through it, which is good. He said afterwards he was tired as he ran in the morning. I said that's no excuse as I've done an eight mile run this morning. I advised him that he shouldn't let a fighter know if he is hurt or tired. I told he that he can move around the ring, feint his opponent, try to walk his opponent down with a high guard. There was many ways not to show if you are hurt or tired but that comes with experience.

I sparred one of Floyd Mayweather's sparring partner's as well. Which was good work. I had eaten three plates of food at the Buffet in the morning and my food hadn't fully digested. He was attacking me with body shots so I moved around the ring and countered. We'll definitely do more rounds when I come back next time.

His trainer commented afterwards that I'm the only British fighter to come to the gym and represent. Normally in his words "British fighter's get fucked up". I told him that I represent worldwide.

I weighed 150.5lbs today on the scales at Mayweather's boxing gym, which is great.

Floyd acknowledged me whilst I was there which was cool. I know he notices that I study his moves and his workouts.
Floyd had a great sparring session today. I was talking to his sparring partner the day before and he was saying he was better than all the other five fighters in the gym as Floyd's sparring partners. He said he lost to James Degale three times in the amateurs. He was confident he would do better than the other fighters who had entered the ring before him, he did himself proud. Even Roger said he had given Floyd the best work so far. He took too many shots but he also caught Floyd with some good shots. Floyd is sparring fully fledged middleweights who fight at 160lbs and walk around at 180lbs. Floyd is hurting them and taking their shots as well. Floyd is a well conditioned athlete. I am in great shape for my fights but there are a few things Floyd does that I can implement in my workouts, to add to my game.
Going to the Mayweather gym will also help me as over the past three days I sparred with five fighters from Mayweather Boxing Club.

Roger had an argument with a coach at the gym, Rafael Garcia's assistant. The assistant tried to tell Roger Floyd is open for the left hook and Roger went off on him. "What the fuck you know about boxing? You don't know shit about boxing. You've never fought. What the fuck have you done in boxing?"

The guy walked off saying he wasn't going to argue. Roger told the coach's fighter to be careful that he doesn't get you killed in the ring as he doesn't know shit about boxing.

I spoke to Boza after Floyd was finished working out. He said he was shocked I didn't campaign more in the States after my fights with Delvin Rodriguez and Danny Garcia as I had put in good performances. I told him that when I beat Lenny Daws for the British title. I only had planned to do it for one fight but then I wanted to keep the Lonsdale belt so I chose to stay for three defenses but I wanted to come straight back to the States afterwards. He felt like there could be some good fights for me over here in the States if I made the move more permanent.

Boza was welcoming and told me that I know where they are now so come back.

Everyone showed me love. As my taxi came to pick me up Floyd was outside with the money team. I gave the taxi man my training bag and went over to Floyd. I told him thanks for everything. We shook hands and we hugged.
I pounded and shook hands with the money team members which included Leonard Ellerbe, Nate Jones and a few others then I jumped in my taxi.
They know who I am now so as long as I would keep winning I

could work with Mayweather promotions in the future.

Sunday 18th March 2012

Today is Mother's Day in the United Kingdom. I can honestly say without my mother I wouldn't be who I am today. The struggles she had raising me as a young mother then after my parents split when I was in secondary school. Dealing with the pain and heartache I gave her through my teenage years. She is a special woman who stood by me. At times I look back and I wonder why. Most mother's would have put their child into government care but my mum loved her boys so fought her hardest to do her best for them.

My Godmother, Dorothy Edwards was another special woman in my life. She foresaw my path of glory as a young child. She would tell me I was going to be a successful champion. I never believed her but she believed and that means a lot to me.

Yesterday I was up at 5am running along the Vegas Strip and this morning I was running Flatlands in Brooklyn. I completed eight miles on both days just with different scenery. The same burning desire is in me where ever my feet pound the pavement. It was a total different environment but one that filled me with hunger to be successful.
How many fighters in the world can boast to be doing what I am doing. One day I'm in Las Vegas. Training at Mayweather's Boxing Club, the next I'm at the world famous Gleason's gym in Brooklyn where world greats, Muhammad Ali, Mike Tyson and Emile Griffith have trained. The atmosphere is different in these gyms. You feel anything is capable. You just have to put in the work.

Back home in London, I still train at All Stars boxing club as it fills me with the young enthusiasm and hope I had as a kid. I remember when I was like those amateurs. Hoping for a better future, hoping to follow my dreams and achieve them. Very few youths do actually see their endeavors through as it is a long hard journey and as an amateur you do not know the business side takes over from the sporting side of it once you turn professional.

I've been professional for nine years now and I will be happy to have a 15 year career. That is my goal. To finish with multiple titles, more great wins at world level, achieve my monetary goals, end my career with fifty wins and my health still in working order.

Monday 19th March 2012

I received a letter from the British Boxing Board of Control today. "Promoter Frank Maloney advises that the British Light Welterweight Championship, Theophane v Williams, will take place on Saturday, 19th May 2012 at the Aintree Equestrian Centre, Liverpool."
My fight with Steve Williams is official and has been confirmed.

Wednesday 21st March 2012

Today I sparred with Dean and Scott Burrell. I have been sparring them since December 2009. So for my fights with Danny Garcia, Delvin Rodriguez, Lenny Daws and Jason Cook we have completed rounds together. They are lightning fast and have a good arrange of skills. They keep me sharp.
I had given Harry $100 as yesterday he said he was going through a sticky moment so he asked if I had spare money. I had

$300 in cash to last me for the next week that I was in New York City, so I gave him $100.

I'm sparring with the twins and I've been supplying myself with fluids in between rounds as Harry was wrapping Alexis, a female boxer's hands. I wear the face protection head guards with a bar going across my nose and mouth.

I always tell Harry to give me the bottle and I will put it in my mouth as its easier. Harry goes to put it in my mouth and I told him just put it in my hand. Harry replies, "What have I told you about talking to me like that?" I replied "whatever." He fires at me with abused language. "Fuck you Ashley." I ignored him and carried on my sparring session with the twins. It affected my concentration for a while as everyone saw us square off against each other. Harry walked off to deal with his other fighters and I finished off my ten round sparring session with the Burrell Twins.

I went to hit the heavy bags for five rounds then three on the speed bag.

I had to go where Harry was sitting as that was his station in Gleason's gym. I ignored him and just spoke to Jihad. Jihad told me to go into Bob Jackson's office as we had to talk it out.

"You're interrupting my training session, Jihad." I wasn't pleased but I smiled and sat on a chair. Harry said how he had told me earlier in camp that he wasn't happy how I spoke to him and that I never spoke to the white officials at the fights the same way I spoke to him. I told him I see the officials three times a year so of course everything would be fine with them. I said it doesn't matter what color you are, if I have an issue with you I let it be known. I went on to say I'm not any of his other fighters who need abusive language thrown at them and pushed to train or work hard. Some hate stepping on the scale to see their weight. I'm always on point. I don't fly from England to mess with girls, slack in training or eat junk food. I come America to work, to bust my guts. I haven't had a day off in a month. The guys in the gym, all sleep with the women who come here to do keep fit, not me. I told

Harry he is respected but I speak to him the same way I speak to my family and friends, so he is no different. I went on to say your name wouldn't have been mentioned in the meeting with Ricky Hatton and Richard Poxon about flying you over for every fight, if you wasn't respected. I said I'm just me and I can't change that. I said if jihad did something I don't like, I would let him know. We shook hands, hugged it out and that was that.
On my way out Jihad said Harry was going through some issues at the minute. I could tell. Such is life!

Thursday 22nd March 2012

I woke up thing morning weighing 149.6lbs which was fantastic as that is what I wanted to weigh in a week's time, so maybe now I could be 148lbs by next Thursday when I fly back to London Heathrow.
My stomach was turning all morning so I had to let Ajose know that I would not be able to make sparring. At the same time I emailed him. He had text me to say that he had been invited ringside to watch the world WBC title fight between Erik Morales and Danny Garcia. They are just keeping the belt warm for him.

Sunday 25th March 2012

Danny Garcia won the WBC world super lightweight championship against Erik Morales last night. I am happy Danny won as it just shows that I am capable of achieving that same feat as there was just a round in it between us and many boxing fans still contact me two years later to say how they thought I won. Danny himself thought I won. I wasn't impressed with either man's performance last night. Marcos Maidana made Erik look better than he was as Marcos struggles against boxers as his performances against Demarcus Corley and Devin Alexander have shown. That's why I believe I would beat him.

Ajose Olusegun was flown out by HBO to sit ringside and watch the fight and he must know that Danny is just keeping that belt warm for him until they meet in the ring.
Danny has not improved much since our fight two years ago even though he has beaten Mike Arnaoutis, Nate Campbell, and Kendall Holt during that time. I was the fighter who caused him the most trouble.

I feel good today. Delvin Rodriguez is currently world number five, DeMarcus Corley is currently world number fourteen and Danny Garcia is currently world champion. That says a lot about me and my record as I beat two of them and dropped a controversial loss to the now world champion.

Imagine what I could do with promotional backing. Majority of what I achieved was as a self managed fighter and I've never had a promoter pushing me to the World stage.

I've signed with Hatton promotions but they seem to have lost the enthusiasm to promote me.

Maybe I'll do a month in Manchester with Joe Gallagher and a month in Las Vegas at the Mayweather gym. Right now these are just thoughts running through my mind. I have to beat Steve Williams before any of this is possible. Getting the knockout win is important as they will rob me if they can.

Jihad thinks I should go to the IBF offices in New Jersey and state my case for a higher ranking. I'm not too bothered about doing that. I'm happy to keep winning and work my way back up.

He thinks I have nothing to lose which is true as I was dropped from number four for no apparent reason.

Monday 26th March 2012

Jihad called me today and said that he called the IBF offices to make an appointment for Wednesday. He feels with Vernon Paris, Victor Cayo and Tim Coleman getting knocked out recently I should be ranked higher.
My last lost was to WBC world champion Danny Garcia and I have beaten WBC world number fourteen Demarcus Corley and I was IBF world number three Delvin Rodriguez's last loss. I shouldn't be number 15 that is for sure. Hopefully, they place me in the top ten.

Tuesday 27th March 2012

Sparred with Ajose Olusegun this morning, I did a six-mile run just after six in the morning as we were not sparring until midday.

Ajose just arrived from Houston last night so I appreciated him doing some rounds with me.

We completed six rounds and it was great work. Jihad commented whilst we were sparring that I definitely have his number. Jihad has watched our last two sparring sessions. They were both on my last week in training camp so I am and was in better shape than Ajose currently is and was. I believe Ajose will win the world title and I will be very happy for him as I am very proud of his journey. He has come very far and is on the verge of making big moves in America. I told him today. All he has to do is win the world title and he will be amongst the big names in the sport. Timothy Bradley is fighting Manny Pacquiao and Victor Ortiz fought Floyd Mayweather after winning the WBC world titles. Ajose is good enough to mix it with those guys.

I'm ready for my meeting tomorrow at the IBF offices. I just hope I get everything out that I want to say. Jihad said Harry was coming. I asked him why. He said he asked him to come. I reckon he wants Harry to come so Harry doesn't think he is trying to push him out. Jihad has done ninety percent of the work with me for this camp. Harry spreads himself too thinly with fighters. He has too many and most of them do not pay him anything. When I come New York, I expect to be a priority. I think he thinks cause Ajose will fight for a world title soon he will jump on his bandwagon but Ajose does majority of his training in Nigeria and he has commented that he wants to start basing himself in Wildcard as he prefers the weather on the West coast.

Wednesday 28th March 2012

What a great day I had. I completed twelve rounds on the pads with Jihad and Harry in a marathon three-hour training session. Watching Floyd Mayweather train in the flesh has definitely inspired me. I inspire many New York and London people, but I am also inspired by many people around me such as my mother, Mr. Akay and Rene Carayol.

Jihad and I went off to the IBF office in New Jersey. Harry didn't come as he was working with Jeremy and Emmanuel who have important fights this weekend.

Jihad and I have always got on well whilst Harry and my relationships are very rocky at this minute in time.

It took us just under an hour to get to the office.
As we walked in the building. I collected my thoughts as I knew I had to get various information out in the meeting.

Jihad rang the buzzer and a blonde middle-aged woman came to open the door. Jihad said we had a meeting with the President. The receptionist asked us to make ourselves comfortable in the waiting area. Jihad did just that, stuffing his face with the candy they had for visitors. I wanted to but I'm watching my weight I had to watch him enjoy himself like a child in a candy store.
After a couple minutes Mr. Daryl J. Peoples introduced himself as the President. We shook hands and he led us into a conference room.

He showed us to our seats and sat opposite us. He said to me "what can I do for you?" I replied "I have come to discuss my ranking in the IBF." He sat interested and let me speak. I told him that I am currently 15 in the 140lb rankings and I was number 4 18 months ago but I have been dropped through the months. I let him know that my last loss was over two years to the current WBC world champion Danny Garcia and that I was the last person to beat Delvin Rodriguez who was third at the time but is now fifth up at junior middleweight and I let him know I have beaten Demarcus Corley who is a former world champion and currently 14 in the WBC. He asked if I had been in active as that maybe the reason why I was dropped down the rankings. I told him I was offered a world title eliminator but I couldn't take it as I was going through managerial problems. He said that was the reason why I was dropped as if you reject a world title eliminator opportunity you get put out of the Top 10 for six months. Over 18 months has past so that is not valid. I told him since then I went back to Britain and beat the British champion and a former European champion. I let him know I'm fighting the same night as Amir Khan and I will be part of the UK Sky Sports coverage leading to Amir

Khan's fight with Lamont Peterson. I mentioned that three of the top 15 had been knocked out recently. I said I know Zab Judah is next in line but I would like to be in the next round of world title eliminators. He listened, he nodded, he responded well. He said he would speak to another member of the IBF and get back to me. Jihad and I gave him our business cards. I took a photo and we left. I feel really positive about how the meeting went.
I will definitely be in the Top ten in next months IBF world rankings but Top five is what I want. I want that world title eliminator. I feel like I can beat anyone in the world. As I told Mr. Peoples I'm only asking for a chance and I think I deserve that.

It motivates me even more knowing that I inspire so many young fighters and young people to reach for their dreams in life. I've come from the bottom and I was just like them. A kid with a dream, I just worked hard to make my dreams into reality.

I'm looking to make a statement come May 19th. I'm bored of domestic fighters calling me out. I win the Lonsdale belt outright and hopefully I never have to fight a British fighter again.

Thursday 29th March 2012

Jarrell Miller, a promising heavyweight who has been Klitschko's sparring partner on numerous occasions is talented but lacks focus. Whilst I was sparring with the twins. In between rounds he made a comment about sexual intercourse. I said whilst I'm in training camp I don't have sex. He shouted out "no way man." I said that's why I'm the champ.

Tuesday 24th April 2012

I received a text message from Rene saying that Golden Boy had

offered me $50,000 to fight Jessie Vargas next week Saturday on the Floyd Mayweather v Miguel Cotto undercard. I am super fit and I believe I could beat him. I think he is overhyped and I don't see why Floyd would want him. I turned down the opportunity as I am focused on winning the Lonsdale belt outright.
Steve Williams will be a hard fight especially in Liverpool. Comparing our records you have to say I am the clear cut winner but I do not trust the judges so I am training for a knock out. I need to stop him by cuts or knock out. No one who knows him believes I can do that but both Dave Brown and Don Charles have commented how hard I am hitting.

I know Steve is nervous fighting in his hometown and against someone as experienced as me so I have to use all the mental games I can possibly do. Coming back to the United Kingdom was such a big risk as I was ranked fourth in the world at the time but it has paid off so far. I am at the last hurdle and I am doing everything in my power to make my dream a reality.

No British 140lbs fighter since Ross Hale in 1995 has won four British title fights in a row so that is 17 years. The last man before him was Clinton McKenzie in 1983 so it will be 29 years that only three men have achieved that feat. I feel even more motivated to achieve that become a great, British champion.

Thursday 3rd May 2012

I finished working with Dave at All Stars to see a message from Rene that Richard had text him about a $100,000 pay day in Russia. Of course Richard wanted me to take the offer. It was for sometime in June. I had already booked my vacation in Jamaica but there was no way I was going to Ukraine unless for a world title shot.
Two offers from Golden Boy in a space of a week. First to fight Jessie Vargas on the Floyd Mayweather v Miguel Cotto show

and now this. My name is floating about but I want the big fights against the big names.

Richard does my head in. I have been signed to Hatton promotions for eight months and I am yet to fight on a show of theirs.

I am just focused on beating Steve Williams in Liverpool as there will be major fights when I get through him.

Tuesday 8th May 2012

Lamont Peterson has failed his random drug test and his fight with Amir Khan on the same night as my fight is looking like it is not going ahead as the Nevada State Athletic commission will not give him a boxing license.

My name floated around on the boxing forums as a possible opponent for Amir Khan as we are fighting on the same night and I am ranked by the IBF.

On Saturday my cousin Carla who is married to Mark Harnell asked me if I got the memo about the press conference that was happening today and if I was coming. I said I did not get the memo and I wouldn't be coming.

I don't know if the press conference went ahead but in the evening James who works for Frank Maloney called me and told me that there would be a press conference on Thursday in Liverpool and if I was getting driven to Liverpool or taking plane or train. I said Rene was the person to speak to as he deals with that stuff. When I got off the phone with him I emailed Rene as he was in Amsterdam on business.

I let him know I wouldn't be cutting my training short for Frank Maloney to promote his show.

Frank is bringing me to Liverpool in the hope I lose to local lad Steve Williams. His team also did not want to give us any tickets for my family. It took us three weeks to get them. Jakub, Rene's driver had to drive to their offices to get the tickets. They also never got no posters for my fight with Steve Williams. Everything was for David Price v Sam Sexton.

I refused to promote his show or make him money by promoting it. He is paying me wages way below my value so I will do what I am contractually obligated to do.

Wednesday 9th May 2012

Penny, Rene's PA contacted James Russell who had called me about the press conference. Frank Maloney promotions said that they were paying for me to stay in a hotel on Friday and Saturday. They would also pay for my train costs.

They expected me to pay for my journey to Liverpool for the press conference and do a six hour round trip for it. They are so penny pinching it is amusing. They have no shame with their game. Of course I will not be attending the press conference. Even when I thought they would be paying for it I was not going to go. Finding out they expected me to fund the trip to Liverpool to promote their show is hilarious.

I completed my last twelve round sparring session today at All Stars Boxing gym with Obi, Remi and Arash. Arash Hagh did the first three and last three with Remi and Obi doing the six in between. Arash is perfect sparring for Steve Williams and he is a middleweight so he is strong. He has improved over the years and he gives me quality work. He is also a genuine nice guy.

Rene messaged me whilst I was working out saying he needed to talk to me as Frank Maloney is insisting I come on Thursday to the press conference as Sky Sports need me there for interviews. I'm not missing training for Sky Sports or Frank Maloney promotions. I need every day to workout and get my weight on point. Rene wants me to go but I said if I go, I am basically risking losing my title on the scales as I won't be able to train to reach my target weight. If need be I will take a fine but saying that, my contract says I don't have to be there until Friday and I'm not going to help Frank Maloney promote his show. I dislike working with him and I will not be going to Liverpool for longer than I need to.

Thursday 10th May 2012

I woke up in the middle of the night and saw an email from Rene. He always tries to calm the situation down by saying how much he is doing for me and how far I have come since knowing each other. Everything he said was true but he thinks that I do not want to do the press conference because of my stutter and that is nothing to do with the situation.
I stutter but I do not let that hold me back from what I want to do. I always face my fears.

Ashley,

First and foremost, I'm ALWAYS on your side and know you well enough to understand that you really HATE press conferences, and I also think I understand why.

Part of my role in working with you is to ensure that you can be the best that you can be, and as I keep telling you, you are far better than you think you are – at EVERYTHING you do.

I know you notice, but I'm not sure you always see the extent of the change in you since I met you; your outlook has moved massively, you have a much more calm and balanced disposition, our conversations have stepped up incredibly – I can talk to you about anything and everything and do, your writing is a completely different class to six months ago – you have picked up the rhythm that we both write to, your vocabulary has changed markedly, you are so much less pessimistic about everything – yet, still strong and outspoken, you are a happier man – and fabulous company, you have entrusted me with your trust – and I'm privileged and proud that we have achieved that huge and vital milestone, (way ahead of the schedule I'd conservatively set), but most of all, we are friends, and that means more to me than anything.

I hope you have noticed that I have tried to treat this as both a special, and strategic relationship. I'm massively commercial, as you know, but I see our relationship as a deep partnership. I have tried to support you emotionally, tangibly, financially, but most of all as a mentor, not a manager.

I have a dream that you can compete at the very top level, and just perhaps win a world championship. I live that dream. I promised you that I didn't want a penny from your earnings until they became significant. I hope I have proved that.

Ashley, we are on the verge of everything we both have dreamed of. I can't ever explain how much your success, and on-going positive story means to me. I just can't let you down.

I've been carefully and subtlety nudging you forward, but I always knew that we would have some very uncomfortable moments. Your dalliance with the fight for Miranda was a real moment of truth, I'm still not sure you understood how angry and hurt I really was. We overcame that, and maybe because of that incident, we have built something very special.

The Saturday lunches I always look forward to. The blogs light up my week, (much to teams frustration, as they never get your speed of turnaround from me). I am sure you understand that I put off my major clients in order to keep your blogs contemporary. My housekeeper, Dily, who is managing the ticket sales from my study, remarked "why does Ashley's work always needs to be done immediately?" – she's learning that ALL work needs to be done immediately.

So forgive the long diatribe, but we have a learning point, and an important moment that we really need to cross right now.

I have watched and seen you feel really raw, and nervous about your (diminishing) stammer.

It hardly comes about when you are with me, in fact It never does at all. We need to start asking ourselves why?

You are smart, articulate, and massively eloquent, but if you don't mind me saying, can get anxious in perceived hostile environments. However, you are overcoming those brilliantly.

It's time to start trusting yourself, the way I trust you. You are ultra-intelligent, but have not yet accepted that. Your slight doubt in you as a speaker, stands a world apart from your self-belief as a boxer, yet you know you are brilliant when talking to the kids in school?

We now need to step up to the plate – you ARE world championship ready; so we need to believe, act and behave like a world champion in the making.

Your profile is absolutely key to this, and press conferences are your 'bread and butter'. We just can't duck them anymore. Your personality and authenticity is our anchor. And believe you me, you have motivated and energised me. If the stammer appears, it will just add massive value to your brand, but I doubt that it will, BUT it's a necessary part of the brand we designed and have built. Stop worrying about it (easy for me to say, but we have already engineered authenticity deep into who you are and will be).

You are more than ready. It's your moment. Step up. You are so capable, and you are at your very best, just being you.

That's all it takes, just you my friend. You are more than ready and it's your moment. This is so much less painful than that 'popped finger' in the Corley fight.

Floyd takes his press conferences very seriously, as did Ali, Tyson and all our boxing heroes, despite their perceived shortcomings. Floyd is the same. They make the most of who they naturally are, as does Beckham. This is your time and your moment and this is a key part of the drill – you will be so much better than any other British contemporary boxer.

Believe me, we have both put in the work, and you are more than ready. I've had the pleasure of witnessing your personal growth up close and personal. You are superb!

Let's do the press conference – it's your time.

I'm so confident that you will be absolutely brilliant!

René

When I woke up and had thought about the situation. I replied to

Rene's email:

Rene

As I stated I'm not missing my last training day to fight in a place I don't wish to fight or promote a show I care little about.

The show is about David Price not Ashley Theophane.
My stutter has zero to do with why I don't want to do it.
If I can go on the television I can do this. Speaking in front of an audience of kids which I want to do in the future is my only thing I haven't been able to do successfully and that is more about having a structured speech I can say.
I stutter but at the same time. I don't run from the fact. I'm 31 so I've lived with it my whole life. I know how hard it is for anyone to do public speaking or a kid at school who has a stutter and has to read in front of his classroom. So I represent them and show them that we can still do it even if we stutter. My stutter is mild but still there.
If the press conference were in London I would do it but it is in Liverpool so I find it unreasonable for me to have to go there the day before I'm supposed to.

I've looked over the fight contract and it says Friday and Saturday I have to be in Liverpool.

My preparations come first so section 12 of my contract says I should do reasonable engagements for the promoter.
To be in Liverpool a day before I need to be and miss my last hard day of training is not reasonable. I will not be at the press conference.
Sky Sports can interview me on the Friday.

I hate fighting in Britain and I have nothing to say about Steve Williams.
He can speak to himself as Lenny Daws did last February.

There is nothing you can say to change my mind.
I need to make weight and as I stated I need my day in London. They chose to have the show in Liverpool so it is not a reasonable request Maloney promotions is asking of me. I'm going by the contract I signed. It is unreasonable!

Yes I have grown over the past year and learnt loads from being around you. You have helped me grow as a person.

I'm fortunate to have someone like you supporting and helping me. You are truly helping me achieve what I want in life.

Even if we were to stop working together I still value as a friend first and foremost. You are one of my best friends and we can speak about anything.

I even appreciate all the work Jackie, Penny, Dominic and Jacub do for me. I like all of them. They are great!

Your help has been much appreciated.

As I said yesterday I will stand alone of this one.

Ashley

Whilst I was working out at Jubilee sports centre in Mozart Estate which is situated in Queens Park. Rene sent me an email saying that he would deal with the Maloney promotions press conference situation. Imagine they want me to make a six hour round trip for a thirty minute press conference. Why they don't do it before the weigh in on Friday, I don't know.

I'm not contractually obligated so there is not much they can do to me.

Rene said Richard Poxon, matchmaker at Hatton promotions had been in contact with Marco Antonio Barrera's people and they said he would be interested in fighting me in July. That would be amazing so we will see what happens with that.

Friday 11th May 2012

Dereck Chisora was in the gym today as he is getting ready to fight David Haye in a fight that has sent shock ways through the British boxing industry as Dereck is suspended by the British Boxing Board of Control and David has got a license with them. The Luxembourg commission has sanctioned the fight and gone over the heads of the BBBofC.
This is a sticky situation which could end the Board's control over British boxing.

I had my last official check weigh in today. I was allowed to be 147lbs but I was 145lbs which is fine. I had just eaten so I knew I would be a bit heavy but I was under the maximum weight allowed.
The Boxing Board of Control official Nick Bond said he had been upgraded and would only be doing European and World title fights so he will see me after I win the Lonsdale belt.

He said I don't need luck as I have worked hard enough to get to where I am and my talent alone will get me through.
It is so nice to have a British boxing board of control official believe in my talent like that.

After finishing a two hour plus workout with Charles, I had an email from Ricky Hatton. It was nice to receive a message from him as last time I spoke to him was after I beat Ben Murphy. He was heading out to the WBC convention in Las Vegas. This was December 11th so exactly five months on I get contact from my promoter. It is not perfect but after I win the Lonsdale belt outright. My career can move back onto the world scene.
I've had loads of support from boxing fans throughout the UK. It feels great that they believe in my talent.
It has been a long hard road for me but the hard work and dedication through out the years are starting to pay off. Steve Williams could be a hard or easy nights work. I'm prepared for both. When you look at the tale of the tape between us, It is a mismatch but I train for the best possible Steve Williams. I expect him to be in great condition for our fight. I am prepared! I have taken him as seriously as I took Jason Cook, Nigel Wright and Lenny Daws. The talking is drawing to a close and our fists will do the talking.

Email from Ricky Hatton went as follows:

"Alright Ash. Hope the weigh in goes well today. Hope your training camp has gone brilliantly. Due to the lack of dates we had and situation with what has happened recently with dates I'm sorry I haven't had chance to bang the drum for you like I said & wanted but rest assured, do the job Saturday my mate and come next time we'll have new dates in place and I promise I will really get your career rolling.
Good luck Ash. And still."

Sunday 13th May 2012

The surest way not to fail is to be determined to succeed. I just can't imagine me losing on Saturday. I am better at Steve at everything. My skills, my speed even my power.

I'm loving life right now. I'm living my childhood dream. My occupation is one that I wanted to do as a five year old kid. I push my body to it's limits and beyond. That has got me some fantastic results in my career. Steve is not important to my career. Winning the Lonsdale belt outright is and being only the third man in 29 years to win in four straight British title fights. What I will do on Saturday hasn't been done in 17 years. I'm joining the history books as a great, British champion. A dominant one,
I even met Clinton McKenzie's son Leon the other day in the gym. I love good omen's like that. Clinton was another great, British champion as I'm looking to achieve a feat he did back in 1983.

Ricky Hatton has big plans for me. I'm looking to fight the best 140lbs fighters just like he did in his career.

Monday 14th May 2012

At 4pm I received an email from Rene that Steve Williams had pulled out of our fight. My mind could not comprehend what I was reading. This is the second fight in a row that this has happened to me.
Later in the evening I found out Steve had a chest infection. When I fought Lenny Daws in our British title fight I was

bedridden the week of the fight. I did not attend the press conference as I did not want him to know I was poorly.
When you want something you have to do whatever it takes to make it happen.
Steve pulling out just shows me that he is not up to the job of beating me.

Tuesday 15th May 2012

The British Boxing Board of Control head Robert Smith said he would be flexible with me regarding an opponent as the difficult situation what I am in was out of my control.
Frank Maloney on the other hand did not try and find suitable opponents for me.
The one and only time I worked with Maloney promotions was my last British title defense. It was the most unorganized and penny pinching promotion I've ever had to deal with and it was a pain from start to finish so I was not happy when I found out he would be promoting this fight. Sometimes boxing is a stressful business. I'm basically twenty-two thousand pounds out of pocket if I do not fight on Saturday.

Rene told me that Darren Hamilton was given approval by the Board. Don Charles was happy with that as he feels I beat him up in sparring. Darren has a record of eleven wins and two loses but he is Southern Area and British Masters champion. He beat two time British title challenger John Watson a couple weeks ago so he is obviously in good shape. He was due to fight in three weeks time against Chris Evangelou so he is ready for this short notice fight. He will believe he can win.
I'm ready anyway!

In the evening I was contacted by Tom Brown from Goosen Tutor. He asked me if I was interested in fighting Josesito Lopez in an IBF eliminator on June 22nd in California. I would love to but it is four weeks after my fight with Darren.
I have got three IBF eliminator offers over the last two years so another will come.

Goosen Tutor Match maker Tom Brown even mentioned about doing another show in Saint Lucia. I would love that. I told him to stay in touch as that would be something that is really appealing to me.

It is crazy the difference 24 hours can make. Yesterday my head was all over the place. I did not have an opponent for my fight on Saturday so it looked unlikely to happen. Now I have an opponent and been offered a world title eliminator. I'm feeling very positive!

Wednesday 16th May 2012

I have been getting much abuse from little known fighter Adil Anwar's fans. As they feel I have ducked him. These guys just don't understand I am in another galaxy to them.
I like to fight boxers I admire or respect as a fighter.
Campaigning as British champion is all about winning the Lonsdale belt.
Lenny Daws, Jason Cook, Nigel Wright and Steve Williams are probably the best fighters that I could have faced. It is not my fault Steve and Nigel pulled out the week of the fight.
Just last night I was offered a world title eliminator in America. No one knows Adil Anwar out of Leeds. You would think he is the second coming of Prince Naseem.
Frank Maloney has just signed him so he went public saying I

turned the fight down.
If I had fought Adil then Darren Hamilton and his team would say the same thing.
I can only fight one man at a time.
During my reign Frankie Gavin, Curtis Woodhouse, Peter McDonagh, Adil Anwar, Steve Williams and Darren Hamilton have all mentioned a desire to fight me. Unfortunately for them they all have to wait their turn.

I'm looking forward to moving back to International level as it is boring just hearing lesser guys mention my name.
They will never fight at the level I do. So they can hate on my career from afar because win or lose I will have loads of opportunities Stateside after I win the Lonsdale belt.
I can't wait to move on. I only wanted to fight Lenny Daws. All these other guys are not very good and I lack motivation fighting against them.

Adil Anwar and Frank Maloney both released press statements saying I turned down the opportunity to fight Anwar.
Frank Maloney has deducted my purse of two thousand pounds because I am not fighting Steve Williams.
Frank has been blamed as the man who sent Darren Sutherland to suicide. Darren was a top boxing talent and I've heard a nice guy so it is a shame he lost his life so young.
I have now worked with Frank twice and they have been the two worst dealings with a promotion.

All this week I have been receiving abuse from Adil Anwar's fans.
I've been through this before so I just ignore it.
Frankie Gavin, Curtis Woodhouse, Nigel Wright and Steve Williams fans have all abused me during my British title reign so I

am used to it now.

Floyd Mayweather gets accused of ducking fighters all the time and he has been accused through his career of avoiding certain fighters. If you have got haters, you are obviously doing something right. I'm in good company!

Thursday 17th May 2012

The bookies have me as a 12-1 favorite and he is a 6-1 underdog. They seem to really believe this is a formality but I think he is better than the odds give him and I think he will be a harder fight than Steve Williams would have been.

There is good odds on me stopping Darren after 8 rounds. 2-1 is a decent price. The bookies seem to think I am likely to stop him within 8 rounds. Maybe I will have to wait until 8 rounds to knock him out.

Ladbrokes gave odds for Darren Hamilton to knock me out on round betting anything from 150-1 to 100-1. If I was him and actually believed I could win. I would take those bets. He will definitely have a go. I'm not foolish to think he is coming to lay down.

Friday 18th May 2012

I've dropped 24lbs over the last four months. It sounds a lot but really it is one pound a week which is nothing.

I weighed 140.6lbs on my bathroom scales which is great. Last time I weighed that a morning of a fight was the bout with Jason Cook. By the official weigh in I was 138lbs.

I wanted breakfast and I knew Jakub would be driving me up to Liverpool. It is a three hour journey so I knew I would want to drink some fluid.
I went for a light jog but in the end I did my 10.5 mile run I normally do on Mondays. It took one hour twenty minutes so I did not go at a crazy pace just steady. It is weird.
After the 10.5 mile eighty minute relaxing jog I weighed 137.8lbs. I had breakfast and some fluid. I now have 36 hours rest until I will fight so that is more than enough time.

Charles told me on the journey to Liverpool that Spencer will tell Darren to try and unsettle me. He said he will deal with the situation so not to get involved.
I said there was more chance of Adil Anwar's team and supporters being a nuisance.
I can't be intimidated by a boxer so I'm not really bothered. I will weigh in, do my interviews, take photos then eat and drink.

I've had guns held to me and people try to kidnap me. Boxing is a sport and one that I kill my body to get conditioned for. Trying to intimidate me is sure to lead in failure. I've seen some bad stuff in my life and I'm just focused on being the best I can be.
Spencer Fearon will be Darren's undoing as he will tell him to jump on me from the first bell. His best bet would be to try and box me.
I am ready for their tactics.

Dereck Chisora is coming to support Charles and I tomorrow when I defend my belt against Darren.
Frank Maloney must be happy with that as he is trying to build David Price up as the next Lennox Lewis.
Charles is not sold on David Price as he says he has watched him at close quarters in sparring sessions with Dereck.

We arrived at Aintree around 2pm. The British Boxing Board of Control's officials were not best pleased with the challenger leaving the champion waiting. Neither where SKY Sports, they found it disgusting that Darren was given a British title opportunity and he would be late to the weigh in. Leaving the television network, the officials and the champion waiting.

Nigel Benn's former manager Ambrose Mendy arrived on the same train as Darren Hamilton and his team. He is an advisor to Spencer Fearon, who is Darren's manager and they have been trying to get me to fight Darren for the last year so they have their wish.

Ambrose left with us and Jakub dropped us off at the Village Hotel in Fallows Way. I was shocked, it was a nice hotel. It was just in the middle of no where.
I told Ambrose that he wanted to hang with us now and he is with the enemy.
He replied "you can learn much from being with the enemy. Darren has a bad hand and he is really struggling with his weight." Don Charles said, "That will not change our game plan. We will set out to do what we plan and if those things are true. They will show up with in the fight."

Ambrose spoke to me during our ride to the hotel about my upcoming fight with Darren Hamilton. Rene wanted him around to make sure that I was fine and that Frank Maloney was not a nuisance. The boxing promoters know to come correct with me so that would never be an issue. I may seem quiet but they know my past. No more needs to be said. Even though I dislike Frank Maloney and many of his workers says he knows nothing about running a business. He has had success so you have to respect that. Me as a fighter would never sign with him as he is so penny pinching and unprofessional. I would only work with him if I have to and I obviously have to as he won the purse bid for the Steve Williams fight. Ambrose told me "You are on the verge of fulfilling your potential. Hamilton stands in the way of that. Even if Darren has improved over the last year, that should have no affect on how you should be able to beat him as my experience alone is something Darren can't pull onto." Ambrose asked me if I had seen the venue where I was going to fight in. I said no. He went on "before your fight. Go and check out the arena. See where you are going to walk. Look at how the ring is. Soak in the atmosphere." I listen as I respect Ambrose so much. He guided Nigel Benn who I was a massive fan of. I remember being a kid watching Ambrose with his jerry curl on the television. I won't check out the venue, the ring or soak of the atmosphere as I do not care about those things. I am too focused from when I get into the venue that whatever they try do to unsettle me, will have no affect on my mood. I can't be intimidated or mentally unbalanced. Like when Don Charles said Spencer could try and make Darren try be aggressive towards me. If they did that, I was have smiled and walked away. As long as you don't put your hands on me, the situation will stay calm.

Darren and Spencer have been respectful. Darren came up to me and shook my hand at the weigh in. Spencer has been saying through the media and social networking sites that he is happy for the opportunity and there is no need for trash talking which is very unlike him. He has shown me support and I have shown him support in his endeavors so it is love and respect. I'm happy for him that he got a television deal with premier sports and he is rising in the boxing world as a promoter.

I believe Spencer and his team believe Darren can win because of the Ben Murphy fight. Darren is awkward but no Ben Murphy. The bookies are sometimes wrong but they know he hasn't got a hope.

Spencer thinks it is meant to be as last time they didn't take the late notice fight but this time they are as Darren beat John Watson in Liverpool two weeks ago on short notice and he was in training for a 10 round fight which is two weeks away so he is in shape. Really it is perfect timing for Darren. Being short notice isn't a big deal to him as he's in hardcore training anyway.
What they need to realize is I'm not John Watson. Darren couldn't stop John, but lightweights Gavin Rees and Anthony Crolla did. He also only won by one round so it was a close fought fight.
Talent and experience wise I'm in an alien world to Darren. I'm from another galaxy. I always find it amusing that these British level fighters think they can beat me. Just accept the pay day and enjoy the experience.

I shared a taxi with Spencer to Liverpool City centre. He said to me. "Ash, whatever I'm saying to the boxing media and on social networking sites, we are just coming for the money. We all know Darren is not going to win." I told him "That maybe the case but I take every opponent serious. There will be no upsets around here." I know Spencer's game. He knows aggressive talk will make me even more focused towards them so he thinks doing the friendly game will make me leave my guard down. Excuse the pun. I believe they think they can win. I want to and expect to stop Darren. If our fight goes as our sparring has gone, he won't make it past round eight.

Saturday 19th May 2012

My trainer Harry Keitt has been in Liverpool since Thursday morning. He said that he had sat and ate with Frank Maloney, but they did not mentioned the weigh in to him. So he ended up missing it. I hadn't spoken to Harry over the last seven weeks, so we had a quick catch up over breakfast. Harry said that Charles told him that I had beaten Darren up during sparring a couple times. I said that you know I don't see sparring as no big deal as I normally just go through the motions so for me to beat him up in sparring is saying something. I told Harry I was not going to go by our sparring sessions. I will box him and try break him down just like any other opponent I fight.

When we first sparred, Spencer Fearon made a big deal about it so there were people with their cameras and a small crowd came to watch. I sparred with Darren Hamilton, Larry Ekundayo and Alex Dilmaghani. Four rounds each so I could get a twelve-rounder in. When the television cameras are on, the bright light beaming down on us, the crowd booing and cheering. That is when your performance matters. Personally I feel like Darren will believe he can win. So will Spencer. Spencer was in Danny Williams corner when he beat Mike Tyson in America. That is doing the seemingly impossible. Sometimes an underdog has a moment, a chance to do something great. Most underdogs never do this, but it only takes that one time. Darren Hamiltons one time will not be tonight.

I stayed in my room all day. I had a big breakfast which consisted of a bowl of porridge with bananas and honey. Scrambled eggs, baked beans, mushrooms with two brown bread toast. A bowl of fruit and yogurt finished it off. I washed this down with some fresh orange juice.

Through the day I snacked on pistachio nuts, protein and carbohydrate energy bars and drinks. By fight time my body will be full of energy.

Last night Mark Harnell told me that I would be fighting after David Price which could be 11.15 to 1130pm as Sky Sports coverage would be live from 1030pm after the Champions League final between Bayern Munich and Chelsea.

A great result for Tottenham Hotspur fans would be for me to win and be the first British 140lbs fighter to win four British title Championship fights in 17 years and only the third man to do it in 29 years.
Then for Chelsea to lose as Spurs finished fourth place in this seasons Premier League and to guarantee a place in next season Champions League we need Chelsea to lose in the final as only four British teams are able to qualify.

I'm going to do my part of the job. Let's hope the Germans help us Spurs fans out.

Before all my fights I watch my favorite fighters.
Marvelous Marvin Hagler vs John 'The Beast' Mugabe always gets viewed.
Hagler was a great champion and took on all challengers. I'm from the same mold.
My reign as British champion is something that will be remembered. I want to knock out all of my challengers. Darren Hamilton tonight and Steve Williams next, then I can own the Lonsdale belt and move back onto the world scene.

Sunday 20th May 2012

To my shock I did not get the decision last night. I still believe I won, without a doubt. I was calm all the way through the fight because at no time did I think I was losing. He was doing his jab thing. I was the aggressor, I was the champion and I was landing the quality shots.
He threw 670 to my 665 but we landed with the same amount of punches. It was a 21% success rate. Jim Watt who was a Sky Sports commentator had me winning by one round. Two of the judges had me losing by five rounds. That is scandalous. To me

there were dark forces at play, you can say I'm a bad loser but maybe the British Boxing Board of control did not want me to make history as the first man in 17 years to win four British title fights in a row.

Don Charles was in my corner and he trains Dereck Chisora who is going against the BBBofC in his fight with David Haye. Don Charles has a letter to the board threatening legal action if he is banned for taking part in the event. He went on a television show during the week to speak about the situation and this morning he is in the national papers as David Haye is boasting of breaking his jaw when the scuffle happened in Germany.

An employee at BoxNation who wanted to interview me on Monday even said that with Ricky Hatton being dropped by Sky Sports that they could have had power in the decision as well. If I would have won that would have been one less British champion on their screens as Ricky has been talking to BoxNation and Channel 5 about televising his fighters.

I received loads of supportive messages and loads of hate mail but the loss gave me a sigh of relief as I was proud to be British champion, I just hated fighting the British fighters. I had no drive or motivation and that showed in this performance. I did enough to win but I was going through the motions.

Ricky Hatton promised me an International title fight in July and I want to see if they will support me and help me bounce back. They have failed in their roll as promoter so far. Now is the time to step up.

Josesito Lopez is fighting Victor Ortiz on June 22nd as Kendall Holt pulled out of his fight with Lopez and Andre Berto failed his drug test so can't fight Ortiz.

I have been offered fights with all three of these fighters in the past. Now I can accept them as the British title is not holding me back.

I had zero motivation fighting the likes of Darren Hamilton and Ben Murphy. You can look back and think maybe I should have taken the Lopez fight as I could have won it but I was a proud British champion.

I can go back to the world scene. I'm disappointed to lose but I'll be back bigger and better. It is amusing how the British boxing fans do not respect my boxing resume. All they know me as is British champion when I was successful before I held the title. Darren Hamilton will achieve nothing else in his career. I will be all his career is about.
Muhammad Ali, Mike Tyson and Sugar Ray Robinson lost to nobodies when they were left uninspired or motivated by their opponents. I'm no different!
I'll take a two week vacation in Jamaica and think about my next steps. I would be up for the International title fight in July, Hatton offered me before the Hamilton loss. Will have to see what Hatton promotions have planned for me.

Tuesday 26th June 2012

Losing to Darren Hamilton was a stain on my record. He is the first British fighter I have lost to in my nine year professional career. It is the first time I have lost in Britain since 2005. That is a long seven years. Many boxing experts and fans believe it was a close fight and it could have gone either way. In my mind I won that fight. I controlled the fight from beginning to end. No doubt there are some rounds I lost. I believe I won eight to Darren's four rounds and that is me being generous. I felt in control all through the fight. When Don Charles told me to step it up at the end of round six to make it convincing. I did! Don Charles, Harry Keitt and Dave Brown had no doubts that I won. My cut-man Mick Williamson thought I lost. I feel safe when he is in my corner and I trust him with my life when it comes to cuts, bumps or grazes

sustained during the fight. When I have my team around me I am ultra confident. I will retire believing that the British Board of Control went against me in the fight because of Don Charles association with Dereck Chisora and Frank Warren. Maybe even Sky Sports had something to do with it as I am signed to Hatton promotions and they have just dropped him as a promoter meaning this would be my last appearance on their channel for a while. I will never accept that I lost through my own lack of performance, just like with my loses to Judex Meema and Oscar Milkitas seven years previous. I have never been a fan of British judging system. That is a reason I chose to fight abroad.
Germany gets stick but I feel Britain is just as bad if not worse when it comes to home town decisions and poor officiating.

I am waiting to see what Hattons plans are for me. They may want to renegotiate my contract but there will be none of that. They failed me as a promoter. I signed with them eight months ago and I've fought on Frank Maloney shows twice. I have been paid half of what I should have got paid for both fights which is nothing to do with Maloney but the lack of organization at Hatton promotion. I want to fight in America again but I'm not going there as a loser. I want two comeback fights first. I would be ready for July and October then I would love to fight Jessie Vargas on Mayweather's undercard. It is possible but Hatton need to get active. I've not been happy with how they have treated me. I was supposed to fight Barrera in July but that will not happen. If I fight in July I want a Welterweight fight as 140lbs takes too much out of me.

Rene has not said a word to me since Monday so I assume he is having problems with Hattons as they probably want to offer me less money or even void our contract. Whatever the weather I am not bothered.
I must say that as British champion I did not enjoy being the

favorite. I enjoy being the underdog and proving people wrong. I can only get that feeling on the world scene.

It is amusing how Amir Khan is fighting Danny Garcia on July 14th. Danny is a man I clearly beat but once again boxing politics did me dirty. They are trying to make Danny out to be some threat but I believe I could beat him more convincingly now than I did two years ago. Boxing is full of fakes.
I'm determined as ever to fulfill my ability. I have 31 wins and 5 loses at the minute. My target is to reach 50 wins. I will be retired by the time I am 40 years old but until then my life is dedicated to boxing. Losing is a part of any sport and it is how you come back that determines you as a sportsmen. I've comeback strong in the past and I expect to comeback again. Roger Federera and Rafael Nadal on the odd occasion lose to lesser players on the tennis circuit. We are human and have odd days where our form slips but all true great players bounce back and I believe I am a great, British fighter. I am one of British boxing best exports right now even if they hate to admit it.

Ambition and determination is something that I have abundance of. You have to have those to achieve what you want as you will have setbacks in life. Determination will get you to your destination in the end.

After my British title loss, I received loads of criticism but just as much praise and love. Just walking around London, people would stop me and show their appreciation for what I am doing in my life.
I'm from a place where we are not supposed to achieve anything. I'm showing everyone that we can.

Training camp with
World WBO lightweight champion Ricky Burns

Monday 27th August 2012

I arrived in Glasgow around 10am. Billy Nelson, trainer to Ricky Burns picked me up and dropped me to his gym straight away. No rest just thrown into sparring with the two weight world champion Ricky Burns. I was shattered but I got through eight rounds with Ricky. He's in great shape but I used my boxing brain, skills and heart to get through it. Everyday will get easier now.

Bradley Saunders the former amateur world number one is currently training with Billy Nelson. I watched him spar when I was waiting for Ricky to come. He is a world class talent. He'll easily be British champion. He has the talent to be world champion but as I told him he'll have to stay dedicated and train hard to get there.
I went for a thirty minute run with Bradley in the evening. I was so tired but I knew come bed time I'll get a good nights sleep.

Tuesday 28th August 2012

If Ricky can handle me he will have no problem with Kevin Mitchell. I expect Kevin to get knocked out or the referee to stop the fight. Kevin has beaten John Murray and Bredis Prescott but been knocked out by the limited but strong Michael Katisdis. I have beaten Demarcus Corley, Delvin Rodriguez, Lenny Daws and Jason Cook.

Wednesday 29th August 2012

I went down to Alex Morrison's gym midday with Michael Robert Senior and Junior.
Michael Junior was sparring with Derry Matthews who is taking part in the next installment of Prizefighter in just over a month's time.

It was the first time meeting Derry but he said if I ever needed sparring I was welcome to come up and stay at his place and we could get some rounds together.

I bumped into my old foe Craig Docherty whilst I was there as he trains at that gym now and then.

Thursday 30th August 2012

I turn 32 years old today and I didn't show signs aging in sparring. I let it all out with Ricky today. He seemed to feel the session more than the other two sessions we have previously done.

I told Billy Nelson on the first day that I would get better with each session over the week. Maybe he did not believe me when I told him, he replied, "Of course you will Ash."

Ricky has a reputation for running guys out the gym through his intense sparring sessions. He is full on and in great condition but that is also my strength.

Boxing reporter Tom Gray who watched our sparring session said that Jim Watt asked him a boxing trivia question in Vegas to test his boxing knowledge. He repeated it to Billy and myself. "What British fighter fought for three world titles over three weights but never won his world titles challenges in the 1980's." Billy and I looked at each other. I fought about the top British fighters in the 80's. Tony Sibson came to mind and I just blurted it out. Tom couldn't believe I got it so quick. It was a lucky guess if I'm honest.

Billy said, "Guess this one then. What British fighter won a world title but never won it in the ring and was just awarded it." I was stuck. I replied "I have no idea." Billy replied "I'll give you a clue. He's a wanker." Straight away "Alex Arthur" just out of my mouth. Everyone started laughing and told Ricky that the clue was that the fighter was a wanker and instantly I said, "Alex Arthur'. I don't know Alex but being in Scotland. His name just came into my head. They jokingly called him "Mr. MBE." We laughed it off, but it was amusing.

End of a relationship

Thursday 22nd November 2012

On Saturday 27th October, Richard Poxon announced it on Twitter that I would be fighting on the Ricky Hatton show. That is how I found out.

In the morning I had a change of heart and told Rene I'd go through with the fight. Sometimes to take a step forward, you must take two steps back. Keeping busy is the most important thing.

Hatton promotions are in breach of contract.
Rene is working closely with Hatton promotions on Ricky's comeback so you could say he is in conflict of interest but without him I would not be on the show.
He also paid £1000 on flying Jihad out here and putting him up in a hotel. He has also paid for my and Dave's travel to Manchester from London which set him back just over £200. All these expenses should be Hattons. Mick Hennessey covered these costs when I challenged Lenny Daws and defend the British title against Jason Cook.
Sometimes the grass is not greener on the other side. In hindsight I made the wrong move to Hatton promotions.
They don't rate me as a fighter and I'm just part of the furniture now.

I was interviewed on Sports Live TV on Primetime on Monday. Tim Witherspoon was a guest on the show and even he praised me for my style of fighting. He said he'd watched me twice and had been impressed at how I was confident enough to give away a few rounds to figure out my opponent then dismantle them. That was nice to hear from a former world heavyweight champion.

Gary, trainer for four years to former British cruiserweight champion Leon Williams saw me in the gym and told me that he is impressed by my mental strength and that is my biggest attribute. He said you came from the bottom and not many fighters can fight their way through the club circuit to the championship level. In his eyes what I've done is a true Rocky story. Sometimes it is nice to hear these kind of words from experienced people on the circuit. Makes the hard work worthwhile and for people to notice my success has come with hard work, dedication and a never say die attitude. He told me to keep doing what I'm doing as I'm there now so just reap the benefits from it.

Dean Powell, the WBO's matchmaker of 2012 sent me a message in the build up to my fight with Chris Truman. He said, "Stay Dedicated mate, It will pay off! You are a great example to all our young boxers!" Frank Warren offered me a deal just before Hattons but he seemed more interested in me fighting Frankie Gavin and I had no interest in that fight. So I signed with Hatton promotions as Ricky said he would back me in my pursuit of big fights but he has failed to do that after fourteen months.

Jihad believes in my talent and he will get my mind right for the fight. I know Harry isn't happy that he will not be in my corner but we are a team and Jihad has earned a trip over here.

The great Michael Phelps once said, "There will be obstacles. There will be doubters. There will be mistakes. But with hard work. There are no limits."

I push my body to its limit and beyond so it is all mental now.

Friday 23rd November 2012

Rene sent me a text message on my way to Manchester. It read "Ashley, I'm sure everything is on point. Let me know f you need ANYTHING? I'll see you tomorrow. René PS met the Golden Boy crew yesterday. They're very interested in you. They shared the Garcia memories with me." That message motivated me even more to put on a show. Golden Boy have some of the best 140lbs and 147lbs fighters in the world on their roster and I want some of that.
I need to be an animal tomorrow. I've been vicious in sparring and I need to be that way in the fight. Chris will give it a go but I have to punish him and win.

The Ricky Hatton weigh in was an event in itself. I've never seen a crowd the size that fitted in a Town Hall. Al Berstein, MC Michael Buffer and WBA welterweight champion Paul Malignaggi was in the building. It is dawning on me that 19,000 fight fans will be watching me fight tomorrow. It will be amazing! Chris believes he will raise his game. He will need to. If I raise my game. We will see a knockout win from me.

Jihad had contact with Tony Bellew and his team whilst in Manchester. They've asked him to be part of the team which is fantastic. I was hoping that would happen with us bringing Jihad over here. He deserves recognition as he is a good trainer and Tony Bellew is getting a lot of exposure from Sky Sports at the minute so that will also shine a light on Jihad. Sharing success is not always through monetary gains. I don't pay Jihad and Harry a lot so I always recommend their services to fighters when they want to go New York City and train. Ajose Olusegun is another fighter I've sent their way. I'm glad I could bring Tony Bellew and Jihad together.

Saturday 24th November 2012

I did not end up fighting as Ricky Hatton lost his match and I was a floater on the show. I still got paid but I wanted to fight. I had basically wasted eighteen months with Hatton Promotions. I had no fights under their promotional banner. I was more disappointed in Ricky as he sold me a dream at his house and when it came to directing me to big fights, he did nothing. I blamed Richard Poxon as he ran the company and would put his fighters ahead of me.

Friday 1st March 2013

I was on my own again, but I was used to it. I had no one I could count on in this boxing game. I was getting shafted by promoters, managers, and commissions.
I went to Luxembourg for a fight just after Christmas then I plotted my next move. I had lost the British title so there was no interest in me in Britain. Frank Warren and Eddie Hearn wouldn't work with me. I thought about fighting for the IBO world championship as it was vacant. Then a lightbulb went off in my head. I'll go back to Las Vegas and see if I can get on to Mayweather Promotions. Floyd Mayweather was friendly towards me and the whole gym was welcoming when I went last year March. I saw Ishe Smith win the world championship and he was with Floyd. He had a similar record to me and was two years older than me. I was going to Las Vegas!
I was in the last chance saloon. I had nowhere else to go.

British Boxing Board of Control

I've never really had a good relationship with the British Boxing Board of Control. I have always abided by their rules and regulations but they seem not to protect or support their license holders.

I remember back in 2002 when I first applied for my boxing license with them. I had an appointment with the Southern Area council. They were around twelve men sitting round a rectangle table with the head opposite you and the other members down the sides. They asked me questions about turning professional. Why did I want to turn professional. What was my amateur record. They asked me some of the rules and regulations and wished me luck on my chosen profession. Of course they did not believe I would achieve what I have in my career. No one in the amateur or professional codes did.

I was fortunate that I had Rene in my life by this stage of my career as the resources Rene had at his disposal, I was protected as much as I could possibly be. The BBBofC didn't back me when the EBU banned me from competing for the European title and Dave Coldwell didn't go by our agreement. How many Ashley Theophane's had been failed by the Board. I'm sure there were many more which is sad as they are there to protect our rights. Too many fighters are exploited by managers and promoters. It is a shame that the commission we pay on a yearly basis takes our money but does little to regulate and enforce their own rules.

I arrived back from my vacation with my brother at 730am after nine long hours on the plane. We would not get home until after 10am. I simply put down my suitcase. I showered and got dressed for the British Boxing Board of Control hearing that I had waited ten months for.

I expected the hearing to last two hours instead it was just under five hours.
I had my legal team from Mishcon de Reya and Mick Hennessey had his legal team who were supposed to be also good.

My legal team pointed out to the Board that Hennessey Sport had broken not one but three of their rules whilst dealing with me.
During the hearing it felt like we were destined to win as everything was on our side.

Hennessey's barrister had to quote cases from 1890 and 1910 to bring relevance to his case it was that weak. Hennessey had admitted breaking the BBBofC's rule of not paying me straight but their argument was that they believed Cestus to be my manager and I never said they were not at any time
Mick Hennessey spoke very highly of Cestus like they had worked magic with me when in reality they had tried with all their might to turn me into an opponent. I had turn down loads of fights which would have been certain to be a loss.
The two British title fights I had at Wembley under Hennessey were my favorite fights in Britain at this stage of my career.

Les Potts sent a letter a week later summarizing what went on in the hearing;

REGULATION 9.37, 24 & 25 HEARING

On Wednesday 6th June 2012 you appeared before the Southern Area Council represented by Counsel Daniel Saoul and Solicitor Liz Ellen of Mishcon de Reya Solicitors. Promoter Mick Hennessy also appeared represented by Counsel Tom Cleaver.

The Council were advised that you had lodged a complaint against Mr Hennessy that you had fought on a Mick Hennessy promotion on 23rd July 2011 against Jason Cook and following your contest Mr Hennessy had acted contrary to your instructions and the rules of the Board by paying the sum of £6,250 from your purse to Cestus Management a New Jersey based marketing company.

The Council heard evidence from yourself, Mr Hennessy and witness Vicki Squirrel of MHSL. Documentary evidence was also submitted and considered by the Council before closing statements were heard from Mr Saoul and Mr Cleaver.

The Council then deliberated and decided that the Regulation 24 complaint against Mr Hennessy (MHSL) should be dismissed.

The Council found that there was some form of global management agreement in place in 2009 between Ashley Theophane and Cestus which they were not satisfied had been terminated and which gave Cestus the right to 25% of the purse direct from the Promoter. This was given effect in relation to the contest against Lenny Daws by MHSL making a payment of 25% of the purse direct to Cestus on the instructions of Mr Theophane. The Council found as a fact that Mrs. Squirrel of MHSL liaised with Cestus regarding management services for Mr Theophane in the normal way up until the date of the contest against Jason Cook and neither she nor Mr Hennessy were aware (if it be the case) that Mr Theophane had terminated the management contract with Cestus or had given different instructions as to MHSL making direct payment to Cestus of 25%. They had not been told by Mr Theophane or any other person that the instruction by Mr Theophane to pay 25% of his purse direct to Cestus had been withdrawn. They were made aware only that Solicitors, Mischon de Reya would be acting for Mr Theophane in legal matters.

The Council were not satisfied that the evidence relied upon by Mr Theophane, including either the letter from his Solicitor or the omission of the signature of Gina Lacovou from BBBofC documents, was sufficient to discharge the burden on Mr Theophane to bring to the attention of Mr Hennessy/MHSL that in relation to the Jason Cook fight he should not give effect to what had been the agreed arrangement that Cestus would again be paid 25% of the purse direct. As a principal, Mr Theophane had an obligation to notify Mr Hennessy/HMSL clearly of the termination (if this had happened) of such an arrangement with his actual or apparent agent, Cestus, and of the withdrawal of his instructions to pay 25% direct, if it was to render Mr Hennessy/MHSL liable for making such payment. The Council were satisfied that Mrs. Squirrel and Mr Hennessy acted in good faith and had no intention to favor Cestus over Mr Theophane in relation to the matter.

The Council found with regard to Regulation 9.37, which provides for payment of the purse to the Boxer himself or to the Boxer's duly authorised representative if the Boxer so desires, that the Lenny Daws and Jason Cook contests were both part of a 'course of deciding' in which Gina Lacovou of Cestus had been held out expressly or impliedly by Mr Theophane as being Mr Theophanes Manager and entitled to be paid commission direct by the Promoter, pursuant to some form of management agreement made between Cestus and Mr Theophane in August 2009. Having regard to this, there was no breach of Regulations 9.17, 9.20 or 9.37 which provides as previously stated, because the payment was on the express or implied instruction of Mr Theophane so far as MHSL were made aware.

The Council also considered a request for costs from Mr Cleaver and after consideration decided that there would be no order for costs. The Chairman also outlined the appeals process which is detailed below:-

Regulation 28.4. Notice of appeal shall be in writing stating the grounds upon which the appeal is made and must be received by the General Secretary within 14 clear days of the receipt or deemed receipt by the Appellant of the decision or order of the Tribunal. Every appellant shall deposit with the General Secretary a sum at the prevailing rate at the same time as notice of appeal is given. If the appellant is unsuccessful such sum shall be forfeited to the British Boxing Board of Control Charity unless the Stewards of Appeal otherwise order.

Yours sincerely

Les Potts
Area Secretary

EUROPEAN BOXING UNION

I never had no aspiration to be European champion until I beat Lenny Daws and I noticed he was number one in Europe.
My team got in contact with the European Boxing Union a few days after my win, asking about if I would take the European number one ranking that Lenny Daws had. They came back to us with a flat no and stated that I would not be fighting for the EBU title as I had fought four times in Germany under the German Boxing Association (GBA).

I knew that this was in violation of my human rights as they were stopping me from working in Europe.

I got in contact with some lawyers who work on a no win no fee claim. European Champion Paul McCloskey was about to fight Amir Khan for the world title so I was being refused the right to make a lot of money.

I got in contact with the British Boxing Board of Control. They said they would have a word with EBU at the next monthly meeting. Months went by and the BBBoC never got back to me. They were not happy when Rene got involved with his legal team. The BBBofC refused to back me once again but what did they expect me to do.

EMAILS

Je dois lui répondre que, comme deja écrit au British Boxin g Board, ce boxeur n'est pas classé car il a travaillé sous la GBA et non sous le BDB, féd. affiliée à l'EBU. D'autre part on a deja désigné le co-challenger de Giuseppe Lauri!

Dear Mr Warren,

As already communicated to the British Boxing Board, unfortunately, we cannot consider the boxers that have fought under commissions of Federations not affiliated to the EBU.
We perfectly know that Ashley Theophane has a BBBofC license, but he fought under the supervision of the GBA, which is not the German Federation affiliated to the EBU.

Moreover, we already have appointed the co-challenger to the EBU super-lightweight vacant title, which is Denis Shafikov.

Kind regards
Enza Jacoponi
General Secretary

PS We would like to inform you that all kind of matters must be communicated through the EBU affiliated federations which has the task of informing us.

From: Hoodstripes Entertainment
Sent: Monday, February 21, 2011 1:07 AM
To: Boxing European Union
Subject: 140lbs Rankings

Dear Sirs

Ashley Theophane beat European number one contender and British champion Lenny Daws on Saturday 19th February. Paul McCloskey is fighting Amir Khan for the World Title.

I would like to ask you to allow Ashley Theophane as the new British champion to move into Lenny Daws number one spot and challenge the next available contender for the vacant European title.

It would be an honor for Ashley to fight for the European championship and be champion.

Ashley has beaten IBF World number 3 Delvin Rodriguez, former World champion Demarcus Corley, former Commonwealth champion Craig Docherty, former English champion Alan Bosworth and British champion Lenny Daws.
Ashley is worthy of the number one spot.

Let me know your decision

Regards

Stacy Warren

A few law firms showed interested but when Rene got involved with me, the law firm he uses, Mischon de Reya contacted the EBU and within six weeks they got the EBU to do a U turn on my ban and changing or implementing a rule for the future. If you fight for an unsanctioned commission in Europe, you will only be banned or suspended for a year.

It was great work but very frustrating for Cestus to try and steal Rene and Mischon de Reya's great work that they had done and try say that they had got me a European title shot when in fact I wasn't allowed to challenge for the title until Rene helped me out. By that time my relationship with Cestus was irreparable.

RENE CARAYOL

I met Rene Carayol in Andy's Barbers on Marylands Road in Paddington. I had been going there for twenty plus years and I was just comfortable with the surroundings. Andy would put up newspaper clippings of me, my fight posters and my calendars. I would normally just go there and stay out of the banter. I had seen Rene at Andy's a few times and Andy would say that he is a good man to know. I didn't care who he was or who he was in with. He would always pull up in a Bentley and he came across as if he thought he knew it all. I normally stayed out of their conversations but Andy must have been talking about me to Rene, saying I'm fighting for the British Title. Rene looked at me as I messaged someone on my Blackberry and said, "Is this guy any good Andy?'. Andy said that I'm going to win. Rene said he would buy four ringside tickets so they could go down and watch me. When he left, Andy said to me "make sure you win. I don't want to look stupid". I told Andy "I'm going to do what I do Andy". Andy told me to come with them in the Bentley but I said I was good in the BMW I would be driving.
After I won I went on holiday to Dominican Republic for two weeks with my mother. So when I came back, I went round to Andy's barber shop and he told me how Rene was impressed with my performance and wanted to help me, so he gave me Rene's business card that he had left him. I text Rene a week later, he said how impressed he was with me but no one knew who I was outside of the boxing world. He felt I should be more known. We arranged to meet up the following weekend. He would pick me up and take to his home in Swiss Cottage for a meeting.

When I got to his home, we had to walk up a few flights of stairs.

He had a modern home with statues from different countries placed spaciously around. Paintings and framed pictures of his family were all over. He was obviously a man who was successful and well off and very family orientated.

Rene spoke about what he does and I listened. He had asked to meet me and I just listened because everyone wants to help you when you are in a good place. I had recently had a meeting with Frank Warren. I was British champion and I was being offered fights Stateside. So everything was going well. Cestus management were a nuisance but I could handle them.
Rene said he wanted to upgrade my image as he believed I could be a successful brand. He said he would like to work with me for a month and see if there was a future in this project. If either one of us felt like it wasn't working, we could go our separate ways and I wouldn't owe him no money for the time and resources he had invested in me. I guess I had nothing to lose but walking away from Rene was not so easy. Many times I felt like walking away. I was used to doing things on my own and not being part of a team. Team work was unknown to me. I got used to it but it was a slow and sometimes bumpy process.

I told Rene that I had to give back the Lonsdale belt in the week so he arranged a meeting with his team on the Monday. It was so weird having a team work with me. They all had big ideas of what they wanted to do or what they thought was possible.
At that time I did not believe it possible but working with Rene after a year I did believe anything was achievable with him. Of course I had to keep winning but Tottenham Hotspur did a Celebrity profile on me. They were happy to have me walk out on pitch at Half time during a Premiership match. Ted Baker made me an Ambassador, Wellman who I had been working with for a few years before Rene came into the picture. They made a national campaign featuring me. They did that due to the Rene's rebranding of me. Rene wanted a Beckham type of image where

I am approachable to everyone. My image did improve and a few companies wanted to be part of my team.

Rene and his team made me a new website which alone would get me great opportunities. Many people had said it was the best around in Boxing. Rene sent me to his tailor to get a suit fitted for a photoshoot he wanted to do in a couple days time. He was all full on. I wasn't complaining, I said I would be up for pretty much anything unless it involved missing training.

Jacuk was Rene's driver and he would pick me up to drive me to the Tailors down Saville Row. Being British champion certainly had it's perks.

The Brand Treasure photoshoot was done in Acton with photographer Amit and Naroop. They had done photoshoots with Sugababes, Ricky Gervis, Taio Cruz, Tinchy Styder and Tinie Temper, along with loads of other celebrities and pop stars. Rene did not tell me he would be interviewing me for a Video interview were we spoke about my hopes and dreams. Sky Sports would say that it was the best interview of mine that they had seen. It was a long and tiring day but a day that was the start of something special. Rene and I had been working together for under a week and we had accomplished so much in rebranding me.

I had now met majority of Rene's team.

Rene had a great team working for him. Was he lucky to have great staff or did he have a good judge of character. I don't know but I loved his team to bits. Coming from my back ground, people never really helped me. Maybe they were Rene's employee's so they had no say in working on my project but the love and support they did it with my touching. You know if people like or care about you and I generally got a good feeling about them.

Rene got his Lawyers working on my project which had issues to deal with as being a high level boxer having a legal team around you should be standard but many of us are not educated in business, so we get taken for granted and we end up signing contracts we shouldn't.
Mishcon de Reya would work on many issues in my career and they always did a great job. They helped me get out of my contract with Cestus management. They got me ranked in Europe again and they dealt with the Hennessey Sport situation. Rene would call on Liz Ellen, Mishcon's sport lawyer for anything to do with my career. I was backed and supported to no end. It is scary to think of how much Rene's had invested in me. I guess that is one reason why he wanted to see this project through but we generally got on and if he chose to walk away at anytime we would still be friends. Leaders make leaders and I felt like Rene was making me into a leader. He wanted me to have a business to run after my boxing career was finished. I planned on being a high end personal fitness trainer. Rene had his own plan of what he wanted me to do after boxing.

It was touchy at times when Rene was trying to take control over my boxing career and Cestus management were still in the picture. They were offering me fights Stateside that I wanted. It was just always low paid. Nothing was more than $20,000. A year after working with them I was getting offers that ranged from $50,000 to $100,000.

Hennessey gave Cestus management 25% of my purse for my fight with Jason Cook, which was at Wembley. When I told them that they should be dealing with Liz Ellen and that I was self managed, so to deal with me directly. Cestus had failed me as a fighter. They had got me two of my biggest and most respected results in America but they did not build on that. They still tried to make me an opponent. The direction of my career differed from were I thought it should be going and where they thought.

I asked Rene why he had chosen to help me. He said that someone once helped him, so now that he is in the position to help other people, he does when he can. He said that sometimes people work hard but they don't know the right people or have the right connections. He said he saw something in me and believes that I could be a brand. Ted Baker had come on board. Westminster city homes were interested in opening a gym and using my name and Wellman had ran a national campaign with their sports supplements using my name and image. That would never have happened before Rene. There was much more we could do, but that would take me winning more titles. You will never find someone more hungry for success or determined to achieve their goals than me.

I have been very patient in my career as I believed that one day I would get to the mountain top. My persistence and perspiration make an unbeatable combination for success and I was the perfect example if you work hard, you can achieve something special. With Rene behind me I believed anything was possible. I always pushed myself to be the best I could be and I never was happy with where I was. I always believed I could be better. After 35 fights, I still believed I had not peaked as I needed those fights that would make me dig deep inside myself and find that super power that I knew was within me. I believed I was destined for greatness after somewhat successful fights with Demarcus Corley, Delvin Rodriguez, Lenny Daws and Jason Cook. These were good fighters but I never had to reach deep inside myself. The split decision loss to Danny Garcia which most experts and fans believed I won, showed how far I really could go, as he would go on to beat Kendall Holt, Nate Campbell Amir Khan, Erik Morales and many more. I just needed the right people behind me. I signed with Hatton promotions but after a year of signing with them I was not sure I had the right promotional outfit behind me. They concentrated on their other fighters Anthony Crolla,

Martin Murray and Steve Qiugg, who were no better than me.

I dreamed big as a kid and to be a thirty years old adult and see that I was achieving my childhood dreams, made me very proud of myself. I pushed even harder as I knew I would always be the underdog but with hard work and dedication anything was possible. It is useless to have dreams if you never try to fulfill them.

Once you are a champion you will forever be known as a champion, that is the beauty of sports as us athletes dedicate our lives and sometimes put our health at risk for sport but to be called a champion or champ can makes those risks so worthwhile. I loved being a champion and spending thirty hours a week for many years in the gym sweating pushing my body through pain. Running on the road at 3am or 5am in the morning was all part of the process, that I never regret.

I always said that I make the impossible, possible and nothing is truly impossible. I came from nothing and in my eyes I had everything against me so my boxing career was a success. What I did, what I achieved, was the impossible because no one believed it was really possible even Mr. Akay used to say just give your best but as the years went by and he saw I was getting these fantastic results, he believed in me more. I may not be the best boxer or most talented in the world but I would work so hard in the gym that by the time we have to fight each other, I would believe I could beat anyone. I was never scared to test myself and see what I could do.

I used to watch the youngsters at All Stars boxing club and I would see those dreams in them. I inspired them and they motivated me to be reach the highest heights.

Sometimes people come into your life and you can wonder why they are there or even fight them on it but if they are sincere that will shine through. Within seven months of working with me, Rene Carayol had achieved a huge amount even by his standards. He had got lawyers, Mischon de Reya to overturn my ban from the European Union rankings. I was now 4th in Europe. He had dealt with the break away from Cestus management. It was not yet finished but the relationship was over. He had put the idea of a chain of Treasure's gyms in my head. We had now joined up with Hatton promotions and the future looked rosy, better than twelve months ago when I was squabbling with Cestus management.

Rene would be pivotal in me joining Mayweather promotions. He never let me down and supported me over the next eight years of us working together.

HATTON PROMOTIONS

Jakub drove Rene and I up to Manchester from London. It was a four and a half hour drive, which was tortuous.

Lucky, I had completed an early morning two hour cardiovascular and strength conditioning session so I was a tad bit tired and caught a nap while on our journey.

It was an eleven hour round trip but worthwhile.

I had seen all of Ricky Hatton's fights from when he stepped up to championship level. I recorded everyone at my weight who were at domestic, European and world level, just so I knew what the standard was and you never know who you was going to fight from when you were fighting for titles.

We turned onto Ricky's road and it was very nice. Lovely houses on either side of the road.
At the end of the road, was Ricky's mansion and it was by far the best.
Rene rang the bell and Ricky answered the intercom. Just hearing his voice put a smile on my face. I just couldn't believe I was actually meeting Ricky Hatton at his home.

Ricky opened the door and welcomed us in. I shook his hand and I felt excitement run through my body.

I was actually in Ricky 'The Hitman' Hatton's mansion.

He directed Rene and I to the kitchen where Richard Poxon, who had been negotiating the deal with Rene and Ricky Hatton's business adviser was waiting for us.

There was a lunch laid out. We shook hands with everyone at the table and sat down.

Louise, Ricky Hatton's wife walked in and she greeted us. She was heavily pregnant.

Behind Ricky, you could see his garden, which had sheep roaming outside.

Ricky spoke about the benefits of signing with him. What he had done for his fighters and what he could do and was willing to do.

Richard Poxon spoke about the two dates in November available to me.

Ricky's business adviser spoke about Hatton promotions on a business level. He said there was support there for me as a fighter and a person. If I had problems in any aspect they would help me if I needed help.

Rene spoke about the goals I wish to achieve and why he thinks we can do it with Hatton promotions.
I spoke about what Ricky has achieved and me wanting to follow in his foot steps and try achieve something similar. Ricky had conquered Britain then took on the World. I wanted to do the same thing and Ricky said he would support and help me reach my goals.

I left Ricky's house feeling like he was the right person to take me to the World title.

One month later I would sign the contract. I would have done it sooner but Rene and Mishcon de Reya law firm were dealing with Cestus management. Gina may have had some legal advice but they were not willing or able to get legal representation, so she dealt with the situation with Mishcon. Liz did a great job and, in the end we ended up walking as the contract I had with Cestus was fraudulent and not legal in any case.

As Hatton promotions did not bid for the fight with Nigel Wright, I had to go to County Durham, a place I had never heard of before. Frank Maloney won the purse bids to that fight as he was the only promoter to bid for it. It was good business for him but working with Frank Maloney was a terrible experience. After dealing with him once I never wanted to do business with him again. Penny pincher came to mind. I did not have no communication from him from when the BBBofC announced he would be hosting the fight. I received no tickets or posters for the fight. He chose the cheapest route to County Durham which was the train and the hotel was of the basic sort. I have worked with over ten promoters in my life, at that stage of my career and he was by far the worse.

Mike Michael from Cestus had been quiet for a while as Hatton promotions had told him to take them to court if he thought he had a case against them and Liz from Mischon had them under control. Mike had contacted Frank Maloney, obviously trying to get money from my purse. When Rene had contacted Frank Maloney, he let him know that I was to be paid and no one else.

In the new year I had hopes of some big fights under the Hatton promotions banner. Six months since meeting and signing with the Hatton promotion I felt not wanted or appreciated by the company. They were slow to deal with the Nigel Wright situation. The Boxing Board of control were still saying Nigel Wright was my mandatory challenger, even though he failed his brain scan for our fight on December 10th. They said that it was his livelihood and they would give him a chance to get a second opinion. Well boxing was also my livelihood and I should have been given a chance to make a voluntary title defense or have a keep busy fight but Richard Poxon was slow on the case. I got Rene to ask about giving Lenny Daws a rematch in March. Again! Richard was slow on the case and never finalized anything so the British Boxing board of control released their mandatory fights and said I had to fight Steve Williams by the end of June which still gave me plenty of time to fight beforehand. I went off to training camp in New York and Las Vegas to get myself in shape and shift some excess pounds so I would be ready. When Wednesday 14th came, Hatton promotions basically did not bid for my fight with Steve Williams or the bid was so low that Frank Maloney won again. I was fed up of Hatton promotions by now and just wanted out of my contract. My contract stated I was due to receive thirty thousand pounds for a mandatory and by Frank Maloney bid I would receive half that which was £15,000 and a disgraceful amount of money for me to fight for. If Hatton did not cover the £15,000 they would basically be in breach of contract and I would be a free agent.

In the end they gave me £7,500 and said they would give me a fight in July, ten months after signing with them. That again would end up not happening.

I didn't fight until September which was a year after signing with them. I had no relationship with Hatton promotions. I just wanted the fights they promised me. It was a shame as I did believe Ricky Hatton could get me some great fights, he just didn't. I felt let down by one of the most successful British boxers of all time.

Mayweather's Gym ¤ Las Vegas Training Camp

Monday 4th March 2013

I came to Las Vegas exactly 12 months ago to the day.

Floyd Mayweather is in camp for his fight against Robert 'The Ghost' Guerrero.
Last time he was preparing to fight Miguel Cotto.

I've been working hard myself at All Stars Boxing Club for the last eight weeks to prepare myself. I've dropped 8lbs and I'm in pretty good shape.

Last year I only came for 2 weeks. This time, I'll be here for 4 weeks.
I'll get to meet Ishe Smith, Floyd's first world champion signed to his promotional stable and Floyd Senior, who is now training his son due to Roger's illness.

I have a good vibe about this camp.

I woke up at 5am to get in an early morning run before heading to Gatwick Airport.

I flew with Virgin Atlantic who are usually good to fly with. The flight was just under 11 hours. It did not go quick, but I was comfortable.

As a kid I would watch boxing with my father. The big fights featuring Sugar Ray Leonard, Marvin Hagler and Mike Tyson were the fighters who were hot then. I would never say I'm blessed to be doing my childhood dream as I've worked my ass off and I've had many obstacles in front of me from the start. It has been worthwhile though. I don't do it for the money or the fame. It feels weird that I have fans and people who want an autograph or a photo with me. I'm just doing a job that I love and that I'm very passionate about.

To be respected in America by my peers means everything to me. Most British fighters are seen as soft touches. I've proven that I can mix it with the best in the hardcore American gyms and when it counts under the bright lights.

I visited Mr. Akay in hospital last week as he had a stroke recently.
We had a good chat, that maybe we both needed.

For 25 years, that man has motivated and inspired me. As a 7 year old kid in 1988 to a 32 year old man in 2013. I was just another kid who wanted to box, but as the years flew by, I stood out with my hard work, dedication and resilience. I've never been the fastest or most skillful, but I give my all. Mr. A has seen the growth in me and it means a lot to me that he is proud of me.

Tuesday 5th March 2013

Early in the morning I jogged 2 miles to the 24 hour fitness gym. Worked out for 75 minutes and jogged back. It was a nice start to the day.

Everyone has been friendly to me at Mayweather Boxing Club. It is nice to be back. I never had that feeling to move to New York City, even though I've always felt comfortable there but being in Vegas feels like this is the place to be. I always thought It a weird place for boxers to go to camp but it is a great place. No doubt there is partying and gambling but as an athlete you are supposed to be focused and have tunnel vision to reach your goal. The distractions shouldn't tempt you.

As I watched the fighters sparring and training in Mayweather Boxing Club, I looked at them as prey. A lot of Americans are talented and slick but they lack that mental toughness and conditioning. That's why I wear them down in the end.

A young fighter who is due to sign with Mayweather promotions asked if I knew how to do double ups with the skipping rope. I said of course. He said he never loses. 2 minutes later he had lost. Through the week I would see him beat other fighters. I would yell out "you the man, you a beast." Just to let him know I'm really the man. Andrew Tabiti would go on to challenge for the world championship six years later in the World Boxing Series.

It was nice to see Cornelius Boza Edwards again. He's welcomed me here and made me feel at home. The gym was cleared out for Floyd's sparring but The Money Team allowed me to stay and watch.

Floyd Mayweather Senior is a master coach. He is a friendly man and it's nice to be able to watch him at close quarters and listen to his tactical thoughts on boxing.

Floyd Mayweather beat up world title challenger Sechew Powell today. Sechew did two rounds and had to come out before Floyd knocked him out. Sechew became sick and threw up at the end of round one, he staggered over to Floyd senior who was in the corner of the boxing ring, with his mouth wide open as if he is about to throw up. Floyd points to Boza, to say go over there and be sick which Sechew Powell did. It was hilarious! Sechew had to carry on sparring but was replaced at the end of the round.

Kenyan fighter Douglas Okola, who had fought Nathan Cleverly was poor and he admitted to me afterwards that he was out of shape and that Floyd was so sharp. He was nearly stopped in the first and only round he did with Floyd.

It was good to finally meet Ishe Smith. Our careers have been similar but Floyd got him a world title shot and he grabbed the opportunity with both hands. He said that I'm never in the UK and that I be everywhere. He's a down to earth, humble guy and I wish him the best.

Wednesday 6th March 2013

Las Vegas reporter Chris Robinson had scheduled to do some stuff on me at the gym today. He did a story on me last year but as I'm here for 4 weeks. He wants to do a few bits on me.

He wasn't interested in interviewing me. He said we'd do that further down the line. He just filmed me training and took some photos.

The gym is much busier than last year as that Money Mayweather bug spreads further a field.

I got in a good workout today. Working in the heat of Vegas is hard work but raises fitness levels.

The coach who asked if I wanted to spar with Zab Judah, sent an email to Brad Goodman, head matchmaker at Top Rank to see if they would be interested in getting me a fight.

A novice professional boxer who witnessed me win the double ups skipping competition
yesterday asked me how I got in shape good condition and what my record was. When I told him it was 33-5-1. He replied "you a beast man". He said that if I ever got time to do some rounds he would appreciate it and learn what he can off me.

There is a lot of love and respect in this gym, which I like. Similar to Gleason's gym in
Brooklyn, New York. Everyone wants to help each other.

Floyd started training around 5pm.

He had some new sparring partner at the gym today.
When the fighter was in the ring, Floyd shouted out "welcome him to the doghouse".
The Money Team, fighters and on lookers started to bang the ring apron and barking. For someone who was already looking nervous, now he looked petrified. Intimidation at its finest!
Leonard Ellerbe said, "Time" and the fighter came flying out at Floyd. Trying to hustle and bustle him. He caught Floyd with some shots but hit air on more occasions.
Fighters always seem to forget that Floyd does 5 minute rounds. They fade then Floyd makes them pay. After the round

one, the fighter had put in a respectable performance. He was better and more aggressive than Sechew Powell and Douglas Okola.

In round two, he tried but Floyd punished him with right hands and left hooks. The young fighter staggered all over the ring. Floyd showed no signs of letting up. Boza Edwards jumped in the ring and stopped the onslaught.

Floyd commented afterwards "Boza saved his career before it even started. Then again what fighter has been the same after being beaten by me." One of The Money Team replied "none of them".

Floyd rolled under the ropes, got his gloves changed and started to hit his favorite heavy bag. Twenty minutes non stop.

Whilst he was working on the bag. Leonard came up to me and asked how long I was in town for this time. I told him 4 weeks as the 2 weeks last time went too quick. He replied "good". He asked what my record was now and what weight I was campaigning at. I answered, then he looked at me and said, "you're a southpaw aren't you?" Regrettably, I'm not or I may have got some work with Floyd. Ishe strolled in while Floyd was hitting the bag. Floyd said, "I can get a man a title shot with no fights. They said Ishe was finished but I got him a title".

Ishe chips in "They said my career was over. Look at me now".

Nate Jones and Roger Mayweather were next waiting in the ring for Floyd as he did 15 minutes straight on the pads and body protector with both men.

If that wasn't enough, he went back onto the heavy bags for another ten minutes.

People often say I train too much but that's because they have no idea how hard the best in the world train.

Floyd would talk whilst training. Which I always love, he is pure entertainment. He said,
"critics always say I don't take no hard fights." He went on, "I did that when I was younger, now its all about making that money. I don't care about being the greatest boxer. I want to be known as the smartest boxer. I got paid more in one fight than all of HBOs fighters did in the whole year."

Floyd also provided a masterclass tutorial lesson whilst training. Showing us how to hit the body properly.

What is noticeable for all to see is that Floyd values his team. He is always telling them he appreciates their work and he even thanks his sparring partners after beating them up and verbally abusing them.

Thursday 7th March 2013

Nate said he is going to be announced in the top ten of best trainers in the world in a couple of weeks. He said Floyd doesn't work with me because I'm pretty. He knows I'm one of the best.

Nate is good! I learnt off him last year and this year we have continued where we left off. I'm even better and more fluid now.

He said I know you don't mess with black girls with that movement. I had to laugh as it reminded me of stuff my brother would say.

Nate said all I have to do is fix up my feet placement and I'll be a threat.
I had done 4 rounds shadow boxing, 3 rounds of skipping, 12 rounds on the heavy bags and double end bag then 3 rounds skipping before I did 3 rounds of pads with Nate. I'm definitely in great shape.

I got sparring tomorrow and the kid is real good. He looks strong, skillful and fast. He seems to be in shape as well. This is why I've come here to fight the best. He was in the US National team and I can see why. He looks class. This isn't the amateur code though. This is the professional game. I'm looking forward to it.

Floyd was on form today. Sechew is not good enough to be his sparring partner. He throws single shots and is just not busy enough. He's more of a counter puncher.
Floyd was floating around the ring. He gave his dad a hug with his right hand and banged a jab in Sechew's face. It reminded me of something I would expect Muhammad Ali to do.

Sechew threw up again half way through the second round. He had to come out the ring. I wouldn't hire him to spar with me and I'm Ashley Theophane not Floyd Mayweather.

The fighter from yesterday, came in and did one round with Floyd. Floyd played with him and at the end of the round told some new sparring partner to get in the ring.

Floyd said, "I'm ah break you. I can fight all night". The kid started strong but five minute rounds in 30 degree heat with 30 seconds rest is a killer. The first round he did well but come the second round, Floyd was knocking him all over the place.

Floyd finished up with speed bag, heavy bag work and pads with Nate and Roger.

Just watching Floyd's work ethic alone is something that should inspire and motivate fighters.

Friday 8th March 2013

Celestino Caballero from Panama, former undified super bantamweight WBA and IBF and Super champion WBA. He is also WBA Featherweight champion. He is currently 142lbs and said he'll make 126lbs in 6 weeks no problem.
Boxers punish the their bodies to get into prime condition.

Today I sparred with Semajay Thomas. Former world number 5, two time US Amateur champion and US number one.
I had watched him training as we are both working with Nate Jones. He has power, speed, skills, seems to take a good shot and is in good shape.
I always like to test myself against the best so when I was asked if I was interested in sparring. I accepted! I've sparred 10 world champions, beaten former world champions, former world title challengers and never been outclassed so I'm always looking for a challenge.
The sparring was top stuff. Semajay is an aggressive boxer but he is still young and learning. He tried to push his weight around,

telling me half way through our sparring session, we are doing five rounds instead of the four we had agreed on before we had started. I'm in shape so I can spar all night. I'm a championship fighter so the more rounds we do the more chance my opponent will get drowned.

Everyone loved the sparring and told me how much they enjoyed it. I've been seeing fighters turn down sparring with Semajay so he is obviously feared already. I can't be intimidated. I relish the challenge. We agreed to spar on Tuesday. I'm sure it will be better as we know what we are both about. He has the talent to be world champion. He just has to stay dedicated and keep working hard.

Monday 11th March 2013

My career is a funny one. I got young up and coming fighters who say they want to be like me, who say they look up to me and what I've achieved.

They say I'm the king of the 140lbs division in Britain, even though I'm no longer the British champion.

I've struggle through majority of my career. Boxing is not something I have to do but its something I want to do and if I'm doing something, I like to do it properly.

There has not been many British boxers over the last ten years who have achieved more than me abroad.

You have Ola Alforlabi, David Haye, Ricky Hatton, Amir Khan, Carl Froch and Brian Magee. They come to mind.

There has been hundreds of boxers signed by the top four promoters in Britain; Frank Warren, Matchroom, Frank Maloney and Mick Hennessey. They have had television deals and the resources to produce champions, but their fighters have had little success when fighting abroad.

Some people are impressed by my career, but I've had to do it this way. I wasn't an amateur champion so I had to prove my worth. I've been a professional for ten years now and I probably have five more years left in the game.
There is more success to come. I just sometimes wished that I didn't have to do it the hard way.
My life has always been hard, so I'm used to it but sometimes I wonder what could I achieved if I had the backing that those British fighters had, which didn't even get to my level.

Today I completed a 75 minute run around Vegas and down the Strip. It was the first time I had been near the Strip and I've been here a week. It's my third time here and it's not a vacation so I'm not too bothered about the Strip and its beautiful hotels.

The boxing gym was closed today as they were putting down new flooring and the TV crew was there to film Floyd.

I spoke with Boza, Otis and Terry outside the gym then went to 24 hour fitness for a strength conditioning workout.

Tuesday 12th March 2013

Security emptied out the gym today shouting out "Will anybody who is not with "The Money Team" or sparring Floyd leave the gym."

Boza told one of them that I'm good to stay but when I went to sit down another Security member asked one of the money team members if I can stay. Floyd's cousin and J'Leon Love jumped to my defense and said, "He's staying."

Jleon Love told me he bet with his brother that I'd beat Danny Garcia. He said he knows my career and that he has mad respect for fighters like Ishe and I, as we've had to fight for everything we've achieved. He said Floyd's his promoter and Al Haymon is his advisor, so everything gets handled for him. He reassured me when I'm here that he wants me to be comfortable. For some reason, most British fighters don't have a good reputation in America. I wonder why!

As Semajay and I watched Floyd doing his strength work in the ring, he said he googled me after our sparring session, so he knew I was a good fighter. When I told him my age. His response was "Get the fuck out of here". I took it as a compliment. We had a good chat and there's mutual respect there. He said he saw my tweet about him possibly being a world champion in the future. I told him I did not know his name by I was impressed with him. He asked me if I do talks with troubled kids and I said when time permits. He said he does! We were both involved in criminal activities as teenagers. I said when I was in jail and saw other youngsters getting locked up for life that I decided I was going to give my all to boxing. He said he was the same. I told him that he has the talent and I said that Floyd is backing him so it's all up to him to turn his dreams into reality.

Floyd remembered who I was. He shouted out "UK" to me as he got into the ring and shook my hand. He acknowledged me as he left the gym floor and headed into the locker room.

CBS/Showtime where in the building to film for the build up with his fight with Robert Guerrero. He did pads, bags, speed ball, skipping and some strength workout. It was a private session and I felt privileged to be allowed to stay as only The Money Team, his family and his sparring partners watched.

Today was a great day! I worked out with Roger Mayweather for around twenty minutes on the pads then I did my normal boxing routine which was bag, skipping, speed ball, strength work, abdominal conditioning, shadow boxing and pads with Floyd's assistant coach Nate Jones.
Today I got that Floyd work out in, as I worked with both his coaches.

I arrived at the gym at 1pm and left at 8pm. What a long day, but I've enjoyed it 110%.
If I could move out here I would.

Wednesday 13th March 2013

Another long day at the gym. I arrived at 1pm and left at 830pm. I'm truly living my dream. If I could relocate here I would.

Floyd sparred a Welterweight boxer today, who's record is 27-2. They did four rounds of five minutes with thirty seconds rest. That thirty seconds is just about enough time to walk to your corner, get a sip of water before you hear "work".

Floyd boxed him and was cautious as you'd except. Brian is probably walking around over 170lbs at this minute in time. Floyd is near 142lbs. So that's a big weight gap.

The more the rounds went by Floyd started to get vicious with his punches. He is more powerful than his record suggests.

Floyd did a full workout of sparring, bag, pads, skipping, abdominal and strength conditioning plus went for a run afterwards. People say I train too hard in the UK. That's because they were brought up on the basic boxing workout. The best always do more than the rest. That's why they are the best.

I was out road running with Floyd Mayweather, the money team and a few of his sparring partners tonight. We ran for six miles around Vegas. I had already ran for an hour this morning but it is not everyday you get to workout with greatness.

When I was leaving the gym, Floyd asked me when I was going to fight for a world title. I said I was working towards it. He asked me what was my record. I told him 33 wins, 5 loses and 1 draw.

He started to impersonate my accent. He asked me jokingly to buy him some skittles tomorrow. I will buy him some skittles to see his face.

He said tomorrow we'll take some photos. I didn't ask, he just said it. He's a cool guy! Whilst running he was telling the fighters, run within your limits. Don't kill yourself. I'm a 12 round fighter. If you're a 4 round fighter. Train for that! Be smart. No one remembers a loser. Be smart and do what you have to, to win.

Whilst out running he made a $50,000 bet. Who does that? His team shouted out from one of the three cars following us, some odds and he shouted back at them to put down fifty.

I met comedian Jay Reid from Showtime's The Ladies Night Out tv show as he was at the gym. Ishe introduced him to me. Ishe was saying to him I'm always in a different country and that one day he won't be shocked if he sees photos of me on Mars.
He said if I ever come London I will contact you but knowing you, you'll be somewhere abroad.

The Money Team have opened their arms to me.
Boza told me to go running with Floyd. They see I work hard and I got some talent so they show me love.

Thursday 14th March 2013

Cellestino, what a fighter, I see this man spar any weight and he always holds his own. He has so much skills. I can see why he is a multi-weight world champion.

During sparring, Floyd got hit. Floyd senior said, "Move your head." Floyd replied "I'm not perfect."

Floyd spits out through the mouth piece, to his opponent "I see fatigue setting in."

Whilst in a clinch, Floyd manhandles Brian. "Let's go for a walk," Floyd moves him in the direction he wanted to go. That is ring generalship, controlling your opponent during defense and offense.

Friday 15th March 2013

Today was a great day and one I'll remember for the rest of my life.

Started my day off with a run along the strip and around Vegas.

Early afternoon I headed to Mayweather Boxing Club for my daily workout. I was due to spar Semajay as it was his last sparring session before his professional debut. Vernon Paris started with him and I took the last half.

I sparred one round with Vernon Paris and he just felt like a human punchbag that threw the odd counter back. He was probably tired. Semajay walked through him and tore him up.

I finished up my sparring with some rounds with the number six US amateur. He was tall and rangy. It was good work.
Finished out my workout with pads with Nate, speed ball, skipping and some abdominal crunches.

Floyd started his training an hour later. He did two rounds sparring. Five minute rounds.
Something happened in there as it was cut short. He did pads with Roger and Nate followed with bags then some more pads. He finished up with some fancy skipping and strength work.

I went for a run with Floyd, J'Leon and one of Floyd sparring partners. We only did a short 23 minute run.
Floyd asked me why Ricky Hatton didn't fight me for his comeback fight and why Amir Khan hadn't fought me. He said he could

get me any fight I wanted and that he wanted to set up shop in the UK.

After the run, Floyd was chilling in his car talking to his boys. They called me over and asked if I wanted to go to the Alicia Keys concert with them. I smiled and said yes. One of his security team gave me his contact details.

I got to the Mandalay Bay just before 10pm. Floyd was in suite 4 over looking the stage. The whole team was there.

After the show, I was invited out with the money team. Floyd didn't go but everyone else was there. Ishe Smith, J'Leon Love and Luis "Cuba" Arias among others.

It was a great night. To think I get minimal love in the UK but the pound for pound king has opened his arms to me.
It all felt like a dream but it was real. I don't like to say I feel blessed cause I've worked hard for everything I have.
Otis one of the trainers at the gym, said I'm humble and hard working maybe I optimize Floyd's hard work and dedication slogan. I lived by that way of life even before I heard Floyd say it.

After the concert J'Leon said you know the night isn't over yet. I said I'm going back to my apartment. He said you sure. I thought about it. It's not everyday I get to hang with the money team, so I thought I might as well. It's not like I have a fight confirmed.

We went to a club in the Mirage hotel. It was supposed to be Rob Kardashian's party.
There was around forty of us there. 30 women and 10 men.

Floyd didn't come but majority of the team was there. It was a fun night. I even ended up going back to my apartment with one of the girls who was with us. She was visiting from Los Angeles for the weekend.
We did what adults do. I didn't even ask her, her name until the next time I saw her on the Sunday. She felt offended but I said you didn't say your name and I didn't ask. She seemed like a nice lady. She was a 25 year old social worker.

Monday 18th March 2013

I sparred world rated Vernon Paris for five rounds today. I enjoyed it. Vernon is fighting this weekend but wanted to get one more session in. His trainer was happy with our work rate. There was no let up. We are two fighters both on our own journey.

Floyd trained with maybe ten cameras following him around the gym. That's what you call a superstar.

He did three interviews afterwards for different television stations.

I'm seriously thinking about staying until May 5th, I'm loving this place.

There's no opportunities for me in Britain. Vegas seems to be the place for me.
I was asked about a fight in the Philippines today.
I'm also waiting for ESPN to sanction a fight with Lanardo Tyner.

I arrived at Mayweather's Boxing Club at 115pm and left at 945pm. Normally I'm here for 7 hours but just hanging out with the money team and Floyd is an experience I'll never forget.

Tuesday 19th March 2013

I sparred Celestino Caballero today. What a fighter, so slick! We did 7 rounds in 30 degrees heat. Everyone said that I had done the best against him than anyone else at the Mayweather Boxing Club. I had seen him beat fighter after fighter up. Day after day! He is awkward and has good fitness. What's good for me is that's my conditioning is second to none. So even though I struggled with his style for the first couple of rounds when I got to grips with it, it became an even playing field.

US Olympian Errol Spence Junior was here today to spar Floyd. He was supposed to have put in very good work with Adrien Broner during their sparring session.

There was no let up in the two 5 minute rounds they did. Errol showed good composure and power. I was surprised by his fitness.
I love fighting young hungry fighters as they are always looking to improve. Floyd is no different. He likes to spar these prospects.

After the sparring, Floyd went over to Errol to say thank you as he always does with all of his sparring partners. Errol said something that upset Floyd. Floyd shouted out "let's go again."
Errol had blood coming from his nose and mouth by the end of the round. Floyd asked Errol "do you want to go again?". Errol was tired but still very proud. Floyd said "glove him up, Boza". If it wasn't for Boza, this would have went on all night. Errol is one for the future and I can see him as a champion in a few years time. He is the next generation.

Wednesday 20th March 2013

Errol Spence sparred Floyd again today. He did well for four rounds. Nate said he's going to speak to Floyd as he doesn't need that hard work everyday.
Nate said he'd tell Floyd that I'd been helping his fighters get ready for their upcoming fights. Don, Semajay and Cellestino are all signed to Floyd or so I thought at the time. I'm just enjoying the work. They are good people and show me love. Floyd just needs to rubber stamp the love from the money team I've received already.
J'Leon said today that's he's got me and will have a word with Floyd.

The team went for basketball after Floyds workout. I can't play Basketball so I left them to it. Nate dropped me to my apartment, that was me for the day.

I had already trained for over 2 hours at 24 hour fitness this morning plus a 2 hour workout at Mayweather's this afternoon. My weight was 152lbs which is pretty good.

Cellestino and I finished our workout at the same time so we got chatting in the changing room. He told me he was a two weight world champion and that he had won five world titles and made 11 defenses. He'd never lost in a world title fight. What a fighter! He also asked if I wanted to spar again. To know a champion like him, enjoys sparring with me is a great compliment. We will trade some punches tomorrow.

Thursday 21st March 2013

Celestino Caballero and I locked horns again. I expected us to do seven 3 minute rounds again but when I got in the ring. I was told we are doing 5 minute rounds. I knew the plan what Celestino had in mind. Boxing for 5 minutes is totally different to 3 minutes. It's easy to burn yourself out. It is truly deep end training. Lucky for me my conditioning is second to none. We did a few rounds totaling 16 minutes. Celestino's trainer told me afterwards that one of the rounds were 6 minutes. I enjoyed it and I'm sure we'll do it again.

Friday 22nd March 2013

Errol Spence Junior sparred with Floyd for the fourth time in five days. He is giving the champ great work. He isn't intimidated! A lot of the other guys fade after one or two rounds but his fitness holds up for three to four rounds which is twenty minutes hard work with the best in the business.

Saturday 23rd March 2013

I woke up around 7am, after a nine hour sleep. I've been pushing my body hard so it's
obviously feeling it. I went out for a ten-mile run which normally would take roughly 75 minutes. I went the opposite route to what I did yesterday so when I missed a turn I just kept running. I realized what I had done when I reached Town Square. That was far away from my home destination. I turned back to go home. It was a long run but I felt good. I felt like Forest Gump. Run Forest Run!

Monday 25th March 2013

What a day! Sparred Celestino Caballero this afternoon over four 5 minute rounds with 30 seconds rest in 30 degree heat. It was hard but we worked through it. Afterwards, Celestino said, "I love the work". That's a massive compliment from a 5x world champion. He enjoys sparring with me. He told J'Leon Love that I do everything, box and fight so it is good when getting ready for a fight. He told me I am strong. I said if we were the same weight I would be in trouble. We laughed and I said, "Thank you."

After finishing my work out I watched Floyd spar. He did four rounds or five minutes with his Mexican sparring partner. He looked sharp!
While doing pad work with Roger and Nate, Floyd said, "I'm human. I have bad days in the gym but I've never had a bad pay day."

Floyd was walking out the gym with his running stuff on so I asked him if we are running tonight. His reply was "no champ I'm running from home." We shook hands and he left the gym.

5 minutes later I walk outside to go home and Floyd asked me if I wanted to go running. Leonard Ellerbe, Floyd, Lanell Bellows and I all ran.
Half way through the run it was only Floyd and I left.
Three Money Team cars were following us as usual.
Floyd asked me how long I had been professional. I replied "10 years". He replied "you have loads of time left". I told him that he had been in the game for 17 years and is still going strong so that would be possible for me if I kept working hard".
I asked Floyd if I could be on the show. His reply was he wants to

do shows in the UK. Which he mentioned last time we went running. I said if there was space I'd like to be on the 3rd or 4th May show. He said he'll see what he can do.
My passion is to fight in the States. One on looker in the gym said with the quality of sparring I'm getting in the gym, he knows I'm getting a W in my next fight.

Nate already said he'll talk with Floyd. Boza told one of Floyds uncles on Saturday "we got to get Ashley on the show".
J'Leon also said he'll put in a word for me.
The next man for me to speak to is Leonard.

Whilst running, Floyd told Leonard everyone is saying I beat that boy (Danny Garcia).
I asked Floyd if he was going to Ishe's celebration party for winning the world title. He said he doesn't go out when training for a fight. I like that! A man after my own heart. Focused!

Its good to know the team think highly of me. Running side by side with Floyd is an amazing feeling.

I already did an 8 mile run this morning. Floyd and I completed roughly 6 miles in 41 minutes. Running with Floyd is a bonus and something I'll always remember. Floyd is a genuine nice guy. He treats his friends and family real good. He also shows respect to fellow boxers and fans.

Tuesday 26th March 2013

My weight is 152lbs which I'm happy with. Floyd's is currently 144.5lbs with five weeks to go. He could easily make 140lbs but

147lbs is the glamour division.
Yesterday on our run I told Floyd he looks in shape, around 146lbs. He smiled and responded "I'm around that". I know after training he is sometimes 142lbs so it is incredible that he chooses to fight at 147lbs and 154lbs. If the fans knew, maybe they would appreciate what he is doing even more. Beating up big men.

Rafael Garcia who counts Floyd's punches whilst punching the bag was asked by the
showtime cameraman for the number. He was about to show him when Floyd told him not to. "We show them what we want them to see. We can't have them seeing all my secrets for fighters to try and steal them". I was sitting on the ring ropes watching Floyd's bag and speed ball drills.

Floyd didn't go too hard today as he did a hard workout yesterday.

When I was leaving one of the money team entourage told me "Keep doing your thing. Dedication, baby".

Another day bites the dust in Vegas.

Wednesday 27th March 2013

Everyone who walks in the gym says you don't even have to workout to lose weight in here. You sweat just sitting down. It's that hot.
I got in some good work with Nate today. I'm continuing to learn and add to my game.

Floyd's mum came to the gym to watch her son do his thing. She came with some friends and family. Floyd Senior was there and they got talking. Floyd is a showman and he was telling us how far they go back. "36 years but 38 years if you include some play time". Floyd Snr is a funny guy, a people's person.

When I went outside to go to the store. Floyd's mum was outside lighting up a cigarette. I told her "you're killing my lungs". She made a joke back at me and we started talking about smoking. I told her I wish my mum stopped. She says every year she will, but she never does. Floyds mum said that she stopped for seven years but sometimes gets cravings. She said she takes three puffs then throws it away. That's exactly what she did. She said Floyd doesn't like her smoking. I told her I understand why. I left her with her friend and walked to the store for that bottle of water, I so desperately needed.

Floyd put on a show today against Errol Spence Junior and Sechew Powell. He then did some pad and bag work followed by some strength conditioning. He's in shape already.
"17 years in the game. Eight world championships over five weight classes and that's with me taking a break from boxing." When he boosts of his stats, there's nothing you can really say.

I told Floyd the other day is he targeting Rocky Marciano's 49-0 record as after his 6 fight deal with CBS/Showtime, that is what he will be. He said, "I never look past the fight in front of me."

Floyd started training a bit later than usual. I was at the gym from 130pm to 830pm. It is long days but this is what I'm here for. To put my work in and also learn from the best in the business.

Thursday 28th March 2013

I spoke to Leonard Ellerbe about being on the May 3rd show.
He said that the show was full. He said he had two of his fighters on it and the rest where on Floyd's undercard.
He was cool about it. I said I spoke to Floyd but I know Floyd is focused on his fight.
I said I was happy to be here training, watching Floyd and going out for runs with Floyd. I told him the money team had shown me love and made me feel like one of them. I said Floyd was the Ali of this generation.
Maybe not outside the ring but inside the ring he is. Ali was not loved when he was actually about, as he made a lot of statements about white people but you have to remember his upbringing down South and being around in the 1960s when Martin Luther King and Malcolm X were assassinated.
Leonard said, "Floyd is history in the making". We ended the conversation and I thanked him.

A journalist contacted me today to say he was flying into Vegas from South America to
interview me but he wanted one with Ishe Smith and Floyd. I said you won't get one with Floyd. I asked Ishe and he said he'd do it if he was one of my people. I told him I had done an interview with him before and he's a good guy.

Monday 1st April 2013

Today is April's Fools Day but there was no fooling around in the gym today.
It was packed and buzzing when I got there.
Everyone was sparring. It was quality sparring at that. Ranked

fighter Shawn Porter was in the gym and so was Mike Jones. I'd love to spar both. I asked Eddie Mustafa who trains Mike if we could work. He said no problem. I don't know if he will let me at his fighter though. He sees me working with Celestino and he knows I'm in great shape and hold my own with anyone.

Celestino and I went at it today. We only did three f5 minute rounds but it was so hot in the ring today. I thought we were going to do four rounds but Jeff Mayweather called time after the third.

I had already completed eleven rounds of work before our sparring session. Shadow boxing, skipping and drills on the speed ball.

I went on to complete eight rounds on the heavy bags followed by four rounds with Nate on the pads. I normally do pads with Nate after I've done all my boxing work. I don't know where I find the energy but the adrenaline pumping through my body drives my exhausted body through the workout. Nate makes me think a lot as we are working on a lot of drills and skill work.
After my session with Nate I did some strength and abdominal conditioning.

Floyd Senior and J'Leon Love were cracking on Zach Cooper a young prospect in the gym.
Senior was telling him he's 60 years old but will still whoop his ass. J told Zach why are you trying to pick on a 60 year old man and there's loads of fighters between 140 and 154lbs here. Around six of us said we'd be willing to spar with Zach if he needed the work. Zach backtracked saying that he is resting as he just fought a week ago and he's off on vacation to Los Angeles tomorrow. J'Leon shouted out "vacation, vacation. You only 2-

0 my man. You don't need no vacation from knocking out a janitor a week ago." The banter would go on for ten minutes. It was funny stuff. The guys at the gym work hard but also have a laugh after training, which I like.

Mondays seem to be a day when Floyd is on point. He completed five 5 minute rounds with Errol Spence Junior. Floyd is getting fitter, sharper and more focused with every week that passes. Today Floyd, put on a master class. He was trading punches and outboxing Errol. It was a pleasure to watch this high level sparring.

There was oooohs and ahhhhs echoing around the gym when the eye catching punches where crashing down on Errol's chin and body. Errol may be getting outclassed but he gives a very good account of himself.

Floyd went on to hit the heavy bag, pad work with Roger and Nate, then drills with the speed ball then some light strength conditioning work. He walked straight out of the gym into his Lamborghini. He drove off and the money team followed.

I'm only staying a mile down the road so I normally walk back. Last time I was here I stayed at the Monte Carlo hotel on the strip but I wanted somewhere closer to the gym. Leonard Ellerbe saw me walking and stopped his car. He asked me if I wanted a lift. I said I'm going by the Rio hotel. He replied "no problem".

I jumped in his car and we set down the road on route to the apartment I'm staying. We spoke about Floyd, the fighters at the gym and Leonard's boxing career. He said he was in the armed forces and that they'd taken trips to England. He mentioned that he had very pleasant memories of his trips to the United Kingdom and that the English women where always welcoming. I said British women always like America men. His response was "yes they do". We shared a laugh. We had reached my destination. I thanked him and told him I'd see him tomorrow. He replied, "Anytime".

The respect that the money team show me is very touching. Being in America, I always feel that anything is possible. It amazes me the love I get Stateside but very little back home in the UK.

Tuesday 2nd April 2013

I was speaking to Nate today before training in the changing room and I was telling him about my fights with Demarcus Corley, Danny Garcia and Delvin Rodriguez. He said he knew I could fight but didn't know I had those names on my record.

He said he will talk to Floyd today or tomorrow.

I sparred WBO world number 6 Shawn Porter today. I asked Nate to ask his team if we could spar. I've seen him fight on TV and I watched him spar yesterday. Nate said, "He's 160 at the minute, that's kind of big, you sure?" I said I want to spar the best. He made it happen, I had a great session with Shawn. Nate was impressed and said I boxed beautifully. We have been working on some technical stuff. I fought to his plan. I wanted to stand and fight but Nate wants me moving around and boxing from angles. It worked and everyone watching told me they enjoyed my performance.

Floyd didn't spar today. He did some bag work and some speed ball drills followed up by some strength conditioning and abdominal work. He finished up with skipping and walking into the changing rooms.

Floyd Mayweather, Cuba, Badou Jack and some kid from the Kronk all went for a run around Vegas. You know I was part of the group. It was a steady run. Floyd said we completed just over five miles.

Afterwards we went back to the gym and chilled with the rest of the money team. The New York Knicks were playing Miami Heat on the television, whilst we watched that and clowned around. Around 8pm I left out. I had been at the gym since 130pm. Another day bites the dust!

Wednesday 3rd April 2013

I had a good conversation with Nate today about being a British boxer fighting abroad.
I told him that most "American fighters and trainers don't respect us but after stepping out the ring with me. I'll have their respect. I've seen it many times over. World rated fighters or world champions would go in the ring with me thinking they are in for an easy workout. They have always been surprised. I can box and fight. I'm always in good condition and my chin is reliable.
I went on to say, "That's why I asked you to get me with Shawn Porter. He's 20-0 and super confident as he hasn't been beaten yet."

Today was maybe the best day sparring for me.
Yesterday was good with Shawn but today Celestino and I went at it.

I dropped him in the first round so he came at me to kill me which went against him as these 5 minute rounds are a killer.

Afterwards Floyd's uncle from his mother's side came up to me in the changing room and said, "I saw the knock down man. He was off balance but that left hook put him down." He stared right at me "don't hit me man. I know what you can do". We laughed and he walked away.

Everyone in the gym was watching after the knock down. We go at it anyway but the champion Celestino is, he had a point to prove.

Everyone stopped what they were doing and surrounded the ring. They began to shout out stuff. Some were raring Celestino on. He caught me with some good body shots but I'm 100% conditioned. I walked through them. Celestino's corner were saying, "Crack his ribs." A spectator said, "I know his body hurts." I was 100% fine. I'm used to fighting bigger men.

The session was so intense and we did not hold back. I loved it and thanked Celestino afterwards. He had a cut by his nose from the first round from my jabs or my elbow, either way our tactics were working.

I told Nate I want to spar all the money team fighters around my weight and beat them up.

Next on the list is Mickey Bey and Mike Jones.
Not sure their trainers Floyd Senior and Eddie Mustafa Muhammad will be too keen as they have seen me in action.

Eddie Mustafa Muhammad said I could spar Mike last week but he's been quiet on the subject this week.

I like Nate though. He shouts out "step your game up" and "we're taking on all names".

Thursday 4th April 2013

Tony Martin, is a British coach based in the Philippines and Las Vegas. He represented
England in the Olympics. He's a proud East Ender.

As I walked into the gym he said to me "that was a lovely right hand you knocked Celestino down with. I was happy as you are a Brit and you are showing them we can fight. It was a knock down, make no mistake about it." I thought it was a left hook but hey, who cares I knocked down a five time world champion and controlled the sparring from start to finish.

Celestino said that the sparring with me has been very technical but very hard. He said he's going to go on and win his fight. I told him that he is ready and that he will win. "Train hard, fight easy." I don't think that we'll be sparring often next week. Maybe one more time. We have worked for 3 weeks straight and it has been no holds barred. Each session has gotten better and more physical each time. It's been a great experience for me to share a ring with a man of his caliber.

Today I got my wish. Mickey Bey was walking past us and Nate said, "He wants to spar you". Mickey and I shook hands then discussed a time for Monday.
When Mickey walked off, Nate said this is how you show them you belong in the money team. He said Floyd would love a UK Money Team member its just asking him at the right time. Mickey is managed by Floyd's cousin as well so a good performance will get back to Floyd, as they are pretty close.

Nate said that Mickey is sneaky and quick. If I can handle Semajay Thomas, Vernon Paris, Celestino Caballero and Shawn Porter. Mickey Bey will not be a problem. I watch him on the pads with Floyd Senior. He can do those pretty pad work but that doesn't impress me. Majority of those guys can't fight. He's been a professional since 2005 but only had 20 fights. He has 18 wins, 1 draw and 1 no contest as he was found guilty of testing positive for PEDs. He pleaded his innocence and said it was a mistake from the doctors he went to for fatigue. He got a small fine and three month ban. He will be fighting on May 4th.

Friday 5th April 2013

Today was another day just doing boxing drills, no sparring. I sparred for three times on the trot so 3 days of straight boxing would be good for me.
Lanell Bellows, one of Floyd Mayweather's fighters, has maximum respect for me. He always says, "You a hard working muthafucka, Ash". Nice to know my hard work is noticed.

Floyd talked to himself during his heavy bag workout "keep pushing myself, I'll be ok." He walked over to the mirror and looked at himself and spoke out aloud again "43 had a game plan and failed. The game plan is come and get your pay check." Everyone laughed when Floyd said that.

Floyd put in a phenomenal training session today. Just under three hours of hard work. If people think I work hard, Floyd is a man who inspires me to push harder.

Saturday 6th April 2013

Today all roads lead to Ishe's BBQ. He is holding a meet and greet for the Las Vegas community.
He was signing autographs and taking photos with fans. There was also free food for everyone and games for the kids.
It is great that he's giving back. I went for a morning run followed by a workout at the Mayweather boxing club.

Sticknmove.co.uk flew in from Peru to interview me, so we did it at the gym and I told them to come Ishe's BBQ and I'd get them interviews with the money team.

'Dan the man' picked me up from the gym and we headed off to Ishe's BBQ.
Dan would become my closet friend during my time in Las Vegas.

A whole bunch of the fighters and trainers from the gym where there, which was good to see. We were there for a few hours then we left Ishe and went bowling at the red rock hotel and casino.

I came last out of ten of us and was the laughing stock of the competition but to be fair, I've haven't bowled for over 15 years.

I'm having a great time in Vegas. Everyone is here to try make their dreams reality. I will be sad to go but I have four weeks more to make the most of it.

Monday 8th April 2013

I was looking forward to today as I was due to spar Floyd Mayweather promoted fighter Mickey Bey. Mickey is trained by Floyd Senior and managed by Floyd's cousin.

Nate told me that Mickey is fast and supposed to pack a punch. I went in there and did what I do. First round we boxed and when I saw he had nothing for me to be worried with, I started to walk him down. I've been sparring for five weeks now so I'm in great shape. This was Mickey's first session so he was obviously rusty and not as conditioned as me. We completed three five minutes rounds. I've been doing these with Celestino for a couple weeks now so I prefer the longer rounds.

Floyd Senior was shouting from the corner "you can out box him easily, man". I shouted back while boxing Mickey. "You crazy, Floyd."

It's not just about the fighters competing against each other. The trainers are also competitive and want to get the better of the other trainer. I can say this now. Nate has a winner and he knows it. I've held my own with everyone so far.
I'm on operation money team. I'm sparring with anyone from the team who is near my weight and all the top fighters that walk through the gym doors.

Welterweight prospect Zack Cooper said after watching my Sparring session, "For a man with a girls name you can fight."

Floyd put in a good workout session which included four 5 minute sparring session, bag and pad work followed by some strength

conditioning.
Afterwards some of us stayed behind and watched the Basketball game between Michigan and Louisville as it was the college finals. Floyd had flown to Atlanta for the final four which is the semi finals over the weekend.

Floyd likes to joke around with the guys. It is nice to see that side of him.

Tuesday 9th April 2013

Roy Jones Junior and Jean Pascal were in the gym today. Roy is my all time favorite fighter so it was a pleasure to meet him. I believe, pound for pound he could have beaten any fighter in his prime. I've never seen a fighter blessed with so much ability. I look like a school kid in the photo I took with him.

I looked at Roy watching Floyd train. This is two of the greatest fighters ever. Floyd didn't pay them no attention until he finished his workout. That's what you call focused.

Whilst I was walking back home with my backpack, a white Ferrari pulls up to me. I stop, I'm wondering who it is. I walk up to the car and see its Floyd.

He asks where I'm going. I said just past Rio hotel. It's a mile away. He says jump in.
I got in the car and he drops me home.
Three Money Team cars were following us. I waved at them and walked into my apartment building.

In my wildest dreams, I could never have imagined that. I don't care what people say about Floyd. He has showed me love and respect while I've being here. I'm just another fighter who respects him and admires his accomplishments. It says a lot for a man who helps people who can not help him.

Rene Carayol is another man who fits that mold. Truly inspiring and motivational!

Wednesday 10th April 2013

J'Leon came up to me whilst I was hitting the heavy bags and said, "Big dog (Floyd Mayweather) asks how did you do with Mickey. He's watching dude. Keep doing your thing."

While Floyd was training today he shouted out "I'm the ghost buster." Referring to Robert Guerrero being known as "The Ghost".

I was told today by one of the fighters "Some English dude is putting in crazy work, that's the word around the gym."

Mickey Bey and I put in some good work today. We completed three five minute rounds. I felt comfortable during the sparring session. Nate was happy, his feedback was that, I did a lot of what we've been working on. Beautiful foot work and slipping shots.

Floyd Senior was shouting out instructions at Mickey. I feel like I was born to be in this
environment, surrounded by the best brings out the best in me.

"Dan the man" was telling Mike and Badou Jack that I've never been a strip club before. They want to corrupt me! It's never been my thing.

Thursday 11th April 2013

Mickey told me he's fighting a Southpaw now so we won't be sparring anymore. I'm tempted to spar him as southpaw. I'm not 100% comfortable in that stance but I feel I'll still have enough to contain him.

Celestino's trainer thanked me for the great sparring I gave him and said he needed that work for his comeback fight.

It was my pleasure to share the ring with a fighter who has achieved as much as he has.

He went on to say that my two performances against Mickey were good. "I know he wasn't expecting all that pressure from you".
I told him Mickey is fighting a Southpaw now so we won't be sparring no more. His reply with a laugh was "of course, he is". Meaning Mickey is relieved he won't be working with me anymore.

Larry King was at the gym today. I was with the money team, Floyd's friends and family watching. One of the security asked me to leave and Floyd said, "He's alright". I told the security man that you always getting on my balls. He said he was told everyone was supposed to leave.

It was a good interview. Floyd came across as likable. He stayed on a positive vibe. He said he never thinks about losing as winning is what he does. "I'm a born winner" is what he told Larry.

Friday 12th April 2013

My weight is the lowest it has been whilst I've been in Vegas. I weighed 151.5lbs today, which I'm happy with. I left London weighing 158lbs. I want to touch 149lbs before I leave. That's easily done!

Floyd's cousin who manages Mickey Bey and works as assistant with J'Leon Love and Floyd asked me if I'd move out here.
I said if Floyd put me on I would be able to. He asked if I had approached Floyd. I said I asked about May 3rd and May 4th cards. His reply was he wanted to do some shows in Britain.
I told Floyd's cousin that you guys know I can fight so it's what you say to Floyd that counts.

J'Leon told me that Floyd knows that I'm putting in the work as everyone is telling him. He said that don't wait for the right time. Just ask Floyd if you can get on Ishe's card. He'll look at me and know that I want it.

Floyd put in a good workout sparring Errol Spence. He is looking sharper every time he spars.
He went 30 minutes straight on the heavy bag followed by some pad work with Roger and Body bag work with Nate.
Ishe asked me when I was leaving. I told him after the fight. He said, "I'll miss you man. You have been everywhere with us". I said I want to stay but I need Floyd to put me on a show. I asked

him to ask Floyd. He said he'd ask Leonard (Ellerbe) and Floyd.

The Money Team fighters are good people. There's definitely mutual respect there. This is what I like about boxing. Though my career I've made some good friends all over the world.

Saturday 13th April 2013

The Money Team's Lanell "KO" Bellows always says to me "you're a hard working muthafucka, Ash". I take that as a compliment. Floyd Mayweather sets the pace and I'm just trying to push myself and improve.

Everyday is a different car for Floyd.
Monday was a Lamborghini. Tuesday was a Ferrari. Wednesday was a Rolls Royce. Thursday a Silver Mercedes and Friday a white Mercedes.

Monday 15th April 2013

I started my day with an 11.5 mile run down the strip and around Vegas. It took 82 minutes. The Vegas weather is very hot now, so that helps build up a nice sweat.

I headed to the gym around 130pm. I like to get there a little early to complete all my workout before sparring with Mickey.

I completed my shadow boxing, skipping, speed ball drills, abdominal and back crunches before my spar with Mickey. Today we completed four 5 minute rounds of sparring and that played in my hands due to my high fitness conditioning. Mickey did well as he dug deep but the third and fourth round was all me. He was practically backing off and on the defensive for the whole of the round until his team shouted out "30 seconds left" and he threw some Sugar Ray Leonard style flurries.

I boxed, I fought, I used great movement.
At the start of round two I went over to Mickey's manager and whispered to him "This is easy work". He laughed!

Floyd Mayweather Senior said after our sparring "No one here (Mayweather Boxing Club) in his (Mickey Bey) weight class can compete with him. So its real good work."

It's good to know one of the best trainers in the world, appreciates my talent.

Nate wanted me to throw more shots but Mickey is waiting to counter me, so I have to time him and break him down. Bit by bit! That's what I did. In the fourth round, he was running around the ring. I was walking him down and jogging after him.

Mickey said he enjoys sparring me as I'm really strong and pressure him.

Nate told me "you boxed beautifully. Tomorrow you won't do no heavy bag. I want you to work on your feet cause when that comes together. You are going to be real nice."

Everybody stops what they doing to watch us and they turn off the music whilst we in the ring. They only do that for the top boys in the gym. J'Leon Love, Badou Jack, Ishe Smith and Floyd Mayweather.

All Floyd's boys were here today watching, so I'm sure word will get back to him that I got one of his fighters under pressure.

Some guy came up to me and said Nelly and P Diddy are starting a promotional company and they'll be interested. I'm not sure about that one. We'll see what happens.

Whatever happens I'm leaving my mark here.

People without visions, hopes, dreams, ambition, or desire to win will go out of their way to kill yours.
I'm just trying my best and putting in work. What will be will be!

Tuesday 16th April 2013

When my alarm went off at 430am, I thought it was a mistake. When I got up to turn it off I remembered I was going to Mount Charleston with Dan to run with the guys from the gym.

Dan picked up Badou Jack then we headed up to Mount Charleston to meet everybody else.

J'Leon Love and Luis "Cuba" Arias just made it for the 6am start as Eddie Mustafa Muhammad who trains world champions Chad Dawson and Ishe Smith was taking us and he has a reputation for being a tight time keeper. If you're not there on time, he's gone.
Dangerous Don Moore also came. Chad Dawson was supposed

to come with us but his driver was late so he ended up, doing it on his own.
9000ft above sea level. That run was hard but I still came first. It took me 53 minutes. J'Leon, Badou, Luis and Don headed the group. I was at the back as I was waiting on Dan to put his stuff in Eddie's car. Within 5 minutes I was behind J'Leon at the front. Don had made a joke that J would kick my ass in running as he's supposed to be a strong runner. I'm competitive so I wanted to see what I could do.

After ten minutes I was leading the pack. J advised me to pace myself as we still had a while to go.

I just ran at my pace but it was hard. All up hill and the air was getting thinner. I could hardly breathe but I was determined.

I refused to look back. My destination was forward so that's where I was looking.
30 minutes passed and J'Leon was back by my side. I told him I thought you'd be way back. His reply was "nah dawg, I'm right here." The hill became steeper and the air thinner. I had to dig deep and fight it. I pump my arms for a minute and whilst doing that I opened a gap between j and I. I never looked back to see where he was. It wasn't a race. I was running against myself. Pushing myself! That was the hardest 5 miles I've ever completed. What would normally take 35 minutes. Took me 53 minutes. I came first which I was proud of. J'Leon, Badou and Dan finished together. Dan surprised me. I didn't know he had that in him. He said that was the first time he's ran since last December when he done the Las Vegas marathon on a last minute decision.

We all did a boxing workout in the afternoon. My legs were tired but I got through it. Floyd only did a light workout at the gym. One of his assistants, David Levi said that might mean they'll get the call at midnight to come back to the gym.

Wednesday 17th April 2013

Eddie Mustafa Muhammad, trainer to Ishe Smith and Chad Dawson walked into the waiting area in the gym where everyone was hanging out before the media workout started and said to everyone. "My man Ash ran like someone stole his pocket book in Brixton" We laughed and Eddie walked into the gym to sit down.

The media workout was crazy packed. Floyd Mayweather is a rock star. Press from all over North America came. The Money Team fighters all worked out before Floyd.

When Floyd came in, the press become like obsessed fans, all trying to get the best photo of him. It was just another day at the office for Floyd. He did a live interview with ESPN, then he started his work. It was what I usually see but just condensed.

After training Floyd did some more TV interviews. I was at the gym from just after 12pm and I left before 7pm.

I got some interviews in myself which was also good and the money team fighters invited me in for some photos and video interviews. They treat me like one of the guys.

We got to downtown Las Vegas at The D hotel at Fremont Street swiftly. The boxing ring was outside, surrounded by hotels and

casinos. We met up with a few of the guys from the gym. Roger Mayweather was doing the corner with his Asian female fighter. I've never seen her fight so I wasn't very optimistic about her chances. She lost in the first round.
I was freezing and bored as the fights were low level stuff.

I was ready to go when Dan noticed Roy Jones Junior and Jean Pascal about to walk into the VIP section. He called me over, I'm thinking he wants a photo with them but no we were walking in with Roy Jones and Jean Pascal, along with their two female and two male friends. We were ushered to a table and we all sat down. That was us for the night. Hanging out with my favorite fighter of all time, Roy Jones Junior. He was sat next to me and Jean Pascal was opposite him on the table. Roy is still the man. People kept asking him to take a photo with them.

I got a photo with UFC President Dana White. I knew the name but not how he looked as I'm not a fan of UFC.

It was a long day and one I'll always remember. Roy and Jean treated us like friends. Dan's "TMT" T-Shirt went very far. Even journalists through out the day were asking him for permission to do certain things.

I was supposed to go hiking with Dan and his friends in the morning but after two long days, I'm shattered.

Thursday 18th April 2013

Floyd didn't come in today as yesterday he was weighing 144lbs. He still has two weeks to go. He's already sharp and in great shape so taking a day off will do him some good.

I had a good days training, 75 minute run around Vegas and 2 hours plus boxing workout.

Friday 19th April 2013

Today J'Leon brought me into the changing room when Floyd had finished his workout.
Normally after he finishes he goes in there, followed by his team. They talk, he showers then they come out and chill with everyone else or Floyd leaves. Depends what he has going on.

Sports Illustrated were in the changing rooms to do an interview with Floyd. Afterwards he did a photoshoot in the media room. I saw a little bit of it. Floyd was dancing and joking around. Music was blasting out. It felt more like a get together then a photo shoot.
Floyd's fiancé Miss Jackson was in the building today.

Floyd was again very respectful and down to earth with the interviewer. Floyd said, "I like lavish things. Money is there to spend and I have money". Floyd didn't seem comfortable talking about how much he earns but he is reported to be getting a minimum of $30 million dollars a fight off showtime.

Floyd talked about being poor, being raised by his grandma and his life as a kid. He said he liked doing regular stuff what kids do. Shooting pool, playing ball or going down the mall with the guys.

I was in the locker room with ten of his team members. Leonard Ellerbe, his photographer, his coach Nate Jones, his publicist Kelly Swanson, Miss Jackson, Badou Jack, Lanell Bellows, J'Leon Love, Kitchie and David Levi. Listening to the number one fighter with only his closest people around him was incredible. The security guy who always gives me a hard time didn't want to let me in but J'Leon told him "He's always okay, man. That's my man, Ashley".

"Money don't mean nothing if you don't have freedom and there's more important things than money." The interviewer didn't expect to hear those things come out of his mouth.

When the interviewer left, Floyd told the fighters "Boxing is all about politics and who you know. If I do a talk for a governing body, do you think they are going to go against me. I pay them what sanctioning fee I want to give them. There's no way they are getting a percentage of my money. They can have their belt back if they want it."

Floyd asked if his sparring partners were still there. One of his team members called them into the locker room. He gave them all a bunch of hundred dollar bill notes then he asked J'Leon if his sparring partner was still there. He came in the locker room and received some money. Floyd then said, "You know I got to give my fighters some money" he then gave Luis, J'Leon and Badou some hundred dollar bills as well.

Personally I think Floyd is a cool guy. He looks after his friends and family.

Whilst we were all chilling in the locker room.
J kept saying, "Ashley is putting that work in. Running up Mount Charleston, sparring everybody. Wow! You a bad guy, Ashley." J was making Floyd aware of my presence for me to say something. Floyd interrupted J and said, "I am not running no Mount

Charleston. That shit isn't helping you in the championship rounds when I'm beating down on you." Floyd was referring to Robert Guerrero, as he has been doing Mount Charleston in preparation for their fight. I told Floyd it was snowing on Tuesday when we did it. He response was "I don't care if it's snowing or not. That shit is not helping you in a fight. You see these guys wearing those altitude face masks. When you get punched in the face all that stuff goes out the window."

Floyd went on to tell us about why him and 50 Cent really stopped talking. He said Fifty was always trying to compete with him and that he never paid his bills at hotels or tipped people. Floyd said I always tip a minimum one hundred dollars so when he said he wanted to go 50/50 on a promotional company. I was like "hell no". I been building my brand for 17 years and you want half of that. "No way". He said Fifty was seeing the cheques he was getting for Pay Per View and he wanted some of that money. Floyd went on "Fifty did a deal with Vitamin water and Coco Cola so he should be okay. I don't know what is going on with his finances. He has to fly 17 hours across the world to make 100,00 dollars. Not me!" Being around Floyd is definitely enlightening. It's like a different world here.

J'Leon has been really cool to me and is helping me out. He told me my mum always said, "A closed mouth, doesn't get fed". Him and Ishe are trying to help me get on a Mayweather promotions card in the future. I need to step up and handle my business. It's not easy when ten people are in a room and Floyd is always busy or doing something but time is running out and I'm running out of opportunities.

Saturday 20th April 2013

Eddie Mustafa Muhammad was playing that good soul music with 8 of us squashed in 4 seats in the back of his SUV, whilst he drove us to the starting point on Mount Charleston. There was 10 of us running today which was good. A bigger group from the gym. This time WBC World champion Chad Dawson was there on time so he started with us.

J'Leon started fast again, like it was a 400m track race. I stayed on his tail. After about ten minutes he dropped off the pace and I kept going. Even though I want to come first, I was just running at my own pace as no one challenged me. Dan came out of no where and was on my shoulder 30 minutes in. I shouted out "Dan the superman" and put in an explosive burst which left him.

Whilst running the mountains there was a beautiful view, I took some quick photos. I looked behind me and saw that the guys was a good distance behind. I did some star jumps, bunny hops, side strides to show off. I did this a couple more times. It was amusing. On one occasion I turned round and gave them a salute. We are all a team and pushing each other so it's all love out there and in the gym.

In the evening I spent time with the money team's J'Leon and Luis at Badou's apartment with Dan to watch the Canelo Alvarez and Austin Trout fight. J'Leon asked me if I spoke to Floyd last night. When I said not yet, it wasn't the right time. He went off on me "Yo dude, you got to say something. He already told you that he can get you any fight you want. He doesn't say that to everyone. Badou asked Floyd to put him on and give him a chance.

You got to do it dawg. You are in a position that many fighters dream of. Take your opportunity."

J is right. I've tried! I spoke to Floyd about getting on the May 4th and 3rd cards but his reply was that they are full and that he wants to do a show in the UK. I'll ask about Ishe's card but time is running out for me. Floyd is a very busy person and always on the go, so getting his attention and time is real hard. As Dan said to me on the way home "I'm making opportunities for myself to ask him. There's no right time but it's finding the best time."

Sunday 21st April 2013

Today The Money Team threw an appreciation party for Floyd at the M resort and casino just off the strip. It was an all white party. These parties are legendary.

Monday 22nd April 2013

When I walked into the Mayweather Boxing Club this afternoon. Badou Jack, J'Leon Love, Nate Jones, Mickey Bey's manager Dejuan Blake and a host of others asked where I was last night at Floyd Mayweather's appreciation white party.

I didn't get an invitation off Melissa, mother to Floyd's daughter Yaya so I thought I couldn't come. Everyone said, "Why didn't you call me?" Even though I'm not officially part of the team. They treat me as part of the team. I know for next time. Badou said, "It's the best party I've ever been to". That was nice of him to tell me that information.

J'Leon said him and Floyd went out running straight from the party. Floyd said he does those type of things as he knows his opponent isn't doing that.

Floyd is looking sharp at just the right time. He sparred four five minute rounds with Errol this afternoon and he was letting his hands go. Punches in bunches.
Whilst he was doing pads with Roger, everyone started to clap at the amazement of his speed, power and accuracy on the pads. He stopped to tell everyone "Why ya'll clapping? Where was ya'll 17 years ago?" The gym went silent and he went back to work. After finishing a near three hour workout, Floyd walked into the locker room followed by the money team. J'Leon told me that Mickey Bey told everyone at the 'White Party' last night that he was off the show as he'd hurt his hand. J said, "Now is your time dawg. God is making an opportunity for you. Its up to you now to say something and take it." I told J I'd do it today just get me in the locker room. As we were walking to the locker room. J walks in and the security steps in my way and blocks me. When J notices what's happened he comes back out and says, "He's good man, I keep telling you".

I just think he likes messing with me. J'Leon and Boza always tell him that I'm good. It's weird as we actually get on. He's only doing his job, I guess. He says, "It's only supposed to be the money team in there."

So there's like ten of us in the changing room with Floyd. Floyd is having a shower and getting ready to go home. He starts talking about his time on the Olympic team and the Olympic park. He said he didn't really get involved with all the partying with the other athletes as he was focused on getting his medal. He was saying his training routine of making 130lbs. He went on to talk about his upbringing and how he wasn't focused on making

money. He just wanted to be a champion. He said friends, family and boxing associates have always been jealous of him and he always found it weird as he wanted the best for them. He talked about working with the first man to officially beat Julio Cesar Chavez, Frankie Randall. He also spoke about being sued numerous times for things that had nothing to do with him but his name was associated with. He spoke about his grandma working hard and always making sure he had healthy food.
He spoke for an hour about many very private things I will not mention out of respect for being allowed in his inner circle. All I can say, Floyd started at the bottom and with working overtime he has become the star he is now. He said that a reason he works so hard is because he knows that so many people close to him want him to lose, just to say I told you so. I feel a lot of similarities to what he has spoken about. As I spoke JLeon later that evening, he mentioned how hard I train. I said I've always had to as I've never had a promoter who had my back. I've had to be the opponent and cause the upset.
Floyd was proud of the fact he had got Ishe Smith a world title. He said, "Boxing isn't about how good you are but about who you know and who you are with. It doesn't matter how good you are. You could be winning a fight but as long as the fighter with the right connections is still standing at the end, he will win."

When Floyd had finished talking and was going outside to go home. J looked at me and said, "Now". I tapped Floyd on his shoulder. I had his attention now. I told him I'd been sparring Mickey Bey and that Mickey was injured. If I could take his place on the card. He tapped Leonard Ellerbe and asked him if that was true about Mickey being injured. Leonard said yes. Floyd said, "Take his number". I thanked Floyd and he walked off to speak to his family. I gave Leonard my number. Leonard said that the slot was probably gone as it is a huge event. J came up to me and shook my hand. I thanked him for backing me and getting me in the locker room. Outside the gym everyone was talking and hanging out. Leonard came up to me and said that he'd made a call to see if they'll take the fight at 142lbs as I'm currently 150lbs. I told him I could make 140lbs. He said he didn't want me dead on my feet. We shook hands. For Floyd to personally give me the go ahead is a major thing. I've gone running with him around Las Vegas and running up the mountains with his fighters. Everyone in the gym sees me put in work and I've sparred anyone who is anyone, that has a reputation of being good.

Tuesday 23rd March 2013

After training I was 150.2lbs. I was very happy with that as yesterday I was 152.9lbs. I can make 140lbs by next week. It will be hard but I can do it. I dropped roughly the same for my fight with DeMarcus Corley in around the same time and I won that fight.

Floyd is really looking good in sparring. He completed four 5 minute rounds with Sechew Powell then he did some bags and pads. That was him for the evening.
Leonard came up to me and said Jose Hernandez could only do 138lbs. I thanked him for the opportunity I left it as that. I told J'Leon as he had been backing me on getting on the card from when I first arrived. J said can't you make 138lbs. I said I'd never been that weight.
Really Hernandez was the opponent so he was never going to beat Mickey Bey on a Mayweather show. J told me to tell Leonard to make the fight at 138lbs then if you don't make it, you'll take a fine, fuck it. I went and spoke to Leonard again but he said the fight went last night as he knows my fighting weight is 140lbs.

I knew it was a long shot in the first place. I'd done everything I possibly could to get on the show. One day I'll make a great manager. The contacts I'm making and the lengths I'm willing to go. I am proud of myself. I'm having business discussions with some of the most influential people in sport. Many people can't get in contact with them, but I can. They shown me nothing but respect in dealing with me.

Wednesday 24th April 2013

Today I had a great sparring session with WBO world number six Shawn Porter. Last time we sparred, Nate wanted me to box and move and make angles. It worked well and we felt like we got the best of the session. This time Nate wanted me to stand and fight him. He was shouting at me "don't back up". We again felt like we got the best of the session and it was the total opposite of our first session. I was backing Shawn up and ripping him with my hooks and uppercuts. The jab was keeping him off balance. I was looking real nice. Everyone afterwards told me how good I looked.

We will spar again on Friday. I look forward to it.

Floyd didn't train today at the boxing gym, well they said he was planning to come at 3am when no one was around.

Friday 26th April 2013

What a sparring session with Shawn Porter this afternoon, sparring and training in America definitely is for me. I seem to flourish over here.

Just before Shawn and I sparred, Nate told me that I'd learned more in the last few weeks with him than Shawn had been taught over the last ten years. Nate's final instructions before the bell rang was "go out there and box. Use your legs." On Wednesday, he wanted me backing Shawn up, today he wants a bit more foot work. Nate went on to say, "You have thirty something fights, you should be able to do everything." And I can.

Shawn was over an hour late, so I had done my whole workout before our sparring session. 10 minutes skipping, 10 minutes on the speed ball, 5 rounds of shadow boxing, 6 rounds on the bag and 1000 abdominal crunches.

To put in the performance that I did after all that work in such drenching heat shows the conditioning I'm in. We completed seven 3-minute rounds with 30 seconds rest.

Whilst we were boxing Nate shouted out "Floyd needs to sign this kid." We stood and traded, I worked my defense, I used my jab and combinations. It was a good performance.

Nate shouted at Shawn's trainer who is also his dad, Kenny. "You know if this was a fight, you'd be losing."

Nate told me afterwards "For an ugly muthafucka you boxed beautifully."

After Floyd had left after his workout, his personal assistant Kitchie invited me to his BBQ on Sunday. That should be fun!

Saturday 27th April 2013

I started my day with a 10 mile run which was nice and relaxing. I headed to the boxing gym for 1pm for a light workout. When I got there, Nate said they want you to spar Errol. I asked him what he thought. He said its good work.

Floyd's uncles said they had contacted my friend Dan to try get hold of me to spar Errol.

Errol had been giving Floyd real good sparring and the rumor is he wobbled Adrien Broner in their session. I saw him spar Cody Crowley, a Canadian fighter on Monday and he nearly decapitated him. They only managed two rounds but onlookers were shouting at the Canadians coach to stop the sparring which he never. It wasn't pleasant to watch.

Prospect Zach Cooper had been asking me for sparring for the last few weeks so at first we were due to spar today but then he said he had work but he had finished early so he came. He started sparring Errol first. I shouted at Errol and Boza "Oh you guys want the easy work first then hard work afterwards, I respect that." Everyone was laughing. Nate joined in asking Errol why didn't he do 141lbs in the nationals. Errol's reply was its easy work in that division. Nate's fighter Semajay Thomas won the 141lbs division so it's a joke they always do back and forth. Errol whilst sparring Zack asked Nate if he had any fighters in the 141lbs division. Nate said you know Semajay Thomas. Errol's reply was never heard of him, probably didn't get past the quarter finals. Everyone was laughing as Semajay and Errol have sparred and were in the US team together.

Speaking out loud I said, "I came here today expecting easy work with Zack but now I got real work with Errol." I laughed and told Zack I'm playing with him.

When it was my turn to spar Errol, I was alert from the start. He wasn't Floyd chief sparring partner for no reason. He is a powerful fighter who throws a nice variation of shots. I used my jab and combinations. I put in another good performance.
I know Nate is happy with my performances, every week they get better. Errol could be a world champion in the next four years.

I was asked to spar Errol for a reason, I've been putting in respected performances over the last eight weeks and I know they wanted to see what I could do with Errol. I did what I was supposed to do. My defense was on point. I stood and traded, boxed and moved. After all this great training I'll be going back to Britain. My talent is truly wasted there. I need fights on the world scene. That's where I shine and thrive!

Sunday 28th April 2013

Today was the BBQ which was thrown by Floyd and The Money Team. It started after 3pm and finished around 9pm. It was a great day out of the gym, socializing with the other boxers.

Floyd spoke to around 15 boxers who train at the gym about being a fighter, promoter and manager. The downsides and upsides of the business, he also said that he had put Heavyweights out of business. He praised Boza as a champion who had fought the worlds best and a man who knew boxing.

Boza asked if I could spar Errol Spence again on Monday.

Boza told Nate "Ashley is part of the team. We want more of that in the future." Nate responded with his humorous self "We want this work, Monday, Tuesday, Wednesday, Thursday." Errol with his big grin responds "I'm fighting Friday." Nate comes back "You don't want it then." I'm laughing by now. This is what Nate does but I love him for it. He chats a lot of smack. He's a great hype man but he believes in my talent. Nate went on to tell me "I've added to your game and I'm not finished yet." I said, "I could box before working with you". Nate replied "not like this you couldn't" Kevin Newman a young boxer at the gym joined in "you looking real nice now man. You wasn't doing that before." Nate asked me if i wanted him to stop adding ingredients to the stove. I said continue to add. Nate went on "I'm cooking you up right now and adding in all these nice spices. When I'm finished with you. You are going to be a killer." Nate has added to my game. Just being in this environment is something that can only bring the very best out of a fighter. I've noticed whenever I come back to the UK it's like my skills are dormant. They awaken when I'm in the States. I'm happier as I'm doing what I always wanted to do. I could easily live here and ply my trade.

Monday 29th April 2013

I sparred Errol Spence Jr. again today. It was a good session. We started off by doing a three minute round then Boza extended it and made us do a further three four minute rounds. Errol is strong, well conditioned and has a good array of boxing skills.

The point that the money team requested me to spar Errol shows they think highly of me as Errol was giving Floyd very competitive work throughout camp.

Tuesday 30th April 2013

Floyd asked Dejuan and Nate how my sparring went with Errol. It is good that the champ is taking notice of the work I am putting in.

In the gym there was a fighter who came in and Floyd remembered him and started to speak to him. Floyd told him "before you join the team you have to go through initiation." Then speaking to all the boxers around, he asked "Who are you going to go through in the doghouse?" J'Leon and Lanell shouted out "give him that Ashley Theophane work."
So Floyd called me over, there was a lot of talk going on. Two other fighters offered their services but Floyd said he wants him to receive some overseas beat down.
Normally they give initiations to an amateur who goes by the name of Memphis. Ladarius "Memphis" Miller would rack up a professional record of 21-1 from 2014 to 2020, beating future world champion Jamel Herring in the process.

Wednesday 1st May 2013

I was supposed to spar that kid who was mouthing off to Floyd yesterday but I arrived at the gym late as I thought it was closed as Floyd had his press conference earlier in the afternoon. The gym opened up afterwards. I had called Nate to find out what time Floyd was training as I wanted to watch, he told me to hurry up and come to the gym. By the time I got there, they were in the ring already. I put on my workout clothes but Memphis didn't want to share the limelight. I got to spar with a 6ft southpaw. He was young and flashy but those 5 minutes rounds drowned him and he ran out the ring after two five minute rounds. I'm no joke!

Oliver McCall and Tony Tucker were in the gym today. Oliver even sparred with one of the young fighters. Tony has been coming every day this week to see Floyd workout.

The Media workout at the MGM Grand lobby went smooth. All the guys had worked out
beforehand, then they went to sweat out for the fans.
The press conference in the morning was good. I sat with the team whilst the fighters were on stage speaking about how they felt about their fights.

Some British media was in the house so I spoke to them about how my time was going. Kugan Cassius from iFilm London got me to interview Lanell Bellows, I was out of my element but I'm proud I swam and didn't drown.
Floyd put in a late night workout. I headed back to the gym with Bob Ware after the team did their media workout at the MGM Grand to watch it. He started around 9pm and finished 11pm. After his workout, Floyd was signing some papers on the table in the lounge area when I asked Ishe if he was going the fight. Floyd looks at him and says, "I got you, you're coming." He calls over Jeffro, one of his security team and tells him to give Ishe, Kitchie's number to tell her to sort his ticket out.

Nate told me to ask Floyd for a ticket as he would give it to me as he knows all the work I've been putting in with his fighters.

I've not only learned from Floyd about great work ethic but how he treats his fans. He shows them the utmost respect and appreciates their support. He signs boxing memorabilia and take photos with them all the time.

Floyd generates an estimated 100 million dollars over his fight weekend. 250,000 people will fly in for his fight. Floyd helps the Las Vegas economy with his fights.

Thursday 2nd May 2013

The Press conference at the MGM Grand for the undercard went smoothly and without any real hitches.

J'Leon put in a crazy workout today. We would later find out he was 9 - 12 pounds heavy. He completed 6 five minute rounds sparring with Luis. They were in great shape but I think it was too hard a workout to do before their fight.

Floyd didn't start training until 10pm. I was told he would be in from 8pm but I knew it would be nearer 9pm as I was here the night before. Floyd hanged out in the chill out area with Adrien Broner and the rest of his close people who came to watch him fight.

Floyd put in a good workout. He started on the heavy bag. He completed around thirty minutes straight on the bag followed by twenty minutes pad work and body bag work with Nate. He then hit the speed ball, showed off his skipping skills and did a quick strength conditioning workout. He went straight through for around ninety minutes.

Everyone was chilling outside the gym until 12.30am. I ended up leaving as I had to workout in the morning.

I got speaking to world champion Adrien Broner. He asked me "when next you out?" I told him that I was fighting May 18th. He replied "Easy money". He is due to fight Paul Malignaggi. We took a photo and parted ways. I'd never think, three years later that we would be fighting.
Anything is possible!

Friday 3rd May 2013

The boxing gym is closed today and for the rest of the weekend due to Floyd's fight. I'll only be doing one session today as we have to get down to the MGM Grand for the weigh in at 1pm and pick up our credentials.

I ran down the strip and around Vegas, It was longer than my usual run. 1 hour and 45 minutes, which was about 15 miles.

Nicole who works for Mayweather promotions sorted out our credentials which we picked up at the MGM box office.
The Weigh in was attended by around 8,000 people. It was an event in it self. Mexican music was played to entertain. The weekend being Cinco De Mayo which is a big Mexican holiday. Floyd is no idiot! He has fought on this weekend for years now as it is a very profitable. Soon he may run out of Mexican fighters to beat up. Saul 'Canelo' Alvarez stands out as the best right now, but at 22 years old is far from ready for Floyd but it would make a mega amount of money.

Floyd came late as usual so the co main events were weighed in before him. Floyd scaled 146lbs which is easy for him as he weighed 144lbs for the last four weekends.

All of the fighters made weight except for J'Leon. I was told he was 9 - 12 pounds overweight 24 hours ago. All this week he has been training in s sweat suit. He did an intense sparring session with Luis what was not even needed. JLeon was 2 pounds overweight after killing himself to make weight. When walking with Badou Jack out of the Arena we saw JLeon and the team rushing back to make within the hour given. J looked like a dead man walking. He made 160lbs.

Dinner with Badou Jack was the plans for Dan and I. Badou had twelve of his Swedish friends over the fight so we went to an Italian restaurant for a meal. We had a good time. The food was nice, if not a bit heavy for my waist line.

After the meal Dan dropped me to the MGM as Floyd's assistant had my ticket for me to pick up from the VIP lobby.
When I got into the VIP lobby, some of the fighters were there hanging out and some other friends and family of Floyd were coming to pick up their tickets. Leonard was there and tickets were all around so I text Dan to come inside as he'd been trying to contact Leonard all week as Floyd had promised him tickets to his May and September fights as a thank you for sending him a letter whilst in Prison last summer.

I picked up my envelope with my fight ticket and thanked them for the love. Dan walked in and spoke to Leonard. Leonard pulled a ticket out of his inside pocket and gave it to Dan.

I was happy for Dan that he got his ticket as he'd been my wing man for majority of my trip.
When I opened my envelope I was surprised to see that I had three tickets worth $1500 each and not the one I expected. I don't know who I'll give it to but I'll decide by tomorrow.

We hanged out until 4am. We had a good time. We met a few group of girls on their hen night. One set from Boston were a funny bunch who wanted to show off their strength by banging out press ups in their high heels. They did great! One doing twenty press ups and the other doing thirty. They were all taken, be it engaged or in a relationship but they were entertaining.

Saturday 4th May 2013

I only had four hours sleep but I was still excited for my day ahead of me. 90 minute run was the best way to start my day. Sun beating down on me.
I decided after my run to give my 3 extra tickets to Ohara Davis. He was an amateur from London who'd come to Vegas for three weeks. I was impressed with three out of the four sparring performances I saw him do at the gym and I knew how happy it would make him. Floyd made me happy by inviting me and I wanted to pass that love on. He went to the fight with his coach Tunde and Anthony Yarde.

You can tell a man's character by how he treats people who can not do nothing for him. Ohara thanked me and told me he wouldn't forget what I'd done for him.
Funnily enough, four years later he would turn professional and call me out after Floyd laughed at him being WBC Silver champion. When Ohara told Floyd at a meet and greet with fans, about his titles he'd won. Floyd would reply he only has gold ones. After Floyd's talk, Ohara would confront him about what he said.
Ohara's PR guy, Charles Sims who was in with Eddie Hearn would make sure that Sky Sports gave it loads of media attention. Ohara had told me he would call out the other TMT guys, but they were fairly unknown to the UK fans so he had to call my

name. It didn't bother me. I had just fought for the world championship and headlined in Las Vegas, which very few Brits had done. Why would I fight him? Only for the money and Eddie Hearn was offering less than what I was making with Mayweather Promotions. One offer was so low, Leonard didn't tell me and Ohara would say at his fight press conference I turned down the fight with him, when Eddie had offered money that would barely pay for my training camp.

Dan had bought two $800 tickets as back up just in case we did not get tickets as we'd hoped and expected. That's nice to know he would have treated me. He's a true friend. He sold one ticket and gave the other to Armando from the gym. He was an 18 year old kid who's always training. Dan wanted to do the same as what I did and pass the love on. He could have easily sold his ticket he bought but he chose not to.

We got there early and watched all the boys. Lanell Bellows, Luis Arias, Badou Jack and Ron Gavril. Luis had a hard fight but he showed heart and determination. J'Leon had me scared. It should have been a routine win but with that drastic weight loss I was now worried about what would happen. My thoughts turned to reality as he had a life and death fight. After ten hard fought rounds and being dropped. He won a split decision. He was booed by the crowd in a scene I'd never witnessed before. As Floyd always says at the gym "It's who you know." J needs to take his weight seriously from now on or he'll never achieve what he is capable of.

I didn't pay much attention to the two co-main events even though the fight between Ponce De La Leon and Abnar Mares looked like a great fight. I mingled and spoke to some of the money team, took a few photos with fight fans who recognized me and just waited on Floyd to make his entrance. We had a great view of the ring.

Floyd walked out accompanied by the money team and Lil Wayne. The fully packed MGM Garden Arena was excited and making so much noise. I never expected to actually come Floyd's fight and to be invited by the man himself was a testament to my hard work and dedication. He had rewarded me for it!

Floyd seemed so relaxed in the ring like he knew he was on another planet to Robert. I told everyone that it would be a late stoppage. Some people thought a wide points win as Floyd had not stopped no one in years.

Dan and I went backstage with Roger Mayweather, his grand mother and Boza to meet the rest of the guys.
Floyd attended his post fight press conference with his fighters sitting behind him. I stayed in the background with the rest of the team.

After the press conference Floyd stayed in the lobby for thirty minutes autographing his fans items and taking photos.

We followed him to his SUV and he noticed me standing there with the team.
He shouts out to the media, "I got fighters in the money team from the UK." Floyd called me over and we took a photo with Badou Jack and Ishe Smith. Floyd left and jumped in his SUV and headed home.

I ended the night with Dan, Bob Ware, Lanell Bellows and a bunch of girls at a lounge at the MGM Grand.

Afterwards Dan and I went for breakfast at another hotel. He dropped me home and we said our good byes. It was after 6am now. I wanted to stay up and go gym at 9am but I finished packing and collapsed asleep. I'd been up for 24 hours. The excitement had been exhausting but this is a training camp I'll never forgot. I'm living my dreams here. Anything is possible but you have to pursue your goals and not wait for them to come to you.

Sunday 5th May 2013

I've spent 9 weeks in Las Vegas. 63 days of training and being amongst the best fighter of my generation. The highest paid athlete in the world. I've learned so much from being in his presence. I've soaked up everything. From the talks and advice he gave to me on our runs. Plus the wise words and life stories to the money team and I in the locker room. He admits that to be where he is today, is a lot to do with having smart people around him. For people who don't know Floyd and want to bash him because of what they have read or a clip they have seen on the internet, don't judge a man until you've been around him. I've watched Floyd and he is just like anyone else. He had a goal and he worked hard to achieve it. He's inspired me and I'll inspire people who look up to me.

I've had an amazing time in Las Vegas. Before coming here, I wondered about retiring as I have no career and no future in Britain. This was the best decision I've made. Sparring the world's best fighters, getting the stamp of approval from Floyd himself, The Money Team fighters and coaches. I know I have so much to give to the sport and so much to achieve. I won't achieve it as long as I stay in Britain. That's for sure!

Training Camp for Pablo Cesar Cano
on
Floyd Mayweather v Saul Alvarez

Tuesday 11th June 2013

Ladarius "Memphis" Miller who is the Nevada amateur champion told me "I need to work with you as you'll make me improve." I'm not too excited as I hate sparring amateurs but he is a good kid and he is a favourite of Floyd's. He sparred Floyd at the start of the Robert Guerrero training camp. So if he's good enough to do some rounds with Floyd, he's good enough to do some with me.

Wednesday 12th June 2013

This afternoon I was hitting the heavy bag when Floyd came up to me and said, "When do you want to fight?" Mike was taking off my gloves. Floyd told Mike "I'm going to get him a fight." All I have to do is keep working and stay patient. My time will come. Floyd continued to walk around the gym.

Saturday 15th June 2013

This morning I was up at 430am as we were going to Mount Charleston for our weekly run.
Eddie Muhammad leaves at 6am sharp, no matter who you are, he is leaving.

J'Leon, Luis, Badou, Ron and three others from the gym came along with myself to complete the run. I finished in 47 minutes and came first as usual. It was 5 minutes faster than my previous fastest time and I haven't done it in 6 weeks. I've come back here in great shape. It is a mind over matter run. You are not going fast but the mountains are hard on your legs and the air is thin as we are 9,000 feet above sea level.

Wednesday 19th June 2013

Today was another productive day. I sparred with Mickey Bey's sparring partner Rashad Ganaway (14-3-1) and LaDarius Miller who had kept on asking to work with me. We did two five minute rounds and I stopped him in the second round. He pulled a no mas. He wanted no more. He quit in the fourth minute but we told him, you can't quit in a fight, work through it. He walked around for around a minute. Then Dejuan said 60 seconds left he came at me banging away. I covered up and retaliated. He soon backed away!
Afterwards he told me how tomorrow he was going to kick my ass and throw some elbows in my face. I told him I wouldn't be losing any sleep. Rashad is okay. He has some skills but fades badly.

Ishe Smith said it was disrespectful for LaDarius to ask me for sparring as I'm an experienced professional and I'm no joke.

Ishe went on to say that me and him had exactly the same career and all I need is that chance and I can be a world champion.
I told him I felt the same and that is why I was so happy for him when he won the world title. It was nice of him to say that and recognize we've had pretty similar careers.

He said I basically beat Danny Garcia and if he didn't have a chin I would of stopped him. He said look at Danny now. You are that level!

Mickey Bey is due to fight two weight world champion Jorge Linares in a WBC eliminator. None of the top ten want to take the fight for the vacant belt vacated by Adrien Broner, who has gone up to Welterweight to fight Paul Malignaggi for the WBA world title.

Mickey has asked me for sparring in the lead up to the fight. His words where "sparring with you will help me get the knockout win I want as you are super strong".

Mickey isn't even ranked and Floyd has got him a world title eliminator. He did the same for Ishe, he got him a world title shot when he wasn't even ranked. He would later do the same for me and get Badou to jump the queue ahead of mandatory challenger George Groves.

As Floyd says, "I run boxing".

It is important to surround yourself with positive people and positive things will happen.
Surround yourself with negative people and negative things will happen. I cut myself away from a lot of people I grew up with as I couldn't be around them and the criminal activities they were doing. You're guilty by association. I rather be by myself, working towards a goal than be around negative energy. Right now I am in a positive environment where everyone is rooting for one another, that feeling is priceless.

Monday 24th June 2013

Don't let doubters and haters break your dream from becoming reality. Let them fuel your fire and desire to achieve your dream.

Last week someone in Las Vegas said to me "Ashley, you're a Superstar". I guess coming from where I'm from. I am.

Ishe was giving advice to the young fighters in the locker room and he used me as an example "This game is unforgiving. Ashley basically drew with Danny Garcia who is getting millions of dollars a fight. When last you fight Ashley? You getting millions of dollars a fight? Nope! Case closed!"

Tuesday 25th June 2013

Mickey Bey told me that he wouldn't be using Rashad for sparring anymore as world title challenger John Molina will be his opponent on July 19th "You strong as hell so you will be all I need to be ready"

Wednesday 26th June 2013

I completed a 45 minute run this morning followed by an hour strength conditioning workout at 24 hour fitness centre. I had a four hour rest period then I headed out to the Mayweather Boxing Club. I completed an hour of work in 40 degree heat before even sparring Mickey.
Skipping, Shadow boxing, speed bag drills and one thousand abdominal and back crunches.
I started off sharp working my jab. Then I started countering

Mickey. I controlled the pace with Mickey fighting on the back foot. It was competitive rounds. We got through four rounds of five minutes and I was happy with myself. I noticed that Mickey was not getting out the ring and he was sipping water. It wasn't over yet. If I was tired, I know he was. I went over to the corner got my head wet with water. We fought through our exhaustion. We had Nevada professional referee's in the ring with us. We hardly clinched so their work was easy with us. We finished strong and completed five rounds of five minutes. That's just over eight rounds. I went on the heavy bag for four rounds whilst Mickey hit the speed bag. I weighed 149.5lbs afterwards. I'm happy with my weight and condition.

Thursday 27th June 2013

J'Leon has his hearing tomorrow for failing the drug test for his fight on Floyd's undercard against Gabriel Rosado. I've told him a little fine and three months suspension will be a good result. He's in good spirits, we went out for a meal with some of the guys after training.

Friday 28th June 2013

J'Leon got banned for six months and a ten percent fine of his last purse, so that's around $10,000. He will be out until November so he can still fight at the end of the year.

I sparred Mickey today. Beforehand I had completed a 12 mile run, an hour weights and 15 minutes of swimming.

As usual I put in a good performance. I feel I have so much more in me though. Mickey asked me what I ate as I seem to have good energy levels and never get tired. I just train hard, so my body is used to the hard work. Mickey said he normally takes over half way through fights or sparring but not with me as I'm consistent with my performance.

Dejuan said that there's a good chance I'll get on the September card and that he's been trying to get me on Ishe's card but its full.

Ishe was sparring Luis when Luis timed a picture perfect left hook. It hit Ishe under his
eye brow. Luis turned away and shouted out, "You're cut!" When Ishe turned his face towards my direction, I yelled out "oh shit". All I saw was blood.

We rushed Ishe to the hospital and waited for him to get stitches. Ishe wanted to still fight but Eddie said the fight is off. Ishe was down at first but Eddie said it happens in our business. Muhammad Ali was injured before the George Foreman fight in Zaire and that fight was postponed. Eddie used to be a sparring partner to Muhammad Ali.

Maybe Ishe can get the Miguel Cotto fight now instead.

Leonard Ellerbe said the show will still go on with Mickey and Badou moving up into the televised fights.

Thursday 4th July 2013

Today is Independence Day in America. I've never celebrated the day before as being British, this day marks when America broke away from Britain. The two countries have maintained a healthy relationship through the years.

We started our day off with a 5am start. LaTondria came to pick me up as usual. We met the guys at Mount Charleston for 6am. We arrived early as usual which is good as Eddie will leave you if you are late.

I came first as expected which was no surprise. It is not a race but there is a couple of strong runners in the field who try and test me. As normal they failed and I finished first. I am the Floyd Mayweather of the mountains. Undefeated!

The time was 5 minutes slower than the previous week. Arash was not there so I could take my time with it. No matter how fast you run it. It is a hard run!

Afterwards we went to Baby Stacks Cafe where Eddie picked up the tab. Everyone says I eat as if it is my last meal and I'm about to go to the electric chair. We had a good time as always.

Eddie Muhammed told me that once Floyd sees me spar he will get me a fight. Badou
interrupted and said Floyd already told Ashley he will get him a fight. Eddie replied he is a man who is true to his word, he just takes his time but he always comes though.

Some of us would meet up a couple hours later and head down to some doctor's house down Anthem Country Club. He had a beautiful place. It is always nice to meet different people. They were friendly and we all had a good time. Good company, good food and some fireworks. It was a fun day.

Today my status of getting a work visa, came up twice in two different conversations. It sounds like it could be a hard task. Rene is on the case but the US government have clamped down since 9/11. I'm a sports man. I'm entertainer. My future lies here. The guys have said if I need a place to stay whilst I organize my future I can stay with them. We are truly friends if not family.

Friday 5th July 2013

Floyd passed by the gym today whilst we were working out.

I had just finished putting in work with Mickey, shame he wasn't 10 minutes earlier as I was looking unstoppable.

Whilst I was hitting the bag he came up to me, touched my glove and said I need to get you a fight.
I said I'm here waiting Floyd. He began to walk to Mickey who was also hitting the bags, he turned round and said I need to get you a fight, repeating it to himself. Reminding himself!

He spoke to Mickey and I continued to work.

Afterwards training, Mickey told me that he put in a good word for me with Floyd. Telling him that I'm strong and that I've given him the best work he's ever had.
He said that Floyd laughed when he said, "He's as strong as hell". He's from down south. It's a term they use.

I told Dejuan afterwards what Floyd said to me when he was dropping me home. He said I've been telling Floyd about you so he knows you're ready.

I told him it's only a matter of time.
Everyone is talking about me and has nothing but good to say about me.

Saturday 6th July 2013

Floyd was hosting a party at the Gallery night club in the hard rock hotel and casino tonight.

There was around twenty of us. Floyd made sure drinks was flowing for his family and friends. I don't drink so I stayed on water for the night. Ty Barnett who I'd tried to get a fight with a couple months ago was in the club and hailed me out. I didn't know who he was at first but Luis called me over and said Ty Barnett wanted me. He was drunk and on a hype. I know he wanted a confrontation but I wasn't going to give it to him. He said I called him out. I replied, "You didn't want the fight at 140lbs so forget about me." He told me to tell my boss (Floyd Mayweather) to make the fight. I was willing to go to his hometown of Washington DC and fight for $5,000 as it was an easy win. I'm not giving him a pay check. Dejuan saw the commotion and called me over. Dejuan told Floyd that Ty was trying to start something with me and that we can open the gym now and you go and beat him up.

J'Leon told me afterwards that he had told Ty the same thing to come to the gym and get that work. Ty wasn't having none of it and wanted to get paid. That ship has sailed.

The situation ruined my party for me but Floyd made my night but telling me in front of everyone that I will fight on his boxing card on September 14th and that I'll get one beforehand. I'm so happy! The hard work has been worthwhile but I have to continue the form I've shown in the gym. I'm ready for this. It's what I've always wanted.

Wednesday 10th July 2013

I put in my best performance today in sparring with Mickey. I was sharp, worked my jab,
countered effectively, digged in some painful body shots and let my combinations go.

We were supposed to do five 5 min rounds but Mickey came out the ring after four rounds. It is very hot in there so I was happy when he took his head gear off. I walked to Todd Harlib who was doing my corner and asked him if Mickey was doing another round. He replied that he's taking off his head gear. I was relieved!

Afterwards Mickey said that he'll keep telling Floyd about me as I've got him in the best shape he's ever been in and given him the best sparring he's ever had. He said every session is harder than any fight he's had. I do appreciate that so much. Everyone is routing for me and showing me love. Mickey said I deserve the big money fights and I do.

Mickey said Floyd was happy about what he told him about me and asked questions about me.
He said we go hard but there is no malicious between us.
He's a good guy and just like what Eddie, J'Leon and Ishe said amongst others. Floyd will come through and always sticks to his

word.

I just have to keep doing what I do. Todd said to me afterwards that I'm always consistent in sparring.

I've noticed that Floyd and the Mayweather promotion boxers get criticized a lot on the forums and social media. I guess I'm going to have to get used to that as well now as I am affiliated with the team now, even if not officially with them.

Without Rene none of this would be possible. I know and appreciate that! Whatever happens this is an experience of a lifetime. I personally know the number one boxer in the world and one of the greatest fighters ever. He knows who I am. This is incredible. I never imagined this possible, but this is my life now and I will work my hardest to make the most of any opportunities that arise.

Tuesday 16th July 2013

I'll remember this day for the rest of my life.

Today was the day. Floyd Mayweather continuously has said he will get me a fight, so I was worried about sparring him. It could have gone two ways. I get beat up like most of his sparring partners or I could advance my movement into the Mayweather team.

I did a workout beforehand as I didn't think I'd get the call, as there's four or five other guys here. Boza told me to be ready just in case, so I put on my gloves and head gear. "Champ wants you" is shouted out towards me. My heart is pumping fast, but I wasn't nervous. Floyd gave me his gloves to spar in "Money

Mayweather" embroidered across them. I couldn't wear my face guard as Floyd doesn't like hitting the bar which goes across the face.

I went in the ring and across from me was Floyd Mayweather. It was a dream come true. We had the champ waiting for a few minutes as Boza fixed up the gym head gear on my head.

I've watched Floyd spar loads of guys and I'm happy just watching, as there is somedays he puts a beating on his sparring partners. Today wasn't to be that day.

They were talking about me in the locker room afterwards. Dejuan and Nate said you have to get him a fight. Floyd replied "he's on my card."

His personal assistant David Levi, gave me a ride home and told me that Floyd said after our session in the locker room that I have "crazy man strength".

I spoke to Leonard and told him I want to get on the Mayweather team and that's why I haven't fought this year as that's been the goal. He gave me his personal number and said call him tomorrow morning. Dmitriy Salita my good friend had put in a word for me and so had Mickey Bey. Now that Floyd has tested out my skills. It seems to be a done deal.

Everyone who was watching said I did well, I wasn't fazed and held my own. I hit Floyd with some good shots but he has super speed and reflexes. I loved it! He was doing his classy defensive moves. I'm a fan, I loved it even more as he did it against me. I made a few mistakes which Floyd took advantage of. He's not the number one fighter in the world for nothing.

Hassan, one of the young boxers who I hang out with when we are not at the gym said that Floyd respected me in there as he didn't trash talk me that much.
I remember him saying during sparring "we already know what happened the last time I fought a British fighter."

Boza told me afterwards that he loved my confidence in there and that he was proud of me.

Rene Carayol believed in me. Anything I achieve is because of him because he made it
possible by giving me the resources for this trip.

We not there yet but we took a giant step today.

Wednesday 17th July 2013

Today was media day for the guys on the card but I got to do some interviews with a few websites about my next move.

I'm due to sign with Mayweather promotions but Leonard told me today that I need an email from Hatton promotions saying I've been released then we can move forward.

Nate said that I surprised him yesterday and did much better than he thought I would do. I told him "you don't believe in me talent!". He replied "Floyd is a great fighter."

Friday 19th July 2013

Ron, Luis and Badou won. All put in good performances. It hurt me that Mickey lost as I helped in his preparation but setbacks are lay ups for comebacks. He was winning nine rounds and in the tenth and final round got caught with a couple shots after letting go of a blistering 30 second combination. All he had to do was last the final 60 seconds and he would have been fighting for the WBC 135lb title on Floyd's undercard. Now he has 60 day suspension. Other than that it was a great night for the team.

Saturday 20th July 2013

After a long night at the Hard Rock Casino and Hotel, I wasn't happy to come back home and see that the electricity was out. I went straight to bed and woke up after seven hours to put in a 9 mile run.

A few hours later I was in the Mayweather Boxing Club putting in some hard work. Being a sparring partner for Floyd Mayweather I cut my workout short by four rounds so I only do eight on the heavy bags and pad work with Nate. It doesn't sound a lot but it adds up after ten rounds on the speed bag, skipping and shadow boxing plus my abdominal and back crunches.

I ended my day with fellow professional boxer Zach Cooper, who is undefeated in three fights. He invited me to Las Vegas against Seattle Lingerie Football League's clash. He is from Seattle and knows one of the girls in his State's team. It was an enjoyable night. Afterwards he dropped me home. Never a dull day in Sin City.

Sunday 21st July 2013

Today Ishe had his birthday dinner. It was at a restaurant near the Red Rock Casino and Hotel. We had a good time. It is always fun hanging with the guys outside of the gym. Dejuan said that I'll fight on the 13th or 14th. I just want to fight!

Monday 22nd July 2013

In the locker room Floyd asked me when am I fighting. I told him I'm waiting on you guys. He turned to Leonard to ask him what is going on. Leonard told him he's working on it.

I stayed for Ishe's workout. I was at the gym for eight hours. I did my workout, watched Floyd then watched Ishe.

Tuesday 23rd July 2013

Today I spoke to Leonard about my P-1 visa. Rene is dealing with it in London with Mischon De Reya. I am just worried about my past as a criminal. When you are a kid and you are doing these stupid things that you think are cool, you never know in the future it could affect you. Floyd Mayweather wants to sign me and get me fights. This is the only thing that can mess it up.

Wednesday 24th July 2013

Another beautiful day in Las Vegas, the sun is shinning and it is another day of
positivity.

I completed a four mile run followed by an hour strength conditioning workout at 24hr fitness centre. I had a couple hours rest, ate and headed off to the boxing gym. I completed my 90 minute workout which consisted of 22 rounds of work; skipping, shadow boxing, speed bag drills, pad work with my coach Nate Jones and heavy bag work. I finished up with one thousand abdominal and back crunches.

As a Floyd Mayweather sparring partner you never know if you are sparring Floyd. You get your sparring gear on and you get told as he gets ready into the ring so you need to stay ready. Right now there is seven of us.

The sparring partners who don't get picked normally hit bag for twenty minutes. That's not good enough for me so I rather workout beforehand and rest for an hour to recover and if I spar Floyd I'll be okay.

Floyd put in a master performance today. He spar Dequan Arnett who had just been in camp with
Keith Thurman and was supposed to of done really well against Keith. He told me he was thrown out of camp as he was beating Keith up. He said he had asked Al Haymon who manages him to get him that fight. So I expected him to do well against Floyd.

Floyd is not Keith! There's Floyd Mayweather then there's other

fighters.
Floyd beat him around the ring. Observers were saying that Dequan won't last the whole camp with Floyd and that Floyd could shorten his career before it has really started.

I want to get in so badly and test my skills against Floyd and see if he can do what he does to these other fighters to me.

Watching Floyd at close quarters five days a week is such a great experience.

I can see why he is the best. It isn't by luck. He works extremely hard.

Afterwards Floyd did a range of interviews with different pay per view channels promoting the fight. Listening to him talk he never forgets to praise his team which includes Al Haymon, Leonard Ellerbe, his father and his uncle Roger Mayweather. As he says, "Family first".

Floyd Mayweather is a rock star. I see close hand the amount of cameras that follow him and the amount of fans that come to the gym in hope of seeing him.

After training I hanged out with Ishe Smith for a bit and had some words with Leonard Ellerbe.

Leonard told Ishe that I'll probably get on the Friday show before Floyds at the Cosmopolitan hotel.
Leonard asked me if I could make 140lbs. I said I'm 150lbs now and that you just have to tell me I have a fight. He said it could

come soon as he was talking to someone 1am last night and thought about me but doubt they wanted that work off you as they were looking for an easy fight. He went on to say that, "You'll never get a call from me saying that there's a fight next week. We make the opportunities but you just crossed my mind last night."

When you surround yourself with positive people, positive things happen.

Friday 26th July 2013

Floyd put in a blistering performance in sparring today. One of his sparring partners only made it through one round as Floyd busted his nose. Blood was everywhere! "Get out the ring. Bring in the next one". Floyd barked out!

Stepping in the ring with Floyd is like death row for most of his sparring partners. It is a pleasure to watch. The man has it all.

The second sparring partner tried as they all do but Floyd punished him. Sweat and blood flew from his face as Floyd hit him. He shouted at Floyd "I have heart". Floyd answered back with brain damaging combinations and told him "heart doesn't win championships, skill does".

As I was hitting the heavy bags, Floyd came up to me and started lightly punching me in the back. I didn't know who it was so I just kept working away. I'm dead focused whilst working out.

It was a good day in the gym. Afterwards I went down to an amateur tournament with some of the money team fighters to watch some amateurs from Mayweather boxing club compete.

JLeon, Luis and I went down to the Mall as they wanted an outfit for Doralie's birthday dinner and party. I was tempted to go as the fight isn't for another seven weeks and I've been in training so I'm good but I wanted to be at my best in the morning for the Mount Charleston run.

There's a time to work and a time to play. Its work time right now for us.

Saturday 27th July 2013

Ishe came for me at 530am and we met Eddie for 6am. Tony and Arash also ran with us. I came first as usual. We did a very good time of 46 minutes. We didn't race but ran together which was still hard but we helped one another.
Afterwards I went to the boxing gym and hit bags for an hour.

Leonard called me whilst I was in the gym. He asked me how I felt about fighting Zab Judah. I said I'd love that fight. He asked me what I thought of Danny Garcia, what the scores where when we fought and where did we fight. I told him that Danny hadn't improved much since our fight and that the scores where close just a round in it and that it was in Texas. His response was that I basically won the fight. I said that's boxing for you. He told me not to say anything but he was trying to have it signed by Monday.
I wanted this fight for so long and it looks very promising. Mayweather promotions have the money to make it happen. I want this so bad. He maybe riding on a high from his loss to Danny

Garcia but that won't help him. He's ducked me three times in the past going back to 2008 when he fought at Madison Square Garden on the Roy Jones - Joe Calzaghe show. I was supposed to be his opponent. I believed I could beat him five years ago so now is no different.

Sunday 28th July 2013

I was awoken by a loud bang on my door this morning from Todd Harlib, who assistants me with my training. It sounded like the police were at my door which was confusing to me at 7am on Sunday in Las Vegas with me being a sportsman.

We headed down to the local track where we met Nate. It was a lung busting session. I didn't know what to expect but it was hard with a capital H. 20 laps of the track. Sprint one lap and jog the next for recovery.
I had to push myself but with most top athletes, you have to be self motivated and drive yourself to the top. Your team can only do so much for you.

I had three hours rest before world champ Ishe Smith came to collect me to go Bikram yoga. Everyone knows I do yoga so he wanted to see how good I really was. Anyone who does Bikram knows how hard it is. It was my first time trying this type of yoga. It was ninety minutes. From start to finish I was dripping of sweat.

It's been an intensive week of training but one that has been quality on all levels. Working with Nate, watching Floyd Mayweather and just being around the money team.

Monday 29th July 2013

Today I got some great news on my next fight. We are just waiting for my opponent to sign the contract then it will be announced.
I don't want no easy warm up fight. I've wanted this fight since I beat Demarcus Corley back in 2008 so I'm more than ready. I've had four months of excellent sparring which has seen me spar 5 weight world champion Floyd Mayweather, two weight world champion Celestino Caballero, former world champion Luis Collazo, the money team's Mickey Bey, Olympian Errol Spence, world rated fighters Shawn Porter and Vernon Paris. It gets no better than that.

Every time I've jumped into the deep end and fought the world's best I've pulled out career best performances.

I'm not someone who gets excited but fighting on September 14th at the MGM Grand against one of the world's best fighters. I'm ready!

Floyd sparred me and Leonard watched closely whilst Floyd and I sparred so they know what I'm made of and what my capabilities are.
I have to thank them for the opportunity as I'm just a kid from London and they have shown me love and respect always.

Most importantly Rene Carayol believed in me from when he saw me knock Lenny Daws around the ring. Two and a half years later we are about to do what we believed I could achieve.

Tuesday 30th July 2013

Leonard called me just before midday and said that the Zab Judah fight doesn't look likely. I brought up Kendall Holts name. He is a former world champion and just challenged for the title. Leonard said his name had been brought up but he lost badly to Lamont Peterson so it's not an attractive fight. Leonard then asked me what I thought about Humberto Soto. I said he's been on my list of opponents I'd like to face for years so if you can make it then make it.

I win then the IBF world champion Lamont Peterson would be next.

I was the chosen one today. "Ash, you're sparring."

Today Floyd came full throttle at me.

I guess because they giving me a hard fight so they want to see what I was made of.

His team said I did good as I hit him more than the sparring partners normally do. Floyd hit me much more than I'm used to. I can hang with him physically and fitness wise but his skill level is on another planet.

Nate said I did very good and he was disappointed in Floyd, as I hit him way too much and I was confusing him with my movement.

Shit! I'm just trying my best and trying to match him. I show him no respect in there and I know he likes that.

When I get in there with Floyd I believe that this is the level I belong at. No doubt he got the better of the session but I put up a good fight and that's after a 6 mile run, 75 minute strength conditioning session in the morning then a 90 minute boxing workout. I'm in great shape.

Wednesday 31st July 2013

Leonard called me in the evening to say that Humberto Soto wasn't interested in fighting me.

He asked me what I thought of Pablo Cesar Cano. I've seen his fight against Erik Morales a couple years ago. I remember thinking whilst watching it that I could beat Erik and Pablo. Now it is a possibility.
I said yes. He said he'll go to work and try make it happen.

Thursday 1st August 2013

I just had a meeting with Leonard and Mayweather promotions at the Mayweather Boxing Club.
They sat the fighters down and told us the rules and regulations. USDA will be doing random drug tests with us.
Leonard told the fighters that I'm officially part of the team but don't say anything as he's working on a big fight for me.
If I get the fight that Leonard is trying to finalise I'll get paid $100,000. A career high pay day for me.
He also recommended Boza as my assistant coach as he's been world champ and worked with Mayweather Promotions for years. Boza and I get on. He believes in me and has been supportive so

that's cool.
Pablo Cesar Cano is interested in the fight so it could be finalized very soon.
Leonard gave a nice talk about me today about me supporting the team and the younger fighters should come to me for advice as I've been around for a while.

I ended my day by going for a run with Floyd around a park. I thanked him for signing me.
We had a chat about boxing and life. It's been a great day!

Friday 2nd August 2013

Leonard told me today that the fight with Pablo Cesar Cano is confirmed at 143lbs for the opener of the PPV card. All I have to do is sign the contract so they can announce it.
Floyd and Leonard are giving me a big opportunity. I have to take it.
Nate said, "Prepare for this fight as if it is your last".
There can be no excuses. This kid has lost every time he has stepped up. He has given a good account of himself. Many even think he should have got the decision against Paul Malignaggi but he lost regardless. This will be his fourth loss.

Saturday 3rd August 2013

Ishe picked me up for 530am and we headed out to Mount Charleston. We met Eddie there for 6am. He was there with Ron Gavrill and his manager. Arash, JLeon, Badou and Cuba were expected but for whatever reason did not come. I was relieved as it was my turn to foot the bill at Baby Stacks Cafe afterwards. The bill was just half of what it could have been.
They weren't missed!

No one normally does anything after the run as it is so damaging on your legs but I try do something at the boxing gym just not any intense work. Daquan Arnett is a talented fighter and managed by King of Boxing, Al Haymon. He was due to spar with Memphis. I walk in after their scheduled time and he looks let down. I asked him if he wanted to work with me. He perked up and ran to get his sparring gear. He's currently 11-0.

Rumor has it he dropped Andre Berto and beat Keith Thurman up. So his reputation and confidence is sky high. My name wasn't added to his list of sparring victims. He is a good strong fighter but my conditioning and experience was the key. He gave me a good workout and I'm sure we'll go again over the next five weeks as he fights the day before me.

Rene gave me the all clear to sign the Mayweather promotions contract. Even if on paper it wasn't the best. It is worth the risk as their reputation in looking after their fighters is good. In January my head was heavy with thoughts on where I was going to go in boxing. No UK promoter showed me love and I didn't have the finance to come to the States.

It looked bleak and six months later I'm about to sign for Floyd Mayweather's boxing promotions. As they say, "Never give up".

Monday 5th August 2013

Over the weekend Ishe and I joked around about sparring together, he told me to bring my arm bands as he was going to bring me out to deep sea and drown me. I replied that I was looking forward to going deep sea diving.

I don't change my workout for anyone so I completed an 8.7 mile run in the morning. Before our sparring session I completed an hour workout doing shadow boxing, jumping rope, speed bag drills, abdominal and back crunches.

Ishe warned me before sparring "you shouldn't have done that 8 mile run in the morning. You're going to need your legs."

Ding! Ding! Four rounds of five minutes with 30 seconds rest. That's just under seven rounds.

Ishe caught me with some good shots to the head and body. Dejuan Blake shouted out to me "move your head Ash". Its easier said than done. Ishe isn't a champ for nothing.

I held my own catching the champ with some nice punches. Sparring bigger guys is what I need for this fight. I may take more punishment than I'm used to but as the saying goes "train hard, fight easy".

Afterwards I did ten minutes on the pads and ten minutes on the heavy bags. I finished up with some strength exercises and I was done.

Floyd came in to start his workout. I normally stay in the background but I heard someone call my name. I looked round and it was Floyd calling me over. He asked "you see the opponent I got you?" I responded "Thanks Floyd." I shook his hand and let him get on preparing for sparring.

To know that Floyd Mayweather knows my name and wants to help me in my career.
That is unbelievable!

Tuesday 6th August 2013

Leonard told me today that I will make $100,000 for the fight. That's £70,000 in Great Britain pounds. The most I've been paid before is £25,000 which is around $34,000.

I had a hard but productive day with Nate. We put in some quality work. After training we waited round to see if Floyd was sparring. He wasn't so I got in some extra sparring with Al Haymon fighter Daquan Arnett. We completed four 5 minute rounds.

Today I weighed 149lbs. With just over 5 weeks to go there is no issues with my weight. There never is!

Wednesday 7th August 2013

Another quality session in the gym with Nate, my combinations are working a treat and the game plan he wants me to use come fight time is a work in process.
After training, eight of us went out for a run with Floyd. At least once a week I try to run with Champ. It's just a bonus to do what I already do.

Thursday 8th August 2013

The announcement that I was on "The One" card was announced today. I have a tough Mexican in front of me but I'm confident in

my abilities, my training and my team.
I'll win and look good doing it.

Friday 9th August 2013

I woke up this morning to an avalanche of tweets, Facebook messages and Instagram likes and followers.
People keep saying it's a big event but that's not even a factor in my mind or training. I always train hard. I don't know no other way. I'll continue doing what I do as that got me signed in the first place.

Saturday 10th August 2013

I was up for 445am as Ishe was picking me up for 530am. We got to Mount Charleston for 6am and Eddie was waiting for us. Arash who is fighting Argenis Mendez, is a good runner and the only one who can compete with me on these runs.
No matter how fast you complete this 5 mile run it is hard. We run up to 9000ft above sea level. I completed the course in 47.35 minutes which is good. My fastest time is just under 45 minutes but that was when Arash and I were racing up here.

I had a few hours rest then headed out to the boxing gym.

I sparred over 5 minute rounds with 30 seconds rest. That's what we do here. Train hard. Fight easy. Afterwards I hit the bag and pads then finished up with my abdominal and back crunches.

In the evening the whole team went to the Monte Carlo hotel as the Nevada Boxing Hall of Fame had their event on. Floyd won fighter of the year and Ishe picked up an award for being the first Vegas born fighter to win a world title.

Mike Tyson, Sugar Ray Leonard, Julio Cesar Chavez, Michael McCallum, Bob Arum and Don King were all in attendance.

Larry Holmes acceptance speech was funny as he joked that Bob Arum wouldn't pay him the money he deserved and Don King would.

All of there greats spoke and it was enlightening and inspiring to hear it.

Floyd thanked his staff as always, plugged his fight on September 14th and told everyone how he believed in his fighters.

Sunday 11th August 2013

Yoga and a strength conditioning session was how I started my day. I then got a 90 minute massage.
I'm ready for the week ahead. My trainer Jihad Abdul-Aziz will be flying in from New York to assist Nate.

September 14th we will be putting on a performance. Pablo is a good fighter but he has shown his limitations in his fights with Mosley, Morales and Malignaggi. It will be a very entertaining fight and I'm happy to open the show for Floyd Mayweather.

Monday 12th August 2013

I sparred Duquan Arnett today as Floyd didn't pick me to work. I had already completed my daily 90 minute workout so I was happy with my performance. After 15 minutes of work, Duquan said he'd had enough.

Tuesday 13th August 2013

I did some rounds with Arash Usnamee who challenges world champion Argenis Mendez next Friday. His pressure was relentless. He will need to do that for the 12 rounds if he is to win next week.

Wednesday 14th August 2013

The PPV fighters did a Conference Call with the media this morning. Danny Garcia, Lucas Matthysse, Ishe Smith, Carlos Molina, Pablo Cesar Cano and I spoke about what it meant to be on a card this size and how our training had gone so far.

I sparred Floyd Mayweather this afternoon, he laughed and said he was playing with me. "I'm only working my defense today." I took this tool from him when I'd spar other fighters, mental games can mess with many fighters head. Throw them off their flow. Afterwards he told me "Some fighters I signed cause I like them. I signed you cause you can fight."

Rene Carayol flew my trainer, Jihad into Vegas from New York today.

Friday 16th August 2013

Ishe and I had an Interview on Fox 5 news. It went well. We promoted the "Back to school drive" that we are doing at the gym tomorrow as well.

Saturday 17th August 2013

The "Back to school drive" went well. Loads of kids turned up and it was nice to put a smile on the kids and parents faces. We also did some interviews which was cool.

Wednesday 21st August 2013

The Magic Show at the Mandalay Bay over the last three days was fun but hard and tiring work.

I had to spar Dequan Arnett yesterday. I asked him to go light and we ended up going hard. I started it though so I was to blame. Floyd, the money team and a couple hundred people were watching us. They promoted my name and "The One" card.

Rap stars Ty, Rick Ross and Jim Jones were there.
It is the biggest Trade Clothing show so it is a huge networking event.
Standing around for three hours followed by a two hour workout at the Mayweather Boxing Club was hard but I got through it.

Thursday 22nd August 2013

I got up 30 minutes early today as the BBC were calling me for an interview.

A few minutes afterwards Nate called me moaning that he wasn't happy that I wasn't giving him ten percent for the training fee.
He said I got signed because of the work he had done with me over the last few months. I told him everyone had a part to play in me getting signed. Dejuan, Ishe, JLeon, Mickey and Boza all put a word in for me with Floyd.
I also told him it was a team thing and that it isn't a Nate Jones thing. Its all about getting me a win on September 14th and we move onto the next one.
I told him he should be happy Jihad is here as when Floyd is working, he doesn't work with me.
He said I was right and wouldn't mention it again.
I told him I don't want to fight with my team, we are supposed to be working in the same
direction.

Rene informed me that my P-1 visa had gone through on Mayweather promotions side. I just had to attend an interview in London for it to be rubber stamped. I've been worried about this for weeks so it is a weight off my shoulders. I've been coming to the USA for eight years and I've never been in any issues, so it should be straight forward from here onwards.

Thursday 29th August 2013

Today was maybe my best performance in sparring. I started my day with a 4 mile run followed by an hour strength conditioning session and hour yoga at 24 hour fitness. That alone was hard but that's just the starter.

The main course was sparring with Cortez Bey. We worked on Saturday after the mountain run and it was quality work. I did well but today my legs and body were fresh. The sparring was vicious. I was in my zone. With something like 18 days to go. There are no games in there.
Eddie Mustafa Muhammed who now trains Cortez barked orders at him and tried to motivate him by saying I was tired at stages. I don't know what tired is. I have Floyd Mayweather to learn from. I see the work he puts in. I follow his lead, carving out my own reputation as a hard worker.

Nate shouted out his own instructions. "Where's the referee?" "Stop the fight." "Ash, you're killing him." It's all good preparation for the fight but I never pay attention to what's going on outside the ring. I'm focused on my opposition inside.
We completed 21 minutes of work. Three five minute rounds and one six minute round with 30 seconds rest.

I helped Mickey Bey get ready for his fight and now his brother, Cortez Bey is helping me get ready for mine.

Whilst watching Floyd workout I noticed there was some commotion going on outside. I later found out that Hasim Rahman had come to the gym with around twenty guys, some tooled up with guns. He brought Luis "Cuba" Arias to the gym and feels like he's owed some money for his troubles. He said he invested in Cuba, flying him out to tournaments and helped him out financially.

Friday 30th August 2013

I'm 33 years old today. I still feel the same. I don't feel any older. I feel great. I've never been a better boxer. I'm at my peak right now.

Pablo Cesar Cano has had three big fights. Losing three to Mosley, Morales and
Malignaggi.
They were all close affairs on the scorecards. I can't afford to lose as I'll never get another chance again. I'm pushing myself to my limit. Fitness is the key! If I can hurt him then I can beat him.

Saturday 31st August 2013

I completed ten rounds sparring today, after running up Mount Charleston with Ron, Badou and Ishe.
Ishe thinks I'll leave it in the gym but I'm used to training when tired. Different strokes for different folks. All the hard work is done now. Two more weeks until the world will be watching.

Monday 2nd September 2013

This is the last hard week of training.

In the morning Nate took me and two other fighters to the track. We completed a very hard session. I'm right where I want to be, fitness wise. I don't know what tired is.

A few hours later I went to the boxing gym. Its Labour day which is a bank holiday in America but to us boxers it's just a normal day.

I had another quality sparring session with Cortez Bey. I love the work that him and Daquan Arnett have given me recently, two young hungry lions.

I did some bag work, skipping, shadow boxing, speed bag drills and abdominal crunches as well.

An older gentleman commented on my fighting style and how I don't waste punches. He said I can do whatever I want to do in that ring. He said if I fight how I'm sparring not many fighters will be in a rush to fight me. It's always nice to be appreciated for the hard work you put in and the skill set I possess.

My trainer Harry Keitt from NYC arrived last night. He will be staying until the fight. I'm ready to rock and roll.

Tuesday 3rd September 2013

Started my day with a 9 mile run. Running down the strip got me thinking. I'm days away from opening up a mega show. One of the biggest fights in the last 30 years. Floyd and Leonard believe in my talent. Ishe Smith believes if I bring my sparring performances into the ring on September 14th, I could stop him. I'm so focused its scary. I respect him as a fighter, but I believe I'm better on all levels. This is my 40th fight and my 10th anniversary. What an event to be a part of, this is a career defining fight.

I sparred Ishe Smith today. Working with a world champion two weight divisions above me a week before my fight is great preparation. We go at it like we hate each other but its all love. We believe in each others talents and want each other to do well.

I worked with Nate on the body bag and Harry on the pads. I did some heavy bag work to finish off. Shadow boxing, speed bag drills, skipping, abdominal work and some strength training is what the rest of my training consisted of.
Another great day down, I weighed 144lbs after training.

Wednesday 4th September 2013

I started my day with a 5 mile run around the streets of Las Vegas, followed by a strength conditioning workout. We went hard at boxing today, we didn't rest. Its continuous work, be it for 5 rounds at a time or whatever the routine is that day. We go straight on bags, pad work, speed bag drills, skipping or shadow boxing. Only time we stop is to hydrate ourselves.

3 weight world champion Adrien Broner was in the gym working out today with his team.

Thursday 5th September 2013

Being a few pounds overweight with more than a week to go is a great thing. I haven't even reduced my food this camp. I've just eaten healthy. 3000 calories a day is the normal target. I start my day with porridge, raisins and sliced banana, drizzled in honey. That is packed with energy and leaves me full for most of the morning. I normally snack on fruit and yogurt. After training I have a protein shake and then maybe some fish or chicken with vegetables.

Adrien Broner was in the gym again. There's talk of him setting up camp in Vegas.

Friday 6th September 2013

I finished off my Nevada State Athletic Commission medical today with my MRA/MRI scan. I completed the physical, blood tests and optician tests weeks ago. I'm good to go.

My trainer Harry Keitt from New York has been here since Sunday now and its great him being here to assist Nate.
Harry has been working with me since I beat Demarcus Corley in 2008, so he's had some role to play in the biggest fights of my career. Dropping a split to current world champ Danny Garcia. Beating world number 3 Delvin Rodriguez and becoming British champion. Tell me who Pablo Cesar Cano has beaten? I don't know them either.
Who'd think that 6 years later, he beat world champion Jorge Linares in the first round by knock out. He truly carries bricks in his hands.

Wherever I train. Be it New York, London or Las Vegas. My work ethic is always congratulated. That played a big role in me getting signed by Floyd.

I completed 10 rounds of sparring today. I had already put in miles on the road and done a strength conditioning session in the morning so I'm in great shape.

Pablo Cesar Cano on record is a devastating puncher. 20 knock out wins in 26 wins but when you look at his wins. He knocked out nobodies and beat nobodies. Okay he gave Paulie a hard fight but I gave Danny Garcia just as hard a fight. You can't live off one performance. You have to look at a man's record and I have the better record when it was time to step it. To beat him I have to be on top of my game but I feel on top of my game. Show time is creeping up on us and winning this fight will be career defining as Floyd and Leonard want to throw me in against some very big names in my division. I started boxing for this. I always believed I would get here now its time to prove I belong at this level. Sink or swim time!

Saturday 7th September 2013

What a long day! It started just before 5am. I woke and got ready for our last run up Mount Charleston. Ishe came for me around 530am. Luis, Ron, Ishe and I were the money team fighters making the trek up the mountain.
As always it was hard. 5000ft to 9000ft above sea level. Hard on the lungs and hard on the legs, fitness should never be an issue for any of us.

Afterwards Eddie Mustafa Muhammad, Ishe and I headed to Baby Stacks Cafe. I always look forward to the delicious food they serve. That's my cheat meal for the week.

I got a 75 minute massage in the afternoon and took a trip to the barbers. Jumped in the shower and headed to the Palms hotel for the appreciation dinner in honor of Floyd. Floyd helps many people day in, day out. He helps people achieve their dreams and he is trying to help me achieve mine. He'll get you the opportunities then it is up to you to perform and get the result.

It's always nice to get dressed up. The food and dessert looked lovely. It was a four course meal. I only had two course, the chicken and salad had to make do for me. I left around midnight. Another long day tomorrow!

Sunday 8th September 2013

I woke up before my alarm of 7am went off. I put in a gentle jog along South Valley View. Afterwards I completed my weekly yoga, strength conditioning and swim at 24 hour fitness.

I chilled for a few hours then set off for the money team picnic. Everyone was there. There was an abundance of food there again. I stayed on my water as I had already eaten for the day. I'm only a few pounds over my weight limit so I'm good. I only started reducing my food today so all through camp I've been eating around 3000 calories which has seen my weight drop slowly. I put in a camp with Mickey Bey when helping him get ready. Now it's all about me so the intensity was kicked up a few notches.

I don't see why some 'experts' would have me as an underdog. I've beaten better opponents than he has. Giving someone a hard fought fight but still losing doesn't mean nothing. I've fought bigger punchers than him and I've fought fighters in great shape like Lenny Daws. This fight could be hard but it could also be easy.

Sparring Floyd was a huge mental challenge. You're in the ring with the best in the game but you have to stay composed. I've seen Floyd beat sparring partners around the ring. That experience of being in the ring with one of the greatest ever and the current number one fighter in the world will help me perform. It's all mental now. I've put in the hard work. Many people in the gym say I'm the hardest worker in the gym other than Floyd. I've been stopped on the street in Vegas and people have said how they've witnessed the work I put in and wished me the best. I even had a guy at the 24 hour fitness who asked for a picture and said I'm his idol. It's nice to be appreciated for the hard work you put in but you have to produce when it's showtime. September 14th is due to be the biggest PPV event ever and I'm the sole British fighter representing and as a money team fighter. It doesn't get no bigger. When I win, a world title shot will be next.

Tuesday 10th September 2013

Today it the dream of being on a Floyd Mayweather card got real.

In the weeks leading up to the fight I just focused on training and didn't think much about my opponent or the event. Journalists kept saying how big the event was but watching it and being part of it is a whole different story.

I arrived at the MGM Grand Hotel and Casino at 1pm as I had to meet Mayweather promotions before hand as I was walking with the rising stars of the promotion.

Andrew Tabiti, Luis Arias, Lanell Bellows, Ron Gavrill and I got in our Limo just before 2pm. We drove to the front of the hotel where the fans were waiting. There must have been a couple thousand. All the rising stars walked one by one to the stand along the red carpet. I was told to wait. It was my time to shine. I was shocked to see photos of me that fans wanted me to sign. I took photos and shook hands. This was superstar shit. I was nervous but I had my sunglasses on to hide it. I joined the team on stage and took photos with them as the photographers snapped away. The rising stars were lead away and I was told to wait for Pablo Cesar Cano. I was the opponent. I couldn't believe it. What bullshit had Mayweather promotions done. I'm used to being the opponent in America but this was my promoters show. I didn't understand this.

Cano arrived after signing photos and taking photos with fans. I didn't acknowledge him. He posed for photos just like I did beforehand. We were told to stand closer to take photos next to one another. Then we were told to look at one another. That's when it became serious. He looked in my eyes and I looked at his. No one was willing to budge. We just stood there ignoring the crowd, focused on one another. We were broken apart and told to stand one either side of the stage. Carlos Molina was next followed by Ishe. I showed no love to Carlos and Ishe showed no love to Pablo. Danny Garcia and Lucas Matthysse came and stood by us as well. The atmosphere is something I'll never forget. I feel like I was born for this stage but I'd lie if I wasn't a tad bit nervous, not about fighting Pablo Cesar Cano but the event itself. It gets no bigger than this. This fight is set to break all the records in America.

Saul Alvarez came to the stage a while afterwards. He had left by the time Floyd came. As usual Floyd was late but he's never early. He arrives on his own time.

I did interviews with Boxnation TV and the sun newspaper then I head to the gym with the team to start our own workouts.

I felt good and put in a 75 minute workout. Skipping, shadow boxing, speed bag drills,
abdominals and strength conditioning plus thirty minutes straight on the pads. 15 minutes with Nate followed by 15 minutes with

Harry. That's ten rounds! I started pads with Harry but he annoyed me when I was working my jab so I told him to get out the ring and I told Nate to come in. This is fight week. I'm wound up tight and have a short fuse. I'm so focused right now. Pablo and I are going to go to war. He thinks he can break me down but I'm stronger than he thinks. After training I weighed 145lbs. I ran this morning and I was 143.2lbs when I finished so I'm cool. Weight is no issue for me.

After training, the money team guys were chilling in the locker room with Floyd. He told me "just get your win and I'll get you a world title shot. You know I can make it happen." Ishe told Floyd that Shane Mosley broke Cano's heart and that I can do the same.

Floyd laughed and said, "Canelo is going to get this work. He may give me good sparring when I'm bullshitting but when those lights are on, no one can mess with me."

Being around Floyd motivates me.

Thursday 12th September 2013

I woke up weighing 144.4lbs, so I was very happy with my weight. That's just 1.4lbs over the weight limit I have to be.

I went for a 7 mile run and weighed 140.8lbs. I ate breakfast and went to the MGM Grand to meet the Showtime TV guys. Steve Farwood, Al Bernstein and Paul Malignaggi were there. Paulie has fought Pablo Cesar Cano so he knows what I'm up against. We basically spoke about signing with Mayweather promotions, sparring Floyd and my fight with Cano. I pointed out he has 26 wins and 20 knockouts but they are against nobodies. I let them know I had beaten the better opposition. Afterwards I went to get my head shots for the Shobox PPV. I got the Mayweather promotions limo back to the hotel and chilled for an hour before heading back for the press conference.

Harry met me at my apartment for 1215pm and we set off for the MGM Grand. I had to take some photos with fans and sign some autographs but its part of success.
When we got to the MGM Arena where the press conference was being held. I did some interviews with British and American press. The fighters were called to the stage and we went to where are names were. I was next to my boy Ishe. He inspires me so much. I'm hard headed and often listen to nobody but I respect him as our journeys have been similar. All I need now is that world title he has. Ishe told me not to go boxing today and I didn't. What would another day of boxing do? Nothing! We've worked hard for months and in my case since March.

The Nevada State Athletic commissioner Keith KIzer was sat next to me. Golden Boy CEO Richard Schafer opened up proceedings. Keith Kizer was next up to speak about the event. Richard Schafer said he wanted to put together the best undercard ever for Floyd Mayweather vs Saul Alvarez and he said that he has done that. He said all these fights could be main events in their own right.

He introduced Leonard Ellerbe. Leonard spoke about Andrew Tabiti, Lanell Bellows, Chris Pearson, Luis Arias then introduced me. He said how I offered any fighter with a name out for sparring. Which ended up with me sparring Floyd Mayweather. He said I was an old fashioned boxer that did it the old fashioned way, going into my opponents backyard.

I walked up to the podium, shook his hand and began to speak. I thanked Leonard, Floyd and the whole of Mayweather promotions. I spoke about how it was a big event and it was an honor to open up the PPV for three world champions in Ishe Smith, Danny Garcia and Floyd Mayweather.

I told the listening journalists that I started in London and I've made my way to Vegas after ten years and 39 fights. I told them how dreams come true. I let it be known that Pablo Cesar Cano was a hard fight but he always lost when it counted. Knocking out 20 nobodies means nothing. I was surprised how long I spoke. Many journalists said I stole the show and that my story was touching and that they wished me the best. Some said it was a good speech but I spoke too long. Speaking in front of a room full of people was always a nightmare for me as I have speech impediment but I've learnt to face my fears as you only succeed and become a better person that way. I thanked Leonard and Floyd again, then sat down.

Pablo Cesar Cano came to the stage after me. Richard Schafer said that he'd never be in a boring fight as his style is all action. Cano was simple and said he will let his fists do the talking.

Angel Garcia went at Team Matthysse hard but he praised me, saying I was Danny Garcia's first test and how I was a good fighter.
He normally goes at everyone was that was surprising but appreciated.
After the press conference I did interviews with journalists from radio, magazines and websites.
I headed to my room and called it a night.

Badou Jack was fighting. My thoughts were with him to start the money team's winning streak.
He got a draw but the statistics showed he should have won. He at least proved he belonged at world level as Sakio Bika had just won a split decision against Periban.

Friday 13th September 2013

The show continued as today was the weigh in. Once again, watching a Floyd Mayweather weigh in which I did in May is a totally different thing than being in one. There was eleven thousand people in attendance at the weigh in. It was basically a mock ring walk that I had to do with my team.

I was the only fighter out of the eight who stopped and took photos with the fans, signed t shirts and boxing gloves. I soaked up the atmosphere as this is a life time achievement for me. I'm living my childhood dream. Many people in the UK never believed I'd get here but the Americans showed me love all the way from 2005. They just liked me and respected my grind.

I walked to the stage where superstar fighters like Shane Mosley, Amir Khan Peter Quillen, Bernard Hopkins among others where waiting.

I'd watch the big fights with all the fighters I mentioned believing that I was good enough for that stage. I'm finally here! Hard work, persistence, always believing in myself and giving my all is what got me here.

Harry and Nate where walking behind me and when I got to the stage I noticed they wasn't there.
Richard Schafer asked me where my team was and I just said they were just here. His reply was "they probably got caught up in the moment."

My name was announced for weigh in. I started stripping to my underwear. I had got the times mixed up about being there before 2pm so I forgot to put on my superman socks and boxer shorts. I'll just wear them for the fight instead.
I had on some wore out green under but the show had to go on. I weighed in at 142lbs. That was perfect. I had made it. When I checked my weight at the gym 3 hours earlier I was 143.2lbs.

Pablo weighed in at 141.5lbs. He looked weak and drained. His team had to give him a chair to sit on as he waited for me to weigh in. A year before he fought Paul Malignaggi for the world title which many people thought he should have got the decision. I think it was a close fight. He didn't make the 147lb weight limit but you come in at 141.5lbs for our fight. Somethings up there. Doesn't matter to me anyway. It's going to be the same result.

Bernard Hopkins called us to do the stare down. We looked to the crowd then looked at each other. There was no blinking, no moving from either of us. The fight could be like that.

He went to shake my hand and I turned my back on him and walked away. The arena erupted, loud boos echoed around. This is how the fight will be. It will be full of Mexicans, he's a Mexican and it's a Mexican holiday. It is what it is.

This is a career defining fight for me and a life changing opportunity. I'm not being friendly with someone who wants to knock me out. We are here to fight not be friends.

As long as the judges are fair, that's all I care about. He can't outbox me, outfox me or out fight me. I'm better at everything than this kid.

He did an interview with showtime on stage and then I followed. Jim Lampley told me that how do I feel about the booing. I simply replied "I've beaten American boxers in America before. I'm used to it." I tried to sooth the crowd with a "I love Mexico anyway". If it worked or not we'll find out.

As I got off the stage, Amir Khan showed me acknowledgement and I walked off.

David Haye, Carl Froch and Amir Khan have all done great over the years on the world stage. I've watched and admired their achievements. With David I've been proud and inspired as I've known him since we were 15 years old. I finally get my time to shine against a fighter who has lost his last two fights.

Harry later told me that security wouldn't let him and Nate on stage so they were arguing.

Ishe came in at 151.5lbs. That was super light but better to be under than other.

The rules were you could only walk with two members of your team. Saul Alvarez followed that but I knew Floyd wouldn't. He walked with his whole team. It was such entertainment. I fell in love with the sport 28 years ago watching Mike Tyson, Floyd Mayweather has brought that excitement back. He is a superstar.

I messed up and walked with the fans outside of the arena. At first I blended in but then a group of girls recognized me and that was it. I couldn't move for the next 20 minutes. As I took one photo with a fan another would come. I would walk a couple steps then be asked again. It took around 45 minutes of my time. I've seen how Floyd treats his fans so I'm following the lead of the champ.

After the weigh in I refueled with my electrolyte and protein drinks. Harry and I then went for a meal. I bought two meals. I ate half there and half later that night. Salmon, chicken, pasta, rice and vegetables. That's as healthy as it comes.

I went back to my room and relaxed. My cousin Lee and my childhood friend Malchus had made the trip to see me fight. They supported me from my 1st fight so it was nice to see them here for my 40th.

I didn't go sleep until 2am but I was in bed from 11pm. I hardly sleep in the lead up to the fight so I'm glad I'm sticking to the routine.

Tomorrow is Saturday 14th September. It is a record breaking fight on many levels. From the gate receipts to the PPV takings and I am part of it.

Devon Alexander wished me all the best and told me to fight hard. I introduced my cousin Lee to world champion Peter Quillen in the MGM store. Peter tried to pick Lee up for the photo I was about to take. It was funny. Its great to have these fighters backing me.

Saturday 14th September 2013

Today was the day that months of hard work and dedication would come together. I didn't get the result I desired but as David Haye said when he messaged me after the fight. "It's good to be officially "World Class", so you never know what title shot may arise!"
I proved with my performance that I could still mix it with the best. Pablo Cesar Cano had just lost close decisions to Paul Malignaggi and Shane Mosley that could have gone either way, now he won a fight against me which was a split decision in his favor. I felt that I did enough to win but he felt the same way. Together we've fought Danny Garcia, Shane Mosley, Erik Morales, Demarcus Corley, Paul Malignaggi and Delvin Rodriguez. That's some very good opposition, our fight was always going to be close.

I was relaxed through the day and warming up for the fight backstage I felt confident. I feel like I was born for the big stage so this was my time. The walk in front of around 10,000 fight fans was what I always hoped for. I was ready for Pablo Cano. He entered after me. He was also confident. The plan was to box him for the first half of the fight and take it to him the last half of the fight. With all the Mexicans in the crowd, Nate told me I was the opponent and had to pressure Cano. With two rounds to go, he told me to go for the knock out. If Shane Mosley couldn't knock him out I had no chance but I knew I could hurt him. It was a great fight and you always want to be in fights where you have to dig deep and see what you are made of. Cano hit hard and is by far the biggest puncher I've faced during my career. I used my boxing skills to win rounds which saw judge Richard Ocasio award me the fight 96-64. Unlucky for me judges Richard Houck and Patricia More Jarman thought otherwise.

Ricky Hatton gave me his stamp of approval afterwards saying, "That was a great performance at world level."

Floyd Mayweather told me after he beat Saul Alvarez that I'll be alright and that he still has love for me. During his post fight press conference he told the world media that, "Ashley fought like a champion, I'm still proud of you."

Rene Carayol flew from the UK to watch me fight and he was proud of me also. As he said, "The dream continues".

Sunday 15th September 2013

In the evening Floyd Mayweather had a victory celebration at his mother's house. Family, friends and his team came to show love. It was a good night. He asked me "when are we going to London?" I replied "I'm waiting on you".

We watched his fight against Canelo. Whenever someone of the team would appear on the television, he'd shout out their name. When I was shown on the telecast. He shouted out "Ash, Ash". He's such a cool dude. He's brought me into his family and I have nothing but good things to say about the man.

My first victory with Mayweather Promotions
Ashley Theophane vs Robert Osiobe

Monday 14th October 2013

I always believed I would make something of my life. To say I had doubters is an understatement. Very few people believed that I would beat former world champion Demarcus Corley who gave my promoter and one of the greatest fighters ever, Floyd Mayweather a competitive fight. Two time world title challenger Delvin Rodriguez was supposed to beat me then fight Saul Alvarez. I beat him against all the odds when he was world number three. He went on to fight three weight world champion and Puerto Rican boxing legend three years later, Miguel Cotto. On the world stage I've only lost to number 140lbs king Danny Garcia and two weight world title challenger Pablo Cesar Cano by split decisions.

If you are willing to do the work, you can achieve anything.

There's no substitute for hard work.
There's no short cuts in the American Dream and I've put in the necessary work. My biggest achievements have been to be signed to Floyd Mayweather, fight on the record breaking PPV event headlined by Floyd "Money" Mayweather and Saul "Canelo" Alvarez and make the grade to be a Floyd Mayweather sparring partner and assist him in his 45th win.

I've been officially signed to Mayweather promotions since August 1st. I'm due to have my second fight under their guidance. I showed I belong at the top table with my performances on the world scene.

There are big fights out there for me in America and over the next three years, those will be what my team and I pursue. Exciting times ahead.

Tuesday 15th October 2013

It's good to be back!
December 14th is supposed to be the date in London that the money team will fight on.

Wednesday 16th October 2013

Mickey Bey said that Gavin Rees was mentioned as an opponent for him.

Thursday 17th October 2013

J'Leon was happy that he got his opponent for the December 14th date. Gary O'Sullivan. He doesn't know who he is. It doesn't really matter. He lost to Billy Joe Saunders in a shut out loss so I expect the same from J if not a stoppage win. He sparred today and looked really good.

Everyone is hyped around the trip.

Monday 21st October 2013

IBO World champion and former IBF world champion Joseph Agbeko flew in to Vegas on Saturday to prepare for his fight with Guillermo Rigondeaux on December 7th in Atlantic City.

Shawn Porter who I sparred with in the lead up to joining the money team is training here for his world title challenge against Devon Alexander.

The gym is currently buzzing.

Tuesday 22nd October 2013

I went to the social security office today to get my social security card. That is a national insurance number in the UK which will allow me to pay taxes in the US.

I'll receive it in the post in up to two weeks.

What a workout I put in today, this week I've built up to 3 rounds of skipping, 3 rounds of the speed bag, 5 rounds of shadow boxing with 10 rounds on the heavy bags finished off with abdominal and back crunches. It's a 90 minute workout. Two time world title challenger Kofi Jantuah has started training fighters. I've been joking around and making fun of him but he has experience at the top level. I worked with him today. After my workout I somehow found the energy in my body and completed ten rounds straight with him, only stopping to hydrate.
It was hard but enjoyable. We'll continue to put the work in.

Wednesday 30th October 2013

Today it was announced that we, the money team will be fighting on December 6th in Seattle.

The plan is to get my first win with Mayweather promotions and end the year on a high. I have 13lbs to lose in 5 weeks. If I'm disciplined it won't be difficult. I weighed 154.7lbs after training yesterday. I want to touch 153lbs this week. So I'll know I only have to lose 2lbs a week and that's a healthy goal.

I spoke to Leonard on Monday. I called him on Sunday. He

returned my call Monday afternoon. He said I'd only be in a keep busy fight. I told him I wanted to fight at 143lbs as I want to target championships in the 140lb division. He was cool with that.

I told him I'll speak to him nearer the time about opponents.

Floyd came to the gym today. Whenever he is present, everyone wants to spar to impress him. There are many fighters in the gym wanting to get signed so this is their big chance. JLeon and Luis were sparring when he walked in and Mickey and I were up next.

I didn't feel like I had a good session. It is still only my second time sparring since my fight. In another two weeks I'll be where I want to be. I love being in that kind of condition where you don't get tired, your body is just at a peak.

Mickey said after sparring that our sessions are like Sugar Ray Leonard and Marvin Hagler working together. World-class sparring! Marvin is one of my best fighters so to be spoken of in describing me as a fighter is the perfect compliment. I can box and fight but my strengths are that I'm hard working, relentless and have a never say die attitude.

Floyd spoke during our sparring session. "Got to have a British fighter on the team." "Ashley, you didn't tell me you was back in town." "You know when we sparred Ashley, everyone told me not to hit you hard and take it easy on you." Floyd tries to put you off your game and see how you react to his words. I just stay focused.
Having the best boxer in the world watching you spar isn't the easiest thing. There's a lot of pressure on you to perform. Floyd has seen me spar Daquan Arnett at the Magic Show back in late August and he's sparred me so he knows what I'm capable of. He knows my weaknesses and strengths.

Today I weighed 153.3lbs. 5 weeks to go and I'm ten pounds over weight. Two pounds a week to drop. That's perfect! I want to be 151lbs by next weekend.

I will be fighting on Friday 6th December in Washington. End the year with a win and i'll be happy.

Thursday 7th November 2013

Sister2Sister magazine 25th anniversary get together was fun. Stars like Bill Bellamy, Lisa Raye and Ronald Isley were there.

Floyd is gracing their cover in December so he attended and brought his team with him.

I haven't seen Ishe since I got back so it was great to hang out.

My weight today was perfect 151.8lbs. That's 9lbs over my fighting weight with 4 weeks to go.

My thumb is sore along with my joints hurting me so I'll take a much deserved morning off as my body is crying for it.

Friday 8th November 2013

Tonight I had the pleasure of going to the Soul Train Awards as part of Floyd's team.

I've heard so much about this iconic event that it was an honor to go.

Floyd is just Floyd to his friends and family but he is a worldwide superstar. It's just crazy and unbelievable that my hard work has got me this far. I still have my doubters but at the end of the day

Floyd Mayweather believes in me and is giving me a chance. That in itself is big and I'll be forever grateful.

Thursday 14th November 2013

Leonard called me at 7.04am to tell me that my opponent is a Nigerian fighter based out of Las Vegas. I've seen him at the Mayweather Boxing Club a few times. He's what you would expect. Decent skills and durable, Robert Osiobe is his name. I checked out his fight with Mark Davis which was in July. Normally he fights at 135lbs so he'll be stepping up a division to fight me at 143lbs.

Monday 18th November 2013

This morning I saw former Heavyweight champion of the world Hasim Rahman in the 24 hour fitness centre.

Newly crowned WBO world champion Demetrius Andrade was at the gym today and he's just called out IBF world champion Carlos Molina who just beat Ishe.

My left thumb has been hindering my sparring and pad sessions for the last two weeks.

I went to the doctors to get it sorted out. I was written a prescription for some antibiotics.

Jihad arrived today and he oversaw my sparring session.
He asked me if I believed I could still become a world champion. I told him yes. Carlos Baldomir, Glen Johnson and Ishe Smith all became world champions in their mid thirties. I don't think age is an issue.

Jihad asked me why I don't respond whilst sparring or during a fight. I said there's no need for a conversation. You talk and advice me, I try to implement the game plan. I'm focused!

Marvin Hagler was always calm and collected in the corner. So is Floyd (Mayweather). Even in my locker room before the fight, it is peaceful. I just like to focus and be relaxed. Everyone is different.

Tuesday 19th November 2013

Today I had a great training session with Jihad. Thirty minutes straight on the pads and 15 minutes straight on the heavy bag. Along with 35 minutes of skipping, speed bag drills and shadow boxing. I finished off with 1000 abdominal and back crunches plus a stretch out with Chris. On days I'm not sparring, this will be my normal work. Flying Jihad out here is worth every dollar. I'm not where I want to be but by fight time I will be on blistering form again.

I lost my fight with Pablo Cesar Cano but I gave him the first three rounds with my running round the ring. They'll be no running in this fight.

Friday 22nd November 2013

I've been putting in some hard work which has become normal now.
I'm where I want to be. I've weighed 148lbs after training over the last three days. I want to be 145lbs after training by next weekend.

I completed six 5 minute rounds on Wednesday which is 10 rounds of three minutes. I'm in great shape.

Today I did three 5 minute rounds and one 6 minute round today with Cortez Bey. Afterwards I did ten minutes of pad work with Jihad and ten minutes on the bag. Plus 35 minutes of shadow boxing, skipping and speed bag drills.

Jihad said he'd watched my opponent. He said he may have speed over me but I'll be too big and strong for him. I think I'll be able to match him on speed and conditioning wise, I won't get tired over eight rounds. Jihad said his team may believe they can cause an upset and I can't afford to lose again in a tune up fight. I know if I loss I'd be off the team. I've worked so hard to get here so I will win in two weeks time. He's not on my level.

Monday 26th November 2013

I'm in my zone now and putting in hard work that is now normal work.
A boxing fan that trains at the gym commented to me whilst I was finishing up on my bag work that, my training is immense and he doesn't see no one train as hard as me here. I replied that I'm the following in the path of my boss.

He replied "many say that but very few live by it. You live by it."
I thanked him and continued my work.

Afterwards whilst on the floor of the ring about to start my strength conditioning work. Otis, the amateur boxing trainer told me that I lead by example. I work non stop then go home.

It's good to know that the work I do in silence is noticed.

Ajose Olusegun started training at the gym since Saturday. I've been a bit frosty to him since he told me he's friends with my opponent. I feel like he's spying on me. There's nothing he could tell him about my weaknesses. He is not Pablo Cesar Cano or Danny Garcia. I'm going to walk him down and break him down. There is a lot of pressure on my shoulders. I know I need to win or my Vegas dream is dead.

Win this fight and I'll have the pleasure to fight on or in the lead up to Floyd's fights in May and September.

Wednesday 27th November 2013

I've been killing myself in the gym. Were as last time I was facing a dangerous opponent in Pablo Cesar Cano, I was confident in victory. This time I'm confident and I'm taking it seriously. I just hope I win or my amazing year would turn out to be a nightmare as well.

On paper this fighter has no chance against me but I am nervous of a slip up, maybe because I know there's so much at stake.

Friday 29th November 2013

Today I sparred with Cortez Bey. We completed 4 five minutes rounds with thirty seconds rest.
I felt in great shape. I was sharp, defense was good and I worked my jab which is the key to any fighter winning.

Jihad left for New York this morning but will meet me in Washington with Harry on Wednesday.

My weight after training was 147.3lbs. I'd love to get it to 145lbs by Tuesday.

The team leaves for Washington on Wednesday 7am and the weigh in is not for 36 hours later. I basically won't eat during that time to make weight.

Saturday 30th November 2013

Badou picked me up for the team's last run up Mount Charleston.

All the hard work is done now, it's all about making weight then getting the win come Friday. When I'm in my groove I feel unstoppable. My nerves are shaky due to my last fight but there is no way this guy is in Pablo Cesar Cano's league.

Monday 2nd December 2013

It's fight week. Business time! Time to get focused. Time to drop those final few pounds. Time to mentally prepare myself.

Jihad told me today "It's Treasure time. You got to win this fight impressively. Show them why you deserve it."

I never look forward to a fight. I work hard in the fitness centre, boxing gym and do my road work. I'm always 100% prepared. Performance is mental. You have to believe in yourself but the fear of failure drives an athlete.

This guy I'm fighting always tries to win. He is just limited. I'm scared but I'm scared of losing to a fighter who is levels below me. I win this fight and Floyd will give me another big opportunity.

All ten of the fighters signed to Mayweather promotions have it all. What a fighter wants in his career Mayweather promotions will back you and help you achieve it. If you don't achieve it, you are just not good enough.

Tuesday 3rd December 2013

Jihad wants me to be more offensive. He feels my defense is good enough. I just need to press the action more.

Leonard was at the gym today to get the fighters to sign their bout contracts.
I made $100,000 for my last fight. This fight I'm getting paid $7,500. That's a big drop. It's all about getting back to that six figure level.
Floyd will be in the audience. He watched me spar but I need to show him I'm as good as he believes I am.

Wednesday 4th December 2013

I left Las Vegas and it was actually snowing. That's a first!

The whole team was on the same plane. My opponent and Chris Pearson's was on the plane and coach to the hotel as they are based in Las Vegas.

I want a big 2014 so it starts now. I need to get him out of the way. He can come to win but records don't lie. He's an inferior fighter to me on all levels. I just have to go out there on Friday and show Floyd and Leonard why they signed me.

Thursday 5th December 2013

I made weight at the first attempt. 142.2lbs. I've competed in the junior welterweight division for ten years now. It doesn't get any easier I just know what to do and what food to get the best out of me.

My opponent weighed in the 141lb region. He competes between 130lbs to 135lbs. Badou Jack and Ajose Olusegun have both said he is tough and comes to fight. The boxing media in Vegas have also said he is tough. I'm not under estimating him but everytime he fights someone who can fight, he loses. I just can't see him beating me. If he does my career is over at world level.

Jihad sees the importance of this fight and understands that I'm in the greatest predicament that any boxer can be in. I'm with Floyd Mayweather's team. It gets no bigger. We had dinner together and spoke about all different things. Harry chose to stay in his room.

As we left each other he promised me he would be "up in my ass tomorrow". Normally I don't need motivating but my confidence is low after that last fight with Pablo Cesar Cano. From when the bell rings I'll be okay but right now my mentality needs to be at its strongest. I've never let myself down mentality and I'm sure I won't now.

Friday 6th December 2013

I won my first fight under Mayweather Promotions. I'm so happy. I love the team spirit amongst everyone. Floyd was ringside for my fight and I could hear him shouting out instructions to me whilst I was fighting "go to the body Ashley." I had neglected Joseph Osiobe's body for the first few rounds then I started to pound his body whilst inside. The referee had said he will let the action flow and he doesn't like to take points off. I told him afterwards "I haven't got any kids yet, he nearly made sure I never have none." He told me that I was doing my own fouling and he let it go. I just smiled and thanked him.

I was determined to win the fight. I boxed, I fought. I did everything possible. I thought I easily won seven rounds of the fight. When I heard the announcer say "we have a split decision." My heart sank! I've lost two split decisions to Danny Garcia and Pablo Cesar Cano so I'm not too optimistic when I hear them. The first judge gave it to me 79-73 which I thought was fair.

After the show the team hanged out at the Island Grille. I ate some seafood linguine, Calamari, Sweet potato fries and a strawberry cheesecake. My appetite was huge after an eight round battle. Joseph was strong or skillful. He was crafty, wild and had speed over me due to him normally campaigning at a smaller weight. I'm a twelve round fighter so those championship rounds are where I normally take over.

Floyd strolled in to the Island Grille and hanged out with the fighters and our teams. We were all in fairly difficult fights. He said to us "I make it look so easy, don't I?"
I'm happy to finish the year with a win and next year I can target some ranked fighters or former world champions again.

Badou Jack and Mickey Bey, I feel are ready for their world title shots, great performances from them.

Saturday 7th December 2013

We checked out and flew back to Vegas. The memories I am experiencing with the money team will always be cherished. Floyd saved my career and he's more than a promoter. I've never been a team player but working with Rene and working with Floyd is something I am grateful to have the opportunity of bettering my life and achieving the life I want for myself.

Training camp for 35th win against Angino Perez on
Floyd Mayweather vs Marcos Maidana undercard at the MGM
Grand Arena

Monday 3rd March 2014

It's the first day back at the Mayweather gym and it was great to see the guys again. I missed the joking around with them.

I've done 4 weeks of training in London and 4 weeks training in New York City so I'm in good shape but the altitude and heat puts Vegas on another level. I started off with ten minutes skipping, 15 minutes shadow boxing followed by 15 minutes on the heavy bag and 15 minutes with Nate. I finished off ten minutes on the speed bag and 1000 abdominal crunches. I'll continue to do this for the next two weeks. I'm in no rush to spar.

Today is the first day of camp for Floyd and having him in the gym is always motivational and educational. Who starts their first training session off with sparring. Only Floyd Mayweather, he sparred a couple rounds and looked pretty good.

He hit the heavy bag and did some pads with Roger Mayweather and body work with Nate Jones. Floyd spoke about his fighters making him look bad and asking for the step up in opposition but struggling to get past them. He said, "My fighters are making my brand look bad." Fortunately for Ishe, Mickey and I we did not fight on Friday.

Floyd finished up with some skipping, speed bag drills and strength work. The first day is down.
Floyd spoke in the locker room about how well the money team merchandise was going. He spoke about how much money he is getting on a monthly basis. His business plans for the future. He's a basketball fan and passionate about it so he was joking around

with the team about advising players on transferring to teams and taking a cut as he's been doing it for free so far.

Leonard and Floyd where talking before the fighters walked in the dressing room about having a team meeting. Lanell Bellows didn't fight on Friday and his rent is due so he went to ask Floyd for some money whilst he was in his car. Floyd said I will look after you but first we will be having a team meeting as I'm not happy about a lot of things.

One fighter is rumored to be smoking marijuana, a couple of fighters go off to Los Angeles for sex weekends during camp and be partying too much. I always tell them not to be in a rush. As you will get the big fights just be patient. They see Floyd getting the big money and the limelight but he's been a professional for 18 years and before that he was a bronze medalist at the Olympics. He's earned everything he makes. We all have the biggest opportunity ever, why would you mess it up with bullshit. It just doesn't make sense to me.

Wednesday 5th March 2014

We where due to have a team meeting today as Floyd is not happy with how the fighters are representing his brand. I wouldn't be happy either. I think it is more targeted to the youngsters who go to the clubs and be sleeping with loads of women.

Being around Floyd is pure entertainment. He reminisces about the past. He told a story how Hasim Rahman hyped up Zab Judah years ago when they were coming up. Zab asked Floyd for sparring and Floyd said, "Sure" lets do it today not tomorrow". He said he took his legs away and his left hand. Breaking him down to the body.
He spoke about how his day consisted of going to the boxing gym, going to the Mall, then going to the strip club, then going to

the normal club. He said I did that everyday. 7 days a week. When his friend, Earl Hayes came into the locker room, he asked him what was a normal day for me? Earl basically told us the same thing. But he said you used to run to the strip club then run back home afterwards to make sure you got your road work in.

Floyd has stories about former girlfriends, stories of the struggles coming up. Whilst we where in the locker room, he asked David Levi, one of his assistants to give his two uncles Gerald and John Sinclair $5,000 each in cash out of his back pack. He told them he values them. I like that about Floyd, always thanks his team.

Dejuan Blake, Floyd's cousin told me earlier on they want me to win a big fight so the team can take a trip to the UK.

Thursday 6th March 2014

Another hard day in Las Vegas, I completed a 4 mile run, an hour yoga and an hour strength conditioning at 24 hour fitness. I had a two hour rest then I headed off to the boxing gym. I did my normal work out which consisted of 75 minutes of work. The gym is hot so it is no joke but train hard fight is always the goal. 15 minutes shadow boxing, 15 minutes on the pads, 15 minutes on the heavy bag, 10 minutes skipping, 10 minutes on the speed bag finished off with some abdominal and back crunches.

I spoke to Leonard today about my opponent and fight date. He said he wasn't sure what date I would fight but it would be either Floyd's or the one just before. Ishe is supposed to fight Lara the one before so I prefer to box on his show then I can enjoy Floyd's but I'm not complaining. I just have to start faster and be more aggressive from the get go.

NBA superstar Ron Artest was at the gym today. He's a real cool guy. We where chilling in the locker with Floyd and he started asking me about my career. He said he wanted to be a boxer, he just doesn't know if he could take a punch.

Friday 7th March 2014

All week the fighters didn't know what was going to be said at this team meeting. For Floyd to want to talk to us, meant something was bothering him. We knew he wasn't happy with the performances from Friday night. Badou lost! Chris and Luis had terrible performances. Luis Arias got tired by the third round. Floyd and Leonard said no one should be getting tired like that.

Basically the meeting was about the young fighters really as they are not taking this seriously.

I told them all week. Stop having sex for at least a month before your fight and Floyd said exactly that. I smiled when that came out of his mouth and looked over to Ladarius.

It was great to hear Floyd say he believes in his team of fighters. He feels like he has a great squad.
He said we are going to lose sometimes. That's boxing! If you lose I lose but just give me your all. That's all I ask.

"If you ask for a certain fighter, you have to deliver". This was more towards Ishe Badou and me as we are on the big fight stage.

He said I want you all to be comfortable, that's my whole thing. If you need anything just ask me. He said my thing is comfort. But you have to give me your all.

Floyd said I may say I'm out with women bullshitting but I'm not. If I have a bad day at the gym that day, I might go back and work

on my defense or my jab.
You have to kill yourself in that gym. If I can, you can.

To hear Leonard say he knows I'm a hard worker. They know I give my all but a few fighters want to be stars but don't want to put the work in.

When it came to Leonard's turn to talk. He basically said. Floyd amazes me, as he still trains so hard. Leonard went on to say everyone can be replaced here and that we receive so many emails about fighters wanting to be part of the team. This is true as Audley Harrison and Carson jones both messaged me about getting on the team.

The Restaurant was nice, with great food. Luis Arias was like they could have called me and told me this over the phone. He's a prime example of a fighter not putting in the work but 99% of what was said was because of him so that's why he didn't enjoy it. These guys beg Floyd for bigger fights but get tired straight away or are not ready.

I thought it was great to hear Floyd talk. This is not a regular thing. It shows he cares.

It's the first week and he trains so hard. I love that as I know I'm on the right path.

Lanell Bellows was mad at Floyd and had an attitude like Floyd owned him something. He's been telling Floyd he needs to fight and I think Floyd gives some of them money to help pay rent etc. He told Floyd I last fought in December I'm ready to fight. Floyd said we gave you a duck which is a bum and you lost. Lanell shouted back, he wasn't a bum he had twice as many fights as me. Floyd said he was a bum. Lanell sat next to me looking like he wanted to fight Floyd. Dejuan Blake, Floyd's cousin told him to relax, he will sort it out.

The meeting finished around 2pm but Ben Thompson from fighthype.com was talking to us about Amir khan and how Amir didn't know who Al Haymon was and how it all worked. He said it was him who put him in contact with Al.

Floyd said at the meeting, Adrien and Khan will fight on his undercard in separate bouts.

Floyd was like I can do anything in boxing as all the organizations want to work with me and he said when you're at my level, it's business first.

I saw the meeting as a peep talk, very inspiring and motivational for me. I loved it.

It's surreal being with Floyd.

Tuesday 11th March 2014

Today I found out that I'm fighting on Friday 2nd May at the Hard Rock Casino. I'll be on the undercard of Ishe's world title challenge against Lara.

Floyd was in the ring about to start pad work with Roger when he ask me "Ashley, when you fighting?". I replied "Leonard is working on it". Floyd shouts out to Leonard. "L, when is Ashley fighting?" Leonard replied on "Friday 2nd, just working on an opponent."
Leonard had got in the ring to assist Floyd with training and came up to me and said, "I told you I'm working on it."

Wednesday 12th March 2014

This was my third day training on my own as Nate had to go Chicago as his daughter was shot in the stomach at a party. She is still alive and will be able to have children in the future.

Floyd asked me if I wanted to spar this camp. I told him yes and that I am here waiting. Since last Monday around 10 people have asked if I'm sparring him and my answer was I don't know. I've been focused on my fight and training so that hasn't been on my mind.

Thursday 13th March 2014

Today Floyd critiqued his fighters. He was talking about how he is good at looking at a fighter and seeing his strengths and weaknesses. Then he capabilities on that, Nate asked him what his weakness was and how would he beat him. He told him that he liked to admire his work too much. Ladarius then asked Floyd what he did wrong. Floyd told him he is too up right. Mickey asked and Floyd replied "you slip punches then don't come back with no shots." I was not going to ask but Floyd offered his view on what I do wrong. He looked at me and said, "Ashley telegraphs his shots. Too wide!" I know this to be true as every trainer I've ever worked with has said that and tried to work on that with me. JLeon wasn't there but Floyd said, "J's best punch is the jab but he doesn't throw it enough". Lanell asked Floyd what he did wrong and Floyd said, "You perform better in the gym than in your fights." Lanell didn't say anything but would complain afterwards that he was judging him on the one fight he lost and said that "Champ didn't even see it." You have to be able to take criticism and from Floyd, the number one fighter in the world, it is truly appreciated by me.

Friday 14th March 2014

Floyd needs better sparring partners. He has punch bags and guys who are too intimidated by him. He schooled this fighter who was supposed to of outboxed Saul Alvarez in preparation for his fight with Floyd. I just don't believe that. He looks too weak and easy to intimidate.

This morning after my work out at 24 Hour Fitness, I received a text from Floyd's assistant, Kitchie. Saying we had to be at the Salvation Army to hand out food. Ishe came to pick me up and we headed down there. We where there for maybe two hours, we gave out 300 packages of food and water. One of the homeless people said it was nice to see the champ down there. It's always good to give back.

Monday 17th March 2014

I spoke to Leonard today about my fight on 2nd May. I'm only doing an 8 round fight as Mickey is co main event and Ishe is fighting for the world title. I am disappointed as the whole point I didn't fight on 28th February was because Mayweather promotions didn't want me doing an eight round fight. The way Leonard told me softened the blow.

Leonard told me that the plan was for me to fight Danny Garcia that's why we were on the September show together.

He said he doesn't want to rush me back into a big fight cause that's how mistakes happen. He said he rather me just stay active and when the opportunity comes I'll be ready.

He said Danny and Lamont want the big money fights so I just stay in the gym and continue to work and improve. Cause the opportunity will arise. He said Danny is vacating the titles to move up to welterweight. He said he knows that for a fact.

So I didn't get the news I wanted to hear but his words where that they still believe in me but just stay ready and I'll be active.

Leonard has been working with Floyd for 18 years so I trust in his experience.

Saturday 22nd March 2014

I spoke to Leonard today, he told me that I would now be fighting on Floyd Mayweather v Marcos Maidana show at the MGM Grand.

Wednesday 26th March 2014

Floyd told Memphis to get a proper mouth piece because he'll get in the ring with a fighter like me and get his teeth knocked out. That's a nice compliment from the champ. He also praised my body work, when he heard about my sparring session we had earlier. He said, 'That's that pro shit."

Tuesday 1st April 2014

I've had two good days of sparring. I've completed my physical and blood work for my fight. I'm 149lbs with just over a month to go. Everything is on point.

Floyd spoke for like an hour after his training session. We where chilling in the locker room with him. He spoke about how fighters are spoilt nowadays. They want everything handed to them and how they don't want to work for anything. He reminisced about walking to the boxing gym in the snow, If he missed a day of training as a kid he'd cry for days. He spoke about coming to Las Vegas when he was a teenager. Nate Jones was back with us and they spoke about altercations they had. Which was timely as Nate and I fell out yesterday during sparring but we made up after my training session.

"I can no longer look at boxing as a sport. When you at my level, It's a business. I'm not

getting in the ring for less than 32 million and then that's not mentioning what I'll get on the back end (PPV)"

Floyd spoke about how Bob Arum said he was the best fighter he'd ever seen when he was with him and when he left him. Bob said that no black fighters could sell PPV. Leonard walked in at this time and Floyd asked him what he'd made since leaving Bob. Leonard said around 400 million. Nate asked what did you make with Bob. Floyd deep in thought said some six's and seven's. Nothing major.

I'm happy that Floyd gambled and walked his own path when many people did not believe in him. He's always inspiring and motivating to me. I just want to make him proud of signing me. I'm trying. That's all I can do.

Wednesday 2nd April 2014

I had to call Dr. Voy who did my physical and blood work on Monday. He said I had an issue with my white blood cells. I told him I was in bed sick over the weekend and I was only getting over it on Monday when I came to see him. He told me that if I continued to get sick or felt tired to contact him again.

In the locker room that afternoon, Floyd said how he'd gone to do his physical today and how the Doctor had mentioned me. "He likes you, Ashley". Floyd has known that doctor since the 1996 Olympics. I just try and be courteous to everyone as word of mouth is a good thing.

Floyd spoke about his relationships with Don King, Shelley Finkel and Bob Arum. These locker room moments with Floyd are priceless. He opens up and tells us all these private and personal things. He is funny but it also shows he was not given the success he has. He earned it. I will keep working hard because even if I achieved 1% of what he has, I would be a success. I'm on the right path and I'm close. It's all mental now. I just have to believe in
myself.

Thursday 3rd April 2014

My final part of my boxing medical for the Nevada State license was completed today. I hate doing eye tests. I always pass them but sometimes my results are good. Sometimes they are bad. I aced the exam other than being told I have 20/40 eye sight.

I paid the receptionist $150 for the exam. Floyd was waiting in the lobby for his exam with his assistant and Leonard. Floyd saw me and joked to the receptionist could I still see with my black eye.

Floyd asked Leonard when was I fighting. Leonard replied "on the same show as you." Floyd enquired who I was fighting. Leonard told him he was working on that. "Look after him Leonard. Make sure he's okay". Floyd stated!

Friday 4th April 2014

Mickey Bey and I completed five 5 minute rounds sparring today. That's one minute over 8 rounds. I'm ready for my fight. I didn't feel good and I wasn't in the mood to pressure him and go all out. I stood off him a few times to see if he would attack me and he is a pure counter puncher. He rarely goes on an unprovoked attack.

Mickey is very fast and skilled. For me it is just frustrating as I'm known as the Marvin Hagler type of fighter. Take them out to deep sea and drown them. I can box though and I get bored of being the one to come forward and break them down. No one has the confidence to attack me down and try to break me down. Maybe because I am in better condition than everyone around my weight division in the gym. People watching thought our session was good. I know I can do so much better so I wasn't happy with my performance.

Floyd gave out some checks to some of the fighters, just to help them out. $3,000 a piece. What promoter does that and doesn't ask for the money back. He's a real good guy.

Jermaine Jackson was in the gym today. He's such a legend. He asked me about my boxing career and he seemed like a nice guy. His dad Joe Jackson always pops into Floyd's camp. Al Haymon used to work with the Jackson 5 back when Michael Jackson was just a kid. Al Haymon basically runs the boxing industry and has a major influence on the music industry but not many people know that. He likes to stay in the background, not like one promoter that comes to mind.

Tuesday 9th April 2014

Hip hop legend Doug E. Fresh was in the gym today to watch Floyd train. He commented that it was like coming to watch a superman movie.
Doug asked Floyd about his fighters he promotes and Floyd told him some of them are not the best but I'm giving them the opportunity to make some money.

Floyd sparred today and was on fire. It's a pleasure to watch greatness at work.

Wednesday 10th April 2014

Superstar movie producer John Singleton was in the gym today. He's made some quality films like Boys in the hood, Baby Boy, Four Brothers, Poetic Justice, 2Fast 2Furious and Shaft. Floyd was in the ring working on his foot movement with Money Mar and Famous, when a man asked me how old they were. I was surprised to see it was John Singleton asking me. We just casually leaned on the apron next to each other watching the training having general chit chat.

Thursday 11th April 2014

WBO 135lb champion Terence Crawford passed through the gym today and legendary
promoter Don King also popped in.
Seeing these people at the top of the boxing world around me day in, day out motivates me to get that world title belt. I just need the continued support from Floyd.
Spoke with Terence, he said he remembers my fight with Danny Garcia, he felt I won. Many people do, but thats boxing for you.

Thursday 18th April 2014

Today I found out from Ishe that Cuba is off the card. He was found positive in his drug test. Marijuana was in his system. There was rumors that he was smoking going back to August 1st. These fighters don't appreciate the great opportunity they have. They are ungrateful. If I was Floyd I'd drop him.

Chris Pearson is off the card as well. No reason has been mentioned. That's two eight rounds gone now.

Friday 19th April 2014

I had a 60 minute massage before sparring Mickey today. It was the worst thing I could have done. I was sleepy, relaxed and I couldn't get my punches off. Nate and I had some intense words in the corner where I told him that he does not have to give me instructions, he can just do pads with me. I told him I will not be changing up my style so if he does not like it, stop working with me. I tried him movement and running round the ring against Pablo Cesar Cano. I would never publicly blame him for the loss. I take the blame or say I just got my tactics wrong but when I lost the first three rounds I blame Nate as he wanted me to do that. Harry and Jihad know my style, Nate doesn't so we will always butt heads. Nate was loud in the gym when speaking to me saying not to blame him when I went into my shell when I got hit. I told him if you got something to say, say it to me not the whole gym. I don't shout at you, I speak to you.

We finished up with twenty minutes on the pads and 15 minutes on the heavy bag. I'm in good shape. There's no doubt about that. Wednesday I was on form and was happy with my performance against Mick. Today I'm sure he was happy with his. That's how it goes. Good days and bad days but it's all good quality work.

We finished off the night with Floyd's red and black appreciation dinner party. Everyone came, ate, danced and took photos together. I like these events because it's nice for people to show gratitude and appreciation for Floyd. He helps out so many people. The man is a real good guy. He is very funny as well. I think the public don't get to see that side to him.
I went with Dan and left with Ishe. As usual Dan was on the prowl. He ended up bringing a girl he met at the Nevada Boxing

Hall of Fame induction party last week. Dan is going back to Canada soon to work so the clock is ticking. He is putting in overtime to get some love from the ladies.

Saturday 19th April 2014

Three hours sleep and we went back to work. Mount Charleston for 6am start. Ishe was
outside my place for 5.12am. The sacrifices are all worth it. People hear Las Vegas and think the Las Vegas strip, parties and women! I might as well be in the jungle, up in the mountains or in a military base. I'm focused, dedicated and hard working. Every week the goal is to be better than the previous week.

Friday 25th April 2014

Today was the last day of sparring. I've been asking for work off Ishe Smith for the past eight weeks and my wish was finally granted.
Ishe didn't hold back but nor did I. I started fast banging Ishe against the ropes with a hard right hook. It was back and forth work, very competitive. At the end of the fourth round my nose was busted up with a big uppercut. I finished the fourth round. Three 5-minute rounds and one 6 minute round with 30 seconds rest in between. It was a great way to end camp. Sparring like that you don't want to do too often.

For the past three days I've been in bed with a cold so I was very content with my performance. Everyone praised my performance. I'm ready for my fight with Angino Perez. I would love the knockout win. That's my aim!

Saturday 26th April 2014

The last run up Mount Charleston was this morning. I was glad to get it over and done with. My body felt tired and my chest tight as I'm just getting over this chest cold. I'll be okay by Monday. I feel so blessed to be part of Mayweather promotions.

Tuesday 29th April 2014

We are here now. This is when the event becomes real. The fighter arrivals, when all the fighters on the card arrive at the MGM Grand Casino. Floyd Mayweather, Marcos Maidana, Lou Collazo, Amir Khan, Adrien Broner. This is a big event!

There are three British fighters on the show, which is unheard of but great for the British fans who have flown out here to watch Floyd and great for us British fighters boxing on the card.

I worked out before and after the fighter arrivals. It is a long day but I do enjoy them. I started at the bottom. No one ever thought I'd get this far but now I'm mixing with the big boys. Dreams come true but I know I can go further and I'm aiming to.

Wednesday 30th April 2014

The fan workouts and autograph signing was another fun experience. You have to soak up the atmosphere. This is something all fighters dream of being a part of. Very few do and I've been part of the last two Floyd Mayweather shows. I'm a part of history. These are memories I'll always hold close to my heart. If you've been to a Floyd Mayweather show in Las Vegas, you'll know there's nothing like it.

Thursday 1st May 2014

We are nearly there. Two more days until my second fight in Las Vegas over the last nine months.

Sky Sports Ringside mentioned that Amir Khan and Anthony Ogogo where representing the UK on this show but no mention of me. I've always faced adversity and still am. Instead of celebrating how far I've come against the odds they try not to highlight my achievements. It's a shame and a disgrace. I'm inspiring the fighters who started on the small hall shows that they too can reach here one day. What I'm doing is incredible.

It was the press conference today. I got to sit next to the bronze medalist Anthony Ogogo. We had some words again. I think he will go on to do great things. It's all about his mind set. The other Olympians stayed in the UK and signed with Matchroom. The ones who make it on to the world scene will have to come here eventually anyway. Anthony is getting great experience already so when he steps up to the big stage it will be normal for him.

I ran this morning and did a light boxing workout. I weigh 141.1lbs. 1.1lbs above my weight limit. I'm on point!

Friday 2nd May 2014

I didn't eat for 24 hours before the weigh in. I made my contracted weight perfectly. For my last three fights I've weighed 142lbs.

I saw Angino Perez for the first time today. I thought he was 6ft but I later found out he was 6ft 2inches. I was intrigued to see how he fights so I watched a second round knock out win he had. He looked aggressive and throws a nice array of punches. It will be a good fight but I really believe I can stop him. I'll be unhappy with a points win. I've twice as much experience as him.

Floyd was like you know I had to sign me a British fighter. Amir

Khan was right in front of us when he said that. Adrien Broner was sharing the same locker room as us and was hilarious. He does some wild things but deep down I believe he's a good guy.

After everyone made weight I went for a meal with Dan and Badou. Dan has been driving me around all week to all my media commitments. I remember a year ago when we where hoping to get tickets to the fight and I got some $1,500 ones off Floyd so we went. It's been a journey and he was part of it. This time I haven't been able to socialize outside of boxing really as I've been so focused on my fight but he's been understanding. Hopefully we have a long standing friendship. I got him a credential to all the media commitments I had. Hopefully I get tickets for my team and I can give him one.

Saturday 3rd May 2014

"The Moment" has arrived. Nine weeks of work in Las Vegas have come to a close. It is all about show casing my talent now. My opponent is 6'2 so I have no option but to get in close and fight, which was my plan
anyway. I want to break him down and knock him out. He's been stopped before. I'm going to do it again.

Journalist Gareth A. Davis brought tears to my eyes this morning. I was watching an interview he did with Kugan Cassius and he was asked about me. He responded that my career shows what boxing is all about. Coming from nothing and making something of your life, as I write this I am getting emotional. I don't think about my journey a lot. It's just my life and what I do. There are millions of people from humble beings who have refused to be a government statistic. I just wanted to make something out of my life so working hard and going Stateside was the only way I knew how to. My options where limited in the UK and the top UK promoters had no interest in me. As I told Anthony Ogogo at the press conference, if you're are going to make it in boxing you will have to come to America at some stage of your career. People are hard on boxers for losing but great football teams, tennis players and swimmers all lose. It doesn't taint their greatness. They always bounce back. That's the important thing, how you come back from a set back and I always bounce back bigger. Coming from the background I've come from, I've already achieved something that is unheard of. I feel it in my bones, I feel deep inside of me that I have more to give. If people believe or not doesn't matter. I'm used to proving people wrong.

Ishe and Mickey won last night. It's all about the rest of us to continue today and get our W's.

Sunday 4th May 2014

I'm ecstatic. I won last night at the MGM Grand. Angino 'Nightmare' Perez was a very game opponent. Looping wild shots, he had a very good uppercut that I thought broke my nose and right cheek bone. In the end, it was just my cheek bone that was fractured but I had blood coming out of my nose for the next four days.
I couldn't miss him with my jab and his 6'2 height didn't bother me. I've fought fighters six foot and always beaten them so height just like southpaws, never bothered me.

I dropped Perez in the second round with a short jab. I nearly stopped him in the third, by the fourth round he was staggering around the ring. It was just a matter of time until I knocked him out but he was still dangerous. Your power never leaves you. I got him on the ropes and crushed punches into his face. The referee stopped the fight and I was relieved. I felt like I redeemed myself as everyone remembered my Pablo Cesar Cano fight.

Everyone on the team won, which was fantastic. It's never nice when someone loses and everyone else wins. It was great that we had a clean sweep.

Floyd won his fight with Marcos Rene Maidana. Marcos looked very strong. I thought the first half of the fight was close but then Floyd pulled away. I was surprised that people where calling for a rematch as I didn't think it was that close.

After the fight we went to Floyd's locker room, ate food and chilled out. The team moved on to the post fight press conference where Floyd and Maidana spoke. 12 months ago at Floyd's fight with Robert Guerrero, Floyd said I was his fighter. It's been an incredible journey for me.

On the verge of thinking of retirement because I couldn't get any fights in the UK. I headed to Las Vegas and was signed by Floyd Mayweather. It's an incredible story.

Just like last year, there was a celebration get together at Floyd's mums house. Family, friends, celebrities and the team went. Great way to end a hard nine week training camp.

FLOYD MAYWEATHER v MARCOS MAIDANA 2 #MAYHEM

Tuesday 22nd July 2014

After an hour delay on the tarmac of Gatwick I arrived in Las Vegas after a 10 hour flight.
3pm Las Vegas time I was at McCarran airport. I got to my residence by 4pm, showered and head off to the Mayweather Boxing Club. Everyone gave me a nice welcoming. After Floyd finished training, he told me that the guys who wanted to fly him over the UK wanted him to do too much work for what they were paying.

It was Ishe's birthday so Val, his lady invited a group of us to a Japanese steakhouse for a surprise birthday meal.
I was jet lagged and super tired but I wanted to be there for Ishe.

Wednesday 23rd July 2014

My first day back in Las Vegas sure wasn't easy but it was a success. A 5am morning run, followed by grocery shopping at 7am, weights workout at 9am then boxing workout at 1pm. I finished my workout weighing 157lbs which was great as I left London weighing 162lbs.

Leonard wasn't in the gym so I have no idea when I am fighting yet. Everyone except Ishe and I are on 30th August. Mickey is fighting for the world title.

I was in bed by 5pm. I woke up from my nap at 10pm to a text from Kitchie, Floyd's assistant. Floyd had rented out the adventure dome in Circus Circus hotel from midnight just for the team who could bring friends and family as well. I got there around 1230am and stayed there for two hours. Floyd paid for all the food and drink as well, everyone made sure they ate. I just got a Gatorade, as I'm watching my weight.

Saturday 26th July 2014

I woke up at 4am to a text message from Erica Diaz, that she wanted to see me. Unfortunately I had to turn her down as I had to be ready for 530am to head to Mount Charleston with Badou Jack.
I completed the run in 48 minutes, just behind young boxer Tommy Hill by a few seconds. I lead the run for the first four miles but the heat, altitude and toughness of the mountain just got to me in the end. I will only get stronger and fitter.

I spoke to Leonard afterwards. He said I'll be fighting on Saturday 30th August when Mickey Bey challenges for the world title.

Tuesday 29th July 2014

It's great to be back in Las Vegas. Seeing Floyd everyday is amazing on many levels. He likes to have a good time and joke around but he works so hard. I never get bored of watching him work out. I sparred Zach Cooper on Saturday and Chavis Holifield on Monday. Three five minute rounds with one minute rest. One more week of one minute rest then I'll move it down to 30 seconds.

I was at the gym from 1230pm to 7pm. Some NBA stars where in the gym to watch Floyd. I don't watch Basketball so I don't know them unless they are really big names. Everyone in the gym knew who they were though and Floyd loves his Basketball so he was very passionate when he was talking about the sport with them.

Leonard called me when I got in and asked what my weight was. I told him I was 154lbs at the minute. He asked me could I do welterweight. I told him yes but I don't want to fight a big welter. He said that the opponent he is after is a former 140lb champion. He said he's not no welterweight like Keith Thurman. He told me not to mention this conversation to no one. I said there is nothing to say. You've just asked me if I can do welterweight. I'll wait for you to tell me if the fight is confirmed or not. I think it is Vivian Harris, he is trying to make a fight with but I would be shocked if it turned out to be Kendall Holt or Jose Luis Castillo. He said it is a fight I will win but it is a 50/50 fight. In my head I'm favorite to win those three fights. I just can't show them no respect or let the occasion get to me.

Saturday 8th August 2014

Morning Mount Charleston run with the team followed by a sparring session with Cortez Bey. Nate said afterwards that if it was an actual boxing match, I would have stopped him.

Thursday 7th August 2014

Ishe was at the gym today. He told me that he thinks I shouldn't fly back to London after this fight as Mayweather promotions can't plan what they can do with me. I told him that Amir Khan flies back and Golden Boy still plan with him, I'm a phone call away. He told me I'm not a superstar or a millionaire like Khan, even if I think I am.
Floyd wants Ishe to have a fight before fighting Edislandy Lara, so hopefully I can be on that show. I'll speak to Leonard after the fight.

Saturday 9th July 2014

What a long day but 100% fulfilling, I was up a little before 5am to get ready for our weekly mountain run. It was a hard six miles but after a hard week of sparring it was the icing on the cake. Pushing hard day in, day out is what it is all about. Two more weeks like this and I'll be ready for action. It was my turn to treat the guys to Baby Stacks. Pan cakes, French toast, Omelets and potatoes was on the menu.

The team finished the night at the Tropicana hotel for the second Nevada Boxing Hall Of Fame awards dinner. It was nice, among so many greats of the sport. It felt just like family. Mike Tyson even helped get Badou and I parking at the hotel as the valet told us it was full but Mike had a word with him for us and he accommodated us. This is Mike Tyson, the man who lit the fire in me to become a boxer. We walked in the hotel with him, everyone was shouting out "Mike, Mike". "It's Tyson". For someone convicted of raped he still has the love of the fans. Other than Muhammad Ali he is the biggest boxing legend alive.

We walked the red carpet, collected our VIP passes and sat with the team.

Sugar Ray Leonard, Earnie Shavers, Mike McCallum, Kevin Kelley, Shawn Porter, Roberto
Duran, Shane Mosley, Evander Holyfield where all there along with the current number one fighter in the world, Floyd Mayweather and to think I'm there as part of his team. It's just unbelievable.

Cornelius "Boza" Edwards was inducted into the hall of fame and Floyd won best boxer for the second year in a row. Shawn and Bermane where given awards for the success they've had over the last twelve months. They both show that hard work, belief and determination can get you to your goals against all odds.

We left just after midnight. Anahi who I started dating that week met me at my place to finish the night off in style.

Tuesday 12th July 2014

The stuff that happens in the background is sometimes the highlights during camp. Today Floyd was telling LaDarius Miller he has to eat pussy if he wants to become Champion.
LaDarius who is 21 years old was responding that he is too young for that. Floyd told him that he has been doing it for 20 years and that he's been champion for 17 years, so do the math.

Floyd asked me what date I was fighting. I told him I'm on the 30th August.

Leonard should have an opponent for me this week. I'm only doing eight rounds so I don't expect to be fighting a killer.

Thursday 14th July 2014

Daniel Calzada is my opponent. I found out through social media as his team put out a press release. He has ten wins, ten loses and two draws. He is eleven years my junior and his team seem to think he has a shot at beating me. My aim is to win by knock out. He is durable as he has only been stopped once by technical knock out. No matter who the opponent there are some nerves but I've had a great training camp so far.

Saturday 16th July 2014

I woke up at 445am for the weekly Mount Charleston run. Five miles all up hill. There was around twelve fighters today. I finished third. Six of us went off to Baby Stacks café for breakfast. Two hours later I was at the Mayweather Boxing Club sparring Chavis Holifield. I started slow in the first round and he hit me with a thunderous over hand right hand. My legs buckled and some of the onlooking fighters shouted out in joy, as they do. I stayed composed and fought through the first six minute round. I'm used to starting slow, I've been like that my whole boxing career. The second six minute round I was warm, loose and focused. I came out sharp, letting go of my hands. I blocked a body shot from Chavis and he hurt his hand so we had to end the sparring session at the end of the round. I finished up with ten minutes on the mitts with Nate and ten minutes on the bag. Everyday can't be hard. That was enough as I had to partake in a back to school giveaway with Mayweather promotions in Las Vegas.

We had a great turn out at the gym for the back to school drive. Many families came for the free giveaways. It was nice to help and give back. I've been there, my mum and dad never had a lot of money so at the start of the school year it seemed like it was always a struggle around the household.

After we finished, we sat down in the lobby of the gym with Floyd and Leonard to watch JLeon's next opponent Anthony Dirrell win the WBC world title from Sakio Bika and Shawn Porter defending his world title to Kell Brook, which he ended up losing.

Sunday 17th August 2014

With people flying in to Las Vegas for work or vacation, they always want to see me but during training camp, I am a recluse. The only thing I do is go to the gym and go home to recover. Unless I have Mayweather promotions obligations to do, there is zero socializing.

People judge and criticize you when their own accomplishment can't stake up to yours. I've never met a champion who looked down on people who have not achieved what they have. Some of the nicest and most humblest people I've met in sport have been world champions. I spoke to former world champion Lou De Valle who is in Las Vegas working with Badou, he told me in his day if you didn't win a world championship you wasn't shit. I said it's still the same. He disagreed but we agreed that boxing needs contenders and journey men, everyone has their place and boxing couldn't survive without them.

I received a phone call from Dmitriy Salita today. We spoke about how far I've come and I told him I believe he could have achieved much more than he did but the hunger needed to be there, his objective was to make money but in boxing, we come from a poor background 99% of the time so the hunger for success needs to be there or you will not achieve what your talent level will allow you to do. That is why Floyd Mayweather is so great. He trains like he is still poor. Always pushing his body to the limit and this camp, he's willing to add to his training regime, doing new things. You never stop learning. Bernard Hopkins at 49 years old has shown that your body can do extraordinary things if you look after your body.

Dmitriy told me that I will become a world champion. He said with every setback I've had I always come back stronger. Olympic Bronze medalist Nate Jones who works on Floyd's training team and trains me, just told me yesterday I will become a world champion. Twelve months ago Floyd told me that and Leonard publicity stated I will become one too. Stan Hoffman, manager to over thirty world champions and the man who gave me my first fight in the US, also told me that I have many attributes that can't be taught but world champions are born with. So some of the most important people in boxing appreciate what I bring to the table, but it's to do it when it counts. I'm 34 years old on the day of my fight. I plan on fighting until the age of 40 years old. 6 years to go and much more to achieve.

Monday 18th August 2014

I sparred 4 six minute rounds against Lloyd Elliot today. He's a British super welterweight fighter who is undefeated in 15 professional fights. I started my day with a 9 mile run and ended it weighing 149.6lbs, everything is on target. I want to touch 147lbs this week.
Daniel Calzada's team seem mighty confident going into our clash. With a record of 10 wins and 10 loses that is confusing to me. In my mind he is another routine win. Of course I have to go out there and earn the victory but I'm pressing for knock out wins against these kind of fighters.

Wednesday 20th August 2014

10 mile run in the morning followed by 27 minutes straight on the pads with Nate and 18 minutes on the heavy bag. Skipping, speed bag, shadow boxing and abdominal crunches where all on the agenda as well. I put in some serious work and weighed 148.4lbs. I am right on target, 5lbs to go with 9 days until the weigh in.

Thursday 21st August 2014

Floyd showed why he is an all time great this afternoon. He completed five 9 minute rounds of sparring with 30 seconds of rest. It was incredible to watch it at close quarters. He was sharp, fast and used his skills and ring generalship. He is ready for Marcos Rene Maidana now. After the sparring session Floyd walked out of the gym floor and back into the locker room. Bastie Samir is a super-middle weight and easily has thirty pounds on Floyd.

Saturday 23rd August 2014

There was no mountain run this morning as Eddie was in California with Tommy Hill, who was making his debut. I completed an hour run around the streets of Las Vegas then headed to the Mayweather Boxing Club for a sparring session with Chavis Holifield. I only sparred once this week and that was with Brighton undefeated super welterweight fighter Lloyd Elliot. I feel ready.
I'm sparring now just to help with weight loss, as you sweat more.

I had planned to do four 6 minute rounds with Chavis. When Cortez Bey showed up and looked at me in disbelief, he had messaged me two hours earlier to say he wanted to join in but he was late. I was going through the motions with Chavis, happy to get rounds but when coaches and fighters watching started chanting for Chavis. I turned it up, beating Chavis around the ring and shouting out "help him now, talk louder muthafuckas. Help him. Help him"
I shouted to Cortez to get ready. After three 6 minute rounds Cortez stepped in to spar me. We completed another three 6 minute rounds. That was 12 rounds of sparring. I went on to the heavy bag and did 10 minutes tapping away. Cortez said they should be getting me big fights again. I told him I just got to keep winning fights and I'll be back where I want to be.

Monday 25th August 2014

Today was my last day of sparring. I completed three 6 minute rounds with Chavis Holifield, 30 seconds recovery. I'm in great shape. Dave Brown, my coach from London who Rene had flown out to assist Nate took the time of my workouts.

Wednesday 27th August 2014

Oh how I hate media day. Week of the fight the last thing I want to do is talk to the media but it is part of the job so I get on with it and majority of the time I enjoy it.

Thursday 28th August 2014

I woke up this morning weighing 148lbs. The last two mornings I woke up around 147lbs but I had planned to run a ten mile this morning,

Friday 29th August 2014

I woke up in my suite around 6am at the Palms hotel casino, I headed to my apartment at the Extended stay America to change to put my sweat suit on. I went out for an hour run around Las Vegas. My weight was 144lbs but I wanted to have some breakfast before the weigh in.
I came back weighing 142lbs I had some porridge with raisins and a banana. I headed off to get my haircut then went for my weekly massage. I had a protein shake, showered and headed off to the weigh in.

I set a target of 200 miles to run and the targeted weight for this fight was 143lbs. I by passed both of them. Running 226 miles around Las Vegas and weighed in at 139.8lbs. Daniel Calzada was 141lbs. I'll be 10lbs heavier by fight time. I shouldn't even be nervous fighting a fighter of Calzada's level but I am. I've pushed my body so hard that I can be no ready than I am but the unexpected makes you nervous. I've beaten many fighters of Calzada's level, tomorrow will be my 36 win and another one I can be proud of.

Saturday 30th August 2014

Today is my birthday and I'm thankful to get my 36th win. 34 years old but you'd never guess it with that performance. Maybe some of the best boxing I've ever produced, and Floyd was watching ringside cheering me on. I did what I was supposed to do with this level of opposition. Daniel Calzada did not have anything to trouble me with.
Doing what I am doing is extraordinary. I am from a poor community in London where many of the heroes are criminals and it is normal to be just that. As a five-year-old child I wanted to be a boxer. Everybody else wanted to be a footballer, lawyer, or a doctor. I was always different. Always on my own path, back in 1998 I watched Floyd Mayweather win his world championship challenge against Gerardo Hernandez on television in London, I would never have thought 15 years later I'd be part of his team. I worked hard and never stopped believing in myself. Won some fights, and the fights I lost where either controversial or very close fights which could have gone either way.

I left Dave Brown and Harry Keitt around 930pm. The whole team was hanging around the bar and around the lobby. There were parties going on all over Las Vegas, but I just called Anahi and spent the night with her in my hotel room at the Palms hotel and casino.

Sunday 31st August 2014

The hard work is over. 200 plus miles ran. 26.8lbs dropped. Strenuous training every day, not one day off in six weeks. Boxing fans who criticize any fighter do not know or appreciate the hard work they put in or the sacrifices they make, just to fight to entertain the audience watching and make a living.

Erislandy Lara vs Ishe Smith

Wednesday 3rd December 2014

Today while I was hitting the bag as Nate watched on. Dejuan was asking me if I'm ranked or anything. I said, "No. You can't get ranked doing 8 rounders".

He said after this fight he'll talk to Floyd about getting me ranked and on TV for my next fight. He said a KO win would help my case.

Thursday 4th December 2014

I was up after 4am this morning. I couldn't sleep. I went to the fitness gym around 6am for a strength and abdominal conditioning workout.

Ishe took his sparring partners, pad man and I for breakfast at baby stacks.

I didn't go boxing until 4pm. I felt tired but had to get the work done. I rolled up to the boxing club and Floyd was outside. I saluted him and went in the locker room to get ready to workout. By the time I was finished, Floyd was gone.

Dejuan was with Floyd during my workout but came back for Ishe's session.

Dejuan said to everyone "This nigga Ashley waving at Floyd from the cab like some fan. That shit was hilarious".

Everyone was laughing. I said I was greeting my boss. Floyd did seem taken back as he just looked at me and walked into the boxing club.

Dejuan went on to say that he told Floyd that he'd like me on TV next time. I asked what did Floyd say. Dejuan replied. Floyd don't care who's on television but I need you to look good Ash. You fighting a 12-5 guy. He shouldn't go 10 rounds with you. You took too many punches from that 10-10 guy last time out.

I told Dejuan I'll get him out if there. I've been training hard. I'm ready for my fight. I was already planning to knock him out. Now I have more of a reason to.

Monday 8th December 2014

This morning I ran 8.8 miles along the strip and back on to industrial way. I weighed 145lbs afterwards.

I went boxing around midday with Dan. I wanted to put in two hard days of training as we fly on Wednesday and the work will basically be done by then.

I went thirty minutes straight on the pads with Nate and finished up with 15 minutes straight on the heavy bag.
I did my shadow boxing, skipping, speed bag drills as well.

Anahi met me afterwards. We had sexual relations. I had gone two weeks without it so I was disappointed I gave in. Maybe cause I know Miguel Zuniga has no chance against me I did it.

Tuesday 9th December 2014

This morning saw me do another long run. This time 9.5 miles. 143.2lbs is what I weighed on my return. To say I was happy is an understatement.

I did the same boxing workout as Monday except no heavy bag. I went to hit it but I felt a pain in my left fist so I skipped it and started hitting the speed bag.

Boxing News editor Tris Dixon was in attendance as he wanted to interview me afterwards. He said he noticed I'm hitting harder. I told him I was beating fighters like Miguel Zuniga ten years ago. He replied that it's the fighters you take your eye off that can cause upsets. I told him I'm focused and I've trained hard. I'll be fine.

Dan said afterwards that watching me I'm definitely one of the hardest workers in the gym.
I'd say so too.

I watched a fight of Miguel Zuniga for the first time today. The only footage of him available is of Daquan Arnett who helped me get ready for Pablo Cesar Cano. Miguel looks awkward but comes forward pushing the action. Daquan fought on the back foot but caught him with a beautiful left hook knocking him out. It's his only knockout loss. He looks tough but I should be too much for him.

Wednesday 10th December 2014

My iPhone alarm rings out loud at 330am. It's early but I have road work to do before Nate picks me up. I completed 6 plus miles. Just under an hour of work.

I ate some porridge with sultanas and honey drizzled all over it. This was 5am, I had two apples for the rest of the day
Jihad arrived from New York City just before majority of the team arrived from Las Vegas. I stayed in my room other than signing forms with the commission.

I'm looking forward to being back on the TV next year and making some proper money.

Ishe, Badou and Chris who are the TV had a media workout. I went down there to support them. I saw Dmitriy Salita there who is promoter of Steve Martinez, opponent for Chris Pearson. They've come here believing they can win.

Dmitriy helped me make my debut here in the States and flew me over for training camp many times. He told Bob and Ishe's pad man that is his opinion I'm the best fighter on the team.

By 7pm I was tired and went in bed to sleep. It had been a long day. I received a message on my phone. It was from Ishe. I asked him what was up. He asked how my weight was. I said it was good. He told me he was going to Lifetime fitness. I didn't want to go but I knew he wanted me to come. So I asked him if he wanted me to there with him. He said yes so I met him in his room for 8pm. Andy who is a friend of Ishe's and working for him during fight week was there to assist. Ishe did around 20 minutes on the treadmill.

We chilled for a bit then headed back to the hotel. Ishe appreciated me being there. He has a big fight so he needs support. I'm one of the few people he trusts on the team. Bob didn't answer his message and Dejuan was at the NBA Basketball game so that left me.

Thursday 11th December 2014

As I wake up in another strange bed, another hotel. The time zone is two hours in front of Las Vegas. I woke around 4am San Antonio time. My weight was around 144.6lbs when I woke up. If I don't eat or drink until the 2pm weigh in I should be in the 142s. After making weight for 12 years you get to know your body.

The weigh in took place at 2pm. I went downstairs at 130pm to register.

Leonard walked in the room at 145pm. It was like seeing a ghost. I've spoke to him a few times but he's not been in the gym like he used to be before him and Floyds situation became public.

Ishe took the stage at 2pm with Lara. He seemed in the zone and confident. Just how he should be. He showed no respect to Lara. The fans and the experts have him a big underdog but they had him the underdog when he beat K-9 last February. Lara's manager and Ishe went back and forth at each other on the stage.
Lara doesn't speak English. He seemed not to take any noticed of the verbal sparring.
Ishe weighed 153.5lbs. Lara 154lbs. They both looked in tremendous shape.

After the TV fights weighed in it was my turn to step on the scales. I was 143lbs. I made weight. My opponent Miguel Zuniga weighed 140.5lbs.
His team started to talk to the commission and make some noise. They said they signed a contract for 141lbs. I was told I have an hour to lose weight. I made it known that all my fights with Mayweather promotions have been made at 143lbs. Dejuan, my now boxing advisor went over to Leonard and the matchmaker John. They ended up sorting it out with Zuniga's team by giving him a few hundred dollars more. Leonard came up to me and said I've told you that we'll never put you in a situation that doesn't benefit you. Don't worry. Calm down.

I went for a meal with Nate, Jihad and Dan afterwards. A Mediterranean restaurant not far from the Omhi hotel where I was staying.

Friday 12th December 2014

I woke around 6am. I lay in my bed thinking about the day ahead. Law and Order was on in the background. I tend to leave the television on when going to bed.

It was breakfast time. I washed my face and went down to the restaurant in the hotel. It was a morning buffet for $18 which wasn't that bad. I had food that I would normally eat. Porridge, fruit and yogurt was the best on offer and the best for me. The food you eat is the fuel for your performance. Dejuan had kept telling me we need you to look good. We need you to take him out. Ji- had had echoed those words. I never put pressure on myself to look good. I just try to win, that's the most important to me.

Everyone was leaving the hotel at 230pm for the non televised fights. Bob was wrapping everyone's hands so he had to get them done before the fights started as he was also cut-man to majority of the fighters on Mayweather promotions.

I spoke to bob beforehand and told him Dan would be driving me down to the venue for 4pm as there was still over an hour to get my hands done. He told me that was up to me to take that risk.

I arrived at the Alamodome just before 4pm. Texas does no drug testing for non televised bouts so that was great. No urine test, that's always a hassle.

This is my fifth fight with Mayweather promotions. I'm comfortable with the fighters, the staff and the way everything is run.

I'm one of the senior fighters and as Ishe said, "There's only three fighters that is elite on the team. You, Mickey and myself"

After losing on my debut for Mayweather promotions. I've been nervous to be dropped and I've felt like I have something to prove as Floyd believed in me and I lost at the first hurdle with him.

I've kept working hard, stayed focused and determined. I've been fighting fighters I could beat seven years ago, D level fighters but that was important to work on my game and regain confidence.

This was the fourth fight of the show. I was relaxed. I had the mind frame that I wanted to knock my opponent out. That wasn't to be. He was a tough as nails fighter. Daquan Arnett caught him with an incredible left hook. I hit him with some quality shots. Rocking him to his boots. Left shaking, but he'd shake it off and keep chasing me.

I think it was the third or fourth that Nate told me to go forward as it looked like I could stop him. It was like to Bulls meeting each other. He rocked me and tried to go in for the kill. I return to the corner and told Nate, "Let me do me. I know what I'm doing. Boxing him is easier. All I care about is the win".

Floyd shouted out from ringside "You stole my moves, Ashley." "Nice shoulder role." "Win and you'll be back to championship level".

Great motivation words from the boss.

In the last round Floyd yelled out "You've won the fight don't take any risks." I used my feet, moving to the left, to the right, using my defense skills then exploding with combinations.

I won the fight. Everyone was shocked with the boxing skills I displayed.

Floyd senior told me back stage "I didn't know you could box that good. It's the consistency of staying in the gym, working on your craft that has helped you."

In the gym I'm forced to be the aggressor as everyone is a boxer or trying to be like Floyd. So I never get to displayed my skills.

I showered and hanged with Dan for a bit. Afterwards I went to Ishe's dressing room and just chilled with him in there as he prepared for his WBA world championship fight with Erislandy Lara.

Ishe was confident going into the fight and he had a good first half of the fight. In
implemented his game plan. Closing down Lara and banging him to the body when he was on the ropes. Second half of the fight, Ronnie Shields, Lara's trainer must have told him to stay off the ropes cause he went back to what he does. Cuban boxing. Hit and move. Confuse your opponent. It's not attractive to watch but it's hard to fight against and effective. Lara shut Ishe out for the second half of the fight. Ishe gave his all but Lara was the better fighter on the night.

After the fight, Andrew Tabiti, Chris Pearson, Dan and I joined Floyd's team of assistants and security for breakfast at Denny's.

Floyd said Ishe boxed hard and was trying to "kill that boy". There was over twenty of us in the diner at around 2am. The server was shocked to see a man worth hundreds of millions in there. Floyd responded that it's 2am and we need to eat.

It was a hard week for Floyd as he saw one of his best friends Earl Hayes, commit suicide and murdered his girlfriend whilst talking to Floyd on FaceTime.

We got back to the hotel around 4am. I went up to Ishe's room as I didn't go into his locker room after the fight as his head trainer Eddie Mustafa Muhammad told Dan and I Ishe walked straight out of the arena. Which Ishe said was not true when I told him. Danny, Ishe's pad man who also works with two time middleweight champion Jermaine Taylor was up there with Ishe. We talked for 15 minutes. Ishe seemed content. He had tried his best but his best wasn't good enough on this occasion.

We left Ishe to packed our stuff for the airport. I ended up being awake for 26 hours straight.

Amir Khan was fighting in Las Vegas at the MGM Grand. Dan and I where attending that so we had another busy day ahead of us.

I moved to 37 career wins. I've achieved more than I ever believed I would. Ended the year on a high.

Monday 15th December 2014

Ishe called to tell me that he will only be paying Eddie 5% for this fight. He wasn't happy that he was the only one on his team not to come back in to the locker room, walking straight out of the arena where Dan and I saw him.

Ishe said everyone on his team had called him to see how he is but no word from him.

I tried to fight Eddies corner and said that he'd done everything expected of him.

Ishe said Eddie can't do pads so whatever I pay Danny will come out of his money.

I agree with that as I'd pay Eddie 5% but that's something you discuss before camp not afterwards.

I asked Ishe would you miss Eddie if he wasn't part of your team. Image replied "no".

Change is sometimes good when you've achieved so much with one person. Ishe went on. I've been working with Eddie 8 years and never been to his house. This was the first year he invited me for thanksgiving.

"FIGHT OF THE CENTURY"

Floyd Mayweather vs Manny Pacquiao

Wednesday 28th January 2015

After spending exactly six weeks in London, I'm back on a plane to Las Vegas.

Kitchie, Floyds assistant contacted me on Sunday evening about accompanying him on his Australian tour with thirty others. That night I got my Australian visa to enter the country. Due to Floyds prison stint he's currently going through some issues with his own visa. Hopefully it is successful.

I started my day with a ten mile run. I always like to put in some miles before hitting the airport for a long haul flight.
I had an eleven hour flight to Los Angeles then three hours later I landed in Las Vegas.
Badou came to pick me up as I'm staying at his until I fly to Australia with Floyd.
Kitchie has told us Friday we are leaving. I think it's more likely Monday or Tuesday.

Saturday 7th February 2015

Ishe messaged me this morning that Badou seems unsure about his fight with Anthony Dirrell. He's been asking Lanell how his sparring went with him years ago. Ishe's view was who cares how the sparring went, it's sparring.

I stayed at Badou's apartment for a week and all he spoke about was Anthony Dirrell. I could hear him in his bedroom "And the new". He's doing everything possible to be ready for the fight.

I told Ishe, just as I believed in him when he fought Erislandy Lara. I believe in Badou. If he believes he can do it. I believe he can.

Friday 20th February 2015

Floyd has been talking about me lately. He's looking to get me a big fight soon. It's truly a scary thing to have the number one fighter in the world believe in you. You don't want to let him down.

Floyd announced his fight today against Manny Paciquao. The fight world went crazy.

Saturday 21st February 2015

Ishe called me today after he had finished an event he was speaking at that targeted young people involved in gun crime. He saw Jessie Vargas there, who used to be promoted by Floyd and is a world champion signed to Top Rank. They began speaking about the show on May 2nd. Jessie isn't happy that Lomachenko is due to be on it isn't of him. Ishe threw it out there that he could fight me. Jessie said he was up for it and would take it if offered to him.
I'll speak to Dejuan on Monday and throw it out there.

Tuesday 24th February 2015

Floyd's birthday is today. Majority of the guys headed down to Red Rock Casino to the VIP bowling lanes for 8pm. Al Haymon is rumoured to have paid for it Floyd's birthday party.
I gave Floyd a gift, it was a 18 carat white gold dog tag with the money team incrusted in diamonds with his kids names on the back. I told him it wasn't a big gift but he said it didn't need to be. He said he appreciated it.

I was there for maybe three hours. When everybody started leaving for the club I left with the boxers to go home. I had gym in the morning.

How far will you go to find greatness in yourself? How far will you go to help someone find greatness in themselves.
This is something that many people lack or never try to achieve. Floyd is pushing himself to greatness and helping us be the greatest we can possibly be.

Sunday 1st March 2015

I'm fighting 30th April, I spoke to Dejuan today. It ruined my mood as he told me I was off television. This will be my fifth straight fight off TV. I'm not happy. I had intended to speak to Floyd. Even more so now.
I told Dejuan I need a world title shot. He replied "You're old as fuck, we got to get you up there ASAP."

He went on to say, "Don't worry, a big fight is coming." I hope so cause this last year has been a joke. I've always done it the hard way from start to finish.

I've always had to prove my worth. For twelve years I've never had it easy.
I need a world title shot in my career. My story needs it. Win or lose I need the opportunity or I'll feel I never got rewarded for all the hard work, dedication and sacrifice I've offered boxing.

Monday 2nd March 2015

Today is the first day of training camp, 2 months until Floyd fights Manny and until I get my 38th win.

I woke up at 4am. Left out 45 minutes later to complete a 7 mile run.
Headed to 24 hour fitness at 9am to complete a two hour strength conditioning session.

Floyd told his staff to be at the gym for 3pm. He rolled in around 4pm. Started his workout around 430pm. Alex Ariza stretched and loosened Floyd before his workout. Floyd always spars the first day of camp. He sparred a young Mexican fighter trained by Oscar DeLa Hoya's former coach.

Floyd completed three 3 minute rounds. He's been off for six months. I always thought he stayed in shape by exercising religiously but his staff says he plays basketball and does the odd press ups and sit-ups but he takes his time off to relax and have fun.

Floyd hit the pads with Roger. Body bag with Nate. Heavy bag work followed then speed ball drills and some light abdominal crunches.

It was a good workout for his first day back. A legendary camp is in front of us.
I'm looking forward to it.

Tuesday 3rd March 2015

Nate told me that he appreciates my loyalty towards him as I could have easily started
working with another trainer as he is absent when Floyd is in not in camp.

After my workout and Floyd's, I headed down to the Brooklyn Bowl to watch some amateur boxing show.

LaTondria who is the first lady of Mayweather Promotions was there with her friend, Esther. I took a fancy to her and made my move.
We sat down and spoke for a couple hours about her life and mine.
I gave her my business card as I left, she messaged me an hour later. She's thirty years old and very attractive.

Wednesday 4th March 2015

A group of us went for a run with Floyd this evening. We did 5.2 miles in 42 minutes. Floyd spoke as we ran.
"Fighters are always in a rush. Take every day at a time."
JLeon and I left the group finishing first.

Thursday 5th March 2015

I sparred for the first time in three months. I completed two 5 minute rounds and one 4 minute round with Chavis Holifield. Chavis is fighting next Saturday so he is in top shape. I'm just starting.

As Floyd arrived at the gym, I had to go. I had a date with Esther. I went for a 5.5 mile run beforehand.

We went to Cirque Du Soleil at New York Casino and Hotel. I got us front row seats which had us on a sofa. We had a great time. I was brought on stage to do a dance and a sexual routine with a stranger. It was fun. With 1000 people watching I was a tad bit nervous.

Afterwards we went to Peppermill restaurant for a meal. I got back to my place around 1am. We spent hours talking and laughing. Great first date.

Thursday 12th March 2015

Zab and I spoke back about the struggles of losing weight as a fighter in the locker room
before training. He said he's been 157lbs maximum. I've been 169lbs. Even though there's been a few times we were supposed to fight I got no grudge against him. Boxing is a business. If the money's not right then there's no fight.

Nate was watching Floyd hit the heavy bag. Floyd looked over at us. Nate told him that DeMarcus said he was all up in my ass. I shook my head and said it was easy work.

While Floyd was hitting the heavy bag he stopped and asked me "What's different about me to other fighters?" I told him "you have to think with you. I have to stay sharp and use my mind." He asked if I enjoyed the work. I told him "I loved it."

Friday 13th March 2015

Floyd sparred Zab 'Super' Judah today. Zab started good as was expected but Floyd broke him down, drawing blood from his nose and mouth. It was quality work from two welterweight legends. Zab is the last undisputed welterweight champion.
Afterwards Zab told me he's fighting April 11th.

It's an astonishing feeling to be on friendly terms with so many fighters I admired whilst in the UK. Now they know me and we are associates.

Tuesday 17th March 2015

Mickey Bey and I put in some good rounds today. I have to be at my best when facing him as he's so sharp. I caught him with jabs but my best work was to the body. I was relentless there and very successful.

Eddie Mustafa Muhammad came up to me as he was leaving the gym and told me that I just need to double and treble my jab and not lean in with my right hand. Good advice!

I Went for a run with Floyd today, he said one more win and I'll fight for the title.
Which Dejuan told me already but nice to hear it from him so I know it's actually true.

Floyd told me that if you go fast or slow the goal is always going to be where it's going to be. If it's one year, five years or ten years, there's no need to rush in boxing or life.

Show on April 30th is due to be at the Palms casino hotel. I beat Daniel Calzada there on August 30th so that's a good omen for me.

Mickey might be fighting in Russia. Word is the Russians will bid 1.2 million dollars. Floyd wants Dejuan to sell Mickeys contract so he's definitely not going to bid over $500,000.

Today was Tremendous! Hard day of work completed. Put in miles and rounds with two world champions, Zab Judah and DeMarcus Corley.
Surround myself with the Best always. I woke up in a good mood.
Going bed in an even better one.

Thursday 19th March 2015

I ran with Floyd after our boxing workouts today. There was ten of us in total. The first half I just stayed at the back as the guys where hanging off Floyd's ankles wanting to be right next to him.

The last two miles Floyd took off leaving them for dust. I stepped on the gas and caught up to Floyd. We ran side by side for the last past of the run. He slowed down nearer the end saying that you should run just how you fight changing up the pace.
I told him that he burned out the young boys. He replied you got to run at your own level.
We finished together as the fans took photos of Floyd as we ended up back at the gym.

Determination, hard work and persistence is everything. That has got me to where I am.

Monday 23rd March 2015

New week, same mindset! Only room for positivity. Let's do this!

I sparred with Ishe today we completed four 5 minute rounds. It wasn't my best performance with him but I worked my jab well and body shots.

Whilst at the gym I got a message from Esther asking if I wanted to go to the movies. I was planning to go running with Floyd but I'll go running next time with him. Zab went out on the run. It's normally just over five miles that we do.

In the evening I went out to the movies with Esther. Afterwards we went for a meal. The movie was fun, we watched Focus starring Will Smith. She told me Will had tried it on her years ago whilst on a shoot. He did it in front of Jada his wife. She had no issue with it so Esther guessed he had Jada's backing.

Tuesday 24th March 2015

I had the honour to spar two of the best 140lbs fighters during my era this afternoon. Back to back! I completed two 5 minute rounds with DeMarcus Corley then I finished up with two 5 minute rounds with Zab Judah. Everyone knows I've accepted fights with Zab in the past so our work had more tension. Corley and I just worked. Zab and I was like a fight. Both of us hesitant to let loose. When we did we were just more cautious of what was coming back.

Zab and Corley finished up with two 5 minute rounds. It was one round a piece but they both let their hands go. Corley kept catching Zab with big right hooks but Zab would fire back with his favoured right uppercut. It was top notch stuff all around. Over the last two days I've sparred with three former world champions. I'm in a good place right now.

Floyd asked me in the locker room, when did I turn professional and what was my record as an amateur. I replied "I turned professional in 2003 and that my amateur record was 40 wins and 10 loses."

Floyd went on to say, "Ashley can fight. It's only me that can cook him."
Dejuan said I got one more chance. I told him that's all I want is the opportunity and that is your job to get it.
Floyd butted in "Ashley's alright." "He's that guy you want with you in a club when bottles start flying. Tough Muthafucka."

Thursday 26th March 2015

Floyd finished his workout. Went back into the locker room and sat down. Then he spoke! "All I want to do is go home and hang with some fine looking women. That's all I want to do."

He got ready to go out for a run from the gym. There was maybe eight of us that accompanied him. Zab Judah was amongst the group. It's astonishing for me to think back as a teenager and a young man in his twenties. I looked up to these fighters. I get to work out with them now. They are my peers. It's crazy what hard work can truly make you accomplish.
We ran for 5.25 miles and it took us around 42 minutes. It's not a fast pace just a steady
jog.

Floyd spoke in the locker room about coming to an agreement with Top Rank for Mickey Beys first title defense. He said Mickey would get 175k and his opponent 150k. They were due to fight on April 30th as main event.

Ishe would message me later to tell me he's main event now as Mickey turned it down and said he prefers it to go to purse bids. I told him he would likely get around 250k as that's what Ishe got for his first defence. Mickey was very unhappy with that stating if Al Haymons guys are getting 500k upwards, why aren't we.

Friday 27th March 2015

I woke up to a group text message from Kitchie, Floyd's assistant said that he would not be in the boxing gym today. I wasn't surprised to get that message as he didn't have a good sparring session yesterday and his lip was busted by a head butt. Nate said yesterday he would talk to Floyd about taking the day off.

He's been pushing hard this week. There's still four more weeks of hard work to go.

Wednesday 1st April 2015

Today is April's fools so no one was trusted. The work was the only thing that was to be believed in.

I sparred with DeMarcus Corley this afternoon. I wasn't happy with my performance but everyone watching thought I put in a controlled performance. There was things I know I could have done and didn't. I am too strong for Chop Chop though. He had some good moments but I'm an all together better fighter.

Floyd sustained a cut lip on Friday which has stopped him from sparring this week. He sparred on Tuesday but the cut reopened so he said he's taking the rest of the week off from sparring.

During his workout Floyd looked at me and said, "Ashley, You're going to be my final fight." Floyds photographer Pete Young said, "You'll take that Ash? a cool two million."

Thursday 2nd April 2015

Dejuan called me this morning. Today marks four weeks until my 45th fight. I gave a list of ten opponents to Dejuan and he's come back with the toughest one on the list. Mexican fighter Mohonri Montes who has 30 wins, 4 losses and 1 draw. He's an experienced fighter for 25 years old. He's gone 12 rounds with three weight world champion Humberto Soto who I'm also targeting. He gave him a very good fight. Eric Bone also beat him over ten rounds.

Dejuan asked me if I'm sure I can beat him. I told him yes I want my world title shot.

I watched my opponents fight with Eric Bone later that night after training. Eric outboxed him. I believe I can do the same thing. I just need to keep training like I have been doing.

Friday 3rd April 2015

Demarcus Corley and I went at it again. Just before we were about to spar, Esther walked in the gym with LaTondria. That was extra motivation for a top performance. We said hi and she gave me a hug. Esther was wearing some little spandex Nike shorts that barely covered her ass. I know Esther caught some fighter's eyes as they started to swarm around her. She was working out with Bianca and Tokyo so she wasn't interested in that.

After my training session I went over to her and we spoke for a bit.
I completed four 6 minute rounds with Chop Chop. His nose was busted from round one. A couple of his kids were in attendance with his wife. He was wearing a white shirt. By the end of the 24 minute session his shirt was now red. I killed him today. Nate stormed off yesterday when he said tomorrow will be the last time I spar Chop. I told him that's not your decision to make. He said, "Fuck you then" and walked off leaving me to work out on my own. It's okay. Jihad will be flown in soon. His lupus is playing up so I've told him when he's better let me know and I'll fly him out.

Saturday 4th April 2015

445am I was up and ready to hit the mountains for our weekly altitude run. It was only Ishe and I as Badou was not attending for whatever reason. He messaged me last night to say he wasn't coming.

Badou is preparing for his world title against Anthony Dirrell, he finally sparred KO Bellows after weeks of Ishe and I telling him he was perfect work for him. Badou had told me a couple days ago that he's been beating up his sparring partners. I told him that's what you're supposed to do.

Tuesday 7th April 2015

I started my day with a 9 mile run. I had organised sparring with Moo Moo for 1pm. I had a terrible day in there. I got 4 six minute rounds in but I was one paced. Moo Moo was letting off his combinations and caught me with big right uppercuts that lifted up my head a few times.

Wednesday 8th April 2015

The biggest fight in boxing history is getting closer each week.

Floyd sparred again today. He's in his groove now. Today he put in a super long workout. You just sit there thinking he's still working. It's tiring just watching the man.
After training Floyd joked in the locker room about how you have to pick women up and keep them.
When Floyd was about to leave he called me over and asked me if Kitchie had my contact number. I told him yes. He said we'll get that car tonight. I told him "You the man. Thank you."

Thursday 9th April 2015

I've started cryotherapy. I'll be using it for the next three weeks. It is supposed to boost energy levels, reduce soreness, reduction in fatigue and enhance performance.

We'll see how this goes.

Monday 13th April 2015

17 days to go until my 45th fight at the Palms Casino Resort.

I started my day with a 9.5 mile run. I weighed 149lbs which was perfect as my fight is made at 143lbs.
I completed a two hour boxing workout with Nate.
Afterwards the guys where just chilling with Floyd in the locker room.
Demarcus Corley sucker punched Zab Judah in the gym and everything goes crazy.
Demarcus had post something on social media about Zab being a pussy because he wouldn't give him a rematch. I told Demarcus he was in the wrong. He replied "it's just business."
Demarcus has 25 loses so is no longer marketable. His big money fights are long behind him.
Zab ran after Demarcus with a knife and was shouting at the top of his voice that he was going to kill him.
Security wouldn't let Zab back into the locker room to chat to Floyd. Floyd told his staff to get rid of them or call police as the media will blame him for the incident if they find out.

Dejuan told me that my opponent had been changed.
Mohonri Montes is out. Oscar Cortes is in. His record is 25 wins with 2 loses. 13 by knockout. On paper he is another dangerous opponent.

Friday 17th April 2015

Montes is back in. He wanted more money. I don't know if he got it back he's officially my opponent.

Nate and I had a big bust up today. He threatened to attack me. All because I don't want to do his easy track session. I told him your job is to do pads, that is all. He told me "Fuck you. I'm done with you. Just pay me my fucking money." I hit the heavy bag for 45 minutes.

After training I got on the phone to jihad and told him the situation. He said he could be out there for Monday. I butt heads with Harry and Nate. Personally clashes with mine. Maybe cause they used to their fighters doing what they're told. With Nate he wants to accept the praise for wins but not accept the blame for the loss I had with him. Last fight he trained me for one week and goes on like I looked good because of him. I looked good because of the work I put in.

Monday 20th April 2015

Nate phoned me at 8am this morning. I was out running. He must have seen that jihad was on his way to Las Vegas on social media. He asked me what time I was going to be in the gym. I told him "if you are still part of my team be there for midday". I continued my 9.5 mile run. I told Nate on Friday. "With or without you this show will keep moving forward."
Only person on my team that is irreplaceable is Rene Carayol.

Dejuan asked me what was up with Nate and I during training. He said you know Nate family. Don't fuck your opportunity up.

Later on at Cryrotheraphy, Ishe said that Dejuan told him Nate was unhappy with the way I spoke to him. Saying he's only a boxing coach and that I don't want Nate going to Floyd and messing up my relationship with him as Floyd has known Nate for 20 years so is going to side with him. Ishe said I'm very blunt and that Americans are sensitive. He told me not to kiss Nates ass but just tone down my bluntness and choose my words better.

Tuesday 21st April 2015

This is the third 12 round sparring session over the last three weeks. My team where happy with my performance. I started fast with my first sparring partner. Showing him no respect.
Six 6 minute rounds. Then on my second sparring partner. I worked on my defence for the first 3 minutes while I recovered. Then I fired back. He had some good moments but I was always alert and paced myself. At 34 years old, this game isn't getting any easier but I'm continually pushing myself. I'm looking forward to a rest after this fight. I'm super confident of getting this win but I do have a very good opponent in front of me.

Wednesday 22nd April 2015

I was so tired after sparring yesterday. I have one more sparring session to do. Then it's just staying sharp and dropping the final pounds for the weigh in.

The weigh in is 7 days away. I've dropped 12lbs over the last 7 weeks. I have 5lbs to drop over the next week.

I started my day with a 6 mile run, followed by a two hour strength conditioning session. I went to Sub Zero Recovery for a Cryrotheraphy session then headed off to the Mayweather boxing club for my third session of the day.

I threw 1200 punches during 25 minutes of pad work and 2000 punches over 20 minutes of hitting the heavy bag. I really was on form today.

I went back to Sub zero recovery for another Cryrotheraphy session to help my body recover from the four hour training day I had. Last day of sparring is tomorrow and I want to finish on a high.

Monday 27th April 2015

It's fight week. The biggest fight ever is about to take place in Las Vegas.
I'm focused on my fight. Getting my victory and get my money.
I started my Monday as I usually do with a 9.5 mile run. A few hours later I headed to the boxing gym. The gym was packed with fight fans. Everyone knows I'm the most unsociable person whilst I'm training. Do not bother me during my workout. I'm super focused. It's just how I am. Some of the guys talk mess and are very loud. I'm the opposite. I'm quiet. I just work.

I told Nate that we're going to work today. We completed 30 minutes straight on the pads. I felt good and bystanders told me I looked good.

My weight was 145.9lbs after the workout. I have 2.9lbs to drop by Wednesday at 330pm. That's when the weigh in is.

Dejuan called me afterwards and told me he's working on a sponsor for me. $8,000 to $10,000 I'll get to wear a t shirt. I asked him if he knew how much I was getting paid yet. He said don't hold me to it but I'm trying to get you six figures.

Mickey turned down $200,000 for his world title defense. Floyd was willing to pay his opponent $150,000. So he saved 350K. Mickey is now going to get $58,000 as Top Rank promotions won the bid as Mayweather promotions didn't bid for the fight. Floyd got Mickey the world title opportunity and word has it Floyd has given Mickey an advance of $100,000. Mickey supposed to have a gambling problem.

Tuesday 28th April 2015

Today is the fighter arrivals. It's a shame that Bob Arum chose to do his own one at the
Mandalay Bay.

For the first time it was in the MGM Arena. I enjoyed the event for what it was. It was a very pro TMT crowd. Normally at the arrivals you have the cheers and jeers from both fans. It was missing that.

Dejuan told me that Leonard had sent him the purses. My purse was $20,000. I was disappointed. Dejuan said that he spoke to Floyd and he said get through this fight and my next pay day will be better. I've racked up $10,000 in sponsorship so that has help balance out better for me.

Wednesday 29th April 2015

The last 24 hours before the weigh in is always so hard. No food or fluid, just breathing, I even ran this morning for 6.5 miles. Which took me an hour.
I went to the Palms casino resort to weigh myself. I made weight and faced off against my opponent. I'm very relaxed. I believe in myself. Every time he's stepped up he's lost. I view myself as a step up for him.

I checked in to the hotel very late so there was no rooms available. The lady upgraded me to a suite which was very nice of her.

Thursday 30th April 2015

After making 143lbs yesterday I woke up weighing 155.6lbs. I was happy with that. My body just soaked up all the food and drink.

Before heading to the ring, Nevada checked my weight. I was a staggering 160.5lbs. In 24 hours I'd put on 17.5lbs.

I was calm before my fight as always. The nerves don't kick in until I start warming up or the ring walk. I was back on television which was a huge relief to me. ESPN asked me yesterday if I change my style when I'm on TV. I told them no that I just see it as the viewers are missing out on my talent. My talent was made for TV. No loss for me except my pay which is dramatically affected.

I had the same referee as the last time I fought at Palms last August which was a good omen for me. Badou was also walking me to the ring. Last time he did that was 12 months ago when I got my last stoppage win.

The crowd was a proud TMT crowd. There was loads of Brits in attendance. Esther was ringside supporting me. My opponent fought how I knew he would. He was strong as expected. His punch output was low but everything was meant to hurt. He had a nice jab and fast hands. Faster than the last three Mexicans I'd faced. He threw combinations too.

I boxed him and moved. It was not easy but I was doing it. His body shots were affecting me. They hurt. My breathing was getting deeper and deeper each round. One round he really hurt me to the body and I could not breathe.

Dejuan was shouting from ringside. He seemed to be panicking. I looked at him to tell him everything is under control. Nate said I was easily winning and I felt the same.

Going into the last round Bob said I needed to step it up. "Don't go back and throw non stop punches". Nate would be upset with those words. I traded back and forth with Montes. Getting close. I was winning. Closing the show in style. Ten seconds to go. I threw a beautiful three punch combination but left myself open. Montes hit me clean on the chin and my legs gave way. I was on the floor. Shocked and embarrassed. The referee was counting. I got up around the count of seven. I was okay. By the time Montes came at me the bell rang. I felt like I had done enough to win but you never know what the judges are seeing.

The scorecards took long to come in. That is normally a bad sign for the visiting fighter.

"We have a split decision". I'm never comfortable with those words. "96-93 twice and 93-96 the other way. And the winner is Ashley Theophane." I was ecstatic. Back on TV and I won. Fifth straight win with Mayweather promotions.

After showering and taking photos with fans. I went to eat at the buffet with Jihad, Dan and his date.
I met up with Esther afterwards. We'd go to a hookah lounge, listen to music and celebrate my win. She'd spend the night at Palms casino hotel with me, leaving 8 in the morning. It was a perfect ending to my victorious night.

Friday 1st May 2015

We had fought now, it was time for the boss to handle his business.
Weigh in at MGM was a mega event. I held interviews all over the MGM casino resort.
I just can't see this fight being close.

Later that night we head out for dinner at a Moroccan restaurant. Ishe's friend is the owner. It was Badou's surprise victory dinner.

Saturday 2nd May 2015

I ended up watching Floyd vs Manny at LaTondria's house. She had thirty people over there to see Floyd win. After the fight they left to party and celebrate his victory. I stayed with Esther who was staying there.
Dan told me while I was driving to the fight party that he'd buy me a ticket. I appreciated that. Dan's a true friend, I couldn't be bothered to do a U-turn.

The girls screamed during Floyds fight as blows were exchanged. I enjoyed the fight but that's me. I enjoy pure boxers. Floyd is of the mold; Pernell Whitaker and Willie Pep.
Two of my all-time favourites.

Sunday 3rd May 2015

Floyds victory party was at his mothers house as usual.
I skipped it for the first time. I wasn't happy with a few things this camp so celebrating was definitely not on my mind.
Esther asked me if I was going to the party. I told her I'm seeing you. Latondria dropped her off at mine around 10pm.

FIGHT DIARY: FLOYD MAYWEATHER vs ANDRE BERTO

Monday 22nd June 2015

It's the first day of training camp. There's two months to go until my 46th fight and hopefully my 39th victory.

I started my day with a 4 mile run and completed a 75 minute boxing workout. Nate is not around all week so I'll be on my own. It's okay as I'm only getting back into the groove.

Monday 6th July 2015

Ishe called me tonight at 1025pm for 36 minutes. Leonard Ellerbe had just called him to say he wouldn't be fighting in Los Angeles on 29th August and that he wouldn't be on the television on August 22nd as Mayweather promotions are putting Chris Pearson in the TV spot and that Showtime are losing too much money but he'll still be fighting Vanes just not on TV. He couldn't believe it but I wasn't surprised. He thought maybe he was bumped off TV for me.

Sunday 12th July 2015

Training camp is officially under way. I had the pleasure of starting off sparring with the pound for pound king Floyd Mayweather on Sunday. It's been two years since we last worked together so it was fun to be the first person he shared a ring with since he dismantled Manny Pacquiao.

Floyd was sharp, his movement was nice for the first few rounds. His jab and counter right hand was sharp. I ate it a couple times but I had my moments in those first two rounds. His team shouted out whenever he did a nice move but over the last two rounds I put in some good punches which made his audience, his team quiet. Floyd chatted shit to me during the sparring but that's what Floyd does. You just have to enjoy the occasion. It was a pleasure to put in some rounds with him. He gave me $400 as a thank you afterwards.

Monday 13th July 2015

In the locker room after his sparring session. Floyd said I helped him get sharp yesterday. He looked good today as he beat Romain, his sparring partner over the last ten years around the ring.

Boza was very happy with my performance with Floyd. He said he hadn't had competitive sparring in a while.

Tuesday 14th July 2015

I stopped Zach Cooper during sparring today. Afterwards I asked him why was his performance was so bad. He broke down and said his dad had terminal cancer.
I tried to console him but that kind of news would affect anybody. He's going back to Seattle in a couple days to be there for his parents.

Friday 17th July 2015

Floyd knocked out young fighter Thomas Hill this afternoon. Floyd was hitting Tommy during the clinch. Tommy stopped protecting himself and Floyd unleashed a devastating left hook that left Tommy unconscious on the canvas. It was sad to see as Tommy is a nice guy. Floyd rolled out of the ring and started hitting the heaving bag. Tommy was out for a couple minutes. Afterwards he said he couldn't remember it happening.

I received a two thousand dollar check from Boza today. Floyd gave me $400 cash for the session but Boza paid me and the other sparring partners as well.

Monday 20th July 2015

I sparred Chavis Holifield this afternoon. I haven't sparred since Zach so I wasn't sure how I'd feel. It was a good session. Chavis always brings it.

I spoke to Floyd and he said he'd get the car he promised me back in March. He's said, "I just got so much on my mind that I be forgetting." He thanked me again for the sparring a week ago as he said it got him right for day one of camp.

Afterwards I spoke to Boza to see if I was on the sparring team. He said, "Yes or I'll have to fly in another guy." That's $16,000 I'll be up this camp as its $2,000 a week.

Ishe later showed me a ring he wants to buy Valerie. He said its time and she's a good woman. She surely is!

Tuesday 21st July 2015

Floyd bought me a Chrysler 300 Sport today around midnight. He bought the car and I just had to go and pick it up. I'm very happy with it. There's only 11 miles on it and he bought it for $50,000. Kitchie, his PA gave me a call and said to pick up my new car. I had been driving a DODGE Charger rental during camp, Ishe came to pick me up to go to the dealership. Gervonta Davis was there as Floyd had bought him a Jeep to drive around Las Vegas in. We took some photos together, next to our new cars. I had to sign some documents of ownership and left a happy man.

Floyd has bought most of the fighters on the team a car and put the ones who are not from Las Vegas in apartments. He pays for their rent until they are making enough money to do it themselves.

Monday 3rd August 2015

From sunrise to dusk was hard. I woke up before 6am completed a 6 mile run then I headed to the fitness gym and completed an hour workout. I had my regular Monday morning warm body wrap session then headed to the boxing gym for 1pm. Nate is in Chicago as he had to spend the weekend in the hospital for some tests on his heart. I completed my normal workout, nothing too crazy but a good workout.

Floyd arrived at the gym around 4pm and by 5pm he was out on the gym floor ready for sparring. It's Monday so he normally wants hard work. I thought he'd go with me or Lanardo. Bob walked over to us and looked at me. Smiled and said, "It's you today." I'd always laugh with Bob because everyone would say I do good against Floyd but Bob would be the opposite. Saying, "You got your ass beat."
Boza put on my headgear and Chris took out my diamond ear ring.

Floyd was in the ring first. I entered the ring to a gym fully packed with fight fans, Floyds kids, his workers and fighters.

We worked for four rounds of six minutes with thirty seconds recovery. S who is Floyds head of security, during sparring was very quiet. He'd shout out "He's in deep waters now." "He's getting tired." But it couldn't be further from the truth. Floyd and I both had our moments. It was a hard sparring session but I dug deep. We had some nice exchanges. I always love it from start to finish. I'm in with the best in the world.

The onlookers congratulated me on my performance afterwards, I think many were surprised I was so good as Floyd normally beats on his sparring partners. I held my own. I had to give my best though.

Dejuan told me that it's possible I'll fight on Floyds boxing show as the show the week of the fight is in California and not Las Vegas.

Steven Upshaw Chambers looks like being my next opponent. His last loss was to Andre Berto, Floyd's next opponent.

Monday 10th August 2015

I was told I'll be fighting on Floyds card on September 12th at the MGM Grand Arena.
There's no bigger show than a Floyd Mayweather show.

Wednesday 12th August 2015

Floyd dropped a Russian professional in sparring that had a good reputation around the gym. He had been sparring partner to Ishe and had given him some good work. As Ishe said its all about levels. Floyd demolished him. Dropping with a sharp left hook and beating him for the rest of the round. If Floyd brought that mentality into his fight with Berto he would be winning by knockout.

I sparred with former world champion, Yuriorkis Gamboa today. I had completed five hours training beforehand. 6 mile run, two hours of weights and two hours of boxing but I'm on the sparring payroll so when Floyd asked me to spar I had little choice but to oblige. Gamboa started good. He probably shaded the first two four minute rounds but then his energy levels dropped and I

started to find my range and banged him with jabs and opened up with
combinations. I wanted one more round but he was done. It was defiantly good work that I didn't want to do but enjoyed it after we had finished.

Saturday 15th August 2015

I started my day with an 8-mile run along the Las Vegas strip. The Floyd Mayweather
Foundation was doing their annual back to school giveaway at the gym but I was unable to attend for the first time in three years.
I had planned to go to Grand Canyon for the afternoon with a lady friend that was visiting me from London for a week.

Sunday 30th August 2015

I'm 35 today. I don't feel older but I am. It's scary to think one day I'm going to have to retire from boxing. I hope I'll be financially fine. I've made $200,000 over the last two years with Floyd. That keeps me alive and able to live.

I've got one more year on my contract with Mayweather promotions. Hopefully I can get a world title shot and get a $200,000 pay day. Win it and that will be life changing.

I spent my morning and afternoon with Talia. We went to Lake Las Vegas at 11am for Fly Boarding then headed off to the Orleans Casino and Hotel to do ATV driving in the desert. We had fun, I dropped her home afterwards then went home to get ready for dinner.

I picked 24 year old Jessica up at 8pm. We headed off to the Alize restaurant in the Palms Hotel and Casino. She's a nice girl, career driven and goal orientated. Just my kind of woman, we had a nice time at the restaurant and I dropped her back home.

Saturday 5th September 2015

There is seven days until my 46th professional fight. I'm going after my 39th win.
This camp has been perfect, maybe just a little too perfect. My shoulder has been hurting me for the past month but it's nothing too serious. I've still been able to work hard and push myself.

This fight will be my seventh fight with Mayweather promotions. This marks two years of my three year contract with them.
This camp has been very similar to the first camp I had with Floyd. I've been his sparring partner. I've sparred some other great fighters in Yuriorkis Gamboa, Mickey Bey and Steve Forbes. I'm fighting on Floyd's show which is billed as "High stakes". I've been told Mayweather Promotions are trying to get me a world title shot next. These are all things that happened two years ago before I fought Pablo Cesar Cano. I'm super confident just as I was then.
Steven Upsher has fought Andre Berto, Luis Collazo and Eddie Gomez. He lost to all three of them. Other than shaking Berto up in round two he was easily beaten. I don't know how he can beat me. He's never beaten any one of my standard. He was due to fight Adrien Broner on October 3rd until Adrien got offered a world title fight for the WBA so a win for me should bring a very big fight. 12 months ago, Upsher fought Berto then was scheduled to fight Broner. I beat him and I want my big fight. He believes he's coming to upset me. I'm in tremendous
condition. I feel like I'll walk through him. He's had seven to eight weeks notice so he should be in great shape too.

Tuesday 8th September 2015

Fight week is here. MGM Casino and Hotel hosted the fighter arrivals. Mayweather promotions only asked the PPV fighters to attend. That was a mistake on their part as there was long gaps in between. I was the only fighter to attend and that was because I knew there would be loads of press there so I'd get interviewed a lot. I did a couple hours worth of talking to the media. It was a productive and tiring day for me but worthwhile.

Elie Sechback interviewed me and told me that my opponent Steve Upsher is a tough Philly fighter. I responded "Is he?". I hadn't watched him yet. I did later that night. He's tough in the sense he comes to win and can take punishment but I don't see any threat after watching his fight with Eddie Gomez.

His team asked Mayweather promotions if they could raise the weight limit to 144lbs. I agreed! I should have said no and made him struggle to make weight. I was 143.6lbs after my run this morning so I'm good.

Wednesday 9th September 2015

Today was the fan workouts and autograph signing. I did my thing. These days are flying by. I start my day with a morning run then head to sub zero for a cryotherapy session. From there I go to get my wellness wrap.
Everyday is pretty much the same. It's all about the weigh in on Friday.
I've been told I have to report for 10am on Saturday morning. I'll probably fight 1230pm to 1pm. I'll have an empty arena. It will be like sparring to me. It is what it is. Win this fight and I'll be fighting Adrien Broner.

This morning I lowered my weight to 143.2lbs. I'm still eating three times a day and drinking three to four liters of fluid a day. I'm feeling strong. Only weigh in day I'll have to sacrifice.

Thursday 10th September 2015

After my run I hit 143lbs, my weight isn't an issue if I had to make 140lbs I could have made it. Even though the weight has been raised to 144lbs I'm still trying to come in at 143lbs.

Today was the undercard press conference. It went well. Ishe used his time to go at the media for their negative articles towards Floyd when in two years he's created three world champions. He's changed his fighters lives. He was the one that made a big issue about PEDS. Al Haymon is helping to bring boxing back to the mainstream and helping boxers to make money were as in the past promoters sucked boxers dry. Al and Floyd are good for boxing but reporters are never happy.

Friday 11th September 2015

I didn't stay at the MGM Grand last night. I wanted to make sure my weight was good. I woke up weighing 145.6lbs. I went out for a light jog. I came back weighing 142.8lbs. I had a small bowl of cereal. I went to sub zero recovery to get my daily dose of cryotherapy.

Afterwards I headed to the spa to get my 90 minute massage. Then headed off to the MGM for the official weigh in.

Floyd got there an hour after me. He came in with like thirty people so there was chaos around him. His security told the hangers on to go into the stands.

Andre Berto and his small team walked through the sea of the money team supporters.

I saw the doctor, he looked over me. I passed the physical as always. I weighed in around 4pm. I weighed 143lbs. I came in at the weight I wanted to come in at.

My opponent looked smaller than I expected. I've watched two of his fights now. He looks decent, he's just no Ashley Theophane. I don't expect a hard fight but I've prepared for a hard fight.

It's funny how much people are supportive now but when I needed support where were they? When I needed to sell tickets where was they then? The love is so fake but you just have to go with it.

I went out to eat with Jihad to my favourite sushi spot in Las Vegas. Then went to my barber D Cooke to get my hair done. From there I went back to sub zero recovery.
Less than 24 hours until showtime, I'm supremely confident but I want to look good. I want to stop him. It's funny to me he thinks he can beat me. It's time to show how good I am. I believe I'm top level. It's time to show it, this can't be a hard fight.

Sunday 13th September 2015

As I lay in my bed and think of the last 12 weeks. I'm proud of myself. I've won 6 fights in a row. I've beaten some decent fighters. C and D level guys. I've looked better and in doing so. I'm ready to face an A level guy now. Adrien Broner would be perfect. He's beatable and a massive name.
No one would give me a chance against him but no one ever gave me a chance of being where I am now.

Badou fought his ass off last night. I am so proud of him. He messaged me this morning that his wife Yasemin is pregnant. I'm happy for them. They are a good couple together and she's a good woman. Ishe and I are the only two that know so he said not to say anything.

Ishe fought his ass off. He lost a tough fight in a majority decision. He's made a million over the last two years so now I think it's time to step back from the big fights and take some easy ones. Get 30 wins then target the big names.

Al Haymon thanked Ishe for his kind words at the press conference when defending him against the media bashing his name. Ishe said you put money in our pockets so I'm very thankful to you. Al replied "we are going to keep doing what we do." If he helped make Floyd 800,000,000 imagine how much he's made.

Monday 14th September 2015

Ishe took me to breakfast at baby stacks this morning. Valerie his finance and Uriah his youngest son also came.
Ishe told me how one more lose and he'll call it a day.

He said, "I'm going to fix this shit with my kids, make sure my team is together and on the same page, take some tune ups, make one last run at it man, all wheels blazing. I suffer another defeat, think I'm going to call it a day my man."

I told him that you've made a lot of money, been world champ and fought the best. I've always said 10 loses would be the max I'd want to take.

He replied "I am going to come back in the December or January/February.

Either way 1-2 more losses and I'm out it's been a hell of a ride. Accomplished everything I've wanted."

He's content. I win a world title and make some money I'd be content too. Right now I need that world title win. Adrien Broner is the fight I want and I hopefully it's the fight I get.
It's been a long tiring camp but I was successful. Big win on Floyds last ever professional fight. I've had a great career myself. Just one or two things left to accomplish.

WORLD TITLE CHALLENGE:
ADRIAN BRONER VS ASHLEY THEOPHANE

Sunday 18th October 2015

I was in a deep sleep. My lady was sleeping next to me and shook me to wake me up. I heard my phone vibrating so I knew it was someone in America.

Dejuan Blake my advisor was calling me. I switched on the light and said, "What up. I'm sleeping." He started laughing and said, "Wake up nigga. AB just made you famous. Mentioned you during his after fight interview." I started laughing and smiled. "It's on!" Dejuan said he didn't want me to go at him straight away but Adrien mentioning my name, put me out there. I told him I'd be back in two weeks and that AB had just made my night.

I got off our call and looked at my phone. My social media had gone crazy.

If I get it my way, I want to fight in December and get my 40th win then Adrien in the Spring.

Tuesday 20th October 2015

Dejuan called me at 830am. He told me if I want the AB fight. I can have it. I replied that's what we have been working for. Why have another fight in the process, I could get injured and the Adrien Broner fight would be gone. The opportunity is here now so time to grab it. He told me not to post anything regarding it but it will be happening sometime in January. That's just the news I need to hear.

Wednesday 28th October 2015

Mickey Bey started camp for his fight on December 18th today. He told me you're going to be the fourth underdog from Mayweather promotions to win a world title. I told him I know. You, Ishe and Badou wasn't supposed to win. No one believed you could win except for the team and you did. I'm going to do that too.

Wednesday 4th November 2015

I started back sparring today. First time in this camp, first time in two months. I went up against Zab Judah, former undisputed world champ. The last welterweight to hold all titles.

We completed six three minute rounds. My team said I put in good work the last two rounds. It's my first session back so I was never going to be sharp or have my timing on point but it was a challenge to spar Zab as he's fighting next week Friday. I bloodied his nose in the fifth round. It was back and forth work. I just look at where I am in my life. Level pegging with legends of the sport. Respected by fighters I used to look up to as a young amateur in London. It's a wonderful feeling. I want to fight on the December 12th card. My shoulder is no longer injured and I'm feeling good. There's still six weeks to go. The guys don't want me to fight but I'm stubborn. I want my 40th professional win and some Christmas money.

Monday 9th November 2015

Floyd put out a response to Adrien saying, "Fuck TMT" after an awards ceremony. He called Ben Thompson from FightHype.com to put it out.

He discredited Adrien's four title wins saying he had beaten nobodies and should be ashamed to fight for a world title after losing to Shawn Porter.

I was at the gym hitting the heavy bag and Floyd came in happy with himself, laughing about what he had said about Adrien. I laughed with him. "I went in on him." "Yes, you did Floyd." I replied as I hit away on the heavy bag.

Wednesday 11th November 2015

Adrien comes back at Floyd with a YouTube video filmed in his car on his phone. Telling Floyd how wrong he is and how he's fucked up for dissing him. He finished off the video telling Floyd to answer his phone or call him.

Thursday 12th November 2015

I walked into the gym today and everyone was saying I'm a home wrecker and to stay away from their family functions as I break up relationships.

I worked as usual. I know I'm not fighting now as Dejuan said Leonard is saying the show is full. I don't mind as my shoulder is still playing up. I sparred two five-minute rounds with Don Moore and my shoulder went again.

Tuesday 1st December 2015

On Monday, Floyd Snr asked me if I was fighting Broner. I said yes, he said something, and I kept it moving. So yesterday one of his cronies calls me over, and points to Floyd Snr to let me know he wants me. So he says, "You really fighting Broner." I told him yes. He went on to say I can win but I need to work on this and that. I was like cool. Thanks for the input. Told him I'll need to spar with Mickey so he'll see how I'm coming along. I went on to say I watched your interview about Broner over the weekend. Floyd Snr has been vocal about not liking Adrien or his team. Anyway, he asks me who I'm training with and as I walk off, his assistant tells me if I want to work with Floyd for this fight he would be interested. I said I work with Nate so everything has to go through him.

I text Nate afterwards as he's back home in Chicago as he went back for Thanksgiving then had to stay five extra days as he has a hospital appointment on Thursday. I told Nate he needs to be here as it looks bad me working on my own and I have a big fight soon. Everyone like where's your coach. He's been here 1 week. Out of the 6 I've been here.

Some of the guys were like you might need to stay over Xmas if I fight in January. I said with who? Nate won't be here.

When I do comeback after Xmas I need Jihad or Dave here as Nates coming and going is disrupting my progress.

I've lost 10% of my body weight since being here. I went from 168lbs to 152lbs. I'm in good condition but there's only so much I can do on my own.
I'll start working with Floyds uncle the last five weeks of camp. He's good with strength exercises.

Floyd did an interview with DJ Clue this week saying the fight will be in Atlanta sometime in January.
Broner saying Ohio, Floyd saying ATL so we'll see.

Thursday 3rd December 2015

I sparred with Mickey Bey this afternoon. It's always a session that I have to give my all.
We completed four five minute rounds with 30 seconds rest. I threw 394 punches during the session. That's 99 punches over the five minute sessions. I would love to increase it to 150 by the end of camp. Adrien throws around 30 punches on average during three minutes in fights so I need to be throwing twice as many as him. He has the skills but I need the work rate, the punch output. 43 punches is my average punch output so I'm already more active than him but I need to increase it.

Floyd Mayweather senior worked my corner shouting out instructions to me during my session with Mickey. It's an honor that someone of his experience believes in me and wants to work with me. I did pad work with him for just over ten minutes afterwards.

He doesn't like Adrien so I know he'd love to work with my team but I already work with Nate so that would have issues as Nate wouldn't want to be his assistant when he has been working with me for just under three years.

I messaged Nate that night and told him he needed to get back to Las Vegas ASAP as Floyd is trying to take his spot.

Monday 7th December 2015

Nate arrived back today. I never went to the boxing gym on Friday as I knew Floyd senior would work with me and I didn't want him getting too comfortable coaching me.

Nate and I had a good workout. Floyd senior even went up to Nate and started talking to him about me and how he didn't know I was that good.
I joked with Nate afterwards that he's letting you know he wants your coaching position so don't slip up.

Tuesday 8th December 2015

I did the hyperbaric chamber for the first time this morning. I'm doing everything in my power to be the best I can be for this fight. I'm leaving no stone unturned.

Sunday 20th December 2015

I've put in nine good weeks of training in Las Vegas.
A pre training camp. I dropped 16lbs and got myself in decent shape.
I got some quality sparring with three world champions in
Zab Judah, Mickey Bey and Steve Forbes.
My shoulder has improved drastically. I would love it to be 100% better by the first week in January.
I've been getting massages and I have done all the exercises my physio has got me doing.
I'm off to London for two weeks but the aim is to stay around 154lbs and to maintain my strength and cardiovascular conditioning.
I started my day with a 10 mile run, cleared my stuff out of the apartment. When I return it will be 100% focus towards ripping

the title from Adrien. I believe I'm good enough to do it. Only time will tell!

Saturday 15th January 2016

WBC super middleweight champion Badou Jack has been keeping in contact with me to see how training is going on in London.
His strength conditioner coach Angel Heredia asked him to tell me he wants to work with me and I only have to pay him if I win. He wants me to win as he really dislikes Adrien Broner.
Shawn Porters strength coach Larry Wade asked to work with me too.

I'm happy with my team. I work hard as it is. Only the intensity of my work outs needs to change. I will be in top shape for my fight.

I went to bed with the message from Badou
"Pressure and determination and you'll get him. It's now or never, lets get it."
I'm very proud of what he's achieved over the last year. He beat Anthony Dirrell as the underdog then again he was made underdog for his fight with George Groves. Now he's about to fight with Julio Cesar Chavez Jr on April 30th in Los Angeles.
I have the opportunity to change my life with this win. It's up to me to do it.

The Press Conference for the fight in DC

Monday 29th February 2016

Over the last two days I've done interviews with Spike TV and they have filmed my training. We also went to some scenic parts of Las Vegas over looking the city.

They interviewed Floyd, Leonard, Badou and Ishe. The preview show should be entertaining. 13 years as a professional. I dreamed of the moment, it's finally here.

Leonard said just keep talking how I have been talking and don't get involved in his antics. He also said he'll speak to Floyd about getting in his head. He said his main focus is to make sure the referee looks at his fouls and that judges are watching who is working. So he said he'll be putting pressure on them to do their job.

One of Adrien's baby mothers messaged me about walking in the ring with me.

My weight is good. Training is going good. I hurt my wrist and hand against Ronnie Austion yesterday so I took today off from boxing but I went for a 10 mile run and a hot yoga session which had me ready to walk out. I'll continue going as it will helped with my strength and
fitness.

Wednesday 24th February 2016

I started my day with Bob Ware's run up Mount Charleston. It didn't feel that hard but the next day my legs were so sore. Eddies mountain run doesn't have that effect on my legs. 4 miles up and down a hill followed by a 4 mile run on a straight road.

I went home for a nap then went to hot yoga on wagon trail. That was another quality session. It was 90 minutes in 110 degree heat.

I finished my training day with a two hour boxing session with Nate. We did 45 minutes straight on the pads as usual. Everything has to be taken up a notch this camp.
Floyd came by the gym to watch the boxers. He told me "I've done my job. Now it is up to you."

Afterwards I headed to the fashion show mall to buy a shirt for Monday's press conference and a gift for Floyd as today is his birthday and there is a birthday dinner for him.

There was maybe 100 people at the birthday dinner for Floyd. He thanked me for the gift and asked me if I needed any help with sparring. I told him I was okay for work.

We left Nine Steak House just after midnight. The entourage headed to a club. I headed home.

Friday 26th February 2016

Nate called me in the morning from Chicago. He had gone there for the weekend for his daughters baby shower and was going to meet me and the rest of the team in Washington DC on Sunday.

Nate had called Floyd and Floyd had told him I need better sparring and that he was willing to pay for it if need be. I told Nate that I'd had good work style wise for Broner but if there's a fighter Floyd wants to fly in, I have no problem with that.

Floyd had said something like we need to step it up. I said Floyd must have spies in the gym but there is no way I could train harder. It's not humanly possible.

I had a day off from boxing but I still did an hour run in the morning, a two hour strength session, a ninety minute hot yoga session and I ended my evening with a swim at lifetime fitness on West Charleston Blvd. Thats just under five hours of training on a day I have no boxing. I'm pushing my body like never before. Last time I pushed my body so hard was when I was preparing for my British title challenge five years earlier.

Nate agreed with me and said I'd burn out if I pushed any harder. He told me we were much alike and that not to trust any one at the gym as not everyone that is riding with you, is with you. I already know that. I associate with very few people in general.

Saturday 27th February 2016

5am I jumped out of bed and into the shower. I headed to Mount Charleston to meet boxing legend and now coach to boxing champions Eddie Mustafa Muhammad.
There was a handful of fighters as usual. We ran the five miles up, 8500 feet above sea level.
I continued for another 1.5 miles as usual.

We finished and headed to baby stacks for breakfast.

I went off to the gym for a sparring session with 17-0 Don Moore. It was his birthday today. He had turned the ripe of age of 36. We completed four 6 minute rounds. I finished up with ten minutes on the speed bag and 10 minutes on the jump rope.

Whilst I was in the ring about to begin my abdominal, strength and neck workout. Dejuan came into the gym. He had just got off the phone with Floyd. Floyd wasn't happy with my sparring session with Don. He wanted me to know that I have to move my head when inside and not let my sparring partners let go on me, to move away instead. I told Dejuan I thought he couldn't see the ring. Dejuan replied "he can move the cameras now." I told Dejuan that I had ran the mountains in the morning. He said not to come in and spar then.

That messed up my whole mentally before Monday's press conference. I've never been a man to shine in sparring. I'm working on my punch output. I'm doing anything from 70-100 punches inside three minutes which is very good. I want to win this fight so much. Not just for me but for Floyd as he's shown he believes in me.

What Floyd said is true. I messaged Nate that and he called me saying he agrees with Floyd. I said why didn't you mention that then. I've told him it's pointless doing that pretty pad work but wanting me to be mean. That pad work does nothing to aid me in this fight. To me it's a waste of time. I enjoyed the pad work I do with Dave Brown more cause that is how I have to fight in this match. Aggressive and going forward not pity pat with light punches. If I don't get the win in this fight. Nate will probably be the one to go as he's shown he can't change his coaching style.

Dave is supposed to fly in on Tuesday. I've spoken to him but I don't think he has responded or confirmed his flight details with Rene's team. He needs to or I'll have to fly in Jihad.

Monday 29th February 2016

Today is a leap year for February. It happens once every four years and our press conference is today in Washington DC.

My hotel room was the best suite I've ever stayed in.
I went for an hour run before 7am then had some room service for breakfast, an omelet and tropical smoothie.
I went to the hotel gym for an hour then got ready for my press conference.
Spike TV came to my room to interview me before I headed up to the press conference.

Adrien was an hour late so I did interviews with the press that was on hand. He strolled in with HipHop star Rick Ross.
I sat next to Floyd. Leonard opened up proceedings then Floyd took to the mic.
I went first as the challenger. I told the packed house that it's been a long journey and I'm thankful for Floyd signing me after ten years on my own. I said I'm expecting a war and I'm training for that.
Adrien followed me. He started off respectful then went into a tirade. That we are his enemy. "Fuck Floyd. Fuck Theophane. Fuck Nate."

PR Boss Kelly Swanson got us to do the face off and he started to disrespect me. I told him I'm glad you coming to fight so you won't run. He said, "The only time I've ran is when I run up on a nigga." I said, "Yeah just like Maidana." That struck a nerve and he refused to do any interviews and stormed off with his entourage.

I did some interviews with Floyd and some photos.
After we had done I went to see the White House with Dan and Nate.
We got back to Vegas just before midnight. I was tired. It's very mentally draining but it's all part of the job.

Wednesday 2nd March 2016

I finished my hot yoga session at 1pm and noticed Leonard had called me. I called him back but he didn't answer his phone.

I got to the boxing gym for 4pm. Dejuan called me over and said Floyd is flying over Kenny Simms from Chicago and wants me to spar with Devin Haney. He watched me sparring Don Moore the other day and I guess he wasn't happy.

Kenny Simms was Manny Pacquiao's chief sparring partner for his fight with Floyd. Rumor is he was beating the shit out of Manny.
Devin was a sparring partner of Shawn Porter for his fight with Adrien Broner. Floyd wants me to win. He's never done this for any of his fighters so this means a lot to him.

Thursday 10th March 2016

Very good day today, the cameramen that flew in followed me around.
Completed 12 rounds sparring and threw 865 punches. Anything over 800 in the fight I'll be happy with. That will be enough to win the fight. I've been beating my sparring partners up. Adrien throws on average 400 punches but quality. Marcos Maidana and Shawn Porter ran over him. Paulie Malignaggi out worked him.

There was some kid Dejuan wanted me to spar over the last two weeks. I finally did. They think he's a future star. His dad is well off, has a big mansion and has hired video cameras to film his training sessions. I knew him and his team thought they'd come in and be too good for me. He's trained by Floyd senior.

The kid did well in the first round. After that he was running round the ring. I bloodied his mouth. His team were shouting out the time to him as he was dead out there. It was too funny to me. Then come to find out I have to pay him and pay him more than I pay my usual sparring partners that can do all the rounds. Lucky I told a regular sparring partner to come so I got my full workout but ended up paying more than twice as much as I would.

Dejuan was like that's why we gave you the money. They gave me a cash advance of my money to pay for training camp expenses. It's not your job to tell me who to spar or spend that money. It's my money. I won't be sparring that kid again. His team asked Nate "when next?". I told Nate tell them we'll let them know. Then Dejuan paid them cash so messing up my receipts. As I've been giving my sparring partners checks. Told him stay out of my business. Everything is going perfect. He would go on to become WBC world champion. It's funny how things work out.

Dave said Floyd senior could have told me how good I did. I said he expected his fighter to better me and he's sour he's not training me for this fight.
Everything is going perfect in camp. I'm on fire!

Friday 11th March 2016

Three weeks until fight time. I was up at 4am as I had a track session scheduled with Bob for 430am. The camera crew was there bright and early waiting for us. What a painful session it was, Six 800m runs, eight 400m runs, twelve 200m runs. All with thirty seconds rest in between. It was around six miles of running but six minute mile pace. I know Bob was shocked with my fitness as the night before after 12 rounds of sparring I had completed his swimming workout which is also lung pumping hard. I am definitely ready fitness wise for my fight. Whatever Adrien brings I will be ready.

I went to the fitness gym at 9am then my infra red body wrap for 1120am.
I had an interview in an MGM suite as part of the filming the camera crew was doing.
After that I had to Bikram yoga for a 90 minute session.
I finished my night at Sub Zero Recovery for a session of cryotherapy. It's been a hard day of work.

Bob called me on my way back to the hotel room to try talk me in to taking tomorrow off from my mountain run.
He's obviously concerned with me burning myself out and leaving it all in the gym. It's his first time working with me on the fitness side of things so he doesn't know how hard I really train and how quick my body recovers.
He asked me if I fought Adrien tomorrow would I be ready. I told him I believe so.
He said you've had two hard workouts in less than eight hours. I told him next week is my last hard week of training. I compromised as I said the camera crew that Floyd hired is filming me tomorrow run the mountains but I'll take Monday off for you.
That's always the problem with working with new people they are not used to the work load I do. I'm training no different to what I normally do.

I feel in tremendous condition. My aim is to maintain my fitness levels or get in even more better shape. I want to be feeling unstoppable by fight night. Bob wanted me to have two days off so I would feel super refreshed for sparring on Tuesday. I told him I don't train for sparring. As long as I'm getting my rounds in and hitting my numbers I'm happy. I said I'd take the two days off but I won't be doing it again this camp. He agreed and said I just want to see how you feel with the two days off. Two days before my fight I'm cool with. Two days off before sparring is not important to me. I've been feeling great throughout camp but even if I wasn't I wouldn't care cause it's all about putting in the work before my fight. It's not about looking great in camp. It's about looking good and feeling good on fight night.

Saturday 12th March 2016

A grueling 6 mile run was how I started my day. I went for an infra body wrap, Hyperbaric chamber, cryotherapy sessions then I headed to the boxing gym for 4pm.
Ronnie Austion was my sparring partner today. I feel like I'm in the ring with AB when I spar him.

Dejuan came to pick up the $300 he had paid the young man for our sparring session. He moaned at me not to over train. I told him I've been in the boxing gym three times this week. Everyone has an opinion on me and they are people who are not part of my training team. They don't know my training schedule but see me training hard and say I'm over training when they might just see me once that week. Dejuan is never present during my boxing sessions nor is Bob. I have the same training regime I normally have I've just stepped up the intensity and workload. I rest and do all of my recovery
sessions.

I threw 921 punches over 12 rounds. I know I can touch 1000 punches. I feel unstoppable. No one gives me a chance to beat Adrien. I believe I will be able to miss it with him on fight night. I'm going to get hit. Maybe hurt but I'll give as good as I get. If I can throw anywhere near 800 punches I can win.

Tuesday 15th March 2016

My last sparring session with undefeated Delorien Caraway was this morning. We completed 12 rounds of sparring. He wanted to get out of the ring at the 10th round but I offered to give him $100 to finish up.

I ended up throwing 1017 punches during the 36 minutes of work. I'll be happy with anything over 800 in the actual fight. That will be enough to get me the win over Adrien.

I ended my day with swimming with Bob at Lifetime fitness. I had my best session yet with him. My lungs are powerful right now. I'm truly in the best shape I've ever been. I just need to give a performance like I did when I fought for the British title and I'll win. I feel like I'm a better fighter now. I just want to give my best and I feel like it will be enough to hear "And The New".

Thursday 17th March 2016

My last 12 round sparring session was this morning before the media workout was supposed to commence.

Ronnie Austion, who is a clone of Adrien is perfect sparring for him. I threw 988 punches
during the 36 minutes of work. We embraced afterwards. If the fight was tomorrow I feel like I'd win. I bring this work rate into the fight and I will win. AB isn't as powerful as Pablo Cesar Cano or Montes so I believe I'll be able to apply the pressure and let my hands go. I just have to watch out for his uppercuts and left hooks. My whole body feels strong, so I'm battle ready.

Nicole got upset with me for saying the staff at Mayweather promotions are unprofessional. Think her staff didn't like that I called them that in the gym.

I found out about my media workout at 330am and I had already planned sparring for 10am so I couldn't workout during my media workout, I just did interviews with the media.

I said it's the first time I'm main event in two and a half years and I couldn't take part in my media workout as I was told so late. I said you obviously gave the media notice, you are supposed to keep me in the loop.

I told her you know I'm normally respectful but I jokingly said it to the staff in the gym. She said one of them was close to tears. I apologized but I was cool with the staff throughout the media event. At the end I said I won't call them out again and if I have an issue I'll direct it to her.

Otherwise than that, I had a good day. I didn't even think anything of it as I said it jokingly and the staff were cool with me afterwards.

During this camp I've sparred Devin Haney and Teofimo Lopez, they'd go on to win the WBC and IBF world lightweight titles. They were both big talents who believed they would be where they currently are. They both had supportive fathers who did everything in their power to support their sons. As much as I respect these fighters, their fathers have done a superb job. It's possible without them their journey to the world title wouldn't have been so smooth.

Monday 21st March 2016

I flew through the swimming session with Bob tonight. We go 12 times under water. I did 11 lengths, needing just one time to come up for air. I normally take five breaths then continue. The 11th one I did the whole length without needing to come up for air. My lungs are powerful now.

Afterwards Bob said he didn't want to do that hard track run this week, instead halving it. 6x800m, 8x400m and 12x200m. We'll probably do half of it. Short but sweet. It's about quality work and maintaining.

Nate said today "we have no option but to win." This is the mindset we all need. It's a war. I have to be prepare to take punishment and give back.
It's in me. I just have to perform under pressure. "Under the lights" as Floyd says.

Tuesday 22nd March 2016

I had a great sparring session with Ronnie Auston today. Dejuan even woke up early to come in to watch me.
Floyd was watching from Miami.
I threw 887 punches over ten rounds. On that performance I easily would of thrown 1000 over 12 rounds. My last sparring session is Thursday. I'd like to do a similar punch output. 800 is the minimum I'll be happy with. 80 punches a round is the target. In two rounds I threw over 100 punches. On average I got out over 80 punches. Only once did I dip in the 70s and that was 78. I just want to produce this on fight night and I will be world champion.

Wednesday 23rd March 2016

Floyd arrived back in Las Vegas last night and came by the gym. I missed him but everyone is talking about his interview a few days earlier. He told Adrien he was wrong for throwing money in the air and how it was disrespectful to the people in the line and the worker serving him in the supermarket. Saying he doesn't need change and through the money in the air.
Adrien did a response critiquing Floyd for having double standards when just five years ago he was burning money in a strip club.
Floyds game plan is to get into AB's head and distract them ahead of our fight which is days away now.

Leonard came in while I was finishing up my training session and said how he was looking forward to my fight next week and how the talking is over.

I hope I can pull off the win for the team.

I went swimming with Bob at night time. I beat Tuesday's best time. Swimming under the water twice for a whole length, my lungs are really strong now.

Thursday 24th March 2016

Today was my last sparring session of training camp. Ronnie Austion was the man is the opposite corner. The first round he used his feet and moved around the ring, jabbing me and using his boxing skills. I didn't throw more than 50 punches that round. From round two he stood there trying to counter me and box me. He failed! I threw over 900 over the next 9 rounds. The total Marcel picked up was 987 punches which is an incredible number for 10 rounds of boxing. If it was 12, it is possible I would had hit 1200 at the pace. I'm ready. I'd love to be too strong for Adrien but I don't know if I will. Hopefully I'm physically strong enough to fight my fight and I can't see how he will handle 1000 punches flying at him during 12 rounds. That's the only pressure I put on myself. I want to fight the same way I've been sparring. I'd be happy with 80 punches a round in the fight.
I'm supposed to lose. I'm a 12/1 underdog in the UK and plus 2400 over here in America.
I win and it will change my life. I just need to give my best and don't let the pressure and occasion get to me and I believe I'll be world champion.

Nate blew up after the 8th round of sparring when I told him his advice wasn't working. I'm getting hit. He started shouting at me that he wouldn't have me talking to him like that and that he'd

fuck me up. I just went back to work with Ronnie and ignored him. Dejuan said he'd talk to him. I didn't answer his calls or listen to his messages that night. I don't have a girlfriend or child. I don't need drama and I'm not going to let a man stress me.
I went for a massage afterwards. Leonard called me and told me Adrien had an arrest warrant out for him in Ohio. It had made TMZ and was all over the Internet. Adrien Broner was a trending topic. All I care about is that the fight goes ahead.

Friday 25th March 2016

I was up bright and early this morning. 5am start as I had to get in my 6 mile run before completing my morning of Medicals.

I headed to get my MRI scan at 7am. The doctor told me I had passed it which I was happy about.

My next appointment was 10am at Dr Voys office. My blood was taken and I completed my physical. I expected my EKG to be good but it even surprised the doctor and his nurse. 40 BPM (beats per minute). He told me that Floyds was 38 so I was in good company. He said you'll do 12 rounds easy. They got me to do some light exercise to try get my heart rate to the normal 60 BPM but my heart would get to the 50s then go back down. I left his office very satisfied.

Dan came to pick me up, to take me to do my eyes. He drove me back as they dilated my eyes and my vision became blurry.

I got back and went to bed to rest, then headed to Bikram yoga for my Friday night 90 minute session. Afterwards I popped into Sub Zero recovery for a cryotherapy session. It's been a very productive day. 7 days until I'm crowned world champion.

Saturday 25th March 2016

Nate apologized for his outburst on Thursday. At first I wouldn't speak about it then I told him. You're a coach if you can't take feed back from your fighter, you're in the wrong job. I'm not a robot so I have my own opinions on how shit should be done. He was unhappy as I've not been happy with some of his training technics for the fight. I told him if I'm unhappy I'm going to voice my concerns. I'm not going to be quiet. I speak my mind. We can go our separate ways. I choose to work with you. I don't have to. At one stage I thought he was going to attack me as he was standing over me and saying he's going to leave before he does something he regrets but he hugged me and apologized in the end.

Afterwards Dan asked if I wanted to go to watch the fights tonight. I said no I'm going bed now. Then he said let's go Bobs and see his new place. I said nah I'm good. I showered and headed towards my car. Dan came up to me and said I have to get you to Bobs. I asked why. He said they want to surprise you. A send off as not everyone can come your fight next week. I reluctantly went.

Bob Ware was the host. The last two years he's invited me to his house for thanksgiving. His family are good people. His mother told me "even though your family are far away, you can class us as family." I've met some good people during my time in America, they are some of them.
Around 30 people were in attendance. Bob and his family, Ishe and his family, Lanell and his family, Charvis and his daughter. John Sinclair, Dejuan Blake, Nate, Uncle Steve. Everyone I generally mess with so that was cool.

Many of them can't come to Washington DC so they wanted to wish me well.

That was nice of them to do as I tend not to socialize during camp.
I'm not the softest person but I appreciate the love.
Hopefully I can bring the title back to Las Vegas.

Tuesday 28th March 2016

Its fight week, I've woke up the last three mornings weighing in the 144lbs range. After a morning run I've touched 142.4lbs. I'm nearly there! Two days until the weigh in, I haven't had to make 140lbs in four years.

I flew in to Washington, D.C. today. We were supposed to fly 130am but the flight was cancelled due to crew issues, so they changed my flight to 11am. I didn't mind, I just got to miss the media workout that I didn't want to do anyway.
I feel so ready for this.

Wednesday 29th March 2016

I woke up this morning weighing 143.3lbs. I went to the fitness gym and did a 5km run on the treadmill then came back to my room. I was now weighing 142.2lbs. I ate 850 calories through the day and drank half a liter of water, sipping through the day.

During the morning I attended a photoshoot for Premier Boxing. I headed to the final press conference for 1pm with the team. Adrien didn't come until 90 minutes later. He told everyone he wasn't going to attend as the event is nearly sold out. So he's done his job.
Leonard was happy with that comment. Adrien would call Floyd a hater during the press conference. Leonard fired back at him you're not fighting Floyd, you're fighting Ashley. Adrien seemed rattled at the press conference. He changed his first stance that he'd stop me in four rounds to eight rounds.

I told him I hope he comes to stop me cause that means we will be battling me and I'm prepared for 12 hard rounds. We squared off. He told me "it's different when you're in there with me." It could be. Until I'm in there I won't know. This win would be big for me. Floyd would be forever grateful. I hope I can get the win for both of us.

My mum, dad and brother arrived in the evening.

Thursday 31st March 2016

142lbs is what I weighed when I woke up. It was just after 4am so I decided to head to the fitness gym for a 5km run. Afterwards I weighed 140.4lbs.

I didn't eat for the whole morning. I had an interview with the Spike TV crew. Antonio Tarver, five time world champion and first man to defeat my favorite fighter of all time, Roy Jones, Jr. I told him that and he replied "I get told that all the time."

I spoke about my journey from London. Being the underdog and the opponent for ten years before meeting Floyd and him telling me, I want to help you become world champion and here we are now. Dan came to the fighter meeting with me. It was only 20 minutes long. Antonio asked for a photo with me and I went back to my room to relax.

Dave and Nate came to my room at 1130am to head to the weigh in at the Headbangers boxing gym. I did my Medicals and signed in with the commission.

At 1pm I was asked on to the stage as the weigh in was due to start. I waited there for Adrien but he did not show up. So I was told to wait on the side until he arrives. He was in the venue but did not show his face until another 45 minutes. I was sitting next to Dejuan. I told him he's definitely trying to lose weight. Sam Watson had told me earlier that he didn't attend the fighter meeting in the morning and he said, "You can beat him, You just have to rough him up in there and throw all kinds of shit at him." Sam represents Al Haymon so you know Al feels the same, they maybe just think I'm not capable of the performance I need to win.

Adrien showed up around 45 minutes late. My brother would later tell me when he arrived at the venue, Adrien was coming out of the boxing gym with him team shouting out "AB, AB, AB."

I got back on the stage with Nate. I just hoped on my scales were correct. I was 139.6lbs on my scales and it's normally .4 under. I was correct. I weighed exactly 140lbs. I was so happy. Adrien stepped on the scales next, he was 140.4lbs. He was overweight. I didn't care that he was over. I just told Dejuan, he's got to pay. I told him go for $100,000. He got penalized that but half goes to the Washington DC commission. I wanted a $200,000 purse and I got that in the end.

Adrien looked drained and stressed out on the stage. He looked at me and said, "I'm going to beat your ass." I can't see that happening. Unless he's some super talent. He won't handle my relentless pressure and punch output for 12 rounds.

I went to eat with my mum, dad, brother, Dave, Marcele and Dan at Nando's.

Afterwards I headed to meet the WBA officials to sign off on the fight gloves.
The Washington DC commission had told me they wanted me to win. I signed off on my fight gloves in front of the WBA and read some WBA paperwork. Leonard told me in front of them, "You

will be their champion after this fight." I just have to go in that ring tomorrow and fight how I've been sparring. 1000 punches in 12 rounds. I feel even 800 will be enough to win in this fight cause Adrien won't throw more than 400. 500 would be a push for him.

I chilled for the evening then went out to eat with my brother at night time at a local restaurant.
He came back to my room until midnight then went off on his woman hunt and I went to bed. I've got a big day tomorrow. I can turn my childhood dreams into reality. I have an opponent who doesn't seem to be mentality or physically at his best. It's now or never as Badou told me months ago.

Friday 1st April 2016

Dejuan called me at 10.20am and told me he'd had a meeting with the WBA and the Washington DC commission. He said they wouldn't give me the $50,000 from Adrien Broner as its against their rules.

Dejuan said Sam Watson was backing him. I told him Sam wants me to win. So Dejuan ended up speaking to Al Haymon and he told him how I've trained so hard and it's not fair that Adrien gets all this money compared to me. So Al said he'd put the extra $50,000 on my purse.

I got the $200,000 I desired from the start. Now just to get the win tonight and that pay level with continue.

I relaxed in bed all day, watching Marvelous Marvin Hagler fights. Just getting my mind right. I finished up with Adrien Broner's fights against Marcos Maidana and Shawn Porter. I know what I need to do, it's just to do it. Easier said than done but I believe I can win.

I left the hotel around 7pm for the venue.
It came to my knowledge that Floyd bet 100k on me winning. That means he'll pick up a million when I win.

I need the performance of a lifetime to win. Just do what I have been doing in sparring and I'll be fine. I'm ready for a war. I sat backstage listening to music as I knew Nate would be talking out loud about the fight.

Floyd came into my locker room around 730pm to talk to me. He said I'm riding with you. This is one in a lifetime shot. Tell yourself that during the fight. You've worked your whole life to get here. You can beat him. You've fought tougher fighters. You would have stopped Paulie. He's scared now, don't think he isn't. Just go out there and do what you do in the gym. He doesn't like that rough stuff. You throw more punches than Shawn Porter. Just don't freeze out there, and you'll win. He's burned too many bridges. Everyone wants you to win, you just have to go out there and be you.

Badou came in as Floyd was finishing up and said he was in my position a year ago.
Just go out there, fight every round and you'll win.

Floyd said win this fight and you'll be a king back home. I'll come back with you. They don't like him. What you are doing now is history. You're putting your name in the history books.
You can do it.
He said I told you I got your back. I wanted to cry. He said, "Do it for your family. Your mum, your dad, everyone of them."
We took a photo together and he left my room.

Saturday 2nd April 2016

The fight finished in controversy. The referee stopped the fight thinking I was waving my hand to quit when I was saying I'm okay. It was weird. I was not hurt in any way. Adrien had just hit me with an uppercut and I moved away. He came after me and hit me low. At that time I look at the referee. He's looking at me. So I signal to him that I am alright but the referee thought I was asking for help to stop the fight and he stopped it. Such a weird thing, everyone knows I wouldn't quit. I had the won the sixth and seventh rounds. The eighth was close. I felt like there was nothing in it. Nate kept telling me to give more. I said I'd respond I'm giving my all. He'd say, "Okay then, keep doing it." I don't know how the fight looked from the outside but I knew it was close. The early rounds was back and forth. So was the other rounds. He may have been winning by a couple rounds but we had four to go and I could see he was tired. He had a cut over his eye. I was bruised around my eyes. It felt like a war. He had the power but I had the work rate. I was hitting him with everything. He wobbled me a couple times but I'd regroup quick and fire back. There was no way he was going to stop me with a punch. The referee was from Puerto Rico and his English was obviously not very good.

Floyd came to the ring apron and gave me a hug and told me "I'm proud of you. You put up a terrific showing, we'll get you some more wins and you'll fight for the title again. I run boxing, you'll be okay." I felt like I disappointed the whole team but everyone was proud of me as they said it was a great fight and they could see it was a close. The TV replay showed I was hit with a foul punch low, I look at the referee and then he jumps in and stops it, so everyone could see it was stopped prematurely.

Adrien did his after fight interview and called out Floyd. Floyd just laughed it off which was the right thing to do. Adrien just struggled with me. He'd have zero chance against Floyd.

I went back stage. Washington DC do their urine test after the fight. Nevada do it before. So I was dehydrated from fighting. I couldn't fill the sample cup on the first try so Marcel, Dan and Bob waited with me for an hour while I drank some water and went again. Nate had disappeared! He did the same thing when I lost to Pablo Cesar Cano. My urine was the darkest I'd ever seen it but it was just enough.

I went back downstairs to change and we headed back to the hotel. Dan, Badou and my brother were chilling in my suite with me. Dan brought back two girls, one he'd been dating during his time in Washington DC. I didn't really acknowledge them, Badou and I was just talking.

They all left around 3am. My brother stayed and slept on the couch.

I didn't win but I gave everything I had. Dejuan called me around 330am to see how I was. I told him I was fine just mad it was stopped as I felt I the fight was back and forth and those championship rounds may have swung the fight to me. Dejuan said I can fight when I want and that the WBA will allow me to fight for the vacant title so to have a think about that. I said I would.
I let him know I'm going to have two months off so August would be the month I'd want to fight in.

I spent the day with my family. All four of us, that is a first I can remember. I went for lunch with my brother then I went to the local mall with mum, dad and my brother. Stacy and I split up from them. I just followed him around the stores as he wanted to buy stuff. I rarely buy anything as I have too many clothes and no where to put them.

Everywhere we went in the mall I was stopped and asked for photos or people stopped me to say they wanted me to win or that the referee shouldn't have stopped it.

After the shopping trip I went to my dads room and went to sleep for a bit. He had two beds so I was staying with him for the night as my stay at the Gaylord Resort was only until Saturday.
The hotel I got my parents was nice. They liked it!

My brother came for me around 10pm to go for something to eat. I wasn't hungry but he wanted me to accompany him. We went to our regular spot. We'd been there three times in two days.
The waitresses told us about Adrien racking up a $300 bill at the restaurant opponent and not tipping the waitress. They didn't like him. I got a feeling no one did in the city as he was booed after he beat me.

I left my brother in the restaurant just after midnight. Next time I'd see him would be in
London.

My dad thanked me for the trip and said he was proud of me. It was his first time in America at 59 years old. He said he may have never came here if not for me but he had fun.

Floyd Mayweather vs Conor McGregor Diary

Ashley Theophane vs Shoki Sakai

Sunday 2nd July 2017

After a 10 hour flight I was harassed by the US Immigration. The officer told me my visa could easily be revoked. He also sent me to sit down in the corner and wait for the queue to finish then when he called me back and told me. "This is what you have to deal with if you want to come to America."

Badou Jack was waiting for me outside for nearly two hours.

When I got to him, the weather was unbearable. 105 degrees and set to raise to 112 the coming week. I felt like I was on fire. Badou dropped me to my regular hotel, the Extended Stay America on South Valley View Blvd.

Ishe messaged later that day to tell me that he'd been given opponents already. Good to know we won't be having last minutes opponents for this show.

Monday 3rd July 2017

I only had four hours sleep. I went to bed after 11pm and woke up after 3am. I couldn't go back to sleep so I stayed in bed until 5am then went for a run along the strip. 9.5 miles total.
I could feel the difference in altitude and conditions. I got through It, It was nice to be back in Las Vegas.
That run always reminds me of how far my hard work has got me. If I win a world title or not. My grind, my accomplishments have been incredible. No amateur success, no promoter backing for ten years but I made it to the mountain top.

I had my first training session with Lou Del Valle for the first time in 7 months. Lou was happy. He commented that the first round was "shitty" but after that I was sharp.

Tuesday 4th July 2017

Today is a holiday in the USA but as a professional sportsman it's just another day for me.
5 hours sleep but the work has to go on regardless.

8 miles and a bit, down the strip and back to my hotel. I had a few hours rest then headed off to the Mayweather boxing club. Steve was moaning that it was holiday and to make sure I cut him a check after my fight. I gave him twenty bucks as a thank you.

Lou was happy with the shape I came to camp. I told him I've been in the gym since Badou fought James Degale in NYC. I was told I would be fighting March so I stayed in shape, whilst I waited on my date. I'm glad to be working again with a target in mind. Lou and I put in the same work again but I was a touch bit sharper. I could feel the pace though.

Bob gave my car a jump and I was back on the road. Happy days! My car is only 2 years old and just under 9,000 miles on the clock.

Wednesday 5th July 2017

My first day of sparring today, Charvis Holifield is fighting at the Westgate hotel in 9 days so we arranged to work. He should be sharp and it's my first sparring session of camp.

Tuesday 11th July 2017

Today Badou, Ishe, Arjan (Badou's brother in law) and I hit the road to Los Angeles to watch the first press conference of Floyd and Conor McGregor.

I woke up at 4am to start my day with a five mile run. I got to Badou's for 6am. Ishe was late as usual.

It took us four hours to get to Los Angeles. We got our VIP passes from Mayweather Promotions then went for lunch.

The press conference was what I expected but Floyd was more explicit than I've seen him in years.
The build up to the fight will be explosive. The fight not so much as Floyd should win easily.

We were walking back stage with Floyd when "turn off your cameras" was shouted through the corridor. Al Haymon appeared from a room and him and Floyd went to talk for a few minutes. After they had finished, Badou, Ishe and I went to greet him. Al pulled me towards him and gave me a hug. Badou laughed afterwards. Al has always acknowledged me and greeted me when I've seen him at the MGM.
It's just incredible that I work with these people that run boxing. I may not be big in the game but they have given me two opportunities to come out of my level and both times I fell short. I haven't given up and never will.

Tuesday 18th July 2017

Saturday 8th July, Ishe told Badou and I that I was down to fight Mario Barrios. An 19-0 Mexican fighter signed to Al Haymon. I would be on Floyds card.
I was told by Dejuan I was fighting off TV on August 22. So I didn't believe Ishe.

Yesterday, I messaged Dejuan to find out about my opponent. I woke up to a missed call and a text message with the name Mario Barrios.

So Dejuan knew the name for over a week but acted like he was just given the name when Ishe had confronted him at the LA press conference, he acknowledged I'd been given a name but said he was a "killer" and it was turned down.

Dejuan called me this morning. I told him I'd fight him but I have to be paid as I'm the opponent and everything is against me. He said he'd get back to me after he spoke to Leonard. $100,000 is the minimum I'll accept. Ishe thinks I'll get offered $75,000 and they'll keep the rest.

Anthony Joshua visited the Mayweather Boxing Club this afternoon. The whole gym showed him love. I met him for the first time earlier this year when him and Floyd did a meet and greet with fans in London. We spoke for a bit then he went to watch the guys train and hanged out in the lobby area for a bit chatting to everyone.

Rolando "Rolly" Romero's father came up to me complaining about his son's fight activity. He's only had two fights since December 2016 when he made his debut, he told me. Most people are currently inactive, I last fought in December. I told him to be patient I'm sure things will work out. Three years on, Rolly has had ten more fights and is currently the interim WBA lightweight world champion. Loyalty and patience can pay off!

Friday 21st July 2017

I told Dejuan this morning that I wasn't interested in the fight. I hadn't heard anything all week and the money talked about was no where near what I expect.
Dejuan told me that he'd already turned down the fight as the money was too low.
I was happy about that. I don't want to fight some unknown kid as an opponent. I want to fight a name.
$12,000 is what they wanted to give me to fight that 19-0 fighter. Just over a year ago I fought for the world title. Why would I ever contemplate taking that sort of money.

Badou's fight is on the verge of falling through. Again money is the issue. Nathan Cleverly isn't happy with the offer.

Wednesday 2nd August 2017

My alarm woke me up for 6am. I was tired after sparring yesterday and my body needed to rest.

Kenny didn't reply to my email or text message. Normally he responds asap so I know it is possibility I don't fight.
How, as a fighter are you supposed to give your all in training camp when you have no idea what is going on with your fight. Less than 3 weeks to go and no word of an opponent.

I got a text message from Maye this morning whilst I was at the fitness gym about scheduling my medicals. Maye works for Affiliation Management. Dejuan's management company.

Ishé wanted to fire him earlier this year but I talked him out of it.

Floyd came to the gym early today. His security came in before 1pm and told everyone to finish their workout and leave. I told Lou, I'm not leaving. I am finishing my work. We were midway through our pad session.

Floyd walks in the gym, sees everyone working and tells his security to let them continue to work. For two rounds he watches Lou and I do pads. I've been coming into my form this week. Even Badou came up to me while I was on the bag and said, "This is the best I've seen you. Lou is a really good coach." I replied, "Thanks" and continued to work.

After my bag work, I did my abdominal workout and finished up. I then went to watch Floyd finish his workout. He was at the end of his workout so was doing some strength work and abdominal work. He stops, walks up to Ishe and I then says all that altitude training and hyperbaric chamber stuff won't help him, meaning Conor. You either can fight, or you can't. I nodded in agreement, "That's right, champ." It was an inside joke between Ishe and I as he was in the hyperbaric chamber yesterday. Conor is training at the UFC training Centre in Las Vegas and it has everything. Top of the range equipment. He'll be in tremendous shape, but you need more than that to win a boxing match, you actually have to have boxing skills.

I completed three sessions today and my body was absolutely shattered.

Sunday 13th August 2017

Dejuan told me that the last opponent didn't want to fight me at 143lbs and I wasn't willing to make 141lbs so I've got a new one. A Japanese boxer based in Mexico. That's a first, he has 7 loses in 30 fights. Battled hardened as Rene said. He can actually fight. Just not good enough to beat me.

Monday 14th August 2017

Floyd has been coming in early to watch Gervonta spar.
I was in the ring finishing up my abdominal workout. Gervonta was getting ready to spar
Sanjar Rakhmanov. Floyd was standing on the apron.
I walked over to leave the ring. Floyd stares at me and asks "You ready for your fight?" I replied "Yup. All is good. I'm ready." I hold Floyd's shoulder and walk down the steps.
I'm going to miss being part of the team. I genuinely respect Floyd. I've got love for the man. From 2013 to 2016 I've brought in $400,000 thanks to him.

Sunday 20th August 2017

I waited all day to be told what time the weigh in is tomorrow but no one from Mayweather Promotions contacted me. I had to reach out to Ladarius Miller to find out details about the schedule.

I still can't believe when I told Dejuan yesterday how unhappy I was about doing 8 rounds in my fight, he said I could pull out if I want. I spent thousands of dollars to fly here, have a hotel, pay my team and you ask me if I want to pull out after working my ass off for months. What manager/advisor says that? He's an A class idiot. The man is an imbecile.

I just can't wait to fight and win so I can tell them I want to leave.

Monday 21st August 2017

Biggest week of the year in the Las Vegas, entertainment and media networks flew into Nevada. If they were fans of Mayweather vs McGregor or not. It was the place to be.

I kicked off the fight week at Sam's Town Hotel and Casino against Shoki Sakai. A tough, gritty Japanese fighter based in Mexico. He is trained by the great, Nacho Beristain so I knew going into my fight I had a tough nights work ahead of me. Yes, on paper I was the favorite but this 26 year had fought 4 times in the last 12 months to my 1. He had lost 2 by majority decision which he easily could have won, he gave all of his opponents a hard night in the office. You have to believe in yourself but I'm realistic nowadays to know judges make bad decisions all the time so nothing is guaranteed in boxing.

I got to the weigh in for 1130am. Filled out my paperwork, did my medical with the doctor, did a photo shoot with the television photographer as I was told I may be a floater for tv which I hated as it means I have no fight time and just have to stay ready and warm which isn't easy. I told Dejuan to take me off tv but he obviously didn't listen as I saw social media posts from his team through the night.

I weighed in at 144lbs and my opponent was 143.4lbs. I watched his 3 opponents from the last 12 months. He can actually fight. His 7 loses mean nothing. He prefers to box but fighting Mexicans mainly and being trained by a Mexican he can fight in close to. He has heart and a good chin. It's going to be a hard fight. I'm not happy that it is over 8 rounds. He could easily be a banana skin if I'm not on form.

Tuesday 22nd August 2017

I've had 21 fights abroad. 15 in the USA. 4 in Germany. 1 in Luxembourg and 1 in St. Lucia. That's not bad for a man that 15 years ago, it seemed my career wouldn't pass the small hall in London. Now I'm international.

Thursday 24th August 2017

Badou's press conference was today, it went well. I believe Badou will win, possibly by stoppage.
Floyd's last work out was like a party in the gym. Dmitriy Salita. Big Baby Miller. Errol Spence. Adrian Broner were all there to watch him work out.
I dropped Dmitriy to his hotel afterwards and went back to my spot.

Friday 25th August 2017

I met Elie Seckbach and Ben Thompson of Fighthype at the media Centre. We headed off to the T-mobile arena. I went backstage to meet Badou and his team. I walked out with them for Badou to weigh in. He looked in great shape.
Floyd and Conor weighed in 30 minutes afterwards. Carl Froch, Tony Bellew, Chris Eubank Senior, Zab Judah were all there. It's amazing that I've come so far that these fighters I admire, know me and some of them I'm even friends with. I may not be a world champion but the hard work to get this far has definitely been worthwhile.
Gervonta was late weighing in and was 2lbs over weight. He vacated his world title.
Ishé and I went to Badou's hotel room afterwards where his chef had cooked up a pasta dish. We chilled for a bit then left.
Tomorrow is fight day. Vegas will be crazy.

Saturday 26th August 2017

Floyd Mayweather, "The Best Ever" finished his career with a fine performance. Possibly his best since Miguel Cotto in 2012 and outclassing Saul Alvarez in 2013. It had everything. Floyd lost the first three rounds and came back fighting. Changed up his tactics. Walked Conor McGregor down and got the stoppage in round ten.
All through the week I spoke to the media; Evening Standard, Sky Sports, FightHype, iFilm TV, Daily Mail and BET365. I said that Floyd would win by round 9, 10 the latest. I put down $10,000 on the Floyd win. I wasn't going to risk losing $10,000. I won $1,851 which was basically free money. It was a better way for Floyd to finish his career. Fans were upset with the Andre Berto fight while this time it was such an exciting fight, it was the perfect send off.
I've watched Floyd as a fan and now as a team member. It's been a pleasure to see his career up close and personal. He's always treated me well.

Sunday 27th August 2017

I went by Badou's house this afternoon for his victory BBQ. Everyone from the gym was there plus some other fighters from around town.

Afterwards I went to the Thomas & Mack for JLeon's charity basketball game. Chris Brown along with loads of other celebrities gave their time and hopefully money.
I was leaving and Chris Eubank Senior and his son were walking my direction. I asked them where they parked and Chris replied he had got an Uber here so I offered them a lift to their hotel. Chris accepted.

During the car ride we talked boxing and he asked me what is the lure of Floyd as none of his fighters are active and that the only thing you should trust is your bank balance.
He gave me his number and said contact him when I'm back in London as he'd like to get me some fights.
I gave him my number and dropped him to the Encore Casino Hotel.

Leaving Mayweather Promotions

Monday 5th March 2018

I've now been in Las Vegas for 16 days.
Lou was sick all last week so it was just me and Marcele putting in the work.
I've touched 154lbs which is great as I came here at my heaviest weighing 164lbs.

I arrived for Ron Gavril's WBC world title rematch against David Benavidez, he was unsuccessful in winning the rematch, I told him not to spend all his money as Mayweather promotions won't be rushing him back into a big fight.

It was Floyds birthday on the 24th February so I headed to Los Angeles where he was celebrating and having a three day party. I went for the main day with my good friend, Dan. We did a road trip in his Tesla. It was great fun and we got to meet Jamie Foxx and Bobby Brown. Mariah Carey was also in the house. The only other fighters to make the trip was Ron and Badou. That was one of the best parties I've been to. Floyd Mayweather parties are an event.

I had the pleasure to go to NASCAR on Sunday 4th March, which was a great experience. I went with my TV reporter friend Cherney Amhara, she's of Jamaican decent so we reminisce about our Caribbean upbringing. We watched it from the Coca Cola VIP suite which was bursting with energy.

Sunday 18th March 2018

I've now been in Las Vegas for a month. It's been great working with Lou and Marcele.

I've dropped 10lbs so far.

Dejuan has been quiet. He's told me he has news about a fight but has told me nothing more.
Ishe is fighting on May 11th. He has no opponent yet. They are probably trying to mess me about again and give me an opponent last minute and give me a two week notice like my August 22nd fight last year.
Ishe wants to sue Mayweather Promotions. Mickey Bey warned me about working with Dejuan as he's Floyd's cousin and gets a monthly check so he's never going to rock the boat and fight for us about a better deal.

Dave Levi, told me Jessie Vargas enquired about sparring me in the lead up to his fight with Adrien Broner. I think it's a 50/50 fight but I learn towards a Jessie win. Depends what AB turns up.

Thursday 29th March 2018

I've sparred twice so far with Jimmy Williams. A 15-0 fighter from the East coast. I'm in a pretty good place for a 37 year old version of myself.

I doubt I'll be fighting over in Las Vegas again. According to Dejuan Blake, Floyd isn't happy that I lost in August against the level of opponent I fought. The crowd thought I won,
Las Vegas is a place that bad decisions are a regular thing but that's a worldwide issue with Boxing. Bad decisions happen and the fighter has to live with it. Floyd has said he isn't given us no more free money. If I train and fight. The money I'm paid isn't free. This is work. I earn my money.

Saturday 7th April 2018

It was a great night at the Hard Rock casino, Erislandy Lara v Jarred Hurd. Caleb Truax v James Degale, JRock Williams v the Jamaican Galimore and Sergio Mora v Alfredo Angulo. It was a pretty good show. Sat front row with Badou and Ishe. Obviously those wasn't the seats, Ishe and I got from Mayweather promotions but we sat there anyway.

Kell Brook was in attendance, Errol Spence too. They had some words as Kell had recently said he'd beat Errol at the higher weight.
World champions Jermal Charlo and David Benavidez were there. It was a packed house. Mike Tyson even attended.
I had tickets to Martin Lawrence's stand up over at Mandalay Bay but the boxing show was so good, I couldn't pull myself away. By the time I got to the show it had ended and people were leaving. I'd been a fan of Martin since House Party so I was looking forward to it.

Monday 9th April 2018

Floyd went from the fights in Las Vegas on Saturday to a party appearance in Atlanta on Sunday. One of his cars was shot at with Greg, one of his security guards getting shot in the leg.

Sunday 15th April 2018

It's been a great week. I sparred 15-0 Jimmy Williams on Thursday, completing 7 rounds. Jessie Vargas had his media day at the same time. I think he'll beat Adrien Broner next week Satur- day.

I've been speaking to a handful of promoters over here in the US as I want to fight during this trip. My goal is to get a six figure deal back home so fighting will keep my name out there.

Monday 16th April 2018

I woke up to news from a Boston promotional company that they have Larry Smith as an opponent for me, he's fought Gary O'Sullivan, James McGirt, Wale Omotoso, Feliz Diaz, Jermell Charlo among others. I'd prefer to fight a better opponent but fighting him is better than no fight at all. It's all about staying active.

Monday 23rd April 2018

Fight week now. I woke up at 155lbs and went for my Monday morning run down the strip.
Afterwards I was 150.4lbs. I relaxed for a few hours and went to the Mayweather Boxing Club and did my usual workout with Lou and Marcele.

Afterwards in the locker room, the guys were talking about Josue talking mess to Floyd on his Instagram, asking for a release as Mayweather Promotions wasn't doing their job. Some of the guys thought he did right. Some thought he should be quiet. Mayweather Promotions has over 40 fighters, very few are happy at the minute.
Ladarius Miller said he thinks that Lonnie or me will be the next one to attack Floyd and ask for a release. I didn't say anything but I plan to ask Leonard for my release, the day after my fight. No need for me to attack Floyd, he's always been cool with me and done what he's said he would do for me.

This is the first time in 11 years that I'm fighting someone with a losing record. Last time was Rocky Muscus, who I disposed of in one round.

Thursday 26th April 2018

Today was Badou's launch of Ripper Nutrition. I only caught the last 30 minutes as I had to get my final workout in before leaving for Boston tonight.

Saturday 28th April 2018

I fought Larry Smith in New Hampshire in a Ballroom. I went in there thinking I'd blow him away but he was used to fighting bigger guys and gave me a fight for 8 rounds. I won on all the judges scorecards but he didn't lay down.
We spoke afterwards about the sport. He told me how he'd been used and abused by managers and promoters. A story that is told far too often.
Marcele did a good job in the corner. I even had a small cut that he dealt with.
The fighters on the show and fans showed me love. I spent the evening taking photos and having chats with everyone who wanted to speak to me.

Monday 30th April 2018

I spoke to Leonard to ask for a release from my contract as it's not due to finish for another 15 months. I think he was surprised by my call. He told me, he'd call me back to finalize.
Maybe he spoke to Floyd to let him know and what to do next.

Wednesday 2nd May 2018

Leonard called me to say that my contract with Mayweather Promotions was over and I was free to do what I want.

Saturday 5th May 2018

Today is Cinco Di Mayo. My career with Floyd Mayweather's Mayweather Promotions started 5 years ago at the MGM Grand when Floyd told me after his victory against Robert Guerrero, that I was now his fighter. 5 years on, that professional relationship is over. Nicole sent me a release form to sign which basically said it was a "mutual release" for me to seek other opportunities and that I could not sue them.
I don't want to sue Mayweather Promotions, Floyd kept to his word and got me the world title shot I deserved years before signing with them. The last two years they have lost me money, it is time to move on, all good things must come to an end. Floyd has always been good to me on a personal level. He has treated me like a friend and helped my career more than anyone else in this sport.

I saw Vanessa, an employee of Dejuan Blake's Affiliation Management this morning outside 24 Hour Fitness before I went to workout. We spoke for 45 minutes about the current situation of Mayweather Promotions. Alexis, Lonnie and I have all left Mayweather Promotions and Affiliation Management this week. Savannah Marshall left this month also.

Wednesday 9th May 2018

I'm lying in bed and my phone goes off. It's a message from Ishe asking me to come to his media workout at the Mayweather Boxing Club, I didn't want to go but I went to support him.

I had just left Mayweather promotions, so I didn't want to see anyone from the company just yet.

I got there for 1.30pm, I walked in with Ishe and Bob. Said hello to everyone. Dejuan and Leonard were at the back doing interviews. Leonard saw me and acknowledged then Dejuan came to the back where I was and said I can't say anything to him nowadays. I told him I'm here every day. You're never here. He said well I'm here now. What's up? What's going on? I just told him same old. Thinking back he probably wanted me to bring up my release from Mayweather Promotions but it was pointless. I was now free.

Ishe told me after his interviews that Leonard told him why can't the other fighters be like Ashley. Gervonta, Josue and Adrien Broner have been talking bad about Mayweather Promotions, Leonard and Floyd, I've just been saying I'm released to fight back home. I won't talk bad about them as you never know what the future holds. Overall I'm thankful to them and appreciate what they did for me. I'm bitter for the last two years with them, not being kept active but no one was. The boxing landscape in the USA now is currently slow. Many fighters are inactive.

Friday 11th May 2018

Ishe lost tonight against 27 year old Tony Harrison from Detroit. Ishe had a great camp, strength work at Phase One 3 times a week. Mountain runs up Mount Charleston 3 times a week. Boxing work and sparring. There's a fine line between overdoing it and peaking. I've overstrained a few times in my career, it's easily done when you're in the zone. At 39 years old, it could be age. Too many hard fights, his last fight against Jillian Williams was the best I've seen Ishe but at our age those grueling fights can take it out of you. Ishe has said he doesn't want to go out on a loss. I just worry for him that Boxing will retire him. It's hard to walk away from a sport you've done majority of your life. Hence it's so important to make plans for life after Boxing. It's scary but important as many retired sports stars face depression and going bankrupt after retiring from sport.

Friday 18th May 2018

I flew into Toronto, Canada for Badou's weigh in for his fight against Adonis Stevenson, the WBC world champion.

Saturday 19th May 2018

Fight day in Toronto. I had a late night visitor to my hotel room so I got to bed late after leaving the King Edward hotel where everyone was staying.
I met up with Badou and the guys at the Italian restaurant we went after his weigh in yesterday. I met them there around 230pm. I had a seafood pasta dish. It was lovely.

I chilled with Mike for a couple hours afterwards. He went to the barbers and had to collect fight tickets for Badou off Nicole. I also got mine. Section E. Row 7. Seat 7. These where next to Badou's reebok sponsors so these were good. I ended up sitting just outside of the ring. No better seat in the house.
The fight ended in a draw. Badou just can't get a break. Tough fight but respect to my friend. He always goes up against the best.

WORLD TOUR

I've officially parted company with Mayweather Promotions after five years together. I had some great moments and memories with them. I also had some terrible times when I wasn't fighting often or being paid what I thought I was worth.
To be part of Floyd's team, see him prepare for his fights for the last 3 years of his career. Be backstage and hear the conversations with the WBC and TV bosses, meet a whole load of celebrities, meet Al Haymon who was always friendly to me. I couldn't have dreamt my life or boxing career reaching these heights so I'll always appreciate Floyd letting me into his world. All good things must come to an end, as the saying goes.

Eddie Hearn had tried to make fights with a couple of his fighters so I thought I may have got some work with him. It never happened, he offered me Josh Kelly three times and on the third time, I said yes, then they went quiet. I didn't really care as I never got the respect I deserved in the UK.

I would go on a 10 fight world tour over two years. I flew to nine countries, picking up ten victories in the process.

Hungary was the first place I would fight after leaving Mayweather Promotions. I'd never been there before. The promoter treated me well. The other fighters on the card asked me for photos. I picked up a win against Janos Vass. He wasn't very good but he tried. I was surprised he lasted so long. I got the win in the 5th of an eight round fight.

I'd always wanted to go to Africa. Ghana was especially a special trip for me as Isola Akay was from there. He spoke fondly of his country throughout the years. I knew many Ghanaians in London and I really wanted to fight for a Ghanaian championship or African title but we couldn't agree a deal with the promoter. To become African champion would have been as special to me as winning the British championship in 2011. The event was supposed to happen at the Bukom Boxing Arena, I was looking forward to that as I'd heard of the Ghanaian world champions of the past fighting there. It was like the MGM Grand or Madison Square Garden to Ghanaians.

I fought Frank Dodzi at 154lbs, he didn't make the weigh in and the show organisers assured me, he'd weigh in. When we got in the ring the next day, he looked massive. There's no way he weighed the same as me yesterday. He was wild and aggressive. I stayed alert, boxed him and attacked at the right times. I was hitting him with crunching blows. His corner would stop the fight in between rounds. It was the humane thing to do. This was a ten round fight, I won by a technical knockout in the fourth round.

Steve and I had been going to different boxing gyms around Accra. We trained at four or five different gyms. Some were gritty and what you'd would expect and some looked like gyms, I'd expect to see in London, New York or Las Vegas.

We went through some markets, watched singing and dancing shows, hanged out with the locals. They treated us like one of them. They were so friendly and welcoming. I left their country, wanting to come back and appreciating how they made me feel.

The next stop of the world tour, my fourth fight of the year was in Poland at the PGE Turow Arena in Zgorzelec.

Bakhtiyar Isgandarzada was my next opponent. He was from Azerbaijan. It was an 8 round bout that ended in the third round. He shot his load, throwing everything at me and when I was starting to break him down, he quit on his stool.

It was a weekend trip which saw us fly into Germany, get a train to Poland and a car to the hotel. Reminded me of that film with John Candy and Steve Martin.

Plains, Trains and Automobiles. On the way back we had to leave super early to catch our flight home. We were worried about missing our train as we would have missed our flight. We just beat the closing of the gate. That seemed to happen regular with Steve and I.

I headed back to Las Vegas in January 2019 to support my friend, Badou Jack. He was fighting Marcus Brown on the undercard of Manny Pacquiao and Adrien Broner, at the MGM Grand. There was a clash of heads during the bout which caused a big gash in the middle of Badou's forehead. Badou, lost the fight on points. Many referees would have stopped the fight. The referee gave my friend, every chance to get back into the fight. It just was not his night.

I spent a month in Las Vegas, it was good to be back and see my friends. I based myself at City Boxing Club. It was on Sammy Davis Jr Drive which led onto Industrial Road. Ishe and I had the same assistant. Ishe was training there so to make it easier on Marcele, I trained there so he wouldn't have to go back and forth from Mayweather Boxing Club.

Devin Haney had started his career in Mexico, as he was seventeen and couldn't fight in the USA until he was eighteen. I spoke to a promoter he had worked with, out there about fighting in Mexico. He got me an opponent, Ricardo Arce Sarmiento for a show on January 26th. Marcele and I drove down to Tijuana from Las Vegas. Irish boxing legend Wayne McCullough was there with one of his fighters. We spoke about boxing and he wished me well in my career. I won by knockout in the third of an eight rounder. The weekend trip to Tijuana was a success. Start my year with another win and my world tour continues.

Ishe Smith had sued Mayweather Promotions and Affiliation management. He started the process last year. About the time I had left Mayweather Promotions, he contacted a lawyer. Jones Lovelock attorneys would get him one more fight under the

Muhammad Ali Boxing Reform Act, as a payoff from Mayweather Promotions. $70,000 to fight Erickson Lubin in Los Angeles. The week of the fight, he was told by Leonard Ellerbe that he had some medical issues that had showed up in his test results but he'd be allowed to fight but would have to have further examinations if he wanted to continue his career afterwards. He called me, told me the news. I felt bad for him. Mentally he wasn't going into the fight in the right state. He had kids to take care of and he is a great dad. I always loved to see him with them as he put them first at all times. I respected him for that. I drove to LA from Las Vegas with my friend Dan to support Ishe.
From the first bell, I could see he was off. He didn't want to get hit. He was worried. Leaving his partner alone with their kids was his worse nightmare. He quit on his stool and collected his check. I didn't blame him. He is Las Vegas, first world champion so he will forever have that claim. He had officially retired from professional boxing. He'd fought the best, sparred the best and been a part of history.

One month later would be the last time I had contact with Ishe. I told him I was fighting on Badou's boxing show in Dubai, UAE. I still sent him and his family a Christmas card for the next two years. It is a shame he chose to end relationships with three of his best friends. Bob, Floyd's cut man, Badou and me. I have some great memories of him and during my time in Las Vegas, he was a true friend. It's a shame, it ended this way. Life goes on!

I came close to fighting in my Grandmothers homeland of Ireland. I just couldn't agree a deal with the promoter, so I went back to Hungary to keep busy and get another win. I fought in the town of Kistarcsa against Zsolt Friesz. It didn't last too long. I ran through him and got the knock out in two rounds. It was a nice dinner show, much better than the small venue I fought in on my last trip here.

Badou Jack was dipping his toe into promotions. He asked me if I was still doing my world tour and if I wanted to fight on his show in Dubai, UAE. Sometimes working with your friend can cause problems. He had Amer to run the day to day of the company so I dealt with him.
The first weekend of May is always a big weekend for boxing in the USA. So May 3rd in Dubai was a great weekend to have it. Five days in Dubai with many of my friends from Las Vegas, It was a great trip. Malchus flew in from Omar, where he'd been working since 2014 and Dan flew in from Canada. I fought Jun Paderna who had not fought in years but he took the fight a few days before showtime. My opponent from Thailand did not get on his plane to Dubai. Which sucked, so I was thankful that Jun stepped in to save the show. Five Palm Jumeirah is where we stayed and where the event was. I was so impressed with what they put together. I was very proud of my friend. I won in the second round by knockout. It was on to the next.

My long awaited "Homecoming" at York Hall on June 22nd never happened. Last time I fought in London was when I defended my British title against former European champion Jason Cook at Wembley Arena on the 23rd July 2011. I was looking forward to it as I had made my debut at York Hall on June 3rd 2003, my career had come full circle. It was not meant to be. Mr Isola Akay would pass away on Saturday 15th June 2019. He was like a father to me. He was sick for a long time. I had visited him at the hospital earlier that week. It was sad to see him like that but I was glad I could be with him. I met him as a 7 year old child. He supported me throughout boxing and life. He threw me out of the club during my troubled teenage years as I was just too wild and a hot head. I would apologize for arguing with fellow fighters and some of the coaches. I was let back in the club and the rest is history. He will never be forgotten and will forever have a place in my heart. I hope I can touch some youths lives as he touched mine.

My homecoming fight was off but a few days after burying Mr Akay, I fought in Timisoara,
Romania against Ferenc Hafner. He was a southpaw which most boxers hate but I've always been able to deal with them. Probably because of the years sparring Ajose Olusegun, he was an Olympian, British and Commonwealth champion plus world title challenger. I think he underachieved. He had so much talent but was never backed by a promoter. He flew out to Las Vegas to try get onto Mayweather Promotions but it never happened. Hafner put up a fight, he tried. I was just too good. I stopped him in the fourth round. Dropping him numerous times before the referee ended it.
Four fights in seven months, I was on a roll and feeling good.

Eddie Hearn had offered me Josh Kelly three times over the last year. For the undercard of
Anthony Joshua vs Alexander Povetkin at Wembley Stadium on September 22nd. The offer needed to be improved. Then again for November 10th at the Manchester Arena on the undercard of Tony Bellew vs Oleksandr Usyk and finally at the O2 Arena on 20th April 2019. I said yes this time but Eddie never responded. Such is life. The show goes on. Without support from my homeland I was still successful and respected across the globe as my world tour had shown me.

I had agreed to fight in Denmark for October 5th against Kim Poulsen, he would have been my best opponent during this world tour. He pulled out with a month to go. I was given names of new opponents; one was an easy fight, a former European champion or a former world champion. I'll always pick the hardest task. I picked the former world champion, Kassim Ouma. I used to watch him on ESPN Friday Night Fights. He was a child soldier in Uganda. He made it to the USA and became world champion. He had fought fighters like Verno philips, Alex Bunema, Kofi Jantuah, Roman Karmazin, Marco Antonio Rubio, Sechew Powell, Jermaine Taylor, Cornelius Bundrage, Vanes Martirosyan, Gabriel Rosado and Gennadiy Golovkin. He had fought everyone, so it was an honor to share a ring with him. He was a sparring partner for Floyd Mayweather during the Victor Ortiz camp.

The Danish promoter offered me a bonus if I knocked him out within the first two rounds. He didn't like Kassim's bad attitude and he was smoking outside the venue in front of the fans, a couple hours before the fight. I attacked Kassim from the start, I wanted the bonus but he was too big and too strong. I hit him with some power shots. His head would snap back. He just looked at me and kept walking forward. I would retreat, using my boxing skills. Lucky for me I had them in my tool kit or I would have been stuck. Many fighters are one dimensional. He knew how to use his southpaw stance effectively and his size advantage. By the seventh round, I was tired which rarely happened to me. I was known for my engine and my insane work rate. I was 39 years old now. So even though you feel great, you no longer can do what you did as a younger man. I went back to the corner and told Steve, I was tired. He slapped me in the face and told me I wasn't. Dave was also in the corner for the fight. They were very much opposites in their coaching styles. Dave was laid back. Steve was hype and aggressive. He wanted me to push Kassim back. I couldn't and I was starting to get hit. I was on my back foot permanently now. It was the ninth round, I was being backed up through the round. I was breathing heavy. The lights went out. It was pitch black in the arena. I think the promoter did it on purpose as I seemed to be in trouble and they did not want Kassim to win. Not after how he had been disrespectful to the promoter and his team. After five minutes the lights came on and I was fully recovered. The bell rang moments later and I had another minute to rehydrate and get some instructions. I was going to box for the last round. I was surely winning. I won the first half of the fight. I had two or three rounds he may have won. The bell went and we both felt like we had done enough to be victorious. The scorecards were read out. 100-91, 99-91 and 98-92. It was a shut out. Unanimous victory, judging by the cards it was an easy win but it was far from it.

I went back to the locker room, Dave and Steve went back upstairs to watch the rest of the show. I stayed and just sat down until the show was over. I was so exhausted, I felt old.
Kassim had lost five straight now, his last win was three years ago. He seemed up for the fight with me. He didn't come, just for a paycheck. He came to win. Or at least it felt like that in the ring. There's only two years between us and our experience was matched. Two veterans going at it, this win would be a perfect way to walk off into the sunset.
We know fighters rarely retire when they should.

I've achieved everything I possibly could and against the odds. British champion, four International titles, world title challenger, headlined in Las Vegas, 5 year member of
Mayweather Promotions. Sparring partner to Floyd Mayweather for two camps. Fought at the MGM Grand three times. Fought and won in twelve countries. I've spent majority of my career abroad, having 31 fights in the process oversees.
My boxing record; 59 fights 50 victories, 8 loses, 1 draw.
My professional career spanned 16 years and 4 months.

What next? Treasure Boxing Club is my next big goal. To have my own boxing gym. I've seen the good work that they do in communities and so much people it helps. Boys, girls, men and women, I've been to boxing gyms across the world. It's all about the next generation. For my gym to be a home to so many. A place they can feel safe. A place they can make friends and become a family. Stay tuned!

THANK YOU

Lucille Treasure

Thank you mum for going through all the pain to raise me and being my rock. Without you, I wouldn't be the man I am. I could not ask for a more supportive mother.

Zachary Theophane

Thank you for supporting my dream of becoming a professional boxer.
Educating me on the boxing greats!
I still have my first pair of boxing gloves that you bought me.
You took me to All stars boxing club as a seven year old in 1988.
You were part of the process for helping me achieve my childhood dream.

Isola Akay

Thank you for being like a father to me. Supporting me when I needed it and giving me tough love when you had to. You will never be forgotten and I aim to make you even prouder than you was.

THANK YOU

Rene Carayol

You came at a time in my life when I thought I knew it all. You wrapped your hands around me and treated me like a son. I can never repay you for everything you've done for me but I aim to be what you was to me, to someone else.

Floyd Mayweather

You treated me like a little brother. You gave me advice and helped me when I needed it. You showed me another way of life and that anything is possible. You helped me when you didn't have to or need to. Thank you for opening your world to me.

DEDICATION

Tyrone Gavin Theophane: My Soldier For Life

This man had my back from when we were little kids. He supported me in my goals and dreams. Out of all my family he was the only one who came and supported me when I competed in Athletics competitions. Tyrone followed me all over the country, even to the National Federation Athletics championships in Wales. He would support me in my amateur boxing fights, whenever he could. He believed in me. Sometimes even more than I believed in myself.

Tyrone would have been so proud, to have seen me become British champion, or to have fought in our grandparents homeland of Saint Lucia. He would tell people, watch out for my cousin, he'll be big one day. He would have loved to of seen me join Mayweather promotions and be side by side with Floyd. He would have flown out there to support me. Headlining in Las Vegas, fighting Adrien Broner for the WBA world championship. He'd have been by my side.
We'd talk as teenagers about one day having money and not being a product of our surroundings. He'd put me in check if I was ever wrong. He felt more like a brother than a cousin to me. It still saddens me that he is not here. Why him? He had so much more to give this world. He left three children and I hope they can become successes in their own right.

My teenage years, many negative things happened to me. Some of my lowest points in life, he was there. They were low points for him too. We came up in a dangerous time in London.
He had my back and never let me down.

A True soldier. I love you. Losing you, I lost a part of me.

Printed in Great Britain
by Amazon